FROM COHEN TO CARSON

From Cohen to Carson

The Poet's Novel in Canada

IAN RAE

McGill-Queen's University Press
Montreal & Kingston • London • Ithaca

PR
9192.5
.R34
2008

© McGill-Queen's University Press 2008
ISBN 978-0-7735-3276-2

Legal deposit second quarter 2008
Bibliothèque nationale du Québec

Printed in Canada on acid-free paper that is 100% ancient forest free
(100% post-consumer recycled), processed chlorine free

This book has been published with the help of a grant from the Canadian
Federation for the Humanities and Social Sciences, through the Aid to
Scholarly Publications Programme, using funds provided by the Social
Sciences and Humanities Research Council of Canada.

McGill-Queen's University Press acknowledges the support of the Canada
Council for the Arts for our publishing program. We also acknowledge
the financial support of the Government of Canada through the Book
Publishing Industry Development Program (BPIDP) for our publishing
activities.

Permissions: see pages 373–4.

Library and Archives Canada Cataloguing in Publication

Rae, Ian, 1971–
    From Cohen to Carson : the poet's novel in Canada / Ian Rae.

Includes bibliographical references and index.
ISBN 978-0-7735-3276-2

1. Canadian fiction – 20th century – History and criticism. 2. Poets,
Canadian (English) – 20th century. 3. Novelists, Canadian (English) –
20th century. 4. Literary form. 5. Narration (Rhetoric). I. Title.

PS8187.R33 2008   C813'.5409   C2007-906263-6

Typeset by Jay Tee Graphics Ltd. in 10/13 Sabon

This book is dedicated to my parents,
David and Kathryn Rae,
in loving thanks for their encouragement
and generosity.

Contents

Acknowledgments

This manuscript was written with the support of fellowships from the Killam Foundation, the Social Sciences and Humanities Research Council of Canada, and the Max Bell Foundation. Additional support came in the form of a Li Tze Fong Memorial Fellowship and a Gilean Douglas Scholarship in English. I thank these funding bodies for their commitment to independent research and higher education.

Several chapters in this manuscript grew out of a dissertation that I completed at the University of British Columbia in 2002. W.H. New did a superlative job of supervising the dissertation. Eva-Marie Kröller and Kevin McNeilly made valuable editorial suggestions on draft chapters and encouraged me to publish. The commitment of these professors to the production and criticism of Canadian literature continues to be an inspiration.

As mentors and colleagues at the McGill Institute for the Study of Canada, Nathalie Cooke and Antonia Maioni have assisted me in countless matters, both professional and literary. I thank them for their enthusiasm and transcultural savvy. I also wish to express my gratitude to Claus Daufenbach and Sabine Sielke, who gave me the unique opportunity to teach in the Nordamerikastudienprogramm at Universität Bonn, as well as a friendly introduction to German culture.

I would like to acknowledge the Canadianists at McGill and UBC, who each, in their own way, influenced the direction of this project: Sherrill Grace, Laurie Ricou, Glenn Deer, Richard Cavell, Margery Fee, Brian Trehearne, and Robert Lecker.

I wish to express my gratitude to the research assistants who gathered countless articles for me, especially Karis Shearer, whose enthusiasm for the project endured long after she had left McGill to pursue graduate studies. Finally, I would like to thank Jane McWhinney for her careful editing of this manuscript.

FROM COHEN TO CARSON

INTRODUCTION

Framing the Poet's Novel

"One unanswered question of Canadian literature," according to the critic Fraser Sutherland, "is why so many celebrated fiction writers begin and continue as poets."[1] There are many possible responses to Sutherland's question, not the least of which is that the designation "novel" holds the promise of greater book revenues and a broader audience. Indeed, Canadian authors have written sequences of prose poems, such as Daphne Marlatt's *How Hug a Stone* (1983), only to discover that their publishers insist, for marketing purposes, that their poems are novels.[2] Yet sales figures alone do not explain the shift from poet to novelist, because the authors in question have continued to write poetry as well. More significantly, authors such as Leonard Cohen and Michael Ondaatje have explicitly written novels as extensions of their poetic practice, ignoring warnings from literary critics as far back as Aristotle against mixing poetry and prose.[3]

Blurring the boundary between poetry and prose has become so common in Canada that several critics share Allan Hepburn's conviction that "the lyric mode predominates in Canadian fiction."[4] Book reviewers frequently declare that, "in Canada, there is a long literary tradition of poets turning into novelists," but critics have not gone beyond the study of individual authors in analysing this phenomenon.[5] One aim of this study is to demonstrate that a major reason for the abundance of poet-novelists in Canada lies in the reciprocal relation between the contemporary long poem and novel. Even as the long poem attempts to novelize the traditional lyric sequence by introducing competing voices and styles, it has radically transformed concepts of narrative coherence and sequence in the Canadian novel by adapting the devices of contemporary poetry to prose fiction.[6]

I will show that a number of Canadian authors overcame the limitations of their lyric practice by experimenting with the long poem, while at the

same time developing rhetorical strategies that they subsequently used to
shape their novels. In order to illustrate the formative influence of the lyric
and the long poem on Canadian fiction, I present five in-depth case studies
of Canadian authors who have made the transition from poetry to the
novel. Scrutinizing Leonard Cohen's *The Favourite Game* (1963), Michael
Ondaatje's *Coming Through Slaughter* (1976), George Bowering's *A Short
Sad Book* (1977), Daphne Marlatt's *Ana Historic* (1988), and Anne Carson's *Autobiography of Red: A Novel in Verse* (1998), I argue that the way
in which the authors frame their early novels derives from, and expands
upon, narrative forms that they developed in their long poems – forms that
themselves are extensions of their lyric practice. In order to provide a context for these transformations, chapter 1 offers an overview of genre theory
relevant to the poet's novel.

   This study does not survey all of the poet-novelists in Canada. Nor do
the authors included here make up a monolithic school, although they edit,
anthologize, promote, critique, and riff off each other's works. For example, in a taped conversation with Fred Wah in 1980, Marlatt explains that
she admires Ondaatje's *Coming Through Slaughter* and Bowering's *Burning Water* (1980) because "they move in a direction in prose I want to move
in."[7] Similarly, Ondaatje names Marlatt as "one of my dearest touchstones,
one of those companions of opposites that has brought me here."[8] This
companionship of opposites does not necessarily lead to a uniform style.
Marlatt makes extensive use of fairy tales in her work, for instance, but
Ondaatje recalls her editorial objections to one of his forays into the genre:
"I reacted to Daphne Marlatt's *Zócalo* and *How Hug a Stone* and she's
helped me often with my books ... I remember in *Running* [*in the Family*]
Daphne Marlatt saw a chapter that was a retelling of a fairy tale and she
thought it was awful – so that went."[9] Although Marlatt cites Ondaatje
and Bowering as influences on her writing, she issues an important qualification: "The dialogue with these people is as primary as the actual books
are."[10] One of my aims here is to explore the literary manifestations of this
dialogue, which veers off in many different directions.

   I also wish to demonstrate that the stylistic affinities among these writers
are not limited to a single generation. For example, when asked whose
work she admires from a technical standpoint, Anne Michaels replies: "I
think that obviously Michael Ondaatje's narrative moves are extremely
interesting. In some ways I feel a kinship to that kind of relation."[11] This
statement raises a number of key questions: What are Ondaatje's narrative
moves? What kind of "relation" is Michaels talking about? And why
should the kinship between the novels of Ondaatje and Michaels be obvi-

ous? An analysis of Michaels's first novel, *Fugitive Pieces* (1996), helps answer these questions.

Ondaatje's *Coming Through Slaughter* is perhaps the lynchpin of this study, because it is an exemplary and influential text that draws from several different currents in Canadian literature. Ondaatje's lyrical, genre-blending style of writing has become so fashionable in Canada that Bowering proposes, only half-humorously, "that there is a genre called the Ondaatje."[12] Although Bowering proceeds to use this term in jest, his earlier discussion of Leonard Cohen, who, he says, "lives in the DMZ where genres meet," refutes such proprietary claims because it establishes Cohen's status as a groundbreaking poet-novelist who inspired Ondaatje.[13] Cohen is the subject of Ondaatje's only book of criticism, *Leonard Cohen* (1970), which reads like a manifesto for Ondaatje's own aesthetics in the late 1960s and 1970s. Yet as a Jewish poet from Montreal, Cohen was influenced by A.M. Klein, whose short novel *The Second Scroll* (1951), which Bowering lists elsewhere as a great Canadian long poem, is a hybrid of lyric poetry, prose, verse drama, and scholarly glosses.[14] Thus, I return to Ondaatje's *The English Patient* (1992) in my conclusion not because Ondaatje owns the trademark to a genre but because his work is at the epicentre of the debate over the poet's novel. His work also draws from – and has drawn further attention to – the lyric novels of Klein and Cohen, the perspectival shifts of Sheila Watson's *The Double Hook* (1959), and other important innovations in Canadian prose.[15]

While poet-novelists such as Ondaatje and Carson have garnered numerous literary prizes and raised the profile of Canadian literature internationally, they also have many detractors. My concluding chapter responds to Stephen Henighan's attack on the poet's novel in *When Words Deny the World* (2002), as well as to critiques of the same phenomenon made by Philip Marchand in *Ripostes* (1998) and by David Solway in *Director's Cut* (2003). I also address concerns about the lack of coherence in the poet's novel by examining the hybrid novels whose form, Henighan believes, is symptomatic of a national illness. In particular, my final chapter explores stylistic affinities among *The English Patient*, *Fugitive Pieces*, and the novels discussed in the previous chapters.

Working within this cross-genre context has allowed me to dispel the notion that poets who turn to the novel betray their allegiance to poetry. At the Longliner's Conference in 1984, a York University event designed to enshrine the importance of the long poem in Canadian literature, James Reaney lamented that "as poets, we've fought the novel and lost."[16] While the University of Ottawa affirmed the resilience of the long poem by hosting another conference on the genre in 1996, I maintain that the strength of the novel in Canada, in particular the critical acclaim brought to it by poets, is also evidence of the vitality of the long poem.[17]

In the chapters that follow, I make the point that novels by Cohen, Ondaatje, Bowering, Marlatt, and Carson stand in a serial relation to their earlier long poems. Occasionally an author will acknowledge that a long poem establishes the template for his or her novel – as is the case with Bowering's long poem *George, Vancouver* (1970) and his novel *Burning Water* (1980) – but more commonly the long poem serves as a laboratory in which an author develops narrative strategies, elaborates on personal sets of symbols, and refines themes that are employed in later novels. Chapter 2, for example, demonstrates how Cohen embeds poems from *The Spice-Box of Earth* (1961) in his novel *The Favourite Game* (1963) and modifies key motifs from the long poem that concludes *Spice-Box*, "Lines from My Grandfather's Journal," to frame that novel. Chapter 3 reveals how Ondaatje develops a style of narrative based on the painted series in *the man with seven toes* (1969) and the photographic series in *The Collected Works of Billy The Kid* (1970), and goes on to adapt this imagistic technique to the song cycle in *Coming Through Slaughter* (1976). Chapter 4 examines the formative influence of Bowering's "post-lyric" poems on his serial novels, *Autobiology* (1972) and *A Short Sad Book* (1977). For Bowering, the "serial novel" is less a plot-driven character study (as it was for the Victorians) than an expansion of the serial poem, a form that I discuss at length in my first chapter.[18] Chapter 5 traces the gradual development of a lesbian quest narrative in Marlatt's long poem *Frames of a Story* (1968), her novella *Zócalo* (1977), and her novel *Ana Historic* (1988). It focuses on the ongoing revisions of the heterosexual quest narrative that Marlatt derives from Hans Christian Andersen's fairy tale *The Snow Queen* (1844). Chapter 6 examines the combination of lyric, essay, and interview in Carson's long poem "Mimnermos: The Brainsex Paintings" in *Plainwater* (1995) and scrutinizes the expanded version of this format in *Autobiography of Red* (1998). This chapter emphasizes how Carson revises canonical narratives in order to allow the women's voices at the margins of her story to attain a place of prominence. Studying Cohen's motivic variations, Ondaatje's song cycles, Bowering's serial aesthetics, Marlatt's quest narratives, and Carson's mythic frames in this way makes it abundantly clear that long poems established the formal precedents for the novels mentioned.

The manner in which these authors move from poet to novelist varies, however. Cohen and Ondaatje proceed in a fairly linear fashion from lyric to long poem to novel, whereas Bowering and Marlatt produce an early (and for them unsatisfying) realist novel before earning reputations as poets and returning to the novel with a renewed conception of it. Carson, on the other hand, combines these two approaches. She begins as a poet writing primarily in lyric sequences, composes the manuscript of a prose novel, and then, dissatisfied, completely rewrites it as a novel in verse. In each case, an intensive period of work in the lyric and the long poem furnishes the respective authors with the repertoire of rhetorical devices that they use to shape their novels.

Frank Davey anticipated this observation in 1983 when he noted that "in Marlatt, Bowering, Ondaatje, [and] Nichol, we have writers whose prose works are in many respects indistinguishable from their long poems," a trend Davey predicted would grow as the long poem "encroach[ed] further upon fiction – not only on the prose measure, character-relationships, and satire – but on the viewpoint shifts and the jesting hypothetical incidents that have marked ... recent fiction."[19] For contemporary evidence of this encroachment, one need look no further than the shortlist of "Canada's Best Fiction" published in December 2002 in the Canadian edition of *Time* magazine. The multi-authored article surveys the period from 1943 to 2003 and identifies six key fiction writers. Margaret Atwood is crowned "the controversial queen of Canadian letters" for her dextrous ability to write criticism, poetry, and prose in distinct, but equally celebrated voices.[20] Margaret Laurence, Michel Tremblay, Alice Munro, and Rohinton Mistry also make well-deserved appearances. The list, however, features a surprising inclusion: Anne Carson. Carson, who is profiled under the heading "The Love Poet," might seem out of place on a fiction list, but Gordon Teskey explains that she "has written two widely acclaimed short novels, both in verse: *Autobiography of Red* (1998) and *The Beauty of the Husband: A Fictional Essay in 29 Tangos* (2001)."[21] Teskey says that "Carson's experimental magic recalls the work of Michael Ondaatje," but the latter author is a surprising omission from the *Time* list."[22] Ondaatje appears solely through intertextual references to Mistry and Carson, and, in this heavily realist selection, Cohen, Bowering, and Marlatt are not mentioned, even though they have played a major role in pushing the Canadian novel beyond the entrenched conventions of realist fiction.[23]

A number of tropes recur in these novels to explain their unorthodox narrative forms: the spider web, the mosaic, the anthology-in-process, the archive-in-process, the monstrous and multipartite body. Each of these tropes engages with the diverse and partial histories of a multicultural society in which a variety of linguistic and narrative traditions interact. The formal affinities between these novels do not, however, constitute a consistent style or even a consensus about style. In Margaret Atwood and Christian Bök's *Ground Works: Avant-Garde for Thee*, an anthology of avant-garde fiction that surveys the period from 1965 to 1985, for example, Bök states that "contributors to this anthology pursue eclectic, literary interests, experimenting with many varieties of radical fiction in an effort to find a genre appropriate to the sociocultural circumstances of Canada,"[24] but the only generic similarities among the selections are their anti-mimetic stance and their zeal for hybridizing genres. The anthology begins with Cohen's *Beautiful Losers* and includes portions of Ondaatje's *The Collected Works of Billy the Kid*, Bowering's *A Short Sad Book*, and Marlatt's *Zócalo* among other selections. However, in my concluding chapter I demonstrate that the long poems and novels I am considering are not at all homogenous. Thus, my purpose in fashioning a new frame of reference for the interpretation of the poet's novel is not reductive. While I highlight similarities among authors wherever possible, my primary aims are:

1 To challenge critics who dismiss the poet's novel on the grounds that the prose is inchoate or formless;
2 To provide a framework against which one can judge the differences among poet-novelists so that *Fugitive Pieces*, say, cannot simply be written off as a "shameless imitation of Ondaatje's metaphor-laden aesthetic";[25]
3 To highlight the diversity of poetic narratives and cultural resources that the authors discussed draw upon to reshape the realist novel;
4 To demonstrate that what David Solway perceives as the "Great Disconnect" in Canadian writing from the "tradition of forms, themes, principles and hieratic dispositions" of the past is simply a different set of forms, themes, and principles in action – one open to classical and international influences but also firmly rooted in a tradition of Canadian writing.[26]

I

(Un)framing Genres

David Malouf told me recently: "Every novel has about a thousand lost poems in it." I think that's true. My novels don't have that *Ben Hur* sense of looking down and encompassing the full scope. My book may have that kind of scope, but it's pieced together with little bits of mosaic. Each scene tends to be written from the point of view of that private, poetic voice.

Michael Ondaatje[1]

In choosing to work with the lyric, the long poem, and the novel, I have invoked three of the most established – but also the vaguest – terms in literary criticism. The formal innovation that critics identify as a key aspect of the lyric also characterizes the long poem and the novel. Paul Ricoeur remarks that the novel "has, since its creation, presented itself as the protean genre par excellence ... Indeed, it has constituted for at least three centuries now a prodigious workshop for experiments in the domains of composition."[2] My aim here is not to wrestle these shape-shifting genres into submission. On the contrary, their protean qualities are what make them alluring. In a glowing review of *Autobiography of Red*, for example, Jed Rasula celebrates how the form of Carson's novel in verse recalls the German Romantics' vision of the "maverick legacy of the novel as 'total poetic genre'": "Historically, the novel is a genre arising in the seams between other genres, accenting the fault lines within and between them: a genre born to contest other genres. Because most novels forgo this legacy, it has lately become a fetching prospect for poets."[3] The epigraph to this chapter highlights this cross-genre sensibility; Ondaatje and Malouf overstate their case, however, by claiming that all novels derive from poetic sources. No fixed formula can define the lyric, long poem, and novel, but I offer here some evolving definitions of each genre to provide a backdrop against which the reader can gauge the migration of the lyric into the novel in the twentieth century.

THE LYRIC

The term "lyric" derives from the Greek *lyra*, or lyre, the harp-like instrument that accompanied the singing of the original lyrics. The form has adopted and abandoned numerous metric conventions (Shakespeare's iambic pentameter) and formal conventions (Petrarch's sonnet) in response to expanding notions of musicality and the particular needs of time and place. However, twentieth-century free verse dispensed with rigid conventions of metre and structure, and the descriptor "lyric" came to encompass a broad range of styles and sensibilities, including those of prose. In his *Oxford Book of Modern Verse* (1937), W.B. Yeats added line breaks to his favourite passage in Walter Pater's book of criticism, *The Renaissance* (1873), and declared it the first modern poem.[4] Yeats demonstrated that the musical force of language arises from cadence paired with thought and emotion, and not from an imposed rhyme scheme or metrical formula. Daniel Albright interprets this boundary break to mean that the "lyric is a mode, discoverable in odes and dramas and novels and possibly the telephone directory," but the present study retains the distinction between lyrical passages embedded within prose narrative and isolated lyrics.[5]

The lyric is not the only genre in which symmetry and mutability are paradoxically combined. In *The Birth of Tragedy*, for instance, Nietzsche argued that drama, which began as tragedy, evolved from the union of "the plastic, Apollonian arts and the non-visual art of music inspired by Dionysos" – that is, from Apollonian symmetry paired with Dionysian "frenzy."[6] In poetry, one can write Apollonian lyrics governed by regular metre and stanzaic structure, but the Dionysian drive toward ecstasy and change evidently holds sway. Albright notes that "no Aristotle has ever composed a manual prescribing the parts and proper sequences of the lyric."[7] In fact, in the midst of establishing a number of enduring genre definitions in his *Poetics*, Aristotle stated breezily that "what is meant by 'lyric poetry' is self-evident."[8] Nothing could be further from the case for modern critics.

Modern lyrics tend to be short, concise, and characterized by radical associative leaps and abrupt shifts in perception. Margaret Atwood observes that short lyrics generally stress "formal elegance and verbal felicity" by focusing on "objects in space" and "noun-and-adjective accurate description," while at the same time isolating a particular emotion or cluster of emotions.[9] Despite a tradition of impersonal lyrics that ranges from Stesichoros to T.S. Eliot, the lyric form largely continues to assume the classical "I-You" structure of enunciation, even in cases where speaker and audience are one and the same. This apostrophic mode, as Smaro Kamboureli points out, "establishes the priority of discourse over narrative" and encourages readers to imagine themselves as either speaker or addressee, rather than acting as spectators at an event.[10] Influenced by post-structuralist critiques of the unitary self, Bowering triangulates this configuration in *Burning Water* by calling the writer writing the novel "He" and attempting to dissociate Him from the "lyrical self" of his long poem *George, Vancouver.*[11] Destabilizing the lyric ego is thus a major impetus behind the shift from poetry to the novel, but poet-novelists find innovative ways of retaining the intimacy of the lyric address in their prose.

The lyric is often criticized for being a closed and solipsistic form. After the Second World War, and particularly during the Vietnam War, Canadian critics (many of them poets) condemned the lyric for the limited range of its elevated tone, diction, and perspective. These criticisms drove lyricists toward the long poem, which promised a greater range of voice and mood. However, as Brian Trehearne observes in *The Montreal Forties: Modernist Poetry in Transition*, the generation of poets who mentored the likes of Cohen had already converted to extended forms and grown dismayed with the predominantly lyric sensibility of the imagist long poem.[12] In the 1960s, anti-war poets such as Bowering made a show of escaping their lyrical selves, while feminists such as Marlatt reconsidered the gender implications of lyric subjectivity: "Poetry, that inspired making (*poiein*) with words, that wellspring, that temple of the oracular, that lyric construction of the exalted I – women come to it troubled, doubled by the graven/craven images men have provided: Eve of the forked tongue, miss-represented, ma-damned."[13] From Marlatt's uncapitalized "i" to Carson's personae, feminist writers developed means of decentring the exalted subject and displacing its authority.

Rather than abandoning the lyric, however, many of the poets studied here explore latent possibilities within the lyric voice. William Rogers argues that, even in poems where the voice of the lyric "I" is not necessarily the author's (such as Ondaatje's *The Collected Works of Billy the Kid*), a "'doubleness' of voice" permeates the lyric so that the speaker's "anomalous voice functions as something like a symbol of the author's voice."[14] The poet-novelists accentuate this tension through a play of masks and narrative levels. Doubleness is also encouraged by the lyric's propensity for symbol (a consequence of the form's brevity) and the rapid transitions between colloquial *parole* and the more incantatory language that generally sustains the lyric's elevated tone. Certainly Gerard Manley Hopkins had the lyric in mind when he wrote that "poetry is speech framed for contemplation of the mind by the way of hearing or speech framed to be heard for its own sake and interest even over and above its interest of meaning."[15] Such formalized speech makes readers conscious of the musical properties of language and fosters a reflective mood that makes the lyric uniquely equipped to fill the role of meta-commentator in novels such as *Ana Historic*.

While the lyric is usually brief, subjective, and musical, perhaps *the* distinguishing feature of the lyric is its fascination with mutability as form and theme. Ondaatje's "the gate in his head" provides a fine example of the protean energies active in the lyric, because it combines traditional elements of lyric address with a postmodern sense of open-endedness.[16] The poem begins as an apostrophic address to Ondaatje's friend Victor Coleman. Admiring the "sense of shift" in Coleman's poetry, Ondaatje emulates his friend in the first two stanzas by juxtaposing objects in space. The imagistic fragments accrue with only the occasional comma to separate them until, in the transitional third stanza, Ondaatje turns his attention from Coleman's poetry to his own surroundings. The author then describes a landscape of broken, blanching, and melting objects that resembles "some sea animal / camouflaging itself" in transformations. Alluding to the Proteus myth, Ondaatje invokes the porous net, one of his favourite motifs, as a metaphor for writing. A chaos of images streams through the poet's net and the sudden appearance of full stops and more insistent punctuation cannot dam its flow. On the contrary, the poem contrives its own dissolution by invoking a blurred photograph of a gull sent by Coleman in a letter to the poet:

> And that is all this writing should be then.
> The beautiful formed things caught at the wrong moment
> so they are shapeless, awkward
> moving to the clear.[17]

Ondaatje's writing resists the temptation to arrest images in their protean transitions and celebrates "formed things" on the verge of changing their form. The poem lasts just long enough to imagine an alternative to the stasis of its final full stop.

In the same way that poets chafed against the limits of lyric subjectivity, they also grew dissatisfied with the narrow scope of the lyric moment. The lyric generally confines itself to a synchronic fragment of time, as Sharon Cameron explains in *Lyric Time: Emily Dickinson and the Limits of Genre*: "If a poem denies the centrality of beginnings and ends, if it fails to concern itself with the accumulated sequence of a history, it must push its way into the dimensions of the moment, pry apart its walls and reveal the discovered space there to be as complex as the long corridors of historical and narrative time. For the moment is to the lyric what sequence is to the story."[18] Carson, an admirer of Dickinson, corroborates this theory of the lyric in her discussions of Greek lyric: "Lyric [poetry] attempts to enter so deeply into history at a particular point that time stops."[19] However, this resistance to temporal flux did not suit the Heraclitean aesthetics of the *Tish* group that included Bowering and Marlatt, and the denial of temporal flow was often viewed as politically irresponsible. The American poet Jack Spicer, who had a strong influence on the *Tish* group, argued that a "poet is a time mechanic not an embalmer" and insisted that "words must be led across time not preserved against it."[20]

Creating a sense of duration while retaining the intensity of the lyric is a difficult enterprise, and critics often distinguish the novel from poetry in terms of narrative and non-narrative writing. However, Northrop Frye points out that this distinction has little historical basis: "The literary historian who identifies fiction with the novel is greatly embarrassed by the length of time that the world managed to get along without the novel, and until he reaches his great deliverance in Defoe, his perspective is intolerably cramped."[21] From Frye's perspective, the lyric is "the genre which most clearly shows the hypothetical core of literature, narrative and meaning in their literal aspects as word order and word-pattern."[22] Frye's position can be faulted for being reductive, if not short-sighted. Yet his sense that the lyric is a distillation of stylistic codes that undergird the novel finds an echo in Carson's theorization of the novel, which I discuss in chapter six.

Carson also stresses that the intensity of the lyric is bolstered by its protean relation to the temporal continuum: "A lyric aims to capture a moment of change from one time to another, from one situation to another, so it's not that you describe any moment in the day and make it intense, you choose the moment in the day when everything changed because of some little thing or thought or mood. Homer can tell you the whole history of the fall of Troy, he has 24,000 words to do it, and there's no necessary choice of frame, of the critical moment, as there is for a lyric poet."[23] Of course, Homer's epics have an overarching framework, but Carson's point is that the lyric adheres to its mandate of brevity with extreme fidelity. Whereas the epic simile aims to limit description and accelerate the plot by stating that something is like something else, the lyric propensity for metaphor slows narrative down and invites meditation by stating that something is another thing which it is not. Because the lyric is usually configured as a compression of experience that suspends the passage of time, it demands a particularly economic use of detail, and often resorts to a metaphorical overlay of times, places, and/or personae.

THE LONG POEM

When placed in a sequence, the lyric acquires a diachronic dimension. Poets attempted early on to expand the temporal scope of the lyric by experimenting with the lyric sequence. In *Post-Petrarchism: Origins and Innovations of the Western Lyric Sequence*, Roland Greene argues that the lyric sequence presents "the possibility of a thoroughgoing invention of character away from the straits of story, linearity, and causal logic" by treating a single theme from multiple angles and over an expanse of time.[24] This form of lyric fiction permits character development, narrative focus, and a method of measuring time, while avoiding the causal chain of a conventional plot. Whereas the author of a plot-driven narrative cannot lavish too much attention on particular events without sacrificing momentum, the segmentation of narrative in the lyric sequence concentrates all the narrative energy on key moments in the story. In their narrative works, the poet-novelists fragment their storylines in this manner to shave down the transitional matter between key moments.

Barbara Godard notes a similar compression of narrative in the long poems of the Romantic period, when the lyric colonized the epic:

When Wordsworth answered the call to become England's greatest poet, to pick up the mantle of Milton, to write an epic, he was reduced to silence. More precisely, he was reduced to *The Prelude*, the lyrical and autobiographical long poem that was to have been a warming-up exercise but, in fact, became an epic, the model for the Romantic epic. So in British North America, as well, many attempts to achieve epic grandeur, to write long poems, led to lyrical forms. One thinks of the extended sonnet cycles of Charles Sangster, 'In the Orillia Woods,' and Charles G.D. Roberts' *Songs of the Common Day*, as well as of Lampman's *Lyrics of Earth* or Sangster's *St. Lawrence and the Saguenay*. Although they write in praise of mother earth instead of in honour of the idealized courtly lover, these poets carry on the canonical tradition of the single voice which had by this time squeezed out other poetic genres. The epic had become a lyric.[25]

Although Godard continues to distinguish between lyric and epic in terms of personal versus public discourse, written idiolect versus oral sociolect, she sees the interplay of these discourses as being central to the Romantic project in English. This interplay is also central to the poet's novel in Canada and accounts for much of the romantic sensibility of the genre.

On the other hand, many poets embed prose anecdotes, dialogue, and found historical documents into their lyric sequences, a technique that swings the generic pendulum away from lyric toward epic. D.M.R. Bentley argues that English Canadian long poems in particular situate themselves at the intersection of the lyric and the epic because of prevailing concerns about the historical evolution of the nation. In his ambitious essay "Colonial Colonizing" (1998), Bentley traces the commemorative mode of epic across three centuries of nation building in Canadian long poems ranging from Henry Kelsey's "Now Reader Read ... " (1690) to Jon Whyte's *Homage, Henry Kelsey* (1981). He finds that the "encyclopedic ambitions of the epic" are usually counterbalanced by the "self-ish concerns of the lyric," such that the long poem documents both personal and public experience.[26] In this context, the seemingly radical postmodernism of long poems such as Robert Kroetsch's "Seed Catalogue" – in which the growth of the poet, farm, region, and nation are made synonymous through interleaving juxtapositions – builds on an established colonial rhetoric. However, Kroetsch tries to mobilize this rhetoric toward postcolonial aims.

By and large, early English Canadian long poems do not establish a stable myth of origins or arrive at the fated fulfillment of a national destiny, as in the classical epic mode of Homer and Virgil. While Adam Hood Burwell's "Talbot Road" (1818) has the race politics and crusading tone of epic, it lacks the length and scope.[27] Adam Kidd's "The Huron Chief" (1830) has a hero of epic proportions as well as an encyclopaedic mix of songs, anecdotes, battle scenes, and classical allusions, but its hero is ultimately martyred and the poem turns into a lament for the European conquest of the Huron nation.[28] It is for these kinds of reasons that Northrop Frye argues in his 1946 essay "The Narrative Tradition in English-Canadian Poetry" that "Canadian narrative demands a tragic resolution."[29] Frye traces a narrative tradition that begins amid the "philosophical pessimism and moral nihilism" of the nineteenth century and extends as far as E.J. Pratt's *Brébeuf and His Brethren* (1940) and Earle Birney's *David* (1942).[30] Frye surmises that the telos of Canadian narrative is not a triumphal one. However, at the conclusion of the essay, he sees Canadian poetry "hesitat[ing] on the threshold of a new era" in which the traditional storytelling modes of the long poem will adapt to the radio and thus, as Marshall McLuhan would add, take advantage of the non-linear possibilities afforded by electronic media.[31]

POETRY, NARRATIVE, AND ELECTRONIC MEDIA

McLuhan maintained an abiding interest in the dynamic between poetry and the novel. He wrote his Master's thesis on "George Meredith as a Poet and Dramatic Novelist" (1934), and his PhD dissertation, "The Place of Thomas Nashe in the Learning of His Time" (1943), began as an investigation into the development of Elizabethan prose.[32] However, it is in the interplay between print culture and electronic media that McLuhan did his most memorable work. His enquiries into media in *The Gutenberg Galaxy* (1962), *Understanding Media* (1964), and *The Medium Is the Massage* (1967) brought him considerable fame in the 1960s and culminated in *Through the Vanishing Point: Space in Poetry and Painting* (1968).[33]

McLuhan's thesis in *Through the Vanishing Point* is that the simultaneity of the electronic age has rendered traditional modes of representation, in particular the continuous storyline, obsolete. McLuhan equates storylines with the sightlines in the Renaissance art of perspective. He believes that the singular viewpoint of classic perspective has been outmoded by electronic circuitry, and he sees cubism, abstract expressionism, and other innovations of twentieth-century art as expressions of electronic sensibilities. To combat the privileged perspective of the storyline, McLuhan argues, narratives should be configured according to the spatial arrangements of twentieth-century media culture, not the linear configurations of Gutenberg print culture. "In poetry, in the novel, in the movie," he writes, "narrative continuity has yielded to thematic variation," as well as to a renewed zeal for analogy, parataxis, and juxtapositions across intervals.[34] Much as McLuhan's theories of electronic media anticipated the internet universe of numberless, decentred connections that one negotiates through software windows, hypertext links, and keyword searches, his theories of literature in the electronic age shed light on the compositional practices of authors such as Ondaatje, who types the entire draft of a work into his computer and then "relies on the search-string key to isolate repeated motifs" and "look for word echoes and patterns."[35]

In *McLuhan in Space*, Richard Cavell successfully delineates a Canadian "shadow canon" of "verbi-voco-visual" artists inspired by McLuhan, such as bp Nichol and Michael Snow, whose works stand in contrast to the so-called Frye school of mythopoeic poets.[36] However, there is ample evidence to suggest that McLuhan influenced a number of more canonical and mythopoeic authors, such as Ondaatje, who once considered asking Frye to be his MA thesis supervisor, and Carson, who attended St Michael's College at the University of Toronto during McLuhan's tenure. Ondaatje's work is highly ekphrastic, but the selection of an excerpt from a 1909 interview with Louis Jones as the backcover blurb for the original edition of *Coming Through Slaughter* links the visual style of Ondaatje's novel to the questions of orality and form raised by McLuhan. The quotation contrasts the improvisational style of Buddy Bolden's jazz (he could not read music) with the melodies of classically trained John Robichaux: "Buddy Bolden ... was the first to play the hard jazz and blues for dancing. Had a good band. Strictly ear band. Later on Armstrong, Bunk Johnson, Freddie Keppard – they all knew he began the good jazz. John Robichaux had a real reading band, but Buddy used to kill Robichaux anywhere he went. When he'd parade he'd take people with him all the way down Canal Street."[37] The narrative "arches" of Robichaux's music suggest to Bolden the linear mode of organization that McLuhan equated with the architecture and paintings of Renaissance piazzas, and that both Bolden and Ondaatje aim to overcome. This move from visual to oral also defines Carson's novel in verse, where Geryon's "autobiography" begins as a sculpture, evolves into a series of photographs, and concludes as tape recordings and dialogue.

At the conclusion of *The Gutenberg Galaxy* McLuhan implores artists to "strive not towards a point of view but to discover how not to have a point of view, the method not of closure and perspective but of the open 'field' and the suspended judgement. Such is now the only viable method under electric conditions of simultaneous information movement and total human interdependence."[38] McLuhan's notion of the "open field" has many similarities with the poetics of Charles Olson and the Black Mountain school of artists in the United States, who greatly influenced the early work of Bowering and Marlatt. However, by the late 1960s the latter artists had grown suspicious of the race, gender, and nationalist assumptions that sustained Olson's open forms. Instead of pursuing the expansionist poetics of the Black Mountain poets further, Bowering and Marlatt transferred the visceral aspects of proprioceptive writing (such as the breath line) to serial forms of poetry that experimented with conceptual constraints and iterated patterns, which they then worked around and against. This conflation of techniques appears to be contradictory, as if a painter had gone through a Jackson Pollock phase only to revisit Magritte. However, the cognitive studies of Erving Goffman and Deborah Tannen demonstrate that no gesture or utterance can be understood without a frame of reference (e.g., this is play, this is war).[39] In *Framing in Discourse*, Tannen argues that pattern recognition operates at all levels of narrative and linguistic comprehension: "Notions of script, frame, and schema can be understood as structures of expectation based on past experience, and ... these structures can be seen in the surface linguistic form of the sentences of a narrative. Furthermore, the structures of expectation which help us process and comprehend stories serve to filter and shape perception."[40] The challenge of the artist thus becomes not to eliminate all frames of reference but to dismantle the limitations of the old frames of reference and open up alternative dimensions of experience in new ones.

As early as 1969 Dorothy Livesay was working to reconcile Frygian interpretations of poetic structure with McLuhanesque insights into the transformative power of electronic media. In her influential essay "The Documentary Poem: A Canadian Genre," Livesay asserts that "our most significant body of poetry exists in the longer poem" and thereby echoes the famous endorsement of the long poem by Frye: "In looking over the best poems of our best poets, while of course the great majority are lyrical, we are surprised to find how often the narrative poem has been attempted, and attempted with uneven but frequently remarkable success ... We tend to form our canons of criticism on carefully polished poetry, but such standards do not always apply to the narrative, for the test of the great narrative is its ability to give the flat prose statement a poetic value."[41] Whereas Frye contrasts the narrative poem to the lyric, Livesay argues that Canadians "have built up a body of literature in a genre which is valid as lyrical expression but whose impact is topical-historical, theoretical and moral."[42] She argues for "a new genre, neither epic nor narrative, but *documentary*" in its "conscious attempt to create a dialectic between the objective facts and the subjective feelings of the poet."[43] Citing works such as Bowering's *Rocky Mountain Foot* (1968), Livesay demonstrates that the pioneering documentary work of the National Film Board corresponds to a tradition of the long poem that is didactic and factual as well as emotive and lyrical. Ondaatje has dismissed this film tradition, but Manina Jones argues in *That Art of Difference: 'Documentary-Collage' and English-Canadian Writing* that a revised documentary impulse lies at the root of narratives by Ondaatje and Marlatt. I shall demonstrate in chapter 6 that documentary-collage is also a useful concept for evaluating Carson's *Autobiography of Red*.

Livesay's argument is less persuasive in its assertion that the documentary poem is a distinctly Canadian genre – a claim she later retracted – than in its more minute demonstration of the resistance to continuous sequence in the narrative tradition that Frye admired: "My premise is indeed that the Canadian longer poem is not truly a narrative at all – and certainly not a historical epic. It is, rather, a *documentary* poem, based on topical data but held together by descriptive, lyrical, and didactic elements. Our narratives, in other words, are not told for the tale's sake or for the myth's sake: the story is a frame on which to hang a theme."[44] Livesay makes important observations on the relation of lyricism to narrative, but the didacticism of her socialist themes has drawn the ire of Roy Miki and other critics.[45] Furthermore, the documentary elements in Bowering, Marlatt, and Carson tend to be dispersive: they recover historical information while at the same time questioning the dominant media of historical representation, such as photography, film, chronological narrative, and archival systems.

This interrogation of media honours McLuhan's legacy, but bp Nichol in his essay "The Medium Was the Message" cites three further innovations in McLuhan's thought that illuminate the study of Canadian poetry. First, Nichol argues that McLuhan used the pun as a deconstructive tool to decode cultural stereotypes rather than to encode classical allusions in the manner of Joyce.[46] This sort of deconstructive punning is central to Bowering's treatment of Canadian history and myth in A Short Sad Book, as well as to Marlatt's wordplay in Ana Historic. Second, Nichol praises McLuhan's hypothetical thought probes because they "suspend the 'normal' demands that logic or sequential thinking impose on you, shift into a mental hyperspace," and thereby "follow fictional highways to real destinations."[47] Finally, and more generally, Nichol concludes that McLuhan blazed a path for a wide spectrum of Canadian literary thinkers through his elliptical style of argumentation and "the serial leaps of his mind."[48] Appropriately, at the very height of McLuhan's fame in the late 1960s, a type of long poem known as the "serial poem" was growing in popularity in Vancouver. This recursive form of narrative, initially a non-narrative form, which evolved out of poetic interpretations of serialism in music, television, and the visual arts, laid the foundation for many of the poets' fictions and thus demands to be analysed in depth.

THE SERIAL TURN

The serial poem owes part of its popularity in Canada to the presence in Vancouver of Robert Duncan, Jack Spicer, and Robin Blaser, three pioneering figures of the so-called San Francisco Renaissance. Duncan lectured at the University of British Columbia in 1963 and 1965 and became a mentor to Vancouver's Tish poets. Spicer also lectured at the Vancouver Poetry Festival in 1965 (where McLuhan was a featured speaker). Spicer was "offered a position at Simon Fraser University and would have begun teaching there in the fall of 1965" had he not died that summer.[49] Blaser, for his part, accepted a teaching position at Simon Fraser University in 1966 and has lived in Vancouver ever since. Together, these poets developed a unique variation on the lyric sequence: "The serial poem as developed by Duncan, Blaser, and Spicer (who named it) is not simply a series of short works linked thematically and formally as in a sonnet sequence, nor is it what M.L. Rosenthal calls 'the modern poetic sequence' in his book of that name, for that sequence is always, at least in part, lyrical, while the serial poem, at least in Spicer's case, arises outside the self and is 'dictated.' The serial poem may utilize any number of forms, but there is no need to keep a consistent pattern."[50] Although Duncan later left the group and became involved with the Black Mountain poets, Spicer and Blaser took as their models Rilke's *Duino Elegies*, *Sonnets to Orpheus* and Duncan's *Medieval Scenes* because of the dictated quality of these works.[51] They used these examples to theorize alternatives to the lyric ego.

The density, brevity, and musical quality of Spicer's poems would mark them as lyrics, but Spicer objected to the lyric "I" and wished to create "a poetry that would be more than the expression of [his] hatreds and desires."[52] He therefore renounced what he called "the big lie of the personal" in favour of a more decentred subjectivity.[53] In *After Lorca* (1957), Spicer shrouds his lyric voice by writing a series of "translations" of Lorca.[54] He frames the serial poem with an introductory "letter" from Lorca in which the dead Spaniard warns that Spicer has chosen English words that alter his poems' meanings, or inserted new stanzas without warning into the translations, or titled as "translations" poems that are entirely Spicer's own. Spicer accounts for this conceit in his penultimate letter to Lorca by stating that he thinks his own personality will shine through "the lovely pattern of cracks in some poem where autobiography shattered but did not quite destroy the surface."[55] Although *After Lorca* is an early Spicer poem and not typical of his later, more impersonal practice, it exhibits the kind of parodic playfulness that one finds in Carson's translations of Stesichoros in *Autobiography of Red*, as well as in Ondaatje's portrait of *Billy the Kid* – a response to Spicer's 1958 poem of the same name.[56] All these works demonstrate that a common function of framing devices is to make explicit the implicit doubleness of voice in the author/speaker of the lyric. Thus the suppressed lyric "I" of the poet frequently resurfaces in a different guise. And, more often than not, it is strengthened by association with artistic geniuses such as Lorca, Stesichoros, and Bolden.

Spicer and Blaser also seek to overcome the synchronic quality of the lyric's arrested moment. Blaser maintains that "the beauty of the idea that you can write a single poem ... is a lie. The processional aspect of the world has to be caught in the language also."[57] He formulates the most concise expression of this aesthetic in an oft-quoted passage from his essay "The Fire": "I'm interested in a particular kind of narrative – what Jack Spicer and I agreed to call in our own work the serial poem – this is a narrative which refuses to adopt an imposed story line, and completes itself only in the sequence of poems, if, in fact, a reader insists upon a definition of completion which is separate from the activity of the poems themselves. The poems tend to act as a sequence of energies which run out when so much of a tale is told. I like to describe this in Ovidian terms, as a *carmen perpetuum*, a continuous song in which the fragmented subject matter is only apparently disconnected."[58] The poets are thus singers in a song cycle that rejects the stamp of an individual ego, for the self in time is always in the process of becoming other.

In Canada, the serial poem is most prevalent in the west, but the form has gained national prominence, in part through the editorial efforts of Bowering and Ondaatje. In 1964 Bowering established the journal *Imago*, which he intended "for the long poem, the series or set, the sequence, swathes from giant work in progress, long life pains eased into print."[59] Bowering published a large number of his own and other authors' serial poems before he abandoned *Imago* in 1974. Five years later, Ondaatje edited *The Long Poem Anthology* with the aim of mapping "important new directions in Canadian poetry and in the form of the long or 'serial' poem."[60] In his introduction, Ondaatje echoes Frye and Livesay in his assertion that "the most interesting writing being done by poets today can be found within the structure of the long poem."[61] However, Ondaatje also acknowledges the importance of American influences. He devotes an entire section of the introduction to a quotation from Blaser's essay on Spicer, "The Practice of Outside" (1975), and the anthology includes a serial poem by Blaser, as does its successor, *The New Long Poem Anthology* (1991), in which editor Sharon Thesen updates Ondaatje's project.[62]

SERIAL MUSIC

Musical metaphors play an important role in the theorization of the serial poem. Douglas Barbour places the serial poem "in the category of anti-lyric" alongside shorter poems that "deliberately flout high lyric conventions yet have their own, wild or atonal, music."[63] Although Blaser stated in 1979 that "the term serial was not adapted from serial music,"[64] Spicer's biographers insist that Spicer coined the term "with reference both to the serial music of Berio and Boulez and to the radio and movie serials that had entertained him as a teenager in Hollywood."[65] Blaser was perhaps uncomfortable with the comparison of poetry to serial music because only Spicer's "Fifteen False Propositions Against God" (1958) and "A Book of Music" (1958) could be said to mimic serial music in any strict fashion.[66]

However, the recursive phrasing and the avoidance of tonal continuity in Spicer's poetry make the comparison to serial music instructive. Indeed, Blaser argued in 1975 that in Spicer's work there is "a special analogy with serial music: the voice or tongue, the tone, of the poem sounds individually, as alone and small as the poet is ... but sounded in series, it enters a field."[67] Serialism grew out of the twelve-tone method developed by Arnold Schoenberg, in which an "order of succession is established for rhythmic values [and] for levels of loudness, for example, as well as for pitches. All of these so-called rows are then repeated during the course of the work."[68] The rigidity of the twelve-tone system fell out of favour with composers (including Schoenberg himself) following the Second World War, but M.J. Grant demonstrates in *Serial Music, Serial Aesthetics: Compositional Theory in Post-War Europe* that serial modes of repetition evolved into increasingly open forms: "Dependence on the creation of boundaries and their immediate refutation characterises serial compositional aesthetics as much as the music itself, and exists over, above and beyond the systemisation of parameters which may have lain at its roots."[69] Serial composers such as Boulez developed open systems of composition that incorporated chance occurrences into their aleatory loops. Grant also argues convincingly that modern poetry and painting had a profound impact on the evolution of this musical culture, and thus it is not unreasonable to posit a relationship between serial music, painting, and poetry in Canada. Cross-genre comparisons are impossible to avoid in a discussion of the serial poem, and the definition of "serialism" must be interpreted liberally, since Spicer coined the term "serial poem" as a joke.

More significant to this study is the fact that composers such as Berio blended serial techniques with electronica and other genres of music. Serialism became a method for rethinking other forms of composition. For example, the Canadian pianist Glenn Gould cites Schoenberg and the twelve-tone composers as being among his "strongest influences," and his groundbreaking recording of J.S. Bach's *Goldberg Variations* in 1955 is an example of how the principles of serialism might be injected into traditional forms.[70] Gould's irreverent recordings of Bach's aria and thirty variations push the classical pattern of theme and variation to its extreme. Gould's refusal to play legato, his reluctance to use the sustaining pedal, his radical shifts in tempo, and the staccato action of his keyboard very nearly break down the flowing phrases into recurring sets of individually sounded notes. He emancipates the silence within the piece, yet the melody is paradoxically strengthened by the gaps and the threat of breakdown. The musician's peculiar architectonic powers make his *Goldberg Variations* cohere, and in 1955 he converted an obscure work for the harpsichord into a best-selling piano recording in North America.

Of course, a classical pianist would not have toppled Louis Armstrong from the number one sales slot in the United States without some shrewd marketing by Columbia Records. The recording owed part of its popularity to the series of thirty photographs of Gould (one for each variation) on the original album cover. These photographs portrayed Gould in eccentric poses during the recording process and provided a flamboyant contrast to the exacting quality of the music. No stranger to mixed-media endeavours himself, Gould's pioneering sound collages, theories of electronic media (in association with McLuhan), and fame as an artist of world-class stature had an effect on Canadian cultural production from the 1950s onward that is difficult to calculate, but profound and undeniable.[71] For example, Ira Nadel points out that Cohen was asked to interview Gould for *Holiday* magazine in 1963 and he became so engrossed in the conversation that he forgot to document it: "The idea was to interview Gould and record his impressions about a series of cities. The editor was concerned that Gould and Cohen would be recognized and suggested that they wear false beards as they walked around Montreal, the first proposed site. Cohen actually met Gould in the basement of the Hotel Bonaventure in Ottawa to begin the piece but became so enthralled by Gould's conversation that he forgot to pursue the line of questioning he had prepared."[72] Gould's promotion of Schoenberg through CBC radio documentaries and his ability to articulate the ideas that impassioned him almost certainly had an impact on the literary forms of variation that came into vogue in Canadian literature in the late 1960s and 1970s.[73] His thoughts on serialism therefore bear consideration in relation to literary form.

Speaking generally, Gould identifies what he sees as the "two most significant concerns of contemporary musical analysis" and notes that they "seem perhaps rather paradoxical": "They are concerned about the functional intensity of structure, about the motivic muscularity so to speak of contemporary music, and on the other hand perhaps as a kind of therapeutic relief from this, [there is] a curiosity about the relationship of chance to intention, accident to deliberation."[74] Gould sees these tensions clearly in serial composition, which he defines broadly as an "attempt to promote a fractional nucleus of the material into sponsoring, through procedures of

imitation, the entire musical structure."[75] The composition expands from
this nucleus in an iterative fashion, while at the same time never duplicating
a musical phrase. Thus, while early twelve-tone works appeared to make a
radical break with classical music, critics such as Reginald Smith Brindle
interpret serialism as a "skillfully disguised" deployment of certain elements within that tradition, in particular the sonata and Wagner's leitmotif.[76] Although serialism is often viewed as esoteric, Gould maintains that
the fundamental principles of serialism are no "longer even remotely avant-
garde. They are now simply part of the indigenous twentieth-century
approach to art."[77] The dissonance and counterpoint of jazz, for instance,
provide the inspiration for *Coming Through Slaughter*, but the rhythmic
shifts in Ondaatje's novel clearly borrow from the techniques he developed
in his serial poems. Michael Jarrett has also noted the atonal treatment of
tonal jazz in Ondaatje's novel.[78]

THE SERIES AND THE SERIAL

Spicer's conflation of the musical sense of the serial with "the radio and
movie serials that had entertained him as a teenager in Hollywood" creates
a problem of terminology. Hardly less problematic is Duncan's assertion
that by "serial music" Spicer "meant nothing as recondite as serial composition in music might lead one to believe, but the episodic appearance of the
movie serial."[79] In radio, film and television, the "serial" refers to an ongoing sequence of connected episodes of similar duration. These heirs to the
Victorian print serials are strongly plot-oriented and typically feature cliffhanger endings that compel the audience to attend the sequel or tune in for
the next episode. Paul Cobley observes that some serialized television pro-
grams, "particularly in the genre of 'soap opera,' may run for decades while
delaying a definitive ending."[80] In contrast, the "series" refers to a
sequence of discrete episodes that are connected by theme or character (for
example, Sherlock Holmes), but not by an overarching plot. "Unlike the
serial format, the series does not foreground development and progression
towards an end" or seek to delay narrative climax indefinitely.[81] Thus,
when Spicer and Blaser discuss the "serial poem," they borrow the discontinuous and recursive character of narrative from the series and the open-
ended conclusion from the serial.

When one compares the serial poems of Blaser and Spicer to those of the
other authors in the Canadian long poem anthologies, one notices significant differences. Marlatt is suspicious of the exalted "I" in the lyric tradition, but she is not willing to abandon lyric subjectivity altogether, as she

states in a 1970 journal entry: "no Martian (Spicer) writing the poem, tho it is in some sense other (not-me), but energy of the whole stream – sensual in the way as anything alive picks up sensation, reading it."[82] Instead of taking dictation from "outside" voices, she cultivates her own embodied voice and makes it interact with voices that have been excluded from the canonical "inside," such as the voices of the Japanese Canadian fishing community in *Steveston* (1974).

Bowering, for his part, rejects the "continuing" aspect of the serial poem. Blaser considered *The Moth Poem* (1962) to be a continuing sequence whose open form enabled him to expand it indefinitely – the final lyric in the 1979 version, "The Translator: A Tale," was a late addition.[83] In contrast, Bowering establishes strict compositional limits for his poems in advance. For example, he limits the composition time for each of the twenty-six sections in *Allophanes* (1976) to the duration of a single lecture by Blaser, so that the temporal framework becomes one of the limits that the poet works within and against. Bowering explicitly incorporates the frame into the composition of an artwork and thereby takes the *perpetuum* out of the imperial *carmen*, as he explains: "The serial poem – from those guys in San Francisco – is an openended form. It's open*ended*, that is to say, each of the pieces is discrete but it's a series that will decide when it's going to stop and where it's going to go – it could go anywhere. Whereas my sense of the serial is a lot like [Victor] Coleman's sense of serial – and a lot like painters' sense of the serial. Painters say, OK, I'm going to work on this shape, say Roy Kiyooka's Ovals, or I'm going to work in terms of this theme – 'Lovers in a Landscape' by Claude Breeze. That's what I have."[84] This painterly sense of the serial, which embraces the motivic repetition of serial music, fashions a discontinuous narrative out of discrete units as in the television series, and questions its own framing practices in the manner of the visual arts, is perhaps the best analogy for the poet-novelist's technique.

All of the novelists studied here modify serial strategies to create narratives out of seemingly discrete units. These units, which may vary generically from lyric to letter to prose anecdote, are primarily connected through patterns of iteration (of diction, symbolism, and myth), instead of through causal connections between events in a linear narrative. Since the fragmented storyline presents a challenge to realist demands for a causal plot, these novels rely on intricate framing devices to legitimate their apparent discontinuities. These framing devices privilege themes and patterns in the text, but they also inhibit any singular interpretation of that text. Each act of framing is thus an act of unframing, because the authors reconfigure previous stories and narrative techniques, as well as undermining their own media. I refer to this double movement as "(un)framing" because the parentheses emphasize the instability of the frame as a structural device.

THE SERIES IN PAINTING AND PHOTOGRAPHY

The example of Roy Kiyooka is crucial to an understanding of these framing practices. Bowering considers Kiyooka to be "the first Vancouver postmodern poet, partly because he is also deservedly celebrated as a painter, sculptor, and photographer."[85] Ondaatje also cites Kiyooka as his ideal of a multimedia artist, and readers at the "celebration" that began the Roy Kiyooka Conference in Vancouver (1–2 October 1999) included Bowering, Ondaatje, and Marlatt.[86] Kiyooka's connection to Marlatt is particularly important because she began writing *Ana Historic* after ending an eight-year relationship with him. She also edited Kiyooka's memoir, *Mothertalk: Life Stories of Mary Kiyoshi Kiyooka* (1997), following the artist's sudden death in 1994. Marlatt explains in her introduction that she altered the original manuscript to restore some of the linearity and detail of the oral interviews with Mary Kiyoshi Kiyooka, which the artist had rendered as "a free-floating succession of stories [...] linked thematically or verbally, rather than chronologically, sometimes not linked at all, and sometimes repeated elsewhere in the manuscript."[87] I have not devoted a chapter to Kiyooka because he did not produce a novel per se, but it is worth considering his legacy here because his serial artistry, and Marlatt's modification of it, illustrates key concerns about the relation of time to the image in the long poems and novels of his peers.

Kiyooka began his career in the 1950s as a serial painter of the hard-edged school of abstraction, but he devoted most of his artistic energies in the late 1960s and 1970s toward a reworking of the temporal and spatial relationships of chronophotography, which arranges photographs into chronological grids. Initially, Kiyooka explored the linear logic of the grid, as in the photographic sequence *Long Beach to Peggy's Cove* (1971), which documents a trans-Canada trip in a chronological fashion.[88] However, in *Van Gogh and the Bird of Paradise* (1970–75) Kiyooka began to turn the linear organization of the grid against itself.[89] Sheryl Conkelton observes that grids of shadows within the photographs disrupt the linear organization of the sequence. In addition, "Kiyooka had inserted his own photos into the book on Van Gogh" featured in the series, thereby disrupting the subject/object division and turning the concluding portrait of the artist inside out.[90]

Kiyooka honed these (un)framing tactics in *Powell Street Promenade* (1978–80), which consists largely of a grid of photographs depicting a tree and a parking metre against a concrete wall.[91] Most of the photographs also feature a different pedestrian whose walking posture creates the impression of movement and whose entrance suggests the beginning of a quotidian narrative. Yet as one tries to read the first row from left to right, the pedestrians walk from right to left. The direction alternates in each of the subsequent rows. Some of the pedestrian shots also appear a second time in a separate row, thereby contesting the assumption of temporal progress. The shadows of the tree and the people never appear on the wall, suggesting that it is always high noon in the photographs, even though the quality of light and dates of composition indicate that they were taken on different days. The resulting grid pattern infers progression, but time remains as still as the parking metre in each picture; then it leaps – whether forward or backward is impossible to say – between pictures. Furthermore, from the top left corner of the grid to the bottom right one, there is a diagonal sequence of photographs that interrupts the horizontal rows and inverts the perspective of the street scenes by showing the reflection of the photographer in a pane of glass. The series appears to be about the passage of time, but its logic is juxtapositional, not chronological.

This serial logic also informs Kiyooka's long poems. In fact, Kiyooka refers to his poems and photographs as "frames," with minimal distinction between media. For example, Kiyooka's *The Fontainebleau Dream Machine: 18 Frames from a Book of Rhetoric* (1977) pairs poems with collages and captions that parody the convention of poem and illustration. Thus, "**the 1st Frame** shows" but "**the 3rd Frame** (hides)," "**the 15th Frame** pre-figures," and "**the 18th Frame**" offers no explanation at all.[92] Like the hot air balloon that recurs as a motif in each collage, the poem moves with the drift of its lofty language and surreal associations to offer new and unusual perspectives as it traces its circuitous path.

In this sense, the balloon is similar to the insect in Blaser's "The Moth Poem."[93] It is what Blaser called "the gift or the dictated" – that is, the found object that becomes the "one dominant musical note or image" on which the artist performs variations.[94] However, Kiyooka, operating from a painterly sense of the serial, is more self-conscious about critiquing his own framing practices. His poems and collages in *The Fontainebleau Dream Machine* emphasize their extravagant mode of composition. Christian Bök argues that "Kiyooka performs a surrealist exercise that explores the parataxis of the unconscious through an associative logic of jumpcuts and dissolves. The technological images of both the cinema and the balloon

intersect in the semiological genre of a comic-strip, whose bubbles of
thought drift through a pageant of frames – spindrift words in a turbulent
grammar."[95] These frames appear in different configurations in *The Long
Poem Anthology* and Kiyooka's collected poems, *Pacific Windows*, which
emphasizes Kiyooka's playful approach to art. As Eva-Marie Kröller
observes, *The Fontainebleau Dream Machine* "attempts no less than a
wide-ranging, dialectical, and often humorous critique of history in general, and art in particular, as a grand scheme of self-delusion."[96] Both artwork and encyclopaedic prank, Kiyooka's serial poem (un)frames its own
technique in order to further the sense of shift in the narrative.

Kiyooka's rethinking of the chronological grid sheds light on the interplay of photography and poetry, as well as the temporal patterning, in the
narratives of his peers. As Ondaatje maintains in his introduction to *The
Long Poem Anthology*, it is important to take into consideration that
Bowering served as an aerial photographer in the Canadian military. Critics
should also remember that Ondaatje is a photographer and filmmaker, that
Carson is a painter, and that all the authors in this study have composed
works that intermingle poetry and pictorial art. Frye claimed that many
"imagistic poems could almost be described as a series of captions to invisible pictures," and this is precisely what the early lyric series by Ondaatje,
Bowering, and Carson are.[97] Carson's first book of poetry, *Short Talks*
(1992), was originally "a book of drawings with writing as captions – and
the captions proved to be more interesting to other people than the drawings. So in frustration [Carson] put the drawings in the drawer and published the writing."[98] Thus, one could think of the evolution of lyric to long
poem to novel in terms of the evolution of photography into serial photography and thence into film, except that in works such as *The Collected
Works of Billy the Kid* this evolution takes place within a single book, as I
show in chapter three.

DISCONTINUOUS NARRATIVE IN THE
LONG POEM

In contrast to the serialism of the San Francisco poets, the (un)framing
impulse in many Canadian serial poems leads to a reconstitution of the
fragmented storyline in an altered, but still poem-length, configuration. For
example, Robert Kroetsch's "Stone Hammer Poem" (1975), also collected
in *The Long Poem Anthology*, consists of eleven perspectives on a stone
maul.[99] In each lyric the poet conjures associations with the image of the

maul, and these meditations combine to form a brief family history of fathers and sons. The series contrasts patterns of recurrence and disobedience rather than stressing straightforward patrilineage (although rebellion has always been part of this story). Most of the poems begin with a variation on the subject phrase "This stone maul," and then digress in the predicate to create poems out of wordplay and metonymy. As Bowering argues in his essay "Stone Hammer Narrative," the pattern of assertions and retractions in Kroetsch's series suggests "an alternative to narrative, an attack on the demonstrative."[100] There remains, however, a strong sense of the poet operating on the meta-level to configure the individual segments in a narrative arc, as the subject of interest progresses from "this stone" to "my poems" over the course of eleven variations.

In his influential essay "For Play and Entrance: The Contemporary Canadian Long Poem" (1989), Kroetsch examines the narrative potential of the discontinuous series from a critical standpoint. Seeking to defy what he sees as the "ferocious principles of closure" in the modern lyric, Kroetsch endorses a narrative mode based on interruption and delay that he calls "the contemporary Canadian long poem."[101] As the rare novelist-turned-poet, Kroetsch rejects the isolated lyric and promotes the long poem because it offers a more expansive mode of expression. This long poem can combine lyrics with fragments of found documents, symbolic anecdotes, dramatic monologues, epic catalogues, nonsense poetry, visual media, and any number of other genres. While the metaphors of sexualized violence that guide Kroetsch's essay seem to ground it in the ethos of the epic, the concern of "Mr Canadian Postmodern" for counter-imperial discourse, revisionary history, and interrupted teleology belongs more properly to the anti-epic, as he explains: "Homer wrote poems without stanzas. We threaten to write stanzas (fragments, pieces, journals, 'takes,' cantos even) that cannot become the poem."[102] Yet the further Kroetsch pursues the fragmentary quality of the anti-epic, the closer he comes to advocating a modified lyric sequence.

Smaro Kamboureli's *On the Edge of Genre* (1991) seeks to distinguish the contemporary long poem from its modern predecessors. Kamboureli challenges the influential work of M.L. Rosenthal and Sally M. Gall in *The Modern Poetic Sequence* (1983), where the authors argue that the modern Anglo-American long poem, the "modern sequence," is an outgrowth of the lyric: "The modern sequence, then, is a grouping of mainly lyric poems and passages, rarely uniform in pattern, which tend to interact as an organic whole. It usually includes narrative and dramatic elements, and

ratiocinative ones as well, but its structure is finally lyrical. Intimate, fragmented, self-analytical, open, emotionally volatile, the sequence meets the
needs of modern sensibility even when the poet aspires to tragic or epic
scope."[103] Kamboureli cites this passage in *On the Edge of Genre* and criticizes its modernist sensibility by maintaining that "the long poem is definitely not a simple extension or expansion of the lyric ... Rather, it is a lyric
fracturing its 'wholeness,' parodying its own lyrical impulse."[104] From this
point forward in her section on "The Lyric Mode," Kamboureli adopts
Rosenthal and Gall's definition of the lyrical impulse as a desire for wholeness. Like Kroetsch, to whom her conception of the long poem owes much,
Kamboureli defines "lyrical structure" as "a closed world, a strait-
jacket."[105] Operating from an Apollonian definition of the lyric,
Kamboureli cannot accept Joseph Riddel's argument that the "theory of the
lyric, rather than being antithetical to any notion of the long poem, indeed
is the only theory of the long poem."[106] Whereas Kamboureli sees the long
poem as the undoing of lyric form, Riddel maintains that the lyric "undoes
its own frame, or repeats the 'force' of framing with its own metaphorical
violence – a play of displacements which the modern 'long poem' only
makes explicit."[107] Kamboureli complains that such conceptions of the
lyric "exten[d] the lyric beyond strict generic specifications," but she herself argues that critics "might even go so far as to consider the contemporary long poem as a mutant form bearing only traces of the genres it derives
from, a potentially new species or at least a species engendered by generic
shifts."[108] Elsewhere, Kamboureli argues that this kind of "wavering" in
genre criticism is "indefensible," but I maintain that it is impossible to set
strict generic limits on either the lyric or the long poem because the disruption of formal limits is an integral part of their aesthetic.[109] Consequently,
one reviewer of *On the Edge of Genre* concludes that "the long poem's
generic transgressions are exceptional only in their visibility."[110]

  Kamboureli correctly points out that Rosenthal and Gall fail to acknowledge the openness of the lyric sequences they investigate, but she fails to
acknowledge that the chief precedent for openness among the ancient genres was established by the lyric. As Greene observes, the lyric "always con-
dones *aporia* and deferrals of meaning."[111] Instead of separating the lyric
from the long poem, therefore, it seems logical to pursue the migration of
the lyric into the long poem and ask if this "mutant form" can transform
into a novel. In the following chapters, I include a number of interview
statements by the novelists under study here to emphasize that they consciously built the lyric into a narrative mode in this manner.

THE NOVEL

According to M.H. Abrams, the "term 'novel' is now applied to a great variety of writings that have in common only the attribute of being extended works of *fiction* written in prose," although the genre may also incorporate sections of poetry, drama, or historical writing.[112] Etymologically, the novel means a "piece of news," and the genre retains strong ties to the descriptive traditions of storytelling and reportage.[113] In place of the evocative glimpse afforded by the lyric, and the symbolic anecdote presented by the long poem, the novel chooses to accumulate events, meditations, and characterizations. Where the lyricist reduces, the novelist accretes; where the longliner sketches, the romancer embellishes. However, the novel's formal antecedents can be traced to narrative verse, particularly to the romance, which gave its name to the French *roman* and the German *Roman*. It is significant that in their reconsideration of the novel Marlatt and Carson return to the verse origins of narrative to tell their love stories. Marlatt's narrator declares that *Ana Historic* "is / not a roman / ce" and challenges the heterosexual conventions of the romantic plot, while Carson's novel in verse extrapolates from a long lyric poem by the Greek poet Stesichoros that is itself a revision of epic myth in lyric metre.[114] For both authors, lyric form provides the tools for reconfiguring the conventional romance.

In English, the novel emerged as a genre that used realism to challenge the idealized characterizations and settings of poetic narrative. Ian Watt argues in *The Rise of the Novel* that realists dispensed with the poets' mythic plots, settings, and moral verities to privilege an urban, middle-class world constructed through close attention to the sensual input and contemporary life. This new genre was "novel" to eighteenth century readers because its comprehensive rendering of psychological and material minutiae held up a mirror to the physical flaws, social injustice, and moral relativism of their times. Although Malcolm Bradbury argues in *The Novel Today* that the novel has always fluctuated between its "propensity towards realism, social documentation and interrelation with historical events and movements, and ... its propensity towards form, fictionality and reflexive self-examination," the literary criticism and interview statements of the poet-novelists make it clear that they view the realist tradition as the dominant one.[115] For example, Ondaatje complains that "the novel demands a comfort level of realism that is quite high" and he laments that the "equivalent of cubism or abstract expressionism or the subliminal and fluid cutting of film still hasn't been allowed into the novel except on the periphery."[116] The poet-novelists thus shape their novels in opposition to realist conventions, without entirely jettisoning the "comfort" of realist scene craft or reverting back to the certainties of medieval romance.

In the eighteenth century, the realist novel was often accused of being formless because it altered or overturned dominant narrative conventions. Likewise, as I demonstrate in my conclusion, the poet's novel is often accused of being inchoate. It is useful, therefore, to contrast the early innovations of the realist novel with those of the poet's novel, in a general manner. Whereas the realists abandoned mythic plots and settings in favour of quotidian ones, the poet-novelists situate the mythic within the quotidian in order to highlight the shortcomings of both realist and mythic narratives. The realists created fictional worlds out of accumulated details, but the poet-novelists create fictional worlds out of symbolic details (motifs) networked by poetic devices. The realists described what was plainly in view yet not considered aesthetic; the poet-novelists make an aesthetic out of what is hidden, overlooked, or unnameable within the realist tradition. The realists challenged the politics and aesthetics of romantic Beauty; the poet-novelists challenge the political and aesthetic assumptions of what constitutes the real. The realists made the individual, and not the community, the locus of meaning-making. The poet-novelists retain this emphasis on the perceptions and cogitations of the individual through the lyric voice; however, their protagonists are not autonomous. The poet-novelists tell stories about isolated individuals finding and building a community outside of the one into which they were born, and this social transformation is mirrored on the formal level by the process through which the novel's poetic fragments cohere into a narrative.

The fragmentation of the storyline in the poet's novel inhibits the chief innovation of realist literature, namely the development of an individual consciousness rooted in the experience of linear duration in time. As Cobley argues, time in realist narrative is almost "invariably presented as consisting of discrete moments along a straight line; any extended lingering [takes] place in the service of the narrator's exposition or summary rather than as a result of characters' subjective impressions."[117] In contrast, time in the poet's novel is non-linear, recursive, and stylized in a manner that prohibits the reader from depending on the protagonists' actions and consciousness to connect events. The poet's novel thereby shatters the realist tropes of the novel as a mirror walking down a road or as a window onto the world. The poet's novel positions multiple histories in a state of reflection and refraction, and develops a narrative consciousness out of a constellation of experiences. It is partly the reader's responsibility to assemble this constellation from analogous experiences, histories, and images.

Because the novel developed in opposition to poetic narrative, it is often situated at the opposite end of the generic spectrum from poetry. However, George Becker observes that Friedrich Schiller and Friedrich von Schlegel "seem to have been the first to apply the world [realism] to literature," and he documents a tradition of "Poetic Realism" in German criticism of the drama and the novel.[118] German Romantics such as von Schlegel believed that poetry would invest the novel with a new sensibility:

> Romantic poetry is a progressive universal poetry. Its mission is not merely to reunite all separate genres of poetry and to put poetry in touch with philosophy and rhetorics. It will, and should, now mingle and now amalgamate poetry and prose, genius and criticism, the poetry of art and the poetry of nature, render poetry living and social, and life and society poetic, poetize wit, fill and saturate the forms of art with solid cultural material of every kind, and inspire them with vibrations of humour ... Romantic poetry alone can, like the epic, become a mirror of the entire surrounding world, a picture of its age. And yet, it too can soar, free from all real and ideal interests, on the wings of poetic reflection, midway between the work and the artist. It can even exponentiate this reflection and multiply it as in an endless series of mirrors.[119]

While the Romantics' sense of boundlessness is not shared by the Canadian authors discussed here, Ondaatje argues that Carson's writing successfully achieves this kind of internal diversity: "When you're reading her work, you're taking in a huge range of intellect and wit and emotion, which are not usually found in the same person."[120] The diversity of the novel is usually credited to the genre's ability to subsume other genres, including the lyric, but Carson's novel in verse counters this process.

Ralph Freedman analyses similar genre issues in the context of modernism in *The Lyrical Novel* (1963). This study investigates Hermann Hesse's formulation of "narrative as a disguised lyric, [and] the novel as a borrowed label for the experimentations of poetic spirits to express their feeling of self and world."[121] Freedman outlines a tradition of lyrical novels that includes works by Novalis, Rilke, and Joyce before focusing on Gide's *Les Faux- Monnayeurs* (1925), Woolf's *The Waves* (1931), and Hesse's *Steppenwolf* (1963) in order to elucidate a "lyrical" technique of translating "narrative in[to] imagery and portraiture."[122] Lyrical novels, Freedman argues, are not wholly governed by linear narrative – what he defines as "the surge towards that which does not yet exist."[123] Rather, they replace the temporal chain of events with spatial patterns of association in which the "surge toward greater intensity reveals not new events but the significance of existing events."[124] These configurations do not necessarily eliminate the forward thrust of a plot (the events must come from somewhere), but lyrical novels "exploit the expectation of narrative by turning it into its opposite: a lyrical process."[125] This process often involves the doubling of narrator and hero – Marlatt stages her own fictional rebirth, while Ondaatje and Carson blur the boundary between autobiography and biography.

However, Freedman's modernist interpretation of this lyrical process does not suit the postmodern novels in this study. Unlike Freedman, I do not believe that the lyric(al) binds the novel's energy within the poet's design, such that the "world is reduced to a *lyrical point of view*, the equivalent of the poet's 'I': the lyrical self."[126] In postmodern novels, doubling is the first step in a semantic expansion, a multiplication of possible viewpoints and interpretations that destabilizes the unity of the self. In *Breaking the Frame: Metalepsis and the Construction of the Subject*, Debra Malina uses the narratological term "metalepsis" to demonstrate that boundary breaks between narrative frameworks – such as those between frame tale and principal narrative, author and character, or reader and character – produce differences and deferrals that facilitate the transition from the synchronic to the diachronic. Like the juxtaposition of lyric and prose in narrative, the doubling of characters produces dissonance as well as crossover. The intersubjective frameworks encourage, rather than restrict, shifts within the text. Thus, the strategies of (un)framing that I trace in Canadian texts operate by a paradoxical process of multiplying deigetic frameworks in order to create a less bounded text.

Freedman's ideas of lyric form in the novel draw on Joseph Frank's 1945 essay "Spatial Form in Modern Literature."[127] This essay influenced multitudes of critics but also met with considerable criticism. Frank was prompted to issue a response, "Spatial Form: Thirty Years After," which figures as part of a collection of essays on the subject, *Spatial Form in Narrative* (1981).[128] In his two essays, Frank elucidates ideas on spatial form that have become foundational to the study of the novel. He argues that narrative in the modern novel does not conform to an Aristotelean temporal arc but issues "spontaneously from the organization of the artwork as it present[s] itself to perception."[129] The manner of this presentation is spatial, since it depends on the "interweaving of images and phrases independently of any time-sequence of narrative action" to generate a sense of pattern that makes the work as a whole comprehensible.[130] It is the reader's job to decipher the spatial logic of these juxtapositions, rather than depending on the temporal logic of linear narrative to make connections. One cannot eliminate the temporal dimension of the act of reading, or of the reader's plot reconstruction in the process of reading, but Frank maintains that spatial form maximizes the impression of simultaneity in the text by setting up an interplay between the scales of microcosmic and macrocosmic pattern, which enables the form to be grasped "in a moment of time, rather than as a sequence."[131]

The chief problem with the notions of space put forth by both Frank and Freedman is that they continue to treat space primarily as a visual construct. Although Frank issues a short qualification to the contrary and follows Ezra Pound in defining the image as an emotional and intellectual complex apprehended in an instant of time, in practice he subordinates all other senses to the visual and so perpetuates the visual bias he appears to undermine by theorizing an alternative to linear emplotment.[132] Frank is interested in the "picture of Dublin seen as a whole" in *Ulysses*, "extra-temporal perspective" in *Le Temps retrouvé*, and the capacity of "visible effects" to create "pure views" that "fuse ... into a unity."[133] It is precisely this visual bias that the novelists in the following chapters first establish through framing devices and then subvert. Ondaatje's sonography in *Coming Through Slaughter*, Bowering's elaborate system of puns in *A Short Sad Book*, and Carson's concept of the novel as tango in *The Beauty of the Husband* orient their respective works toward acoustic and kinetic modalities that cannot be reduced to Frank's paradigm. Despite the shortcomings of his essay, however, Frank's discussion of spatial presentation establishes an enduring basis for understanding how authors can "substitut[e] lyric for narrative principles of organization in the novel."[134] Furthermore, Frank's argument that spatial form is fundamentally mythic because it operates by processes of recursion intersects with theorizations of myth by Ondaatje and Bowering that have played a major role in the development of the poet's novel.[135]

THE PROBLEM OF EMPLOTMENT

A subplot within the poet's novels often addresses the question of how the author can overcome the limitations of the lyric time-sense and perspective (the very limitations that drove the poets toward prose) and generate a satisfactory storytelling medium. Cohen's *The Favourite Game* is perhaps the

first extended meditation on this problem in the Canadian novel, although
the whole concept of a Canadian poet's novel was satirized by Paul Hiebert
in the story of *Sarah Binks* (1947), the sweet songstress of Saskatchewan,
before the form had become common on the national scene.

The application of a serial technique to the poet's novel poses unique theoretical and practical problems. How can a poet take the associative logic
of the serial poem, in which the storyline is suppressed, and apply it to the
novel, in which the storyline is conventionally foregrounded? Spicer suggests one serial approach to prose in "A Fake Novel about the Life of
Arthur Rimbaud," published in *The Heads of the Town Up to the Aether*
(1962). Spicer's "Fake Novel" consists of a series of thirty short prose
poems that bear numbered chapter titles in the same way that Bowering's
Autobiology (1972) does. The individual chapters can be read as complete
works unto themselves, because in a serial narrative "things do not connect
... they correspond."[136] Spicer's allusive series makes fine poetry, but it
would be difficult to hold the reader's attention through two or three hundred pages of such correspondences. As Spicer's title indicates, the poetic
series does not convey the sense of a world entered and a life lived in all its
tedium and glory that one generally associates with the novel. When Spicer
undertook a novel in earnest in *The Tower of Babel* (published posthu-
mously in 1994), he wrote a conventional detective story in which the
"search for a mysterious new kind of poetry" is part of a linear storyline,
rather than a force structuring the narrative.[137]

If the poet-novelist shifts the narrative emphasis from the question of
what will happen next (which is the force propelling most detective,
romance, science fiction, and pornographic novels) to an examination of
why things happen, or a study of how language affects cognition, then the
author must provide some other means for the reader to fashion a sense of
continuity out of the discontinuous material. A compelling central character may function as a unifying force in the text – and each of the novels
examined in the following chapters presents a portrait of an intriguing individual. However, a character's ability to anchor a non-linear narrative by
force of personality alone is limited, as Spicer's life of Rimbaud also demonstrates. Normally the central character in a novel experiences a crisis that
must be resolved in the course of the narrative. Although a truly linear plot
(devoid of flashbacks and digressions) is rare, to dismantle this rudimen-
tary story arc is to create a problem of emplotment, as Marlatt states in a
1985 journal entry: "the trouble with plot in Ana H. – not wanting a
plot-driven novel but not knowing what shape a looser sense of narrative
might take – don't want a sense of moral order to dominate the characters.

perhaps because I'd rather write something akin to a long poem – something with a more inclusive sense of knowing/narrating."[138] Marlatt is not
alone in struggling to conceptualize a "looser sense of narrative" and
authors generally resort to metaphor in order to articulate their formal
aims. Ondaatje, for instance, endorses Phyllis Webb's metaphor of "narrative form as a kind of necklace in which each bead-poem while being
related to the others on the string [is], nevertheless, self-sufficient, independent, lyrical."[139]

By far the most common metaphor for serial narrative involves a reap-
praisal of the trope of the train, which is conventionally associated with
fast-paced, plot-driven narrative. Marlatt's serial poem *Double Negative*
(1988) recasts "the narrative fictional frame of heading down that track"
by documenting a train trip that she and her then partner Betsy Warland
took across Australia in 1986.[140] The poem consists of three written sections interspersed with collages by Cheryl Sourkes that juxtapose phrases
from the long poem with photographic negatives and black ink prints. The
first written section, "Double Negative," presents a series of lyrics in which
Marlatt and Warland alternate in describing the train trip. The second section, "Crossing Loop," interrupts this lyrical but relatively sequential trav-
elogue with a dialogue between the poets in prose. They reflect on their
efforts at collaborative composition and debate the symbolism of the train.
Whereas Marlatt sees the train as "this powerful industrial monster whose
rhythms and approach are seen as very much like the male orgasm,"
Warland sees it as an umbilical cord "representing our continuous dependency on the earth" and she stresses the cyclical aspects of the trajectory and
mechanics of train travel.[141] The dialogue between Warland and Marlatt
concludes in much the same way that Ondaatje's *the man with seven toes*
begins, with Marlatt asking whether they should "get off the train, get off
the narrative track, and move out into the desert in a different way."[142] For
Warland and Marlatt, this different way manifests itself in "Real 2," the
final section of the book, where, as Sidonie Smith observes, the poets produce "a series of poems that riff seriatim on a line from each of the poems
in the first series."[143] By revisiting the first series in this way, by doubling
back and inverting their initial assumptions, the poets create a narrative
round-trip that replays the "reel" of the earlier frames in a different order.
Mixed-media experiments of this kind compel W.F. Garrett-Petts and Donald Lawrence to argue in *Photographic Encounters: The Edges and Edginess of Reading Prose Pictures and Visual Fictions* that authors such as
Marlatt, Bowering, and Ondaatje create "literacy narratives" that link
visual literacy to new forms of literary composition and reading.[144]

The train also functions as a metaphor for linear narrative in Bowering's *A Short Sad Book*. However, Bowering inverts the gender stereotype that Marlatt describes by composing a circumlocutionary narrative out of riffs on certain keywords, while Angela, his wife and editor, admonishes him to get "going on the [straightforward] narrative."[145] The Bowerings also parody E.J. Pratt's long poem about the building of the Canadian Pacific Railway, *Towards the Last Spike* (1952), by masquerading as Pratt's Sir John A. Macdonald and Longfellow's Evangeline. After Evangeline rides the rails from Acadia to Vancouver, Macdonald takes her mountain climbing and the couple abandon the Laurentian Thesis (the notion that Canadian culture flows from east to west) in Terminal City. Bowering insists that "the CPR has a beginning middle & end but Canada doesnt," and he therefore fashions a mural-like history of Canada.[146] His spatialization of the narrative is highly discontinuous, but he argues that "discontinuity is 'really' an older & wiser continuity."[147] He means partly that he wrote continuous narrative in his early novel, *Mirror on the Floor* (1967), and then reconsidered this youthful technique years later. More significantly, Bowering implies that he is transposing the pre-novelistic concept of lyric *variatio*, and the modern concept of the serial, onto prose narrative. Hence, after making allusions to Spicer and "the great Canadian sonnet" series of his painter/poet friend Greg Curnoe – also "Greg Curnoé" (Curnoe, eh?) – Bowering announces that he is writing a "serial novel."[148]

THE SERIAL NOVEL

Conventionally, the term "serial novel" refers to a novel published in installments with cliffhanger chapter endings. These plot-driven novels, which attained considerable popularity in the eighteenth and nineteenth centuries, take part in "a continuous negotiation between producer and reader in which the final form and content is largely determined by a commercial transaction."[149] Their populist means of distribution (as segments in journals and newspapers) established a broad and regular readership, thus reducing the financial risk of publishing a new work and increasing the number of book titles in circulation.[150] For example, Charles Dickens achieved widespread fame in England for *Oliver Twist* (1837), the first novel that he specifically designed for serial publication. *Oliver Twist* was published in sixteen-page installments in *Bentley's Miscellany*, and each section concluded with Oliver on the verge of some new misfortune. Dickens frequently heightened the suspense of Oliver's predicament by advertising the upcoming installment of the novel, as he does at the end of chapter 2:

"As I purpose to show in the sequel whether the white-waistcoated gentleman was right or not, I should perhaps mar the interest of this narrative (supposing it to possess any at all) if I ventured to hint just yet, whether the life of Oliver Twist had this violent termination or no." For all the wit and political insight in Dickens's novel, the author is well aware that the merit of his narrative will be judged by the thrust of its plot. The novel's selling point is its future-oriented story arc.

Although Bowering is not concerned with Dickens specifically, he plays with the legacy of the Victorian serial in *A Short Sad Book* by periodically interrupting his narrative to assess its progress, by soliciting the reader's opinions on the storyline, and by dramatizing the struggles of a small literary press to publish "The Pretty Good Canadian Novel."[151] Conceived as the final installment of a trilogy that includes *Autobiology* (1972) and *Curious* (1973), *A Short Sad Book* was drafted using the space-constraint of two handwritten pages per section, although these constraints are in fact more rigorously applied to the final form of *Autobiology* than to *A Short Sad Book*. Within each section of these novels, Bowering keeps the reader off balance by juggling a variety of storylines in such a way that one is jolted into paying attention and encouraged to keep pace with the rapid changes in the narrative, rather than expecting a fast-paced succession of events in one particular storyline. Instead of following a single plotline, the reader must decipher riddling wordplays and bridge associative leaps in the narrative. Such a concept of the novel perhaps makes sense of Ondaatje's cryptic assertion that "plot comes out of the language as much as it comes out of the described event."[152] Bowering claims to be subverting the temporality and mimetic drive of the realist novel, and he suggests that if readers want a continuous narrative they should "follow [him] around for a day & make [him] be continuous."[153] Bowering's term "serial novel" is thus a deliberate and humorous parody of the standard term, not a failure to fulfill its criteria. The revised definition proposes a form of narrative consisting of discrete units held together by recurring motifs and formal constraints rather than by event and causal connection.

Toward the end of *A Short Sad Book*, Bowering writes sections of continuous, plot-driven narrative, which he blames on the demands of his wife but which are plainly his response to the broader demands of novelistic convention. Bowering's anti-mimetic claims often mislead, because he remains committed both to a mimesis of process, of recording the act of writing, and to realist scene-craft on a small scale. Indeed, in all of the novels examined here, there is a begrudging but unmistakable dependency on realist dramatization. The poet's novel in Canada is not the antithesis of the realist novel, nor an antidote to all its attendant problems. Rather, it includes within itself a critique of the realist novel, even as it struggles to create a new medium that foregrounds the processes by which individuals and groups fragmented by geographical divides and multiple cultural allegiances manage to tell their stories. The fact that most of the writers in this study draw inspiration from photography for their non-linear narratives indicates that they do not reject the world the realists attempted to capture through linear narrative and verisimilitude, so much as seek a new relation to that world.

This new medium translates the non-narrative techniques of poetry, in particular the serial poem, into the novel. As Godard observes in "Stretching the Story: The Canadian Story Cycle," varieties of the long poem in Canada were initially theorized as alternatives to narrative, but these non-narrative strategies for creating formal coherence were ultimately applied to narrative genres.[154] The resulting narratives experiment with sets of recurring phrases or images, explore vertical linkages in narrative through poetic modes of association, juggle a number of plotlines in rapid succession, and make use of framing devices to establish and then undermine structural patterns.

Leonard Cohen: (Un)framing Narrative

After the distinguished summer of yellow dresses and green pants Lisa and Breavman rarely met. But once, during the following winter, they wrestled in the snow.

    That episode has a circumference for Breavman, a kind of black-edged picture frame separating it from what he remembers of her.[1]

Leonard Cohen

Before Leonard Cohen achieved international acclaim with "Suzanne" on *The Songs of Leonard Cohen* (1967), before he shocked the Canadian literary establishment with the pornographic novel *Beautiful Losers* (1966), even before he seduced poetry fans with his popular collection of lyrics, *The Spice-Box of Earth* (1961), he was interested in the visual arts.[2] His most meticulous biographer, Ira Nadel, observes that in "the 1951 Westmount High School Yearbook, Cohen lists photography as his hobby," and for a short period of time Cohen operated The Four Penny Art Gallery in Montreal in cooperation with the painter Mort Rosengarten (the model for the character Krantz in *The Favourite Game*) and their friend Lenore Schwartzman.[3] The gallery, remembered in Cohen's poem "Last Dance at the Four Penny," distinguished itself by promoting figurative painting in an era of abstraction and by making each picture frame a different colour as a signature gimmick.[4] This fascination with the framed figure may stem from Cohen's early obsession with film. Cohen's father died when he was nine and glimpses of his father in the elder's home movies became an integral aspect of the child's family memory.[5] Cohen is drawn to the framed instant as a means of arresting and intensifying chronological time, as well as transcending its attendant sense of loss. He develops this synchronic framing practice into a central feature of his prose technique in his first published novel, *The Favourite Game* (1963).

    Cohen largely abandons chronological sequence in *The Favourite Game* and creates a sense of narrative continuity through recurring visual motifs (scars, blemishes, picture frames) and romantic scenarios (infatuation with an image followed by disillusionment). Through the pronouncements of his poet-protagonist, Lawrence Breavman, Cohen emphasizes the analogous relation between the heightened images of lyric poetry and painting, but as a novelist he faces the challenge of transforming these synchronic visions into a diachronic narrative. This challenge is more clearly defined in *Beautiful Losers*, where Cohen works ekphrastically from a portait of the Mohawk saint Catherine Tekakwitha and fashions her biography by stringing together hymns, dramatic set pieces, and historical vignettes into "a necklace of incomparable beauty and unmeaning."[6] In both cases Cohen abandons straightforward chronology and adopts a serial treatment of narrative that registers the passing of time through recursive patterning. A similar strategy informs the dozens of self-portraits that document Cohen's aging face in *Book of Longing* (2006). These portraits leap backward and forward in time and interact with the poems in Cohen's collection (sometimes through hand-written commentary).

Born in Montreal in 1934, Cohen came of age during a unique period of Canadian literature. He could claim not only his countrymen but members of his own Jewish community as important writers whose work he would cherish long after he had become a famous wandering minstrel. At the same time, the ranks of Canadian literature in the 1950s were still small enough that a dense ring of talent supported the young writer. At McGill University, Cohen studied poetry under Louis Dudek, the champion of literary modernism in Canada, who published Cohen's first collection of poems as part of his subscription-based McGill Poetry Series. Cohen studied prose under Hugh MacLennan, author of an influential novel about crossing cultural divides, *Two Solitudes* (1945), and MacLennan's teaching of James Joyce's *Portrait of the Artist as a Young Man* influenced the story of an artist's maturation in *The Favourite Game*. Cohen briefly studied law under the poet F.R. Scott, who became an important mentor to Cohen and lent him a cabin in North Hatley, where the early portions of *The Spice-Box of Earth* and *The Favourite Game* were composed. In his friend Irving Layton, "Cohen discovered a Judaic voice of opposition, energy, and passion" whose poetry "forced a new vitality into moribund poetic forms and linked the prophetic with the sexual."[7] These mentorships are crucial to an understanding of Cohen's early poetry; they are well documented by Cohen's biographers, and self-evident from the various dedications of his early poems. Michael Q. Abraham's "Neurotic Affiliations: Klein, Layton, Cohen, and the Properties of Influence" offers a particularly useful overview of how Cohen wrote back to his Jewish mentors.

As J.A. Wainwright asserts in "The Favourite Game: Canadian Literature In and Out," one cannot judge the "narrative insurrections" of Cohen and Ondaatje in isolation but must place them within the context of the changing state of literature in Canada following the Second World War.[8] Mordecai Richler's "satirical juxtapositions of Jewish and gentile garrison mentalities breached the walls of exclusivity" in this period, but the key Montreal influence on Cohen was the writing of A.M. Klein, which suggested a model of linking formal experimentation to cross-cultural purpose.[9] Cohen considered Klein to be the city's leading Jewish writer, but Klein's mental breakdown made his life both an inspiration and a cautionary tale for Cohen. Klein's final seventeen years of silence became a legacy against which Cohen defined his own position as a Jewish writer in Montreal.

THE KLEIN INFLUENCE

Klein's writing impressed Cohen for its attempt to address Montreal Jewry as a unique community while at the same time mediating the divide between the francophone east and anglophone west of the island. As Leon Edel, Klein's friend during his McGill days, remarks: "The background of A.M. Klein was Montreal, and to pronounce Montréal is to speak of a city singular among cities – one that had its east and its west, and the twain at that time not only did not meet but were divided by a ghetto housing Jewish immigrants."[10] Klein grew up in the immigrant strip straddling the Main – the boulevard separating east from west that plays a crucial role in the conclusion of *Beautiful Losers* – and the neighbourhood's liminal sensibility defined much of Klein's career. Educated in Protestant schools, Klein naturally proceeded to undergraduate studies at McGill, where he excelled in politics and classics and added Latin to his command of Yiddish, Hebrew, French, and English. He could have proceeded to law school at McGill in the hope of becoming a "Victorian gentleman of Hebraic persuasion," as Cohen describes the Jews of upper-class, anglophone Westmount.[11] However, Klein had misgivings about the ethnic bias of a university that, in this period, limited the number of Jewish students and reduced the number of Catholics in the French Department by importing Protestants from Switzerland and France.[12] Klein therefore chose to cross town and study law at the Université de Montréal, where racism against Jews was less inflected by class divisions between working-class Jews and Québécois. Klein's professional career would span these divides. He edited the weekly *Canadian Jewish Chronicle* (1938–55), guest-lectured at McGill

(1945–48), and addressed the clients of his law practice in English, French, and Yiddish.

Klein's writing career followed an equally multicultural path. His early poems, such as "To Keats" and "Heirloom," reveal an imagination steeped in the canonical works of Anglo-American and Jewish literatures.[13] Klein's predominantly lyric voice in *Hath Not a Jew ...* (1940) turned satiric in *The Hitleriad* (1944), where he updated Pope's mock-epic *The Dunciad* to critique the rise of the Nazi movement. This excoriation of Hitler established a precedent that Cohen modified in *Flowers for Hitler* (1964), but Klein's long poem failed to awaken much interest beyond his friends in the *Preview* group, such as A.J.M. Smith and F.R. Scott, and members of the Jewish Public Library of Montreal.

Klein's final book of poetry, *The Rocking Chair and Other Poems* (1948), won the Governor General's Award for poetry as well as some of the recognition he sought. *The Rocking Chair* takes Klein's birthplace as its subject and compares his Jewish identity and modes of perception to other cultures in the province, with particular emphasis on francophones. As a two-time Co-operative Commonwealth Federation (CCF) candidate for the federal elections in the Laurier riding, Klein pays close attention to the travails and traditions of the working-class French-Canadians; as a child of the Jewish ghetto, he laments the debilitating effects of the "grassy ghetto" in "Indian Reservation: Caughnawaga"; as a religious poet, he compares his faith with that of the Catholic pilgrims in "The Cripples"; as a multilingual scholar and translator, he celebrates the linguistic confusion of "Montreal," a paean to his city composed of words and neologisms drawn from English, French, and Iroquois.[14]

In "A.M. Klein: The Poet and His Relations with French Quebec," Pierre Anctil delivers the long-overdue evidence that

> the period immediately following World War II saw a profound transformation of the relations between the Jewish community and the intellectual and political elite of Francophone Quebec. The world of the habitant and the snowshoe burst into the poet's work precisely at this point following the tensions of the thirties, when Jews and Francophones learned to coexist on a new basis. One can therefore assume that Klein did not write *The Rocking Chair* in a void, on a mere impulse, but that he responded specifically to a sympathetic undercurrent or at least to the lack of hostility that began to develop between the two longstanding Montreal neighbours – the Jews who had emigrated from the distant Polish or Russian plains, and the Québécois

who had emigrated from the countryside of the St. Lawrence valley."[15]

Anctil's detailed scholarship establishes Klein's pivotal role in facilitating this cultural rapprochement:

In July 1947, Klein published seven of his Québécois poems in the journal *Poetry*, of Chicago. When one considers how little attention the author received in Quebec, even within his own community, one could certainly assume that all of the poems would have ultimately gone unnoticed in Montreal. Shortly afterwards, Klein was offered the Edward Bland Memorial Fellowship, a prize awarded by a black American organization to a collection of poems of high literary quality, whose contents have had an impact on social relations. In its October 1947 edition, the *Congress Bulletin,* the official mouthpiece of the Canadian Jewish Congress, announced Klein's award and republished the prize-winning poems under the new title *Poems of French Canada.* Not content with having published seven poems in this form, the directors of the Congress published the poems again, at the end of the year, in a pamphlet, with yet a different title: *Seven Poems.* In an internal memo dated November 25, 1947, David Rome, editor of the *Bulletin,* wrote to Saul Hayes, the executive director of the Congress:
> I wish to report to you that our release of Mr. Klein's poems has met with a response which, frankly, I had not anticipated. *La Presse* made even more of the story than I had expected. We are receiving a number of requests for copies from Jewish, French-Canadian and English members of the public. We are sending some of them the *Congress Bulletin* which contains these poems.
>
> It is also suggested that the pamphlet should be sent to our list of priests and to doctors, government officials, etc., in Quebec and among those who read French. In order to do this, we would have to reprint the poems.[16]

Although Klein had issued scathing denunciations of anti-Semitism in French Canada in the 1930s, his cross-cultural gestures in the postwar period established a platform for dialogue between francophones and Jews.

The "Splendor erablic" of "Montreal" epitomizes Klein's exuberant mixing of cultural codes in this period.[17] It also anticipates the cultural amalgam that he attempts in his short novel, *The Second Scroll* (1951). Ostensibly, *The Second Scroll* is a quest narrative about a young Canadian

journalist's trip to Israel to witness the prophesied restoration of the Jewish
nation and locate his elusive Uncle Melech. The story derives from journal-
istic accounts of the emerging Jewish state that Klein had published in the
Canadian Jewish Chronicle. In the novel, Klein combines the documentary
narrative with a more symbolic and mystical vision of Judaism derived
from the scriptures and embodied in the character of Melech Davidson,
whose name connects him to King David and the Messiah. Written rapidly,
but the result of considerable forethought, *The Second Scroll* represents
Klein's attempt to mythologize what he initially perceived as the fulfillment
of Jewish prophecy in the state of Israel.

In a 1951 letter to A.J.M. Smith, Klein outlined his ambitions for the
novel: "I desired first of all, a record, a conspectus of my pilgrimage to the
Holy Land, some heirloom to attest to the fact that I had been of the generation that had seen the Return ... I was struck, furthermore, by the similarity between contemporary Jewish history and my people's ancient saga – I
thought I saw in the events of today, in large outline, a recurrence of the
events of the Pentateuch."[18] The Pentateuch, the first five books of the
Torah, supplies the formal model for Klein's novel. Seymour Mayne demonstrates that Klein consciously proceeds from Genesis (a short history of
the narrator's youth in Montreal), to Exodus (the trip to Europe), to Leviticus (the priestly book wherein the narrator encounters the Monsignor at
the Vatican), to Numbers (a stocktaking of relations between Sephardic
Jews and Muslims in Casablanca), and finally to Deuteronomy (the Return
and Restoration).[19] In proper Talmudic fashion, these foundational books
are complemented by a scholarly apparatus, which in *The Second Scroll*
takes the form of glosses containing Klein's poem "Autobiographical"
from *Hath Not a Jew...*, an elegy for Melech, a lyric essay on the Sistine
Chapel, a verse drama in which an impoverished Jew pleads his case to
North African Muslims, and a selection of prayers.

While *The Second Scroll* began as journalism, the slender volume is not
weighty with detail. The work as a whole is gestural, elliptical, and relies on
a dense interleaving of allusions and symbols to give it depth. For a reader
not steeped in the traditions of Jewish ritual or schooled in the mystic symbols of the kabbala, the effect of reading certain passages is roughly equivalent to reading Joyce's *Ulysses* without knowing Homer. However, the
exuberance of Klein's novel, which clearly emulates the verbal acrobatics of
Joyce's prose, overcomes such difficulties.

Klein elevates the journalist's medium to a lyrical and erudite prose style
that approximates his favoured poetic mode as celebrant. In a priestly manner, Klein embeds "the jewels of Hebrew poesy" into his principal narrative

and inserts untranslated selections of Latin into "Gloss Gimel."[20] In "Deuteronomy," the narrator encounters a poet in Israel who takes the extreme position of limiting his poems to one or two lines: "'A poem,' he said, bringing forward his meager manuscript written in a hand that from a distance resembled Uncle Melech's, 'a poem is not a destination, it is a point of departure. The destination is determined by the reader. The poet's function is but to point direction. A poem is not the conflagration complete, it is the first kindling. From this premise it follows that poems should be brief, laconic. Sparks.'"[21] A larger conflagration occurs at the end of the first scroll, where Uncle Melech is "anointed" by Arab oil and set aflame, thereby terminating the narrator's physical quest but not his spiritual or aesthetic one. The narrator's mission to find his Uncle Melech quickly merges with his desire as a translator and anthologist to discover "among Israel's speeches, proclamations, fervours, grumblings, and hopes ... the country's typical poetic statement."[22] The anthology subplot links the narrative to the proto-novelistic practice of embedding lyrics within prose such that the autobiographical appearance of the lyric (in Klein's case the poem "Autobiographical") is thwarted by the fictional frame of the prose. This is a technique originally developed by Dante in *La Vita Nuova* (1294) and furthered by Cohen in *The Favourite Game*.

Since Cohen subtitled his draft of *The Favourite Game* "An Anthology," it is worth considering this trope of the anthology-in-process more closely. Seth Lerer explores this subject in "Medieval English Literature and the Idea of the Anthology," where he asserts that the anthology is the basis of English narrative. Lerer claims that the medieval long "poems that we consider single entities were often read as anthologies of a sort, capable of being broken up and rearranged for individual readers' expectations ... What seems to many distinctive of the postmodern textual condition – the fascinations with pastiche, with the quoted quality of any utterance, with the relativism of the canon – seems also to some distincitve of the medieval textual condition."[23] Lerer maintains that such narratives emerge from societies where notions of nationhood and canonicity are ill-defined, which perfectly describes Canada in the 1950s and 1960s, as well as the new state of Israel. The historical irony is that novels produced in this style, as well as long poems such as *The Collected Works of Billy the Kid*, now constitute a large part of the Canadian canon.

The nephew's account of his trip to Israel becomes increasingly poetic as the narrator nears Uncle Melech, whom he never meets but of whom he hears countless stories. There are so many differing accounts of Melech's character that it seems that he makes a different impression on every person he encounters: a fickle heretic to the Orthodox Jews, a closet Catholic to the Italians, a Zionist martyr to the Israeli masses at his funeral, and a folk hero to the young boy on avenue de l'Hôtel-de-Ville who dreams Montreal into a "pleasant Bible-land."[24] According to Klein's letters, Melech's "sought-for messianic personality is an unidentifiable entity made up of the anonymous fractions of total Jewry."[25] Melech thus embodies the "unity-in-diversity" ideal that Michael Hurley, Andy Belyea, and Tom Marshall identify as Klein's principal theme.[26]

A photograph that the nephew receives of Melech serves as an objective correlative of the multiple dimensions of the uncle's character. An acquaintance of Melech presents this icon to the nephew as consolation for never having met the man:

> All my life I had waited for this picture, and now at last I was to see him, Uncle Melech plain!
> She handed me the snapshot.
> It showed a man standing in the midst of a group of barefooted boys. But his face – Uncle Melech had again eluded me. It was a double, a multiple exposure![27]

Klein thus replicates his cosmopolitan ideal across a number of scales in *The Second Scroll*: in the multiple exposures of the photograph, in the reports of Melech's character, in the narrator's dual allegiance to Canada and Israel, and in the novel's multiple generic frameworks, which ostentatiously flout the conventions of realist prose.

However, for a pious Jew, rewriting the Pentateuch is not the same as parodying *The Dunciad*. The narrator in *The Second Scroll* strives not for mock-epic but to create "word by word, phrase by phrase, the total work that when completed would stand as epic revealed!"[28] This wildly ambitious undertaking is a response to the fervour of Israel's establishment, the return of a traumatized Diaspora to their holy land, and the re-emergence of scriptural Hebrew as a spoken language. The ecstatic tone and optimism of Klein's novel were well received in many quarters and he embarked on exhaustive speaking tours in Canada and the United States. But the fervour was shortlived. Some conservative factions within the Montreal Jewish community criticized Klein for tampering with sacred texts. Although not orthodox in his Judaism, Klein himself began to doubt the wisdom of rewriting the Pentateuch. His exhaustion, combined with the postwar pogroms in Poland, the far from utopian state of Israel in the 1950s, and the ongoing pattern of martyrdom and nationalist demonstration that

Klein imagined ceasing with the sacrifice of Uncle Melech led him into a deep depression. He began to lose sleep, eat irregularly, and doubt his vocation as a writer. According to his son Coleman, Klein grew increasingly suspicious of hidden meanings in ordinary utterances, a tendency exacerbated by an exegesis he was preparing on the multiple connotations of words in Joyce's *Ulysses*.[29] Emotionally overcome, Klein attempted suicide several times in 1954. He survived physically, but in a chilling enactment of the final poem in *The Rocking Chair*, "Portrait of the Artist as Landscape," the poet remained almost completely silent for seventeen years, until his death in 1972.

The exact causes of Klein's emotional breakdown and mental illness are not known. No single incident triggered his decline, and it almost certainly resulted from a combination of fatigue, professional stress, and biochemical factors. But as with the mental illnesses of all legendary figures – such as Buddy Bolden in *Coming Through Slaughter*, who refuses to talk in his asylum years – Klein's sufferings enhanced his mythic status in the public eye. His silence became a canvas onto which artists and critics projected their own fears. For example, Leon Edel argues that Klein resented finding himself "in Hochelaga once more, harnessed to his old round, caught in the old struggles and the conflicts of his art and mundanities of life."[30] This statement might offer some insight into Edel's reasons for moving to New York, but they make no sense in the context of Klein's literary output. Despite the allure of a newly founded Israel, Klein repeatedly defends, excuses, and explains his passion for Montreal in his poetry and through the nephew persona in *The Second Scroll*. Contrary to Edel, Naïm Kattan reports that Klein was haunted by accusations of hypocrisy because he did not support his praise of Israel by actually moving there, and the split between word and deed caused him to feel that words were futile.[31] Roger Hyman offers a balanced survey of the various speculations on Klein's illness in his long-overdue study, *Aught from Naught: A.M. Klein's* The Second Scroll (1999), but one should note Rachel Feldhay Brenner's argument in *A.M. Klein, The Father of Canadian Jewish Literature* (1990). Brenner maintains that after the euphoria of Klein's trip to Israel and the fervour of the novel's composition, Klein was devastated by the political decisions of the emergent state. The nation he envisioned as a synthesis of the fractions of total Jewry imposed restrictive immigration policies that gave preference to Jews from wealthy nations, even as Jews faced continued threats of anti-Semitic violence around the world. Klein's final editorials eulogize the traditions and cultural productions of the Diaspora, and Brenner argues that Israel's "openly propagated and ideologically legitimized denouncement of the

Diaspora ... seems to have dealt the decisive blow to Klein's idealistic vision of post-Holocaust Jewish cultural rebirth."[32] Far from being the "consolation of our people's rescue," as Klein described the Jewish state in a letter to Edel, Israel heaped shame upon the decisions of non-Israeli Jews and severed cultural ties with Klein's Diasporic ancestors, whose cosmopolitan experience he believed was the source of their creativity.[33] This turn of events subverted the "unity-in-diversity" principle that had guided Klein's life and replaced it with a more stringent form of monotheism that preached unity at the cost of diversity. More than at a loss for words to describe the succession of tragedies that befell his world, from the Great Depression to the Holocaust to his failed bids to win the political nomination of a predominantly Jewish riding, Klein seems to have lost his sense of the purpose of words altogether.[34]

This tragic turn in Klein's life had a profound influence on the emerging generation of Jewish writers in Montreal, who followed Klein in making the transition from Yiddish to English. Cohen met A.M. Klein only once, through Irving Layton in 1959. Klein rose to the occasion and discussed poetry with the young writers, but his debilitated state was obvious. Still, only Layton can claim to have had as much of an impact on Cohen's art, as Cohen observes: "[Klein's] fate was very important to me, what happened to and what would happen to a Jewish writer in Montreal who was writing in English, who was not *totally* writing from a Jewish position ... Klein *came out* of the Jewish community of Montreal, but [he] had a perspective on it and on the country, and on the province. He made a step outside the community. He was no longer protected by it."[35] Both Ira Nadel and Winfried Siemerling point to a speech that Cohen gave in 1964 at the Jewish Public Library of Montreal as evidence that "Cohen interpreted Klein's breakdown as the result of being exiled by his community."[36] In this speech, Cohen publicly blamed Klein's silence on the reception of his writing in Montreal. He also blasted the materialism of his Westmount elders and declared that he would henceforth devote his artistic energies to subverting the union of Jewish tradition and bourgeois values. Siemerling's archival work has made Cohen's scathing notes from this speech available, but in a 1990 interview Cohen retracted his more extreme statements. Claiming to have "a certain self-protective amnesia" about this period, Cohen mistakenly asserted that he was upset because Klein had killed himself prior to the speech, which is likely a defensive manoeuvre on Cohen's part, but at least indicates the traumatic impact of Klein's living death.[37]

Another part of Cohen's speech accused Klein of being complicit in his own decline. Cohen alluded to Klein's role as speechwriter and publicist for

Samuel Bronfman (then president of the Canadian Jewish Congress) and argued that the poet "spoke with too much responsibility, he was too much a champion of the cause, too much the theorist of the Jewish party line ... Klein chose to be a priest though it was as a prophet that we needed him, as a prophet he needed us and he needed himself."[38] Cohen's charge was somewhat unfair, because Klein challenged Zionist doctrine and employed prophetic techniques, such as dream visions and blasphemy, in "In Praise of the Diaspora" (1953).[39] Significantly, however, this last, brazen speech was never delivered.

Nadel maintains that Cohen "reformulate[s] the voice of the Jewish poet" by "combining Klein's priestly mien with the prophetic energy of Layton," but Cohen insisted in his library speech that any attempt to merge the priest and prophet "exhausts itself in failure."[40] Nadel is correct, but the contradiction highlights a central tension in Cohen's writing. Throughout the 1960s, Cohen adopted a series of increasingly radical positions in an attempt to subvert his priestly inclinations. As a Cohen, a descendant of the high priest Aaron, the poet's entire upbringing and scholastic training oriented him toward the role of rabbi or community leader. Nadel points out that Cohen's paternal grandfather owned a brass foundry, operated a company responsible for dredging the tributaries of the St Lawrence, and "in 1893 visited Palestine on behalf of a Jewish settlement group, the first direct contact by Canadian Jews with their homeland. [Lazarus Cohen] also became chairman of the Jewish Colonisation Committee of the Baron de Hirsch Institute, which had been organized to settle Jewish immigrants in Western Canada. In 1896 he became president of Shaar Hashomayim Congregation, a post he held until 1902."[41] However, Cohen did not become the president of a synagogue or follow in Klein's footsteps to become a community spokesman. Instead, he became the poet of Klein's nervous breakdown and tried to make a holy land of Montreal.

COHEN AS POET

Cohen's first book of poetry, *Let Us Compare Mythologies* (1956), demonstrates the Montrealer's uncanny ability to anticipate and reflect the *zeitgeist* of an era. Nadel observes that "Cohen's interest in myth coincided with a shift in literary studies, summarized by the work of the Canadian critic Northrop Frye," who, a year after the publication of *Let Us Compare Mythologies*, issued "his encyclopedic treatment of myth and literature, *Anatomy of Criticism*, initiating a new paradigm for the study of literature via archetypes."[42] Cohen's mythologies, cadences, and diction in this

collection are largely Hebraic and European, reflecting his ongoing study of
the Bible and his poetic apprenticeship under the high priests of his particular brand of Romanticism: Keats, Yeats, Dylan Thomas, and Klein, who
sometimes dubbed himself A.M. Keats. In *Leonard Cohen*, Ondaatje criticizes *Let Us Compare Mythologies* for being "too fond of ... an excessive
poesy" that "drowns [its] objects in a rhetoric that does not really fit."[43]
He accuses Cohen of lingering in European monasteries instead of embracing the language and myths of his age. However, Ondaatje's dismissal of the
first collection was too quick, as Stephen Scobie notes: "For a young Jew in
a Christian country, comparative mythology is not an academic exercise
but an immediate fact of repression and prejudice."[44] In poems such as
"For Wilf and His House," where Cohen depicts the Jewish and Christian
communities of Westmount "each in [their] holy hill," he is beginning to
address the complexities of writing in multicultural space, where traditions
overlap and cultural ciphers bear multiple connotations.[45]

Ondaatje prefers Cohen's second collection, *The Spice-Box of Earth*
(1961), which is more spare in its diction and "relies on the strict ballad
form rather than the biblical rhetoric that appeared in *Mythologies* and
was to re-emerge in *Flowers for Hitler*."[46] Ondaatje argues that after the
second collection "Cohen was really becoming a novelist. The best
moments in *Flowers for Hitler*, such as the prose passages or rhetorical wit,
would not seem out of place in a novel," a proposition that Scobie pursues
in his comparison of *Flowers for Hitler* with *Beautiful Losers*.[47] Indeed,
Clint Burnham locates the origin of Cohen's postmodernism (usually
attributed to *Beautiful Losers*) in *Flowers for Hitler* because of certain features of the book: "the notion of the death of the subject, the prevalence of
pastiche, space as a thematico-formal concern, and the dialectic of high and
mass culture."[48] However, *The Spice-Box of Earth* obviously held a special
importance for Cohen because he structured *The Favourite Game* around
its poems.

The opening poem in *The Spice-Box of Earth*, "As the Mist Leaves No
Scar," is a typical Cohen ballad that later serves as the epigram to *The
Favourite Game*. The first stanza of this poem indicates that Cohen has
exchanged his gilded diction for a colloquial voice that acquires the classical rigour he reveres by shaping itself to the ballad form:

> As the mist leaves no scar
> On the dark green hill,
> So my body leaves no scar
> On you, nor ever will.[49]

The musical cadence of the rhyming quatrains in this poem is unmistakable, and Cohen adapted the poem to music on his album *Death of a Ladies' Man* (1977). However, he added the refrain "True love leaves no traces / If you and I are one" to the song, which entirely contradicts the original message of the poem, where an absence of traces equalled an absence of love.[50] This distinction is crucial because in *The Favourite Game* the scar motif illustrates Breavman's preference for his great love, Shell, over his long-time lover, Tamara. Cohen's protagonist falls in love with Shell because she has been scarred by a past relationship and allows Breavman to leave his brand on her, an act he mistakes for love. Tamara's impeccable beauty leaves no emotional scar on Breavman, however, so he abandons her. Yet according to the logic of "True Love Leaves No Traces," Tamara, not Shell, should be Breavman's true love, for they begin to resemble each other toward the end of the novel, and their relationship endures when "one is gone and far."[51] Cohen's themes and motifs are thus evolving entities, not static ones.

COHEN AND THE LONG POEM

The scar motif undergoes further variations in the long prose poem "Lines from My Grandfather's Journal," which concludes *The Spice-Box of Earth*. This seven-page poem reprises the motifs of scars, stars, and mist from the opening ballad, as well as their variations in other works in the collection. However, "Lines from My Grandfather's Journal" signals a radical departure in Cohen's poetry. Cohen had dabbled in the short prose poem in "Poem, en Prose," an early effort published in Dudek's journal CIV/n, and in "Friends," collected in *Let Us Compare Mythologies*.[52] But in his first published long poem Cohen's desire to narrate family history compels him to transform the short form into a diachronic medium.

"Lines from My Grandfather's Journal" examines a deep personal scar in Cohen's life: his feelings of inadequacy in comparison to his maternal grandfather, Rabbi Solomon Klinitsky-Klein, who was "known as *Sar ha Dikdook*, the Prince of Grammarians, for writing an encyclopedic guidebook to talmudic interpretations, *A Treasury of Rabbinic Interpretations*, and a dictionary of synonyms and homonyms, *Lexicon of Hebrew Homonyms*, praised by the poet A.M. Klein."[53] In "Lines from My Grandfather's Journal," Cohen merges his poetic voice with the learned voice of his grandfather to lyricize entries from the elder's journal. The poem begins by equating writing with scarification: "I am one of those who could tell every word the pin went through. Page after page I could imagine the scar

in a thousand crowned letters."[54] The pin reference alludes to a scholarly
game that A.M. Klein explains in the "Sophist" section of "Portraits of a
Minyan," where he praises the erudite Reb Simcha:

> One placed a pin upon a page
> Of Talmud print, whereat the sage
> Declared what holy word was writ
> Two hundred pages under it![55]

In Cohen's poem, the piercing of the pin suggests that the poet's mode of
writing has a vertical dimension to it, as well as the conventional horizontal
one of reading, and that the vertical method in fact sews the fragments of
the journal together. The pin threads as well as inscribes, a phallic practice
that Cohen makes more explicit in *Beautiful Losers*.

Cohen's poem proceeds to offer longer selections from the grandfather's
journal, and each block of prose concludes with an ellipsis. Although the
journal format suggests chronological succession, Cohen avoids making
causal connections between entries, and many of the sentences shift their
focus abruptly even within a single paragraph. Cohen jolts the reader with
powerful but disjointed images of his grandfather's flight from Nazi perse-
cution in Europe, and the reader relies on the obsessive recurrence of key
symbols such as pins, whips, and scars to suggest links between paragraphs. By the conclusion of the poem, the recurring ellipses transform into
pin marks that indicate vertical (generational, ritual, psychoanalytical)
conjunction despite the horizontal (chronological, locational) disjunctions.

The other unifying force in the poem is the grandfather's elevated tone.
"All my family were priests," the Rabbi recalls, but he struggles with a loss
of faith precipitated by the horrors of the Holocaust:

> Do not let me lie down with spiders. Do not let me encourage insects
> against my eyes. Do not let me make my living nest with worms or
> apply to my stomach the comb of iron or bind my genitals with
> cord.
> It is strange that even now prayer is my natural language ...[56]

The Rabbi's meditations and prayers evolve into short lyrics that Cohen
embeds between blocks of prose, much as Klein had embedded jewels of
poesy into his novel. Cohen also underscores his grandfather's shared surname with A.M. Klein by describing his disputatious grandfather in the
terms he would later use to describe Klein, as a man who "stood outside

[his] community" because the "real deserts are outside tradition ..."[57] Like
the A.M. Klein of the 1950s, the aging Rabbi doubts "everything that I was
made to write. My dictionaries groaning with lies. Driven back to Genesis.
Doubting where every word began."[58] In the poem "To a Teacher," from
The Spice-Box of Earth, Cohen imagines himself as A.M. Klein's "honoured son," but in "Lines from My Grandfather's Journal" Cohen weaves
the story of his poetic father-figure into the lineage of his rabbinical grandparents.[59]

Ondaatje hails "Lines from My Grandfather's Journal" as one of the fin-
est poems in *The Spice-Box of Earth*, but I would agree with Ondaatje's
earlier judgement, as well as that of Bowering, that the ballad form is
Cohen's principal strength.[60] Nevertheless, "Lines from My Grandfather's
Journal" is a key transitional poem because it allows Cohen to refine the
short, sharp, lyrical sentences that constitute the bulk of *The Favourite
Game*. The long poem also clarifies the significance of the title of *The
Spice-Box of Earth*. Preparing to invoke the spice-box of the Jewish
Havdallah ritual toward the end of the poem, Cohen defines prayer in
secular terms:

> Prayer makes speech a ceremony. To observe this ritual in the absence
> of arks, altars, a listening sky: this is a rich discipline.
>   I stare dumbfounded at the trees. I imagine the scar in a thousand
> crowned letters. Let me never speak casually.[61]

Here the ellipses stop as the pin sews the beginning and end of the poem
together with a recurring phrase. To make a ceremony of the conclusion,
the speaker (who appears to be Cohen at this point) offers a prayer that he
proposes to inscribe (presumably with the pin) on the family spice-box, an
incense burner whose fragrant contents are blessed and then, as Nadel
demontrates, are "inhaled after sundown on the Sabbath, mark[ing] the
boundary between the sacred and the profane."[62] The emphasis on smell in
this ceremony, as well as the tactility of the poet's engraving, points to the
recovery of the body that will be the focus of Cohen's quest to integrate the
sacred and profane in his novels.

COHEN AS NOVELIST: *THE FAVOURITE GAME*

When Cohen explores his own life story in the semi-autobiographical *The
Favourite Game*, he finds the cultural lineage that structures his long poem
inadequate. The idea of sacralizing the earth of Montreal, and not just the

contents of the family spice-box, poses unique complications for the author, because this corner of the earth bears the footprint of a variety of cultures. Cohen addresses English Canadian, Jewish Canadian, Québécois, and American cultures in *The Favourite Game*, and then adds Iroquois to this grouping in *Beautiful Losers*. The language of Cohen's grandfather – with its priestly tone and emphasis on a single ethnicity – does not suffice to perform this urban rite. Therefore Cohen counterpoints his lyrical prose in *The Favourite Game* with comic and prophetic voices. These tonal shifts enable him to move in and out of cultural spheres and comment on the beauty and banality of each cultural line he crosses.

Cohen began the first draft of *The Favourite Game* in the 1950s and Scobie therefore situates Breavman, the novel's hero, in the context of that decade's cinema and television icons: "The archetypes of popular culture in the fifties – Elvis Presley gyrating his hips out of sight of Ed Sullivan's cameras; Marlon Brando in his black leather jacket in *The Wild One*; James Dean caught in terminal adolescent angst – were all 'rebels without a cause.' It was the lack of a cause, as much as the rebellion, which prevented them from being assimilated."[63] Robert Fulford also sees Breavman as part of this rebellious gang, but in his scathing review of *The Favourite Game* he maintains that such poses had become cliché by 1963: "Lawrence, like most such heroes, has to endure a respectable family (Montreal Jewish, in this case), a good education (McGill, in this case), and a long string of tiresome or tiring but beautiful mistresses. People who do not have these advantages naïvely believe that those who are so favored must lead happy lives. Alas, this belief is mistaken, and no one proves it better than Lawrence Breavman."[64] The charges of solipsism against Breavman are well founded as the narrative action centres almost exclusively on him.

The enigmatic women who populate Cohen's songs and poems also translate poorly into this narrative format, where they play little more than cameo or ornamental roles. "Women may be goddesses" in Cohen's writing, as George Woodcock observes, but as "intellectual beings, as individuals, they are non-existent."[65] Dagmar de Venster concedes that there is some redemptive value in Cohen's ability to shock in *Beautiful Losers*, but she asks in exasperation: "Do you have an orifice and a pair of breasts? These are the essential if not sole requirements for a female character in a Leonard Cohen novel."[66] Breavman's scarcely differentiated succession of trysts in *The Favourite Game* forced one male reviewer to put the book down because "there had been just too many sets of white thighs in too few pages."[67] Although Cohen wrote the novel as a character study of Breavman, another reviewer observes that "repetition could have been avoided if the contest between the lover and the poet, within the heart of Breavman, had been presented in a series of variations reflected in the lives of characters revolving around him."[68] As the novel stands, Breavman's women ultimately blur into one Woman, an essentialized entity to which Cohen continues to refer well into the 1970s.[69] Woman is a vehicle in the male hero's quest, a convention of patriarchal plots that Marlatt deconstructs in *Ana Historic*.

Breavman's relationship with Krantz also deteriorates because of an unequal power dynamic. Krantzstone is the rock, the man of the mountain, the Westmount male whose stability Breavman simultaneously depends on and fears (*il craint*). Their dialectic is really a vaudeville act in which Krantz sets up Breavman for witty one-liners, and Krantz ultimately tires of this supporting role. Breavman's gender, class, and family pedigree instill in him a presumption of authority, such that when he forsakes the mountain for working-class East Island, he characterizes himself as a man who has given up presidencies to see a different side of life. Likewise, Cohen famously informed Adrienne Clarkson in a 1966 television interview that the "time is over when poets should sit on marble stairs with black capes," but he has largely spent the subsequent decades exploring red light districts and abandoned warehouses in the best suits money can buy.[70]

Even overlooking this class distinction, the plot in *The Favourite Game* cannot be reduced to the rebel-without-a-cause template. As *New York Times* critic Charles Poore notes, Cohen is "not only writing a first novel of the youth-in-search-of-a-goal variety, but several kinds of first novels at once ... Such as the one about the unhappy, sensitive poet in a world of crass, if opulent, materialism. Such as the one about the quest for the golden girl. Such as the one about the pilgrim seeking fame, or fortune, or both."[71] Poore lauds Breavman's reckless behaviour for its impressive energy, but he pays little attention to what I take to be one of the key stories within *The Favourite Game*. Its plot is now very familiar in Canada and forms the basis of novels such as Sky Lee's *Disappearing Moon Cafe* and films such as *Mambo Italiano*.[72] It is the one about the ambitious child from a minority background who strives to escape the confines of a spatialized ethnic enclave without entirely renouncing the heritage that he or she alternately ridicules and romanticizes.

To assimilate Breavman into the Hollywood template is to disregard this key story within the story. Only a few reviewers, especially Gilles Hénault, the Québécois reviewer of English Canadian letters for *La Presse*, pay close attention to the problems that Breavman's ethnic background poses for him. Drawing a parallel to the Québécois writers of the Quiet Revolution which anticipates the character "F." in *Beautiful Losers,* Hénault observes that the Québécois share with the Jewish protagonist a sense of existing in a double-bind: "Tout comme Breavman, ils détruisent d'anciens mythes, pour en formuler de nouveaux, plus accordés à leur situation, mais en conservant comme lui la nostalgie de l'appartenance à un groupe ethnique, à une culture, à des traditions. C'est qu'au fond, les traditions ne se nient qu'en se revalorisant."[73] The Jewish identity, which Fulford places in parentheses, is by no means negligible, because it inhibits Breavman's sense of belonging. As a Jew, he does not really fit into Protestant Westmount; as an anglophone, he does not belong in Montréal Est; and as the son of a wealthy factory owner, he cannot claim affiliation to the Jewry of the Main because he is the scion of the powers against which A.M. Klein's father mobilized unions. He is not, like the cinematic versions of James Dean and Elvis Presley, someone who can simply take off his leather jacket and fit into a majority culture.

Cohen calls attention to questions of cultural passing in the fight scene at the Palais d'Or. Having crossed town to chase francophone women at a dancehall, Breavman and Krantz raise the ire of the local men, and the pair are singled out as Jews. An argument ensues in which, as Sherry Simon observes, neither group "has much of a vocabulary beyond the stereotypes they've been taught about each other."[74] Mordecai Richler replays this fight scene in *St. Urbain's Horseman* (1971) to illustrate the historical antagonisms between Jewish and francophone Montrealers. During a period of heightened tension between the two groups, a "St. Urbain Street boy who had gone to the Palais d'Or dancehall to look over the *shiksas* made off with a girl whose husband was overseas with the Van Doos [the all-francophone Royal 22nd Regiment]. The boy was beaten up and left bleeding on the sidewalk outside his house and the story was printed in all the newspapers."[75] The attack on the Jewish boy in Richler's book leads to gang reprisals, a Québécois left unconscious in an alley, the exile of the Horseman, and the closure of the dancehall.

The Cohen scenario, on the other hand, reveals moments of cross-cultural desire even amidst the fighting. Krantz and Breavman want the Québécoises because the women's "racial mystery challenge[s] investigation."[76] The boys' predatory approach to seduction exudes the kind of scientific detachment that marks the subsequent scene where they dissect a symbolic frog at the foot of a war memorial. However, the fact that Breavman cultivates the French stereotype of the *poète maudit* in his behaviour has a destablizing impact on his ethnic identity. When Breavman's assailant yells, "*Reste là, maudit juif,*" the poet takes the insult as a compliment to his rebel image.[77] The slur aligns Breavman with the anti-establish-ment persona of the young Rimbaud and situates Cohen's writing in the Symbolist tradition of prose poems that Cohen admires. (Cohen likes to refer to himself as a *poète maudit*, and Hénault also draws the Rimbaud comparison.)[78] This cross-cultural melee, which Breavman later claims to have choreographed through hypnosis, sets a precedent for Cohen to revise in the political rally in *Beautiful Losers*. Whereas Breavman and Krantz take out their sexual frustrations with their fists in *The Favourite Game*, the narrator in *Beautiful Losers* gets a handjob from an anonymous female spectator at a separatist rally and momentarily finds himself cheering for the creation of an independent, francophone "Laurentian Republic!"[79] Some members of the crowd accuse the historian of being Jewish or English and threaten him with violence, but F. intervenes to certify his "pedi-gree."[80] This statement is blatantly ironic, but part of Cohen's message is that F. and "I," as multilingual orphans, are less conditioned in ancestral hatreds.

Whereas Stephen Daedalus in *Portrait of the Artist as a Young Man* aspires to forge in his soul the definitive voice of his race, Breavman is flip-pant about his priestly heritage and its accompanying roles:

> The Breavmans founded and presided over most of the institutions which make the Montreal Jewish community one of the most powerful in the world today.
>
> The joke around the city is: The Jews are the conscience of the world and the Breavmans are the conscience of the Jews. "And I am the con-science of the Breavmans," adds Lawrence Breavman.[81]

Except for a brief period of repentance in the brass foundry, Breavman acts without the slightest consideration toward his mother and uncles. He is, as all critics note, a person who bereaves others, in particular women. Citing some vague notion of a supreme idea he is pursuing, he abandons the fam-ily business and moves out of his mother's house to participate in the multi-racial nightlife downtown. Yet he cannot escape his heritage, because he achieves celebrity as a Jewish poet. His response to this label is usually ironic. With Krantz he is happy to be a Talmudist, but in the company of Gentiles he sees his Jewishness as a kind of false-front: "He engaged stock-brokers in long conversations about over-breeding and the loss of creative vitality. He punctuated his speech with Yiddish expressions which he never thought of using anywhere else. In their living-rooms, for no reason at all, he often broke into little Hasidic dances around the tea table."[82] Breavman does not define himself by reference to a stable national or ethnic type, but in relation to the people he encounters. He draws on a number of cultural resources and performs variations on the possible personae – King Solomon, *poète maudit*, the Canadian Keats – that each ethnicity suggests.

The goal of all this apprenticeship and experimentation is, for Breavman, to produce something particular to Montreal. Shortly before he flees Montreal for New York, he lambastes his fellow citizens for their colonial mentality:

Some say that no one ever leaves Montreal, for that city, like Canada itself, is designed to preserve the past, a past that happened somewhere else.

This past is not preserved in the buildings or monuments, which fall easily to profit, but in the minds of her citizens. The clothes they wear, the jobs they perform are only the disguises of fashion. Each man speaks with his father's tongue.

Just as there are no Canadians, there are no Montrealers. Ask a man who he is and he names a race.

So the streets change swiftly, the skyscrapers climb into silhouettes against the St. Lawrence, but it is somehow unreal and no one believes it, because in Montreal there is no present tense, there is only the past claiming victories.[83]

Breavman moves to Manhattan in an effort to legitimate himself as an artist of the present tense but, as his *New York Times* reviewer observes, "his best scenes are always in Montreal."[84] He arrives at a similar realization in the course of his journey. After soaking up the cultural offerings of the American metropolis, in particular the music library at the World Student House, he returns to "the Montreal poem factory"[85] and ultimately revises his assessment of racial identities with the tongue-in-cheek salutation: "Hello Canada, you big Canada, you dull, beautiful resources. Everybody is Canadian. The Jew's disguise won't work."[86] The crucial shift that facilitates this transition is that Breavman ceases to think of himself as the embodiment of a bloodline or national archetype and comes to think of himself as a documentarian of a particular cultural space.

The composition process behind *The Favourite Game* highlights these cultural tensions and shifts. In a letter to his sister in 1962, Cohen describes the manuscript as a "subtly balanced description of a sensibility, the best of its kind since James Joyce's *Portrait of the Artist as a Young Man*," and he correctly predicts that this Joycean production would be received as a disordered, "self-indulgent [and] childish autobiography."[87] However, when the American editor of *The Favourite Game* proposed replacing "As the Mist Leaves No Scar" with a Yeats quotation, Cohen responded flamboyantly: "No, no, I refuse, I resist, must we be forever blackmailed by the Irish ... The book will be bare."[88] The American edition was therefore published without the epigraph, an omission that radically changes the movement from introductory ballad to concluding prose poem that defines the Canadian edition. In another poem accompanying his final draft of the manuscript, Cohen announces to the American editor that "Cohen the Jewish Keats" has "been struck down":

> He lies on a couch of snow.
> Therefore blonde dancers
> do not expect him to rise for an introduction.[89]

This passage alludes to the final scene in *The Favourite Game*; yet its proclamation must be read skeptically because Cohen is still announcing the death of the "Jewish Keats" a year later in a letter to Jack McClelland accompanying the manuscript of *Flowers for Hitler*.[90]

Beautiful Losers sounds the final death knell for the Jewish Keats. The second novel captured the sexual and political upheavals of the Quiet Revolution in Quebec and earned Cohen the epithet, "the voice of his generation." However, he rejected this title, much as he had earlier rejected the role of spokesman for the Jewish community. He embraced, on the other hand, the idea of representing a particular cultural geography, of being "the poet of Montreal," in his writing and public persona. In a 1969 interview with Michael Harris, Cohen the singer recalls nostalgically that he became a writer because he wished to "put out [his] work somehow and have it stand for a certain kind of life in the city of Montreal."[91] Thus, in the interval between billing himself as the "Jewish Keats" (1962) and the "Canadian Dylan" (1966) in his letters, Cohen the novelist set himself the task of developing a style of writing that could address the diversity and peculiarity of his birthplace.[92]

Much as Klein pledged multiple allegiances by doubling his scrolls and including a subplot about a Canadian translator, Cohen takes a serial approach to narrative in *The Favourite Game* that allows him the flexibility to explore the various facets of objects, scenarios, and characters. In the serial formations that begin Cohen's book, I believe one finds a crucial clue to the question of why writing novels became a favourite game of Canadian poets from the 1960s onwards. Cohen builds the first chapter out of the central motif from "As the Mist Leaves No Scar" and introduces a series of scars belonging to Breavman's lover Shell, his father, his friend Krantz, and his mother in rapid succession. Cohen offers no explanation of how these separate portraits connect, except for the assertion that a "scar is what happens when the word is made flesh."[93] He fills out the story behind these scars by using the motif as an entry point into a series of related anecdotes. The anecdotes then spin off into longer and more conventional sections of dialogue and descriptive narrative. For this reason, Michael Greenstein reads the novel as poetry: "Although *The Favourite Game* is generally considered a *Künstlerroman*, it may also be read as a long narrative poem since its author and its subject are poets, since its lyrical style is highly poetic, and since it incorporates a number of poems within its text. As a poem, it is divided into four books and ninety stanzas. Just as the 'fact that the lines do not come to the edge of the page is no guarantee' of poetry, so the extension of lines to the edge is no guarantee that the prose is not poetry disguised."[94] In this passage Greenstein is perhaps thinking of Hermann Hesse's definition of the novel as a disguised lyric.

No chronology or causal sequence binds the distinct sections of *The Favourite Game*. Ondaatje observes that from a conventional perspective the plotline of *The Favourite Game* is "non-existent": "We are not reading a formal novel but are looking at various episodes in the life of Breavman. We are not guided along a cohesive time sequence but are shown segments from scrapbooks, home movies, diaries – all of which flash in front of us like 'those uncertain images that were always flashing in his mind.' This style is the most fascinating and successful aspect of *The Favourite Game*."[95] It is also, potentially, the most fraught with pitfalls.

The Favourite Game is an imagistic and elliptical work that unabashedly announces the transition of a poet to prose. The first draft of the novel was sprawling, explanatory, and generously detailed; editors in Canada, England, and the United States demanded a reduction in its length. Cohen responded by bringing out his poet's scalpel, cutting the length drastically, and investing the narrative with the serial logic of the long poem instead of the causal logic of the plot-driven novel. According to Ondaatje, the original manuscript, "Beauty at Close Quarters," was "rewritten at least five times, with the result that its descriptions, dialogue, and portraits are shaved down to an almost poetic form. The book has the effectiveness of a long prose poem, with each scene emerging as a potent and enigmatic sketch rather than a full-blown, detailed narrative. As in a poem, the silences and spaces, what is left unsaid, are essential to the mood of the book."[96] Cohen's prose style becomes more expansive in the second half of

The Favourite Game, but the presence of *The Spice-Box of Earth* remains strong, as he inserts passages from it directly into the chapters set in New York. In so doing, he mythologizes his early poetry, but in devising a poetic form that retains the effectiveness of a long prose poem without becoming a "formal novel," he also blazes a path for Ondaatje's *Coming Through Slaughter*.

Cohen justifies the aphoristic phrasing and fragmented staging of *The Favourite Game* by making frequent reference to visual media, particularly film. He introduces his home movie conceit in the fourth of the early fragments: "Here is a movie filled with the bodies of [Breavman's] family ... Breavman is mutilating the film in his efforts at history."[97] Stan Dragland notes that sentences beginning "We are now" recur throughout *Beautiful Losers* to jolt the story out of the historical past and into the present, and the same is true of *The Favourite Game*.[98] Linda Hutcheon argues that "film is always perceived [by Breavman] as linear, temporal, [and] historical," but she is only partly right, because this kind of film only interests Breavman if he can melt, stain, mutilate, loop, and interrupt it.[99] The reviewer Ian Adam noted in 1964 that the "structure of the work is as much mosaic as lineal (to use McLuhan's terms)," because "the use of thematic and linguistic and scenic links between past and present and future" creates an impression of "simultaneity."[100] However, applying too rigid a notion of "simultaneity" to literature, one that insists upon effects of "unity" and "wholeness," eliminates the possibility of character development in the novel and underestimates the protagonist's adolescent confusion.[101] As T.F. Rigelhof observes, "Breavman never quite knows what movie he's in but he always knows that there's a camera on him."[102] Much of the novel depicts Breavman trying to sort out what movie he's in until he finally takes control of the medium by becoming a writer and cinematic image-producer at the conclusion.

Breavman also associates linear footage with the patrilineal obligations he refuses to meet, and the move away from linear storytelling in the novel may be seen as an attack on a particular kind of patriarchy. Breavman rejects his role as man of the house and upholder of tradition, but at the Communist meeting where he goes to pick up women, Krantz observes that his friend has become the patriarch's alter ego, the womanizer: "These people are half right about you, Breavman. You're an emotional imperialist." Confronted with this insight, Breavman drops his sarcastic front and concedes: "You thought about that for a long time, didn't you? ... It's good."[103] Cohen humorously revisits this scene in *Book of Longing*, where he compares the Communists' "pig-headed devotion / to something absolutely wrong" to his own pursuit of Zen.[104] Breavman, on the other hand, cannot correct his errancy even after his problem is named.

In *The Favourite Game*, Cohen implicitly compares the vivid but choppy effect of his prose to the "slow-motion movie" that is "always running somewhere in [Breavman's] mind."[105] Like the old-fashioned viewfinder that Breavman admires because "each frame glowed with tenderness and passionate delight,"[106] Cohen's halting, frame-by-frame style intensifies his isolated images and vignettes: "Each chapter is a scene, and the feeling one gets in reading the novel is not so much an insight into a character as a vision of Breavman in different poses, playing the lead in several movies. We see him in sporadic, imagistic relationships or histories ... We get to see only the perfect photographic image, and this is why the book appears so romantic. It is Breavman the romantic artist who connects these images."[107] Breavman goes beyond film and studies the paintings of Hokusai, Botticelli, Brueghel the Elder, and Rousseau to hone his skills as a portrait maker. This portrait technique sheds light on the freeze frame narratives, particularly if one recalls that Ondaatje nominates Rousseau for God in one poem[108] and that Breavman "loves the pictures of Henri Rousseau, the way he stops time": "Always is the word that must be used. The lion will always be sniffing the robes of the sleeping gypsy, there will be no attack, no guts on the sand: the total encounter is expressed. The moon, even though it is doomed to travel, will never go down on this scene."[109] Ondaatje's appraisal of Cohen's freeze frames thus applies to his own writing because both authors isolate the lyric moment from the temporal continuum: "This sense of the book being artistic, poetic, being 'framed,' is important because this is the way Breavman sees people – as heightened images or potent highlights of conversation. In spite of the seemingly loose form, the book is, in reality, concrete and sparse. It is a beautiful book and one returns to it several times as one returns to a photograph album."[110]

Echoes of Scott's poetry also shape the passages where Breavman describes the literary scene in Montreal. Whereas Scott satirized the "Virgins of sixty who still write of passion," and chided the unimaginative poets who spring "To paint the native maple" and "set the self-same welkin ringing" in "The Canadian Authors Meet" (1927), Cohen updates Scott's portrait for the sixties: "[Breavman] slept with as many pretty chairwomen as he could. He gave up conversation. He merely quoted himself. He could maintain an oppressive silence at a dinner-table to make the lovely daughter of the house believe he was brooding over her soul."[111] However, many of the people in Breavman's photograph album are dead, and he cannot live in his highlight reel of transcendent visions and high-speed drives, as Krantz's undercutting humour reminds him. Instead of succumbing to delusions of extratemporal existence, Breavman must find a way of creating temporal connections between the epiphanic moments he cherishes.

Breavman's devotion to the lyric moment creates problems in his social life, because he lives *for* the epiphanic moment but he necessarily lives *in* time, with all its hardships and banality. The poet, whose very name suggests brevity, cannot bear listening to his mentally ill mother, who speaks primarily in run-on sentences: "for his mother he's too *busy*, for his shiksa he's got plenty of time, for her he doesn't count minutes, after what they did to our people, I had to hide in the cellar on Easter, they chased us, what I went through, and to see a son, to see my son, a traitor to his people, I have to forget about everything, I have no son."[112] Having "trained himself to delight in the fraction," Breavman cannot endure his family legacy as it is writ in the streets of Montreal, because the physical and social architecture of the Jewish community force him to situate his identity in a temporal continuum.[113] "The Breavman eye, trained for volcano-watching, heavenly hosts, [and] ideal thighs," makes him incapable of sustaining relationships with his lovers, except as objects of his intense but momentary lusts.[114] This inability to embrace the temporal flux of life ruins his friendship with Krantz, undermines his belief in citizenship, and inhibits his work at the factory.

However, one should not equate Breavman's solipsism with Cohen's own, because Cohen constantly struggles to negate the element of narcissism that defines his principal male characters. Cohen is perfectly aware of the problems of Breavman's romantic temperament, and Breavman's friends attempt to curb his obsession with the lyric moment.

Shell, in particular, insists on temporal continuity and detailed characterizations in their bedroom storytelling. She demands an extensive description of the everyday appearance of Breavman's ex-lover Norma, whose name Breavman initially cannot remember. Such quotidian details bore Breavman: "It doesn't matter what she looked like every day. It only matters what she looked like for that important second. That I remember and will tell you."[115] Undeterred, Shell repeats her question: "What did she look like every day?"[116] Breavman then resorts to sarcasm, as he is wont to do when cornered, and paints an absurd portrait of Norma. Shell therefore changes tactics and restarts the discussion of Norma from Breavman's perspective. She penetrates so far into Breavman's psyche that the quotation marks disappear from this section of dialogue:

What did she look like that important second?

  She stands in my mind alone, unconnected to the petty narrative. The colour of the skin was startling, like the white of a young branch when the green is thumb-nailed away. Nipples the colour of bare lips. Wet hair a battalion of glistening spears laid on her shoulders.

  She was made of flesh and eyelashes.

  But you said she was lame, perhaps like Bertha would be from the fall?[117]

Here, Shell tries to dispel Breavman's idealized portrait of Norma by emphasizing the human elements of her flaws and situating her in time and in relation to a community. But such a way of thinking is initially abhorrent to Breavman. He stalls in response, partly out of reluctance to view himself in anything but select moments of grandeur. When Shell demands to know why Breavman refuses to tell conventional stories in bed, he notes that his "voice would depress her."[118] Despite her reservations, Shell cannot resist Breavman's lyrical visions. She falls in love with him and ultimately becomes the victim of her own teaching when Breavman sends her his chronological camp journal.

  The unedited summer journal gives Shell a different perspective on Breavman's psyche. His accompanying letter emphasizes his deficiencies: "I'm not a good lover or I'd be with you now. I'd be beside you, not using this longing for a proof of feeling. That's why I'm writing to you and sending you this summer's journal. I want you to know something about me. Here it is day by day. Dearest Shell, if you let me I'd always keep you four hundred miles away and write you pretty poems and letters."[119] Ultimately, Breavman abandons the love affair, because he is "afraid to live any place but in expectation,"[120] and instead he turns Shell into a character in a novel. Cohen is clearly posing some difficult questions here about the relation of poetry to the novel, and in particular of synchrony to diachrony. He does not resolve all these questions in *The Favourite Game*, but he makes strides toward addressing a problem that clearly haunts him.

  Cohen first articulates this imperative to shape narrative as something more than a linear succession of stunning images in "Lines from My Grandfather's Journal," where the grandfather remarks: "A tradition composed of the exuviae of visions. I must resist it. It is like the garbage river through a city: beautiful by day and beautiful by night, but always unfit for bathing."[121] Cohen thus makes it imperative to reclaim the body from pure vision and abstraction. He resolves to write in a manner that is visceral and not to shy away from the grotesque, as he states at the outset of *The*

Favourite Game: "It is easy to display a wound, the proud scars of combat. It is hard to show a pimple."[122] He must write the body into time, expose flaws in his character, and not succumb to linear design, which he identifies with conformity. The response Cohen devises to this challenge involves shaping the time of the narrative into whorling formations inspired by a child's game. Yet, another child dies before Breavman recognizes the importance of this game.

The death of Martin Stark at the conclusion of the novel highlights the problem of reading *The Favourite Game* as autobiography. Cohen invites such readings by attributing his own poetry to Breavman and by slipping occasionally from third to first person perspectives in his narration.[123] Indeed, Cohen claims in a letter to his publisher, Jack McClelland, that nearly every event in the novel actually happened, and his biographers demonstrate the validity of this claim even as they disguise passages from the novel as journal entries or interview statements by Cohen. The author's half-hearted effort to publish the novel in Canada, and the fact that he did not include selections from *The Favourite Game* in *Stranger Music: Selected Poems and Songs* (1993), as he did selections from *Beautiful Losers* and his books of prose poems, suggests that he regrets these autobiographical elements.

However, Cohen notes in the McClelland correspondence that Martin's death is pure invention. Cohen worked for several years as a counsellor at Jewish summer camps, and he once cared for a child with mild autism, but that child did not die as a result of Cohen's negligence. Cohen therefore rejects the designation "autobiography" and insists that his goal in writing the novel is "to tell about a certain society and a certain man and reveal insights into the bastard Art of Poetry."[124] The disproportionately long section about Breavman's experience as a camp counsellor toward the end of *The Favourite Game* offers the keenest insight into the way Cohen departs from autobiography and fashions a work of fiction. Cohen inserts the invented tragedy of Martin Stark's death into the novel to contrast the negative consequences of the antisocial games Martin and Breavman play with the community-forming game of the title.

Martin Stark is a gifted but shy child who refuses to participate in the camp's group activities. He has an extraordinary facility with numbers, which makes him a freakish hero to his fellow campers. Breavman regards Martin as the embodiment of his romantic ideal of the solitary genius – at once a Wordsworthian idiot boy and a Whitmanesque counter of blades of grass. Breavman even humours Martin's obsessive games of question and answer, despite the boy's lack of physical self-regard:

"What's your favourite store?"

"What are you doing out here in the middle of the night?"

"What's your favourite store?"

Breavman wrapped the sleeping bag around the boy and ruffled his hair.[125]

One day, on his quest to transcend the world of mosquitoes, Martin dies under the blade of a construction bulldozer. His death functions as an allegory for the death of Breavman's youthful ideal, although it takes Breavman many years to come to terms with the damage his negligence has done: "One day what he did to [Shell], to the child [Martin], would enter his understanding with such a smash of guilt that he would sit motionless for days, until others carried him and medical machines brought him back to speech."[126] Cohen, on the other hand, patiently exposes Breavman's tragic flaw over and over again in the narrative. Patricia Morley observes that "Martin's funeral is one of the rare occasions when Cohen has nothing funny to say" and she concludes that Cohen is an "immoral moralist."[127] If the reader has not already turned against Breavman for his libertine treatment of Shell, his "stark" lack of remorse at the funeral and his efforts to deflect blame onto the child's mother discourage any sympathy in the reader. The poet's lack of social concern has turned the children's camp into a death camp, and the boy's quixotic quest to tally and exterminate mosquitoes takes on eerie, Hitlerian overtones, even as it mirrors Breavman's fool's quest for lyric transcendence. There is little evidence to suggest that Cohen wishes the reader to condone Breavman's actions by the conclusion of the novel. In my opinion, the novel depicts what Carson calls "wrong love," desire that mistakes (as youthful desire often does) the nature of its object, much as Cohen's subsequent novel scrutinizes the longings of a loser who loves not wisely and too late.[128] In so doing, Cohen forces the reader to consider the forces of attraction that draw people and narratives together.

THE GAME AS NARRATIVE PARADIGM

The final paragraphs of *The Favourite Game* depict Breavman in a restaurant on rue Ste-Catherine. He is listening to songs on a juke-box and pondering how he might retain his bond to Shell without abandoning Montreal: "He must always be connected to her. That must never be severed."[129] Suddenly he is struck by a memory he feels compelled to write down. The echo of Martin's "favourite" game in this passage suggests that the key to the writer's atonement resides in this vision:

Jesus! I just remembered what Lisa's favourite game was. After a heavy snow we would go into a back yard with a few of our friends. The expanse of snow would be white and unbroken. Bertha was the spinner. You held her hands while she turned on her heels, you circled her until your feet left the ground. Then she let go and you flew over the snow. You remained still in whatever position you landed. When everyone had been flung in this fashion into the fresh snow, the beautiful part of the game began. You stood up carefully, taking great pains not to disturb the impression you had made. Now the comparisons. Of course you would have done your best to land in some crazy position, arms and legs sticking out. Then we walked away, leaving a lovely white field of blossom-like shapes with footprint stems.[130]

This passage is framed spatially by its appearance on a separate page in the text and is ostensibly written on a napkin by Breavman. It is framed temporally by its performative quality, as the reader witnesses Breavman complete a narrative about himself that has until now been told retrospectively in the third person. It is framed tonally, as Breavman writes a kind of prose that, unlike his letters and journals, synthesizes his poetic past and novelistic present. And it is framed intratextually, through echoes of the scenes in which Breavman and Lisa wrestle in the snow; Miss McTavish "fling[s] herself backwards in the snow" after making a failed pass at Shell; and Shell rejects the advance of her sister's boyfriend: "Shell turned and ran. The grass seemed suddenly white, the trees white. She dropped the flowers meant for the fountain because they were white and dirty as bones. She was a spider on a field of ash."[131] But most important of all, the coda re-frames the entire novel by explaining the title and suggesting a paradigm for the whorling movements of Cohen's prose.

Morley observes that the coda "touches on nearly every aspect of the novel's theme," and the plethora of interpretations of this theme underscore the complexity of the prose poem in relation to the principal narrative.[132] Morley maintains that the "pursuit of truth by means of fun is Cohen's favourite game."[133] Loranne Dorman and Clive Rawlins argue that the favourite game is "the 'games' people play with each others' lives."[134] Siemerling suggests that the favourite game is projection, both in the cinematic sense of projecting images onto a white screen and in the psychological sense of projecting attributes of the self onto the other.[135] Desmond Pacey notes that the original dust-jacket of the novel "declares that 'the favourite game itself is love,'" but he objects to this sales pitch as a "serious misreading of the novel. As I read it, and especially the final paragraph, the favourite game is to leave an impression on the snow, to leave behind an interesting design, and by extension I take this to include the novel itself, which is Cohen's design of his own early life."[136] Scobie also reads the game as an allegory of the writing process. Although each of the proposed interpretations finds justification in the text, the latter reading is the most compelling. From the swirl of scar images onwards, Cohen renders time, not as a linear continuum, but as a whorling formation, the webwork of a "spinner," whom he incarnates in the figure of Bertha.

Bertha enters the novel early, right after the scar anecdotes and a tale about a dead pet buried in the flower garden in Breavman's backyard. She reappears as a spirit that Breavman invokes in his twenties: "Come back, stern Bertha, come back and lure me up the torture tree. Remove me from the bedrooms of easy women. Extract the fall due. The girl I had last night betrays the man who pays her rent."[137] Cohen then relates a short anecdote involving a young Breavman and Bertha playing a flute in an apple tree. Bertha challenges Breavman to say something "horribly dirty," to which he responds "FUCK GOD."[138] This blasphemy precipitates Bertha's fall from the tree. She lands on the ground, a bone pierces the skin of her arm, and her body "twist[s] into a position she could never achieve in gym."[139] She is rushed to the hospital, but the subsequent scenes do not clarify whether she lives or dies. She reappears in the text as a spectral presence who haunts Breavman's various philanderings.

At first the story of Bertha's fall seems a blatant imitation of the Genesis tale. Bertha is the temptress, the tree is the tree of knowledge, and Breavman is punished by his father for the incident. The accident convinces Breavman that his voice has magical powers, and he uses these powers to make more women fall for him. Yet the New Testament insinuates itself into the story as Bertha becomes a martyr in Breavman's imagination, and the tree the site of her crucifixion. After they have played a sado-masochistic whipping game with Lisa, Krantz and Breavman pass "Bertha's Tree" and Krantz runs away as if stern Bertha might pass judgement on him.[140] For a while, Lisa and Breavman continue their "games in the field beside Bertha's Tree," but Breavman gradually embellishes the myth of Bertha as a response to the trauma of the accident.[141] The images he associates with her (falling, flowers, torture, burial, resurrection) coalesce into a messianic narrative. Still, he is conscious enough of his imaginative fabrications to warn Shell: "Bertha's Tree is a lie although she really fell out of it."[142]

Breavman later claims to spot Bertha passing on a bus, but Krantz responds skeptically. The friends' conversation makes it clear that Bertha has long since departed from their lives and that Breavman has come to see himself as her messianic double. Breavman calls himself "the keeper" and declares: "They'll all be delivered to me today, Bertha, Lisa. Nobody, not one name, not one limb will be taken away in the dustload."[143] Later, sensing a growing mania in Breavman, Krantz attempts to warn his friend that although he may have the messianic style, he doesn't have the substance:

"You know, Breavman, you're not Montreal's suffering servant."
"Of course I am. Can't you see me, crucified on a maple tree at the top of Mount Royal? The miracles are just beginning to happen."[144]

Only the death of Martin puts an end to these self-aggrandizing postures.

At the end of the novel, Bertha returns as the all-embracing figure who gathers the children unto herself. She gives berth to the children who approach her, and gives birth to the figures in the snow. The meta-fictive author, for his part, emulates Bertha by giving berth to "his" old poetry in the novel and giving birth to new kinds of lyricism in his prose. To read even further into the metaphor: a bertha (or *berthe* in French) can mean a collar of lace; Bertha spins a circle around her in the snow and Breavman loops together an intricate web of stories. The novel is not simply an anthology – etymologically a collection of the flowers of verse – but a narrative in which lives interlace and transform through juxtaposition.

The interjection "Jesus!" which Cohen uses elsewhere in the novel as a conventional blasphemy, takes on the quality of a religious invocation when Bertha enters the scene in the coda.[145] The ceremonial description of the children's game transforms the prose poem into a kind of disguised prayer, but Cohen is trying to make a religion of the secular here, to sanctify a common urban environment. Although the French title of the film based on the novel is *Le Jeu des anges*, and although Bowering travels to a Westmount park to make a snow angel and have "bicultural sex" with her in *A Short Sad Book*, the children in *The Favourite Game* do not play the common game of snow angels, where one blurs the human form into angelic shapes by moving hands and legs in the snow. In *Beautiful Losers*, Cohen defines a saint as one who resists the temptation of such distortion: "His course is a caress of the hill. His track is a drawing of the snow in a moment of its particular arrangement with wind and rock. Something in him so loves the world that he gives himself to the laws of gravity and chance. Far from flying with the angels, he traces with the fidelity of a seismograph needle the state of the solid bloody landscape. His house is dangerous and finite, but he is at home in the world. He can love the shapes of human beings, the fine and twisted shapes of the heart. It is good to have among us such men, such balancing monsters of love."[146] The children in *The Favourite Game* assume the most flawed human postures possible, but the social organization of the game translates these anomalies into beauty.

In the end, Breavman does not achieve Cohen's messianic ideal, but the coda suggests a reconciliation between Jewish and Christian mythologies. This hinted reconciliation becomes clearer if one compares it with a chapter in *The Second Scroll* that it perhaps overwrites. Klein's "Gloss Gimel" chapter consists of a letter from Uncle Melech to Monsignor Piersanti that describes Melech's visit to the Sistine Chapel. When the nephew receives the letter from the Monsignor, it is missing its introductory page and the remainder consists, in essence, of a lyrical essay on Michelangelo's famous frescoes on the ceiling of the chapel. The frescoes, each framed by blood-red paint or architectural protrusions, combine to form a webwork of vignettes from the Old Testament. Melech is struck by the strange geometry of spandrels, circles, and sigils, but declares that "it is not the whirlwind of forms but the tornado of torsos that abashes the little homunculus below, puny before the myriad bodies instant, ambulant, volant, who in their various attitudes and postures are turned and contorted to make of the ceiling the weighted animate corpus of humanity."[147] These prototypical humans impress Melech as "flesh majuscule," and he contrasts them with the miniscule cherubim whose amorous games mimic the central panel of God creating Adam: "Out of upholding heaven, which is their proper duty, they make a game, these gemini in a zodiac of delight ... They embrace, ambivalent *bambini*, and their contacts and touchings are copy, an ingratiating and pathetic imitation, of that first famous fingertouch."[148] As the eye moves away from the Adamic spark at the centre of the composition to the encircling medallions and vignettes, the scenes turn gloomy and foreboding. Images of Noah's drunkeness, Judith's decapitation of Holofernes, and other displays of violence and sin encroach on the carefree realms of the central nudes, such that their "pristine unmarred felicity [is] ever in peril of cicatrice and brand-mark."[149] Melech, whose youthful idealism was scarred by the Holocaust, interprets this design to suggest that the apparently stable composition of the central panels will be unframed by the horrors encroaching upon the panel borders, such that the masses of humanity ultimately represent the "several social heapings heaped to be taken up by the mastodon bulldozer and scavengered into its sistine limepit."[150] Chronologically, the narrative of *The Favourite Game* follows a similar trajectory, moving from the contemplation of flesh and scars to the amorous games of the children to the lasciviousness of Breavman and the death of Martin in the pit. However, Cohen's non-chronological design places the

memory of the favourite game after the death of Martin, so that it offers a
different vision of societal outcome.

Cohen alters the symbolism and arrangement of Michelangelo's masterpiece, or rather Melech's reading of it, by displacing the importance of the
fingertouch, the transcendental signifier, and moving the setting from the
Old World to the New. He brings Michelangelo's fresco down to earth,
letting the bodies create their own imprint on the snow that surrounds the
limping homunculus, Bertha (whose name also means "light"). Cohen
does not disparage the games of the *bambini*, but rather sees their amorous touching as the divine spark itself. The children are not inferior
copies of Bertha, but share her existential experience of being thrown into
a landscape to which they must adapt, and out of which they forge their
sense of group identity. Whereas Martin refused to participate in group
activities, and died alone beneath a bulldozer, the coda emphasizes the
importance of group contact in all its playful, sexual, and cultural dimensions. The sad image of an aging Klein terrified by interpersonal contact
and even by foreign objects entering his home is here reversed, his early
zeal for cross-cultural connection restored by the exuberance of childhood.

The vitality of the children's game also contrasts with the haunting
images of "The Genius," in *The Spice-Box of Earth*. The speaker, after contemplating a variety of roles for a Jew, concludes:

> For you
> I will be a Dachau jew
> and lie down in lime
> with twisted limbs
> and bloated pain
> no mind can understand[151]

When one knows that Bertha has a "Saxon face" and that her name has a
Teutonic root, the boldness of Cohen's naïve vignette becomes clear.[152] He
is writing against the Dachau limepit, against the "circumcision line," and
against the taboo of Jewish-Christian contact.[153]

One gets a better sense of the ends toward which Cohen marshals his
blasphemies in *The Favourite Game* and *Beautiful Losers* by comparing
the conclusions of these novels with the epic telos of *The Second Scroll*.
While the early chapters of *The Second Scroll* confirm D.M.R. Bentley's
assertion that in Canadian literature the public concerns and narrative
thrust of the epic are usually counterbalanced by the private concerns

and verbal virtuosity of the lyric, the conclusion of Klein's first scroll
bears all the marks of classical epic: a journey ends in the founding of a
nation; a valiant struggle establishes the superiority of a race; characterizations gel into fixed epithets; and a stable future is wrested from chaos
and flux. The epic turn in Klein's novel comes when the nephew, in
Israel, remembers his visit to the Arch of Titus in Rome. Titus is a kind
of Ozymandias in Klein's eyes, a tyrant who subjugated the Jews, forced
them to march through the arch at lance-point, and recorded his triumph in friezes on the stone. The narrator recognizes that the Roman
arch, in its ruined state, has an "irony directed against itself."[154] However, he does not consider that the same ironic power might turn against
Israel. He fails to anticipate the problems that will plague Israel in the
ensuing decades; namely, that a nation sprung from the concentration
camps of the Christian West created a diaspora of Arab refugee camps in
the Middle East, or that the fall of the Berlin Wall would be succeeded by
the erection of an Israeli wall deep in Palestinian territory on the West
Bank. Instead, he envisions the establishment of Israel as the end of sub-
jugation and empire. He portrays Israel as Jonah emerging from the
Arab whale to found a nation in a clearing, a tabula rasa signified by the
narrator's memory of a mist passing over the Arch of Titus:

> There had come then a haze before my eyes, and the miracle had taken
> place. The arch was not there! The stone had crumbled. I did not see
> the arch!
> ... And now in Israel the phenomenon was being made everywhere
> explicit. The fixed epithet wherewith I might designate Israel's poetry,
> the poetry of the recaptured time, was now evident. The password was
> heard everywhere – the miracle!
> I had found the key image.[155]

The martyrdom of Uncle Melech sanctifies the new state, which is henceforth governed by "set times."[156]

Cohen modifies this strategy in his novels to make a Zion of Montreal, a
city he sometimes refers to as "that great, golden Jerusalem of the
North."[157] The newly fallen snow in *The Favourite Game* is his mist and
the resurrected Bertha is his messiah. While the spinning game idealizes a
society that produces flux out of fixity, Cohen initially fails to acknowledge
the aboriginal land and history lying under that white blanket. Unlike
Klein, however, Cohen acknowledges the limitations of his vision in *The
Favourite Game* and proceeds to reconsider the unequal distribution of

power among cultures in *Beautiful Losers*. A comparison of spinning games in the prose of Cohen and Klein will make these distinctions clear.

The "Leviticus" chapter in *The Second Scroll* describes the respective encounters of Melech and the narrator with Monsignor Piersanti (the rock of the Church). The nephew and Melech find the Monsignor an alluring but demonic figure. The churchman tries to convert Melech, and when that fails, he tries to convince the nephew that his uncle is a closet Catholic. This appropriation of Melech's spirit takes on a corporeal dimension when Settano (a satanic figure with Communist connections) kidnaps the nephew. The "Leviticus" chapter thus stages a contest between Judaism and the (post-)Christian world that elaborates on a scenario that Klein first scripted in his 1930 short story "The Chanukah Dreidel."[158] Roger Hyman observes that in this tale, written under the pseudonym Ben Kalonymous, the characters "Satanas and Reb Itzik'l Podebosher wage a battle over universal good and evil by spinning the dreidel (a four-sided top traditionally spun at Chanukah), the letters on the sides of which are said to stand for the phrase, the text reminds us, 'there, there chanced a wondrous miracle.' The Rebbe, however, has added his own interpretation, based on *gematria*, in which the letters stand for pairs of opposites ... which signify either matter or spirit on the one hand, or a Christian as opposed to a Jewish vision of the divine, on the other."[159] The Hebrew letters on the dreidel are Nun, Gimel, Hai, and Sheen; "Gloss Gimel" puts a new spin on an old tale. While the stakes of the game in the short story involve the loss of Jewish identity and the looming threat of violence, Hyman demonstrates that in *The Second Scroll* the stakes are "higher because the historical context is Holocaust rather than pogrom, and the loss of Jewish identity now includes the defeat of Zionism."[160] A decade later, Cohen's response to the Holocaust, the Zionist movement, and Klein's silence is to shift the game from an adversarial to a comparative format that precludes such exclusive oppositions and does not produce winners or losers.

In *The Favourite Game*, the spinning game links the spiritual and corporeal. The game is not a Christian imposition, but a favourite pastime of Lisa, who impresses her authority on Breavman when she wrestles him in the snow and demands that he kiss the Hebrew holy books he had dropped. Lawrence (whose name is Latin for "victor") finds his "defeat" at the hands of Elizabeth (Hebrew for "God is my oath") both bitter and "unnatural."[161] Yet the bitterness of Martin's death and the organic imagery of the flowers in the coda suggest that the "unnatural" aspect of Breavman's behaviour was his presumption that authority resides in the male body. (Lisa is, significantly, the only female character who sleeps with Breavman after defining her own terms). Both centripetal and centrifugal, Lisa's spinning game draws characters together and then sends them back out into the world in different formations.

Morley argues that the "childhood game is the novel's final metaphor for the stasis, the immortalizing permanence of art."[162] A more convincing view is that Cohen converts Michelangelo's work of art into a visceral game that can, by definition, be played and replayed. In "Beyond Agonistics: Vertiginous Games in the Fiction of Leonard Cohen," Paul Milton reads the development of Cohen's novels as a process of eradicating the winner-loser dynamic of epic contest and replacing it with a vertiginous aesthetic that installs surprise, paradox, and semantic excess in place of narrative certainty, closure, and stable signification. Whereas Klein's devil and rabbi compete to predict the letter on which the dreidel will fall (and cheat by effacing the letters to change the dreidel's weight), Cohen's children compete to be unpredictable, to create new signifiers (imprints), and to invent local variations of their cultural inheritances.

In *Beautiful Losers*, this vertiginous aesthetic becomes a condition for beatification. Meditating on the virtues of Catherine Tekakwitha and her attempts to bridge European and Native cultures, the historian argues that a "saint is someone who has achieved a remote human possibility. It is impossible to say what that possibility is. I think it has something to do with the energy of love. Contact with this energy results in the exercise of a kind of balance in the chaos of existence. A saint does not dissolve the chaos; if he did the world would have changed long ago. I do not think that a saint dissolves the chaos even for himself, for there is something arrogant and warlike in the notion of a man setting the universe in order. It is a kind of balance that is his glory. He rides the drifts like an escaped ski."[163] The relentless carnality of *Beautiful Losers* emphasizes Cohen's visceral ideas of divinity, but *The Favourite Game* is also visceral in its own way. Although each segment of Cohen's narrative features highly imagistic writing, the reader's experience of reconstructing the fragmented plot is tactile, as McLuhan argued in his theories of audile-tactile space in painting and literature. Thus Poore hails the book as a "churningly avant-garde novel" and Milton maintains that the favourite game is "an artistic practice that represents the body through chance and vertigo."[164]

COHEN'S SECOND SCROLL: *BEAUTIFUL LOSERS*

Nadel's reading of *The Favourite Game* "as something of an artistic manifesto for Cohen" is confirmed by several aspects of *Beautiful Losers*.[165] But in *Beautiful Losers* Cohen revises the power dynamic of the former novel by framing the narrative as a dialectic between two distinct narrators: the anglophone "I," who narrates the first section, "The History of Them All," and the francophone "F.," a political revolutionary who writes the second section as a long letter to "I." These two characters wrap their life stories around a collaborative biography of the Mohawk saint, Catherine Tekakwitha, and then merge in an absurd apotheosis at the end of the novel to produce "IF," the conditional tense of "Magic Canada."[166]

Drawing these stories together in a complicated love triangle, Cohen accelerates the whorling pattern of the first novel. Times, places, and lusts are in a constant state of flux as the narrators' desires radiate outward and then cluster around a specific object, which then precipitates a further dispersal. This pattern is illustrated when "I" portrays his wife Edith filling "her belly-button hole with oil and using her little finger [to draw] the spokes of Asoka's wheel" in a moment of erotic play.[167] F., for his part, claims "there is love on Rue Ste. Catherine, patroness of spinsters," and he mischievously equates the uncanonized Catherine Tekakwitha with the saint whose name graces the Montreal promenade.[168] F. also offers a grotesque version of the spinning game in his portrait of the Jesuit village where Catherine engages in penitential self-mutilation: "Think of the village as a mandala or a Brueghel game painting or a numbered diagram. Look down at the mission and see the bodies distributed here and there, look down from a hovering helicopter at the distribution of painful bodies in the snow."[169] To F., Catherine is a saint because she survives all the negative effects of interpersonal contact: the devastating impact of European colonization on her people, the mortifications of Catholic worship, the pressures from both the Christian and Mohawk communities to procreate. She transforms her suffering into a healing power (according to legend her scars disappeared), a transformation that Cohen interprets as the task of the artist.

Milton is more specific about the relationship of the two novels. He demonstrates that for Cohen games are serious business because they generate new media, which become, in turn, therapeutic tools for a troubled society. Milton focuses on a scene in the lobby of the System Theatre in *Beautiful Losers* where Edith and F. share bits of ice cream that have fallen on each others' clothing and the licking turns into a game: "Games are nature's most beautiful creation. All animals play games, and the truly Messianic vision of the brotherhood of creatures must be based on the idea of the game."[170] This touching game evolves into the erotic "Telephone Dance" in which Edith and F. stick their fingers into each other's ears and share thoughts to which the historian, the genital imperialist, never gets access.[171] The game prompts F. to adopt a pan-erogenous aesthetic and supplies the metatextual authors of the narrative with the trope of circuitry, which they use to reconfigure vertical social hierarchies and linear plotlines. Whereas I demonstrated that the Hasidic and Québécois dances in *The Favourite Game* defined distinct ethnic groups, the Telephone Dance performed by F., Edith, and the pre-conversion Mohawk elders gestures toward a connectivity that crosses the borders of race, geography, and even time.[172] (This messianic notion of time and social circuitry is vital to Michaels's world view in *Fugitive Pieces*, as I illustrate in my conclusion.)

If Milton is correct in saying that "we can read [Cohen's] second novel as a development on the ludic themes of, or even as a ludic rewriting of, the first," then it is worthwhile considering how, in the estimation of many reviewers, *Beautiful Losers* functions as the second scroll of *The Favourite Game*.[173] Indeed, the echoes of *The Favourite Game* in *Beautiful Losers* are too numerous to list. The fascination with the pornographic viewer in *The Favourite Game* evolves into a full-fledged pornographic narrative in *Beautiful Losers*. The homosocial tension between Krantz and Breavman, whose dialectic is a "disguise for love," evolves into a gay love affair and writerly exchange between F. and "I" in *Beautiful Losers*.[174] In every case, the second novel radicalizes the first to a degree that must be understood within the novel's historical context. When *Beautiful Losers* was published, the Catholic Church in Quebec had only recently relinquished its control over book censorship. Outside of Quebec, Morley recalls, Hugh MacLennan's *Barometer Rising* "was banned by the province of Manitoba as late as 1961, and the author received letters denouncing him for his heroine having a child outside marriage."[175] In 1963 *Maclean's* magazine fired the prominent Canadian historian and journalist Pierre Berton because of the public response to an article in which he advocated premarital sex.[176] On the other hand, in an international context, the fetished sex and drugs in *Beautiful Losers* make it very much a book of its era, and comparisons to Jean Genet, William Burroughs, Allen Ginsberg, and Thomas Pynchon are standard. Some critics argue that Cohen's themes and ideas are borrowed, but I agree with Pacey that the first novel "positively bristles with allusions, images and thematic motifs" developed in the second and "can best be seen as the culmination of Cohen's own artistic development, not as the imitation of someone else."[177]

Ondaatje reaches a similar conclusion after surveying Cohen's books leading up to *Beautiful Losers*: "Cohen is dynamiting the delicate poetic imagery of his past."[178] Ondaatje is specifically commenting here on the

"Member of Parliament" scene where F. and "I" *parlent* and masturbate on their way to Ottawa. Cohen replays Breavman's transcendental drive with Krantz across the Shield in order to satirize the vision of the landscape as "poised in perfection for the quick freeze, the eternal case in the astral museum."[179] In *Beautiful Losers* Cohen converts the drive into an elaborate hoax of the perception that the lovers exist "in some eye for a second: two men in a hurtling steel shell aimed at Ottawa, blinded by a mechanical mounting ecstasy."[180] At the moment of climax, *la petite mort*, F. stages a mock suicide and steers his car through a wall of silk, which acts like a photographic shutter: "The wall occupied the whole windshield, first as a blur, then focused precisely as if an expert had adjusted the microscope – every pimple of the concrete three-dimensional – bright! precise! – fast film of the moon's hide."[181] A second later, the car crashes through the painted wall and lands in a field, thereby unframing the caught moment, dispelling the Breavman-like illusion. Whereas Breavman fancies himself a sexual magician, "I" fails to come, exposing the basic impotence of his carnal reveries.

Cohen also hints that *Beautiful Losers* functions as the sequel to *The Favourite Game* by mentioning Lawrence. When F. tries to put an end to the psychological trauma of his working-class past by buying a factory, he breaks down and apologizes to the historian for his failure to achieve emotional closure: "Forgive me. I wanted to taste revenge. I wanted to be an American. I wanted to tie up my life with a visit. This isn't what Larry meant."[182] "Larry" is Tamara's knickname for Lawrence in *The Favourite Game*, where she identifies him as the prototypical beautiful loser: "You're a failure, Larry, but I'm still crazy about your balls."[183] The historian responds to F. by chastizing him for invoking "little Jewish ghosts."[184] Whereas Murray Hill Park and the brass foundry figured as opposites in *The Favourite Game*, F. plans to turn his factory into a private playground. This idea disgusts "I," who insists that "factories, like parks, are public places."[185] A debate ensues over class, labour, and the semiotics of industrial space.

This fascination with exploring a variety of perspectives translates into a recombinant aesthetic that also informs Cohen's diction. For example, the celebrated "Magic is afoot" chant in *Beautiful Losers* elaborates on a scene from *The Favourite Game* in which Breavman watches an ailing firefly and prays for its recovery: "Everybody had to believe in magic. Nobody believed in magic. He didn't believe in magic. Magic didn't believe in magic. Please don't die."[186] In *Beautiful Losers* this looping wordplay evolves into an independent chapter that has been anthologized as poetry and re-issued as a separate, illustrated long poem: "God is alive. Magic is afoot. God is

alive. Magic is afoot. God is afoot. Magic is alive. Alive is afoot. Magic
never died. God never sickened. Many poor men lied. Many sick men lied.
Magic never weakened. Magic never hid. Magic always ruled. God is afoot.
God never died."[187] The ecstatic cadences of this chant prompted the Cree
musician Buffy Sainte-Marie to improvise (after a visit from Cohen) a musical adaptation on *Illuminations* (1969), and she re-recorded the poem with
more elaborate orchestration on her retrospective *Up Where We Belong*
(1996), whose liner notes also feature a picture of Cohen and Sainte-
Marie.[188] In these notes, Sainte-Marie explains the profound impact *Beautiful Losers* had on her. Cohen occupies a rare position in Canadian literature in that his presentation of Natives, however flawed, has inspired
positive and creative responses from Native artists.

Cohen's concerns in the "Magic is Alive" chant are as much semantic as
rhythmic. The experiments in word order are manifestations of his ongoing
inquiry into the sense of recombinant speech, as Breavman makes clear in a
late-night phone call to Krantz:

"The last refuge of the insomniac is a sense of superiority to the sleep-
ing world."
"That's very good, Breavman. Good night."
"The last superiority of the refuge is a sleeping sense of the insom-
niac world."
"Oh, excellent."
"The refuge world of the superiority is a last sense of the sleeping
insomniac."[189]

This recombinant strategy counteracts the linear progression of syllogistic
logic, as Carson also demonstrates in "Appendix C" of *Autobiography of
Red*.

Although Hutcheon dispenses with *The Favourite Game* in a single
paragraph in her haste to discuss *Beautiful Losers* in *The Canadian Postmodern*, the novel warrants much closer investigation by archaeologists
of postmodernism in Canada. Hutcheon is correct in stating that the
"first novel is a familiar modernist version of the romantic *Künstlerroman*" in that it builds to a climactic finale in which the artist confirms
his skill by taking control of the narrative.[190] Yet the metafictional dimension of the novel is much larger than Hutcheon acknowledges, and it subtly revises the modernist paradigms of Klein's epic. While Hutcheon
allows that Breavman's sense of irony "paves the way for the postmodernism of *Beautiful Losers*," I would add that much of the

historiographic technique in *Beautiful Losers* also has its roots in *The Favourite Game*.[191]

For example, Book One of *Beautiful Losers*, "The History of Them All," begins with the historian questioning the standard categories established by his profession: "Catherine Tekakwitha, who are you? Are you (1656–1680)? Is that enough? Are you the Iroquois Virgin? Are you the Lily of the Shores of the Mohawk River?"[192] Whereas the journalist in *The Second Scroll* wished to discover the fixed epithet that would immortalize Zion, Cohen's historian finds that descriptive method too rigid. He wants to engage spiritually and sexually with the many versions of Catherine, even though his starting point is a fixed image on a colour postcard: "I fell in love with a religious picture of you. You were standing among birch trees, my favorite trees. God knows how far up your moccasins were laced. There was a river behind you, no doubt the Mohawk River. Two birds in the left foreground would be delighted if you tickled their white throats or even if you used them as an example of something or other in a parable."[193] The shift from historical facts to conditional speculation in this passage highlights not only the fictive but also the multilayered quality of Cohen's history.

THE BIRDSONG CONCEIT

Cohen does indeed use the multiplicity and simultaneity of birdsong as an allegory of his writing method, one that he first suggests in *The Favourite Game*. Discussing bird whistles with Shell, Breavman remarks:

> "If you tape their whistles, Shell, and slow them down, you can hear the most extraordinary things. What the naked ear hears as one note is often in reality two or three notes sung simultaneously. A bird can sing three notes at the same time!"
>
> "I wish I could speak that way. I wish I could say twelve things at once. I wish I could say all there was to say in one word. I hate all the things that can happen between the beginning of a sentence and the end."[194]

Cohen's birdsong conceit also reappears in *Beautiful Losers*: "Experts with tape recorders say that what we hear as a single bird note is really ten or twelve tones with which the animal weaves many various beautiful liquid harmonies. This he proves by slowing down his tape. I demand National Health! I demand an operation! I want a slow transistor machine sewn in my head!"[195] The number of tones within a single note expands in this passage, as do the number of ethnicities brought into interaction in the second novel. The historian's demands identify Klein's unity-in-diversity principle as a social right, but in his second novel Cohen produces a history more explicitly designed to emphasize the differences within that unity. Cohen sums up his new brand of monotheism in the chanted mantra, "I change / I am the same," which he calls the "truest sacred formula" of Manitou (the Ojibway creator).[196]

The second novel pursues Breavman's ideas on sex and Chinese mysticism further than the first, but its most crucial cultural juxtaposition is between the ancient Greeks and the Mohawks. In the chronology of reading, the comparison between cultures begins with F., who cites "a common belief that every talent must unfold itself in fighting, a love of wrestling, an inherent incapacity to unite for any length of time, an absolute dedication to the idea of the contest and the virtue of ambition."[197] However, the historian grows suspicious of such claims, in part because F. knows little of Mohawk history, but more so because his love of epic contest precipitates his own destruction. Ideally, F. sees his trumpeted "system" of societal transformation as a tool for producing difference: "I want to hammer a beautiful colored bruise on the whole American monolith ... I want History to jump on Canada's spine with sharp skates. I want the edge of a tin can to drink America's throat. I want two hundred million to know that everything can be different, any old different."[198] Sylvia Söderlind is correct to argue that the "lesson F. wants to teach 'I' is the difficult balancing act that consists in seeing particulars when the only tools available are analogous systems."[199] However, F.'s implementation of this method takes on fascist overtones when he takes bodybuilding cues from Charles Axis (not Charles Atlas) and bathes in a pool of human soap with a Hitler look-alike in the Argentine Hotel. F. considers himself a failed revolutionary, and in the end he pleads with "I": "My dear friend, go beyond my style."[200] He reiterates his rejection of the epic mode more forcefully a few pages later: "I let History back because I was lonely. Do not follow. Go beyond my style. I am nothing but a rotten hero."[201] Norman Ravvin therefore maintains that the orgy scene is the "ethical centre" of the novel because the sudden appearance of "Hitler seems to offer an acknowledgement that Nazi processes of degradation and enslavement have become acceptable – even exciting – to the popular imagination."[202]

Edith's proposals for sex games suggest a desire for a comparative, instead of an agonistic mode of social interaction. Hoping to put some variety in her seven-year-old marriage to the historian, Edith (whose skin has been transformed by F.'s soap collection) buys tubes of red grease from a theatre supply store and proposes: "Let's be other people ... It's stupid, she said, her voice cracking, but let's be other people."[203] The historian interprets this gesture as an invitation to go on "a journey only strangers can take, and we can remember it when we are ourselves again, and therefore never be merely ourselves again."[204] He declines the invitation, although it clearly echoes the recommendation of F., who painted a plaster model of the akropolis red in the previous chapter and instructed his depressed friend: "Do you know how to see the akropolis like the Indians did who never even had one? Fuck a saint, that's how, find a little saint and fuck her over and over in some pleasant part of heaven, get right into her plastic altar."[205] Instead of fulfilling Edith's request, the historian takes sadistic delight in rejecting her and witnessing her disappointment. He puts a cruel spin on F.'s words and fucks her over, as it were, in their unheavenly basement apartment. Only after Edith's suicide does the historian realize that the experience of alterity she proposed might cure his problems with constipation, masturbation, and solipsism.

Writing his history after the suicide of Edith, and with the letter from F. in his possession, "I" tries to inject alterity into his narrative by intermingling the Greek cult of the Egyptian goddess Isis with the Huron Andacwandet, or Fuck-Cure, ceremony. In terms of the chronology of events in the characters' lives, this juxtaposition actually begins with Edith and is adopted by her lovers. F. reports that when all the gadgetry of his erotic system failed to bring Edith to climax, he demanded that she reveal her true identity. She replied with the motto of Isis, which translates roughly from the Greek reproduced in the text: "I am Isis, I am all things which have been, and are, and shall be, and no mortal has lifted my robe."[206] F. responds to this pronouncement by kneeling in homage to suck Edith's toes, and the imperative to "fuck a saint" transforms into the command "go down on a saint," which the hitchhiker "IF" does in Book Three when he encounters the woman driving with her skirt hiked up.

The narrator of "The History of Them All" establishes a context for this Isian revelation by relating a surreal legend in which Catherine spills a glass of wine at a colonial banquet and stains all the dinner guests purple. Analysing this legend, the historian intermingles Greek and Iroquois by arguing that the story "is apocalyptic. The word apocalyptic has interesting origins. It comes from the Greek *apokalupsis*, which means revelation. This derives from the Greek *apokaluptein*, meaning uncover or disclose. *Apo* is a Greek prefix meaning from, derived from. *Kaluptein* means to cover. This is cognate with *kalube* which is cabin, and *kalumma* which means woman's veil.

Therefore apocalyptic describes that which is revealed when the woman's veil is lifted. What have I done, what have I not done, to lift your veil, to get under your blanket, Kateri Tekakwitha?"[207] The lifted robe is an obvious allusion to the Isis motto, but as Scobie notes, the cognate "cabin" also links the composite character IF to Osiris, since IF comes down from a tree fort at the conclusion of the novel. Furthermore, Isis "recovered the dismembered body of her brother Osiris from a 'treehouse' (he was concealed inside a tamarisk tree) and brought him back to life."[208] Cohen's treatment of the text as a reconstituted body of fragments thus anticipates the Isian theme in Carson's treatment of the fragments of Stesichoros in *Autobiography of Red* (chapter 6), where issues of time, revelation, and patriarchal contest are uppermost.

The final book of Cohen's novel, "Beautiful Losers: An Epilogue in the Third Person," describes IF's trip from the treehouse in the Laurentians to his apotheosis in the sky above the Main. The quality of the writing in this section is inferior to that of the previous two, but I cannot agree with Dennis Lee's suggestion that one should stop reading at the end of Book Two, because many of the moments prophesied in earlier scenes reach their fulfillment here.[209] IF hitches a ride into the city with a woman who declares, in Greek lettering, "I am Isis," even as the man performs an oral favour for her.[210] She then drops him off in front of the System Theatre where the ekphrastic dimension of the novel reasserts itself. F. had visited this theatre at the conclusion of Book Two and examined the projector beam with a McLuhanesque eye, noting that the "the frames streamed at the screen" and spread their "colourful organic contents over the snow."[211] Having merged with F., the historian is able to analyse the medium, instead of passively accepting the message: "Now he understood as much as he needed. The movie was invisible to him. His eyes were blinking at the same rate as the shutter in the projector, times per second, and therefore the screen was merely black."[212] He thus wrests the cinematic power of projection and hypnotism from its centralized source, and the reel escapes into the street, as F. had hoped.

After paying ludic homage to the Main Shooting and Game Alley, IF ascends to the sky in a cinematic apotheosis as Ray Charles and plays the heavens as his keyboard. This apotheosis completes the re-assembly of Osiris and closes the mythic frame that begins with the novel's epigram, a line from "Ol' Man River" as sung by Ray Charles: "Somebody said lift that bale."[213] Söderlind observes that in "modern Greek, the letter B is pronounced V; carried over into the language of the scripture, the words 'bale' and 'veil' would be homonymous."[214] Charles seems to be the agent of apocalyptic revelation, but the appearance of the American does not tie up the plot with a visit.

Cohen has a genuine esteem for Ray Charles. Nearly three decades after *Beautiful Losers*, he recorded a cover of Charles's "Born to Lose" with Elton John.[215] In the novel, he expresses empathy with African Americans as an oppressed people. However, F. has warned the reader that "nostalgic theories of Negro supremacy" (to which Breavman is prone) tend toward "monolithic" idealizations of an economic underclass and confound the real social challenges that African Americans face.[216] Moreover, in the arcade scene, Cohen had heaped suspicion on American cultural imperialism through his reading of the De Luxe Polar Hunt pinball game. Cohen seems to position Ray Charles as the figurehead of "Magic Canada" for shock value. If Cohen were in search of a world-class black musician from Montreal in the 1960s, he could have chosen Oscar Peterson, but his aim in Book Three seems to be to challenge a sense of nationhood defined by strict ethnic and geographic boundaries. Whereas Lisa's favourite game revolved around a Teutonic light in an economically privileged setting, the "point of Clear Light," the "stem between the two flasks" of the hourglass from which the future streams on boulevard St-Laurent, is black.[217] Thus the efflorescence of a multicultural society in *Beautiful Losers* stems from people of colour as well as whites. One reason for reading Book Three, then, is that it displaces the emphasis on the psychomachia of white masculinities that Lee admires in the previous two books.

Cohen continues to distort Canadian Eurocentrism in the closing paragraphs of *Beautiful Losers*, where he turns the narrative gaze from Ray Charles back to Tekakwitha, the woman whose plastic likeness once graced "the dashboard of every Montréal taxi."[218] Here, Cohen shifts to the second person to mark the transition back to the historical frame of reference that began with the historian's second person appeal to Catherine Tekakwitha at the outset of Book One. Cohen claims that the end of Book Three "has been rented to the Jesuits," although the novel has three endings, each in a different voice.[219] What follows is a petition for the beatification of Catherine Tekakwitha that consists almost entirely of a quote from *Une Vierge Iroquoise Catherine Tekakwitha*, written by the Jesuit priest Edouard Lecompte in 1927. The subtitle of this book, *Le Lis des bords de la Mohawk et du St-Laurent (1656–1680)*, supplies the final words of Cohen's petition. However, as Leslie Monkman demonstrates, Lecompte's book frames *Beautiful Losers* in other ways: the "picture described on the first page of the novel matches detail by detail the portrait of Catherine which serves as frontispiece to Lecompte's book. Quotations ascribed to Fathers Cholonec, Chauchetière, and Remy are also restricted to citations appearing in this volume."[220] Cohen translates the petition phrase by phrase, suggesting that his entire story of Catherine Tekakwitha is a translation of a French text into an English one.

Siemerling also notes that Cohen's quotations from the Lecompte tome interpose English spellings of French words such as *entreprise*, *succes*, and *essentiel*.[221] In addition, Cohen repeatedly spells "Québécois" without the second accent – as do, lamentably, several of his best critics. The fact that these errors have not been corrected in subsequent editions of *Beautiful Losers* suggests that Cohen is playing with variations of phonetic transcription, much as the text reproduces a number of approximations of "Tekakwitha." For his part, F. contradicts the testimony of Père Cholenec (given in French) and informs the reader that Catherine died *mis*pronouncing the names of Jesus and Mary, much as an orthodox Jew is prohibited from uttering the proper name of the divine.[222] Through such deformations, Cohen anticipates the postmodern interest in linguistic pollution that fascinates bilingual poets such as Lola Lemire Tostevin. He also demonstrates the validity of F.'s assertion that "prayer is translation. A man translates himself into a child asking for all there is in a language he has barely mastered."[223] While F. gives "I" an English-Greek phrase book and instructs him to study it and pray with it, Cohen gives the reader a guide to identity translation and hopes the book will facilitate their prayers. At the very least, Lecompte's prayer was fulfilled with the official beatification (but not canonization) of Tekakwitha in 1970. Yet Cohen's description of Catherine's death emphasizes that this official recognition merely confirms a fact established through "*la béatification équipollente*," the simultaneous recognition by a community of a person's miraculous status.[224] The community thus transforms the translator, Catherine, by word of mouth.

Much as the charm of Klein's "Montreal" derives from its neologisms and cultural syncretism, the appeal of Cohen's novel is the zeal with which the characters plunge into the fissures between their cultures and pursue visions of Montreal that err spectacularly. In fact, Cohen perceives error, in its productive guises as neologism, metaphor, narrative ruse, and catachrestic juxtaposition, as the transformative power of writing: "[A poet's] allegiance is to the notion that he is not bound to the world as given, that he can escape from the painful arrangement of things as they are. Jesus probably designed his system so that it would fail in the hands of other men, that is the way with the greatest creators: they guarantee the desperate power of their own originality by projecting their systems into an abrasive future."[225] By making art out of the quirks of bad translations, out of the noise of transmission and the space of loss bounding the framed image, Cohen embraces the potential of error to metamorphose into beauty through a shift in the governing frame of reference. Greenstein sees this method as radically different in effect than that of Klein: "Barely fifteen years separate *The Second Scroll* from *Beautiful Losers*, yet Klein's synthesis of tradition and modernism remains worlds apart from Cohen's postmodern New Jew. The crowd that gathers at Melech Davidson's funeral differs markedly from the crowd that watches the old man's performance in the Epilogue of Cohen's novel. Where Klein's 'Deuteronomy' reveals Israel's rebirth, 'An Epilogue in the Third Person' depicts Montreal's springtime reawakening."[226] According to Greenstein, the New Jews of Montreal "keep and cancel tradition, question a nameless, faceless history, and master paradoxical ceremonies instead of grand narratives."[227] In Cohen's novel, there is no one messiah, but rather a synthesis of New Jewry that disassembles itself as the book proceeds.

To emphasize this instability, Cohen concludes *Beautiful Losers* by abdicating his authorial power. The movement from first person to third person voices in the course of the novel reverses in the epilogue as third person description (of IF's apotheosis) yields to second person petition (for Tekakwitha's sainthood) and finally shifts to first person in what appears to be Cohen's voice in the closing paragraph: "I have come through the fire of family and love. I smoke with my darling, I sleep with my friend."[228] Having passed through these conflagrations of identity, Cohen asks his readers to complete the translation he has begun and arrive at their own destination: "Welcome to you who read me today. Welcome to you who put my heart down. Welcome to you, darling and friend, who miss me forever in your trip to the end."[229] Cohen points the reader in several directions and the only aim of this journey, as Edith established through her sex games, is to end up a different person than one began. Certainly, if readers engage imaginatively with this novel, they will never see Montreal the same way again.

Cohen was not the same after the completion of *Beautiful Losers*, either. In an ominous replay of Klein's experience, he suffered a nervous breakdown in Hydra shortly after completing the manuscript. Nadel shows that a combination of sunstroke, insecurity about potential censorship, and bodily reaction to the amphetamines that had fuelled the writing of it precipitated his collapse: "He didn't eat for more than ten days. He hallucinated and lost weight, going down to 116 pounds."[230] Years later, Cohen would make light of this episode in "A Note to the Chinese Reader," where he explains that "*Beautiful Losers* was written outside, on a table set

among the rocks, weeds and daisies, behind my house on Hydra, an island in
the Aegean Sea. I lived there many years ago. It was a blazing hot summer. I
never covered my head. What you have in your hands is more of a sunstroke
than a book."[231] To date, Cohen has not published another novel.

COHEN THE BALLADEER

Shortly after his breakdown Cohen reinvented himself as a travelling folk
singer, "Un Canadien Errant," as he portrays himself on one cover of a
1838 ballad on *Recent Songs* (1979).[232] This song by Antoine Gérin-
Lajoie, a product of the 1837 Rebellion in Lower Canada, articulates the
longing of the exile for a country lost to him that Cohen expresses in many
of his interview statements. It also encapsulates Cohen's contradictory
nationalist sentiments, as it is a lament for "mon cher Canada" that
includes the provincial motto and nationalist rallying cry of Quebec, "je me
souviens":

> 'Si tu vois mon pays,
> Mon pays malheureux,
> Va, dis à mes amis
> Que je me souviens d'eux.

> 'Ô jours si pleins d'appas,
> Vous êtes disparus,
> Et ma patrie, hélas!
> Je ne la verrai plus.

> 'Non, mais en expirant,
> Ô mon cher Canada,
> Mon regard languissant
> Vers toi se portera.'[233]

In 1968 Cohen rejected the Governor General's Award out of sympathy for
the counter-colonial politics of the Quebec independence movement. However, in 2003, he accepted Canada's highest civilian award by becoming a
Companion of the Order of Canada. Cohen also emphasizes his continuing
regard for the contradictory tensions of Montreal in *Book of Longing*,
which features a drawing and poem depicting Cohen reading *Death of a
Lady's Man* to the ladies' man and federalist champion Pierre Elliott Tru-

deau.[234] *Book of Longing* also features a poem in which Cohen meditates on his life "From a third-storey window / above the Parc du Portugal," close to the corner of St-Laurent and Marie-Anne, where a colourful plaque immortalizes the contributions of Cohen and other Jewish writers to the neighbourhood.[235] Montreal continues to be the emotional and psychological anchor of Cohen's world, as the text scrolled alongside an untitled self-portrait dated 18 November 2003 illustrates. The text begins "back in / Montreal" and then features a catalogue of notable aspects of Cohen's life in exile, none of which seem intelligble to the prodigal upon his return.[236] Another poem in *Book of Longing* expresses this world-weary sentiment more forcefully: "I've been to too many countries / I died when I left Montreal."[237]

As in his writing career, Cohen's singing received early accolades, fell into disrepute, and then was recuperated by a number of influential artists. The novelist Tom Robbins argues in the liner notes to one of the more than thirty-seven Cohen cover albums worldwide: "What matters here is that after thirty years, L. Cohen is holding court in the lobby of the whirlwind, and that giants have gathered to pay him homage."[238] It is appropriate, then, that the Ondaatje novel most influenced by Cohen, *Coming Through Slaughter*, should also feature a beleagured but influential musician as its protagonist.

Narrative form in the Canadian novel would also not be the same after *Beautiful Losers*. Ondaatje describes it as "a gorgeous novel, and ... the most vivid, fascinating, and brave modern novel I have read," although he admits that his appreciation for the intricacies of its narrative structure only developed after a second reading.[239] His first reading led him to believe that nothing linked together the separate episodes of "tour de force writing" and he concluded that the book was nothing more than an anthology of impressive fragments.[240] The dustjacket of the 1966 McClelland & Stewart edition of *Beautiful Losers* fosters this impression by describing the novel as "a love story, a psalm, a Black Mass, a monument, a satire, a prayer, a shriek, a road map through the wilderness, a joke, a tasteless affront, an hallucination, a bore, an irrelevant display of diseased virtuosity, a Jesuitical tract, an Orange sneer, a scatological Lutheran extravagance – in short a disagreeable religious epic of incomparable beauty." On second reading, however, Ondaatje realized that Cohen summarizes the story at the outset of the novel and thenceforth "keeps about twelve incidents going at the same time" even as he appears to ignore the plot.[241] Although F. insists, "Connect nothing ... Place things side by side on your arborite table, if you must, but connect nothing!" neither he nor the historian can resist the associative connections that bridge the gaps of causation in the plot.[242] The "necklace of incomparable beauty and unmeaning" that the historian imagines is produced comparatively, and the reader quickly develops the necessary skills to make sense of the vertiginous narrative.[243] The juggled incidents, circumlocutionary biographies, and sexual perversity confirm F.'s assertion that the "Voice comes out of the whirlwind, and long ago we hushed the whirlwind. I wish that you would remember that the Voice comes out of the whirlwind."[244] The voice that emerges from this narrative whirlwind finally shifts from third to first person and then becomes that of the reader.

Future generations will certainly remember Cohen for his balladry. In February 2006, a tearful Cohen was inducted into the Canadian Songwriters Hall of Fame, along with his songs "Suzanne" and "Bird on a Wire." In May 2006 his first collection of poetry in twenty years, *Book of Longing*, climbed to the top spot on the bestseller list of Canada's largest bookstore (an unprecedented feat for poetry), in part thanks to a Toronto reading and concert he performed with his partner and collaborator Anjani Thomas. But as a novelist I believe Cohen will be remembered for his attempt to find a narrative form appropriate to Montreal, where one culture is constantly being translated into another, and where cultural frames of reference shift with every passing house and shop. Cohen embraced the popular mythologies and anomalies of this *Balconville*, where the stacked balconies, those liminal spaces that figure so prominently in the postcards and literature of the city, have been officially banned since 1927 as an affront to good taste.[245] In *Beautiful Losers*, Cohen spoke affront and contradiction until they became a language. This new language is not free of violence, and it is worth remembering that, as Randolph Lewis shows, Cohen worked from a copy of *Les Lis des bords de la Mohawk et du St-Laurent* given to him by the multilingual Abenaki filmmaker Alanis Obomsawin, who is best known for her National Film Board documentary, *Kanehsatake: 270 Years of Resistance*, about the Oka Crisis in 1990, in which Mohawk warriors blockaded bridges and roads connecting the mainland to Montreal to protest against infringements on Mohawk territory.[246] Although Cohen's cross-cultural gestures are certainly imperfect, his efforts to traverse cultural solitudes have made a lasting impact on Canadian art in diverse languages and media, as well as on an astonishing array of international productions. His translational sensibility demonstrates that the products of culture clash, while sometimes garish or violent, can potentially result in a vibrant, energetic, and beautiful city.

3

Michael Ondaatje: (Un)framing
the Series

There has been a great change in what "structure" is in a poem or in a novel. Or "design." Or the "context" of a novel.

Michael Ondaatje[1]

In this 1984 interview with Sam Solecki, Ondaatje does not clarify what he means by the "great change" in the structure of poems and novels. Although book reviewers frequently refer to his "Booker-winning novel-poems," it remains unclear what Ondaatje considers the relation of poetry to the novel to be.[2] In the Solecki interview, Ondaatje refuses to slot his novels into one category and asserts that "if you're writing a novel then you're writing *against* what you know the novel is."[3] However, he does state that he thinks of the "architecture" of a novel "in terms of repeating and building images and so making them more potent," and not in terms of "the horse race" of plot.[4] In this chapter I examine how Ondaatje develops this architectural principle in his long poems *the man with seven toes* (1969) and *The Collected Works of Billy the Kid* (1970), as well as in his first novel, *Coming Through Slaughter* (1976). Images of frames (picture frames, windows, doors, mirrors) function as self-reflexive motifs for the discrete segments of poetry and prose in these works. But instead of inserting each frame into the chronological grid of a conventional plot, Ondaatje configures his narratives according to recursive patterns of word and image association.

This chapter focuses specifically on Ondaatje's fascination with (un)framing the visual series and transforming it into a song cycle. In *the man with seven toes,* Ondaatje frames his narrative as a series of individual lyrics loosely based on the "Mrs Fraser" series of paintings by the Australian artist Sidney Nolan. Ondaatje expands on the Aboriginal dimension of the Mrs Fraser legend and transforms the painted series into a song cycle by alluding to the Songlines of Aboriginal myth performance. Because song cycles work by correspondence and repetition rather than by linear connection and continuous plot, the poet fashions a disjointed narrative using clusters of lyrics that connect through motifs and recurring themes. The narrative becomes a kind of secular walkabout, in which the mapping of the violent encounters between the unnamed woman and the inhabitants of the desert evolves into a cycle of songs that she performs in public when she returns to Europe.

Ondaatje elaborates on this dynamic between the visual series and the song cycle in *The Collected Works of Billy the Kid*, which is an aggregate of lyrics, photographs, prose anecdotes, and interviews that critics frequently liken to a "picture album" because of its disjointed, visual style.[5] Anne Blott observes that "space throughout the sequence of prose and poetry is bordered by box frames: porch rails, windows, walls, barbed wire fences, and coffins," because Billy attempts to "fix" his world by framing it as a series of photographs.[6] The poet-outlaw perceives the world in arrested images, even as he avoids arrest himself. He portrays himself evading portraits – or rather, the mysterious Canadian "orchestra" shaping Billy's song cycle presents him in this manner.[7] The Canadian artists disturb the fixity implied by the conceit of the photographic frame by performing a song cycle about the process of mythmaking rather than about the historical figure.

In *Coming Through Slaughter*, Ondaatje personifies the dynamic between the song cycle and the visual series in the friendship between the jazzman Buddy Bolden and the photographer E.J. Bellocq. The fictional encounter between these historical figures is structured around the image of the broken frame, a trope that represents the synthesis of the artists' respective talents as well as the process of (un)framing in Ondaatje's writing. The dynamic between the song cycle and visual series – which begins as a relationship between source material and adaptation in *the man with the seven toes* and evolves into a trope in *The Collected Works of Billy the Kid* – functions on the level of metaphor, character, and form in *Coming Through Slaughter*, where the design of the novel is clearly shaped by the rhetorical techniques that Ondaatje developed in his long poems.

Even a cursory look at the architectural metaphors in Ondaatje's writing reveals how the author dismantles the rhetorical artifices he constructs. Ondaatje displays an enduring interest in the architectural order of classical and neo-classical buildings, such as the Villa San Girolamo in *The English Patient* and the Wickramasinghe house in *Anil's Ghost*. The vaults, arches, and portals in these abandoned buildings possess a certain elegance, but they are also laden with explosives and targeted by revolutionaries. They provide a temporary shelter for the artist but they are not a secure destination. After apprenticing in the techniques of classicism, Ondaatje's artist-figures apply their skills to the task of undoing the social order that these buildings represent. Patrick in *In the Skin of a Lion*, for instance, attempts to dynamite the neo-classical waterworks on which he has laboured. In the same novel, Ondaatje dramatizes the construction of the Bloor Street Viaduct and transforms the webbed girders of the bridge into a "main character" and "love objec[t]."[8] However, he contrasts the romance of bridge construction with Patrick's bombing of a Muskoka resort that caters to the Toronto elite who commissioned the bridge and projects like it. A similar scenario configures "Spider Blues," in which Ondaatje's "black architec[t]" – the poet-spider – "thinks a path and travels / the emptiness that was there / leaves his bridge behind."[9] While the poet admires the "classic" control of the spider's architecture, he reminds his reader that these "constructions / for succulent travel" are the product of a "murderous art" in which visionaries – whether the spider, the poet, or Commissioner Harris – lock their victims "in their dream."[10] "Spider Blues" questions the rage for order in Ondaatje's early lyrics, which Stephen Heighton argues were "obsessed with trapping and ordering the flux of phenomenal existence in well-crafted, closed artefacts."[11] The length, shifting perspectives, and self-reflexive tone of "Spider Blues" suggest a re-alignment in Ondaatje's poetics in which he elevates an image into a conceit and then takes it apart.

This (un)framing strategy recurs in many of the heavily anthologized poems from *Rat Jelly* (1973), including "the gate in his head."[12] Bowering regards this poem as a turning point in Ondaatje's career because it marks "a departure, if not in form at least in intention, from his earlier predilection for preserving his objects in the amber of his directed emotions. In [Ondaatje's] poetry since 1973, and more so in his non-lyric works, we have seen him seeking the unrested form he requires."[13] Bowering argues that the poem represents a move away from Ondaatje's "habit of intensifying the world, of fashioning artifice,"[14] but in 1980 Ondaatje was still defining the poem as a work of art: "It's an artifice, it's a chair, it was made by somebody." That somebody, Ondaatje prefers to call "an artisan" rather than a "poet."[15] Whereas Bowering regards "the gate in his head" as transitional, Heighton considers the poem "a kind of manifesto … a clear assertion about what poetry should be and how it can fly by the nets of language."[16] Heighton comes closer to the mark, but one should note the element of paradox in his reading of the lyric. The poem is a clear assertion against clarity: "not clarity but the sense of shift."[17] The lyric frames its own unframing and thereby enacts a paradoxical process that shapes much

of Ondaatje's poetry. Like Carson, who believes that paradox is the essence
of desire, Ondaatje sees paradox as a productive force, precisely because
it is not restive. This preference for motion and change causes Eluned
Summers-Bremmer to interpret "Ondaatje's poetics [as] a continual
re-staging of the mobility of dwelling," which also characterizes his novels:
"In the last few decades transnational displacement has made the novel –
always a kind of conversation with quotidian ways of inhabiting the world
– into a test that must imagine travel, if not in content, then in form, in
order to speak to the contemporary. And not only physical travel, but the
entire (post)modern architecture of displacement from familial, national
and linguistic myths of belonging that Ondaatje's books chart so well, from
Billy the Kid to *Running in the Family* to *Anil's Ghost*."[18] The sense of shift
in the poetry clearly takes on multiple connotations in Ondaatje's novels.

From the perspective of (un)framing, Ondaatje's most concise architectural vision appears in "House on a Red Cliff," a lyric from his 1998 collection of poems, *Handwriting*. Ondaatje uses the image of a flamboyant tree
growing up through the skeleton of a fire-ravaged house to symbolize his
poetic process:

> The flamboyant a grandfather planted
> having lived through fire
> lifts itself over the roof
>
> unframed
> the house an open net
>
> where the night concentrates
> on a breath
>   on a step
> a thing or gesture
> we cannot be attached to[19]

The image of "the roof / unframed" and the metaphor of the "house an
open net" connect this lyric to a number of earlier Ondaatje poems, such as
"the gate in his head" or "King Kong meets Wallace Stevens," where "W.S.
in his suit / is thinking chaos is thinking fences."[20] Solecki analyses the latter two poems in "Nets and Chaos" and argues that the "tension between
mind and chaos is at the centre of Ondaatje's poetry; and its implications
can be seen in the dualistic nature of his imagery, in the deliberate thematic
irresolution of his major lyrics, and in the complex structuring of his two

longer poems, *the man with seven toes* and *The Collected Works of Billy the Kid*."[21] Such dualism and irresolution also characterize the concluding stanzas of "House on a Red Cliff," which contrast long and short, light and dark, horizontal and vertical so as to bring one object into focus against another in a painterly manner. Yet the images gravitate toward dissolution in the final line: "Last footstep before formlessness."[22] The drift is entropic, but the poem as it stands is not formless.

Entropy governs most of Ondaatje's major poems, such as "Letters & Other Worlds," where the poet's father composes "gentle letters ... / With the clarity of architects" and then falls drunkenly to his death, "the blood searching in his head without metaphor."[23] Ondaatje's fascination with the dissolution of form stems from his desire to keep the conclusions of his poems open. Yet this openness is not absolute. He refuses to accept that any single poem represents "a total canning of an incident," but he conjures architectural boundaries when he insists that "there's got to be an open door or something at the end of the poem, so that you can step out or the writer can step out and admit that this isn't everything."[24] In his search for a form that resists closure, Ondaatje admits to being influenced by bp Nichol's concept of morality, "how you have to lead the audience into your own perceptual sense, but then [have] a responsibility to lead them out again."[25] A close look at Ondaatje's first book-length poem, *the man with seven toes,* illustrates the way the author leads his readers into the framework of Nolan's paintings and then leads them out again by unframing the visual series and transforming it into a song cycle reminiscent of an Aboriginal Songline.

THE MAN WITH SEVEN TOES: FROM PAINTED SERIES TO SONG CYCLE

In a 1975 interview with Solecki, Ondaatje touched on why he based *the man with seven toes* on Nolan's paintings of the Mrs Fraser story: "I got fascinated by the story of which I only knew the account in the paintings and the quote from Colin MacInnes."[26] Ondaatje reprints the MacInnes account at the end of *the man with seven toes*, effectively sharing with the reader most of what he knows about Mrs Fraser, since only a modest selection of paintings from the Mrs Fraser series is reproduced in Ondaatje's sourcebook, *Sidney Nolan*:

Mrs Fraser was a Scottish lady who was shipwrecked on what is now Fraser Island, off the Queensland Coast. She lived for 6 months among the aborigines, rapidly losing her clothes, until she was discovered by one Bracefell, a deserting convict who himself had hidden for 10 years among the primitive Australians. The lady asked the criminal to restore her to civilization, which he agreed to do if she would promise to intercede for his free pardon from the Governor. The bargain was sealed, and the couple set off inland.

At first sight of European settlement, Mrs Fraser rounded on her benefactor and threatened to deliver him up to justice if he did not immediately decamp. Bracefell returned disillusioned to the hospitable bush, and Mrs Fraser's adventures aroused such admiring interest that on her return to Europe she was able to exhibit herself at 6d a showing in Hyde Park.[27]

Ondaatje's placement of this synopsis at the end of *the man with seven toes* both frames and unframes his narrative. It provides a basic plot line for his long poem, which is nearly unintelligible on first reading because it was originally written for dramatic performance. The sequence refuses all background commentary, proceeds in brief imagistic fragments, and switches voice without warning among three different speakers: a narrator, an unnamed woman, and a male convict. However, on closer inspection, the painted and written series tell very different stories.

MacInnes's synopsis cannot be used as a rigid template for plotting Ondaatje's narrative. Ondaatje's heroine is not shipwrecked off the Queensland Coast; rather, she chooses to get off a train in the middle of the Australian outback and not board it again (in a move that anticipates Buddy Bolden's decision at Shell Beach). Lost in the arid landscape, the woman escapes starvation by being adopted by a tribe of Aborigines, which is an aspect of the myth barely treated by the painter in his early years and not represented in *Sidney Nolan*. Ondaatje's heroine makes a pact with a convict named Potter, not Bracefell, and the poet concentrates on the sexual and violent aspects of the couple's journey. Nolan, in contrast, gives their wanderings an Edenic quality and emphasizes the woman's betrayal of the man. Only the middle section of Ondaatje's narrative – the swamp scenes and the convict's portrait – appear to derive from the Mrs Fraser paintings. Ondaatje thus unframes the narrative basis of Nolan's series and incorporates certain lyrical and mythic elements from it into his song cycle. The MacInnes synopsis helps to make sense of the theme; however, on second reading one realizes that Ondaatje has largely rewritten the Mrs Fraser story.

Ondaatje's cavalier treatment of source material in other instances has caused critics such as Arun Mukherjee to condemn his blatant "misuse of historical figures,"[28] which is particularly evident in the case of Buddy Bolden, as I shall demonstrate later in this chapter. However, Ondaatje makes no pretense of historical accuracy in *the man with seven toes*; and the whole issue of authentic portrayal is particularly fraught because Mrs Fraser herself altered her story to suit syndication.[29] Following Kay Schaeffer, Beverly Curran has shown that the duration and sexual content of the Fraser-Bracefell trek were fictitious contributions to the imperial market for captivity narratives: "About seven hundred of them were published in America between 1682 and 1800 ... and by the late eighteenth century, pseudo-captivity narratives were appearing in England. Captivity narratives, too, had concerns about fidelity; a version of Mrs Fraser's captivity was promoted, for example, as a 'plain, unvarnished tale, exaggerating nothing, but recording truly and faithfully the particulars' of her ordeal."[30] Furthermore, according to Elwin Lynn, the paintings Ondaatje uses as his source material "only vaguely suggest the stories and myths they are associated with."[31] Nolan veers away from history (or what passes for it) toward myth, since his source, John Curtis's *Shipwreck of the Stirling Castle*, is already "*Embellished with engravings, portraits and scenes illustrative of the narrative*," as its subtitle makes clear. Ondaatje proceeds even further along this mythic tangent, and both artists clearly regard the dismantling of previous narratives as part of their imperative to create anew.

the man with seven toes thus begins with a kind of derailment:

> The train hummed like a low bird
> over the rails, through
> desert and pale scrub,
> air spun in the carriages.
>
> She moved to the doorless steps
> where wind could beat her knees.
> When they stopped for water she got off
> sat by the rails on the wrist thick stones.
>
> The train shuddered, then wheeled away from her.
> She was too tired even to call.
> Though, come back, she murmured to herself.[32]

This lyric is the most straightforward in Ondaatje's sequence, but the movement away from conventional syntax and linear narrative (symbolized by the train) has already begun. The first sentence is a run-on. The connective "and" disappears from the phrase "she got off / sat by the rails," and the dramatic voice intrudes unheralded in the concluding sentence.

The gaps in syntax and storyline widen with the appearance of the Aborigines:

> Not lithe, they move
> like sticklebacks,
> you hear toes
> crack with weight,
> elbows sharp as beaks
> grey pads of knees.
>
> Maps on the soles of their feet[33]

Leaving the linear train of thought behind in these lyrics, Ondaatje arranges his poems spatially, in blocks of images that combine to form a literary map that is as much tactile as it is visual. The map metaphor also recalls Robin Blaser's definition of the serial poem, which Ondaatje cites in *The Long Poem Anthology*: "It has to be a renewed language and information that becomes a kind of map."[34] Like the picture frames with which Ondaatje is obsessed in *Billy* and *Slaughter*, the map doubles as a way of seeing and writing.

"Literary and visual impressions have always gone hand in hand in [Nolan's] work," as Lynn points out, and by writing a series of lyrics inspired by Nolan's paintings Ondaatje engages in an ekphrastic process that reverses Nolan's method.[35] Nolan exhibited his famous Ned Kelly series alongside excerpts from his literary sources and spoke "frequently, until as late as 1947, of becoming a poet."[36] He wrote "short, condensed attempts at poetic prose" and, according to Bryan Robertson, his "habit of writing down visual impressions rather than making preliminary graphic, or painted, sketches" persisted throughout his career.[37] The conjunction of Nolan's paintings with Ondaatje's poems therefore produces a movement that could be summarized as "Verse: Ekphrasis: (Re)Verse," except that this reversal does not retrace the same narrative path. Under close examination, the connections between Nolan and Ondaatje prove to be stronger in style than in content.

Nolan's painterly example shows Ondaatje how to combine lyricism with narrative by developing myth in a series of imagistic fragments. For example, in the swamp scenes evocative of Nolan's paintings, Ondaatje's tone is clipped but his metaphors are layered and dense:

Then swamp is blue
green, the mist
sitting like toads.
Leaves spill snakes
their mouths arched
with bracelets of teeth.
Once a bird, silver
with arm wide wings
flew a trail between trees
and never stopped,
caught all the sun
and spun like mercury away from us[38]

With its vivid imagery, narrow narrative scope, and insistent use of colour, this lyric fits into the larger series like a segment of a storyboard for a film. It offers a succession of glimpses, rather than full-blown descriptions. Solecki observes that the long poem "relies on a form made up of brief self-contained, often cinematic, lyrics each of which explodes upon the reader with a single startling revelation." Similarly Lynn comments that Nolan combines an intense lyricism with "a commitment to sudden moments of revelation."[39] In fact, Ondaatje made a proposal to the National Film Board of Canada to adapt *the man with seven toes* as "cinéma verité in the desert," but "they couldn't see it as one" – with good reason.[40]

Nolan, for his part, never made films but he was conscious of painting cinematically. In the early 1940s, writes Andrew Sayers, Nolan "was convinced that new forms of myth ... would be best expressed through film," and while at work on his Ned Kelly series, he "wrote glowingly of Walt Disney, describing things as though they were sequences from films. As he struggled with his canvases, he dreamed of film, a medium not 'bounded by four straight lines, colour that moves while you watch it and music at your elbow into the bargain.'"[41] Nolan's storyboard technique connects his series to film, but Lynn mentions that it also recalls the "early Renaissance panels that showed various stages of a saint's journey or martyrdom," which are themselves responses to the sculptural narratives on medieval cathedrals.[42] Although Lynn maintains that "it is rare for a series of paintings on a single theme and treated with [such] a sustained, lyrical intensity ... to be preserved as a unit," it was precisely the possibility of sustaining the intensity of the lyric over longer and longer stretches of narrative that interested Ondaatje at this point in his career.[43] To this end, Ondaatje removed a large prose piece on the convict situation in Australia from the final draft of *the man with seven toes* in order to concentrate on the narrative potential of lyric forms.[44]

Both Nolan and Ondaatje make extensive use of image repetition, because motifs can create continuity across the gaps within serial narrative. Nolan's paintings exhibit what Lynn describes as a fascination "with plastic rhymes, with the repetition of similar shapes: the hump of a camel mirrors the hollow of a gully; birds' legs mock the branches of trees."[45] Similarly, all the selections from *the man with seven toes* that I have quoted to this point contain bird imagery. As Ondaatje frequently remarks, myth is created by "a very careful use of echoes – of phrases and images. There may be no logical connection when these are placed side by side, but the variations are always there setting up parallels."[46] Ondaatje's opening simile of the train humming "like a low bird" introduces an image pattern that echoes throughout the song cycle. When the woman encounters the Aborigines, she observes that their faces are "scarred with decoration / feathers" and their elbows are "sharp as beaks."[47] When she encounters their goats, she reacts to the animals' "balls bushed in the centre / cocks rising like birds flying to you."[48] The bird imagery becomes increasingly masculine and sexual when Potter gives his name and a "bird screeche[s] hideously past."[49] The woman later notices that he has a "cock like an ostrich," echoing her observation on the previous page that the eyelids of birds are "fresh as foreskins."[50]

These phallic birds amplify the erotic overtones in the penultimate lyric. Safe in the Royal Hotel – the title of a 1948 painting in a Nolan series on outback hotels – Ondaatje's heroine traces the memory-track of her desert journey across the contours of her body:

> She slept in the heart of the Royal Hotel
> Her burnt arms and thighs
> soaking the cold off the sheets.
> She moved fingers onto the rough skin,
> traced the obvious ribs, the running heart,
>
> sensing herself like a map, then
> lowering her hands into her body.[51]

This tactile mapping connects the woman to the Aborigines who had "maps on the soles of their feet." Her roving hands also reconfigure a European tradition of metaphorical conceits in which male poets, such as John Donne in "Elegy 19," conflate the exploration of the female body with the colonization of foreign territories.[52] The autoeroticism of the concluding lyric dismembers this patriarchal tradition:

> In the morning she found pieces of a bird
> chopped and scattered by the fan
> blood sprayed onto the mosquito net,
> its body leaving paths on the walls
> like red snails that drifted down in lumps
>
> She could imagine the feathers
> while she had slept
> falling around her
> like slow rain[53]

The dream-like image of white feathers falling around the woman while she sleeps raises the question of whether the entire poem is in fact her dream. Indeed, Travis Lane remarks that "it is as if the poem is her dream and Potter, the title-hero, the chief figure of her dream," because the Aborigines resemble "figures of a delirium" more than real people.[54] The dream-like qualities of Ondaatje's visual style thus serve as a bridge to the unconscious, as the meditations on nightmares in *Running in the Family* make explicit.

If the woman in *the man with seven toes* is dreaming, the bird imagery follows a pattern of dream formation identified by Scherner in *Das Leben des Traumes* (1861) and cited by Freud: "In all symbolic dream-structures which arise from particular nervous stimuli, the imagination observes a general law: at the beginning of a dream it depicts the object from which the stimulus arises only by the remotest and most inexact allusions, but at the end, when the pictorial effusion has exhausted itself, it nakedly presents the stimulus itself."[55] This line of interpretation also suggests that the woman's subconscious has superimposed the story of Mrs Fraser onto figures from her own experience. Certainly the nightmarish rape scenes and the castration images of Potter's severed toes and the bird in the fan invite a psychoanalytic reading of the narrative.[56] Ondaatje encourages this reading with the statement that a writer "has to be on the border where ... craft meets the accidental and the unconscious, as close as possible to the unconscious."[57]

However, the attention Ondaatje gives to the Aborigines in *the man with seven toes* suggests another interpretation that is more relevant than a psychoanalytic one to the broader discussion here. Reassessing *the man with seven toes* toward the end of her article, Lane argues that the long poem "presents not a dream so much as history as a dream."[58] This interpretation raises the question of whether the poem presents not so much a dream as a secular Dreaming. The seeds of this Dreaming are already sown in Nolan's series, which aimed to create myth from comparatively recent Australian legends and reflected a particular postwar ideology. In the 1950s Nolan acted as a contributing editor to *Angry Penguins*, a review of literature and the arts which championed modernism and cosmopolitanism, as an alternative to the Jindyworobaks, a group of artists who believed that the cultural malaise of their settler society could be cured by developing a mystical relation to the Australian landscape in the manner of the Aborigines. Nolan embraced myth, but he wished to create myths out of the outlaws and explorers from the more recent colonial past. In retrospect, the chief editor of *Angry Penguins*, Max Harris, remarked that the "time had come … to express a white man's 'dreaming' in terms of poetry and painting."[59] By "dreaming," Harris refers to the Aboriginal myths detailing the creation of the universe, which map the Australian landscape through "Songlines," as Patrick Corbally Stourton explains: "As every story or Dreaming relates to a particular feature of the landscape, series of stories create a track across the land connecting these places and the mystical happenings associated with them. These ancient tracks, which are called Songlines, go in all directions crossing the entire continent and initiated men and women can travel along these Songlines and interact with people from other tribes."[60] In addition to oral performance, one of the principal methods for representing a Dreaming is body painting, which is "looked upon as a great skill, and women practice it widely in most communities."[61] In the Royal Hotel, Ondaatje's heroine creates a kind of body painting from the physical legacy of her journey as she moves her fingers over her skin. The woman both embodies her history and dreams it into the present in altered form. Solecki therefore views the woman/Mrs Fraser as "an Australian version of Atwood's Susanna Moodie, gradually developing from a situation in which she is alienated from the land to the point where she is one with it."[62] Certainly Mrs Fraser, in her various incarnations, has become a kind of Great Ancestor to white Australian art and literature in the same way that Moodie has been accorded mythic status in Canada.[63] The stories of both women serve as archetypes of the European immigrant experience.

Nolan's later portraits of Mrs Fraser have more in common with the Jindyworobaks, as Nolan represents the legendary woman using the design configurations of Aboriginal rock painting. Similarly, Ondaatje borrows from Aboriginal traditions to make his heroine a figure of oral history. She becomes a legend immortalized in song, like Potter, whose first appearance inspires a bush ballad:

> *Potter was a convict*
> *brought in on the GLITTER DAN*
> *they landed him in Adelaide*
> *in a week the bugger ran*
>
> *The bounty men they came for him*
> *they looked for sixty weeks*
> *but Potter lived on wolves and birds*
> *down in Cooper's Creek*[64]

This passage gives us another example of Ondaatje's freewheeling use of historical details. The reference to Cooper's Creek alludes to an entirely separate myth, the deaths of the Australian explorers Burke and Wills, which itself distorts the facts: "Burke and Wills are popularly believed to have died in the desert when in fact they were camped by Cooper's Creek, with no shortage of water, in an area where local Aborigines easily obtained a varied and adequate diet. But by focussing on the horrors of the desert, these myths generated both national martyrs and an expectation that White Australians 'deserved' the land and anything else they could wrest from it, as minimal recompense for the sufferings and death of their heroic representatives."[65] In contrast to these explorers, whom Nolan depicts as awkward and incompetent figures, Potter moves easily between European and Aboriginal cultures and manages to survive. This fact suggests that Ondaatje gives Bracefell the name of Potter because *the man with seven toes* is a "pottage" of Nolan's various series on Mrs Fraser, Burke and Wills, Leda and the Swan, and outback hotels.[66] Potter is another of Ondaatje's beloved mongrels, an inference prefigured by the cover image of "Man and Dog" and by the appearance of the wild dog who accompanies the woman in the second lyric of the sequence.

While Potter's exploits are recorded in the rollicking ballad forms of the outback, the woman's song begins with a melodic verse from the Scottish ballad, "Waly, Waly":

> *When we came into Glasgow town*
> *we were a lovely sight to see*
> *My love was all in red velvet*
> *and I myself in cramasie*[67]

In contrast to the pastoral themes of traditional Scottish ballads, Ondaatje adds two stanzas full of urban images that stress the industrial environment of Glasgow. In the grey and noisy streets of this city, the attraction of the woman "singing with her throat and hands" seems to be her connection to Aboriginal culture and its traditions of oral performance.[68] Whereas the real Mrs Fraser exhibited her scars in London's Hyde Park, Ondaatje's woman sings and acts out her songs. MacInnes deemed the Aboriginals "primitive," but Ondaatje implies that the Scots are also a clannish people with "green wild rivers" coursing beneath their icy "calm."[69] The revised ballad concludes with the formulaic tag of an oral storyteller, which offers a blessing and signals the end of the performance: "God bring you all some tender stories / and keep you all from hurt and harm."[70] The Scottish audience responds enthusiastically to storytelling in song, and their industrial present only heightens their fascination with the mythic past. By staging *the man with seven toes* as a dramatic performance at the Vancouver Poetry Festival in 1968 and at the Stratford Festival in 1969, Ondaatje aimed to reach his Canadian audience in a similar fashion. Yet the poem performs the unique function of putting the ethnicity of the colonizer on stage and making a spectacle of it in the fashion of the Macedonian immigrants in *In the Skin of a Lion*.

BILLY: THE PHOTOGRAPHIC SERIES AND THE SONG CYCLE

This myth-based interpretation of *the man with seven toes* presupposes that Ondaatje had some interest in Aboriginal culture in 1967. I am confident that he was familiar with the concepts of the Songline and walkabout, but he does not allude to any specific Aboriginal myths in *the man with seven toes*. Rather, he tends to collapse myths into myth: "I am interested in myth. Making it, remaking it, exploding. I don't like poems or works that cash in on a cliché of history or a personality. I don't like pop westerns and pop Billy the Kids. Myths are only of value to me when they are realistic as well as having other qualities of myth. Another thing that interests me about myth is how and when figures get caught in myths. I thought Tony Richardson's film on Ned Kelly was marvellous for this reason, better for me than *Bonnie and Clyde*."[71] These comments suggest a bridge between *the man with seven toes* and *The Collected Works of Billy the Kid*. The association of Billy the Kid with Ned Kelly in this paragraph is striking because Ondaatje has stated that he "was previously interested in Nolan's Ned Kelly series" before he began *the man with seven toes*.[72] Like Billy,

Ned Kelly is "a protean figure responding to Nolan's changing styles and attitudes."[73] Also like Billy – who was not included in the general amnesty for the deaths incurred by the Lincoln County War – Kelly "began as a joking saint and as an icon-figure of justice and revenge" and eventually became a "lonely resister, a protester without a programme, carrying out ritualistic murders whose original cause [had] been forgotten."[74] Nolan himself identified Kelly with Billy and, while living in New York, travelled to New Mexico to see the pageant of Billy the Kid to refresh his inspiration for the Kelly series.[75]

Ondaatje cements this connection in *The Collected Works of Billy the Kid* by borrowing Kelly's famous helmet motif from Nolan. Ondaatje's "picture of Billy," the empty picture frame that opens and closes *The Collected Works of Billy the Kid,* strongly suggests the square black helmet worn by Nolan's outlaw.[76] The real Kelly gang hammered metal ploughshares into bulletproof helmets and body armour in preparation for a shootout with police, which they lost, in part because the weight of their armour prevented their escape. Although the historical Kelly wore his iron helmet only once, Nolan paints the head of the outlaw as a black square with an eye aperture in every panel from the Kelly series. Nolan repeats the helmet motif until it becomes Kelly's identity, even as it hastens his demise. Similarly, Ondaatje's Billy shoots portraits and jails his adversaries with his stories, until he himself is jailed and shot. Ondaatje therefore follows Nolan in matching the outlaw's portrait to his way of perceiving (through windows, peepholes, rifle sights) and of being perceived (inside the frame of the artwork, as a "framed" criminal).

Such frames-within-frames focus the audience's vision telescopically, as Nolan makes explicit in the picture *Mrs Fraser* (1947), where the painted borders of the portrait mimic the shape of binocular lenses.[77] In attempting to sustain the allusiveness and intensity of the lyric voice without sacrificing the momentum of narrative, Ondaatje takes a cue from the way Kelly's helmet creates focus and visual rhythms:

Not only does the helmet allow the Kelly legend to be told with the minimum of anecdotal elaboration, but it is also used as an icon of multiple emotions. Through the aperture the eyes blaze with revenge, droop with regret, are haunted with remorse or fade into weary introspection. Sometimes the aperture shows only the land and the sky. This, with the uniformly black, flat silhouette of the helmet, is an optical device to create a vivacious, tangible area in contrast to the smudgy details. When the landscape is concentrated in the aperture – like a picture within a picture – it crystallises, epitomises the impact; at the same time the helmet creates a focal point and gives cohesion to the scattered, dispersed landscape.[78]

In *Billy*, Ondaatje's settings are sparsely detailed, his characterizations anecdotal, and his scenes brief, but he introduces the frame motif to create continuity and emotional focus.

In keeping with Ondaatje's statement that "when you write you create a photograph in some way," his framed compositions in *Billy* combine to form a portrait of the outlaw in the absence of the initial photograph.[79] However, because the significance of this empty frame is not immediately apparent, Ondaatje juxtaposes it with a quotation that he attributes to the book *Huffman, Frontier Photographer*: "I send you a picture of Billy made with the Perry shutter as quick as it can be worked – Pyro and soda developer. I am making daily experiments now and find I am able to take passing horses at a lively trot square across the line of fire – bits of snow in the air – spokes well defined – some blur on top of wheel but sharp in the main – men walking are no trick – I will send you proofs sometime. I shall show you what can be done from the saddle with ground glass or tripod – please notice when you get the specimens that they were made with the lens wide open and many of the best exposed when my horse was in motion."[80] Ondaatje uses L.A. Huffman's commentary here to outline a poetics, in much the same way that he used his friend Victor Coleman's letter and the gull photograph in "the gate in his head." The excerpt foreshadows many stylistic developments in the ensuing text: it is a prose passage that begins in a colloquial voice and then (d)evolves into a poetic tone through fragmentation that elides subjects, verbs, and connective phrases, and favours clusters of nouns. It unframes the conventional syntax of the opening clause and fashions a more vital poetic diction from fragments. Indeed, as Douglas Barbour observes, the excerpt reflects Ondaatje's writing style because Ondaatje composed it. The letter "is really a carefully edited pastiche of two separate letters from Huffman to Perrin Cuppy Huffman, 18 January 1885 and 7 June 1885; the *name* of the person photographed is *Bessie*, Huffman's daughter, and the letters are found in the *chapter* titled 'L.A. Huffman, Frontier Photographer,' in Mark H. Brown and W.R. Felton, *The Frontier Years: L.A. Huffman Photographer of the Plains*."[81] Furthermore, Huffman photographed the disappearing Western frontier in Montana, not New Mexico, so it is unlikely that he would have encountered Billy.

In case readers are not familiar with the history of early photography, Billy's first words alert amateur historians of the frontier to the playful nature of Ondaatje's portrait. In Billy's opening catalogue of the slain, the outlaw claims that he stabbed a blacksmith with a knife at the age of twelve, when in fact he shot a blacksmith named Cahill at the age of seventeen. Ondaatje then changes the name of Billy's victim Joe Grant to Joe Clark, which suggests, not the future Canadian prime minister, who was a backroom politician in 1970, but rather the American photographer of the same name who documented the hill folk of his native Tennessee at the beginning of the twentieth century.[82]

Ondaatje's descriptive passages are also double-coded, such that the actions they describe illustrate the author's formal concerns. For example, the first four paragraphs of the barn scene establish order and harmony with even prose descriptions in which Billy observes the arrangement of objects. Billy avoids the "cobwebs who had places to grow to, who had stories to finish," and he never touches "another animal's flesh, never enter[s] his boundary."[83] He depicts an orderly, almost mechanical universe that suddenly plunges into chaos when some rats (drunk on fermented grain) attack each other. His tranquility disturbed, Billy sits on a window ledge, pulls out his revolver, and kills everything that moves. Only Billy remains when the smoke clears. The framed image of Billy in the window gauging the aftermath of his violence is as emblematic a portrait as any in the text. Barbour observes that the "syntax of the passage is paradigmatic in its dissolution of subject-verb-object connections and its pronominal uncertainty. Billy narrates a self he cannot hold in place: it slips from first to third person, as the peace slips into violence."[84] Billy's Apollonian love of frames thus lays the groundwork for his Dionysian fits of unframing. And the self-reflexive quality of the writing unmasks Billy to allow the reader a glimpse of Ondaatje at his desk in the barn of Blue Roof Farm near Kingston, Ontario, where much of the text was composed.[85] This play of masks in Ondaatje's early narratives inspires Solecki to conclude that Ondaatje "would agree with Anne Carson's suggestion 'All myth is an enriched pattern, / a two-faced proposition, / allowing its operator to say one thing and mean another, to lead a double life.'"[86] The double voice of the lyric thus lends itself to the double life of the characters in Ondaatje's mythic narratives.

Billy also portrays his escape from domestic ties to women as an act of unframing. For example, in a sexually charged encounter with Angela D., Billy gets caught in a sun picture as Angela moves seductively from the door jam toward the bed where he lies:

> she walks slow to the window
> lifts the sackcloth
> and jams it horizontal on a nail
> so the bent oblong of sun
> hoists itself across the room
> framing the bed the white flesh of my arm[87]

Ensnared by Angela's seductive approach, Billy reacts by turning himself into a camera: "I am very still / I take in all the angles of the room."[88] He freezes the scene as a photograph and stops the poem before Angela can take him. As in the visual narrative of a storyboard, the gap between this frame and the next leaves much to the reader's imagination.

Even alone, Billy peers through an endless series of thresholds and portals that mimic the camera obscura, on which the modern camera is based. The connection between Billy and framing is so insistent that the (un)framed composition immediately identifies Billy as the perceiving "I." This critical position, which I have endorsed thus far, can be seen in Nodelman's "The Collected Photographs of Billy the Kid," in which the critic argues that "Billy's artistry is a matter of stopping change – the dead stillness of the actual photographs in the book mirrors the dead stillness of Billy's own perception of the world."[89] Yet, when Billy recalls Huffman's blurred (and fictitious) photograph, he reminds his critics that photography does not necessarily fix its subject: "I remember, when they took the picture of me there was a white block down the fountain road where somebody had come out of a building and got off the porch onto his horse and ridden away while I was waiting standing still for the acid in the camera to dry firm."[90] Like the gull in "the gate in his head," the subject of this photograph moves to the clear. Add mind-altering chemicals to the mix, and the effect is like a dam break, as Billy discovers when he experiments with red dirt marijuana: "I was thinking of a photograph someone had taken of me, the only one I had then. I was standing on a wall, at my feet there was this bucket and in the bucket was a pump and I was pumping water out over the wall. Only now, with the red dirt, water started dripping out of the photo."[91] However momentarily caught, these subjects are not permanently detained, as the suggestion of Billy's escape in the scene of his arrest by Garrett affirms.

The Collected Works of Billy the Kid proves to be less a historical portrait of an American icon than an exploration of "how and when figures get caught in myths."[92] Ondaatje sets the story in a fantasy west that he lyricizes (in Billy's poems), dramatizes (in the interview dialogue), and satirizes (in the comic book legend). This outlaw fantasy began to take shape for the author at around the age of seven, when the photograph of Ondaatje in his cowboy costume was taken. However, Ondaatje insists that in those days "it wasn't specifically Billy the Kid, but *cowboys* that was important ... The question that's so often asked – about why I wrote about an American hero [–] doesn't really interest me cos I hardly knew what an American was when the image of 'cowboy' began that germinating process. I was writing about something that had always interested me, something within myself, not out there in a specific country or having some political or sociological meaning."[93] Ondaatje's fantasy Billy is thus part Ceylonese cowboy, part comic book hero, part Australian bushranger, and part American legend.

Ondaatje's presence behind Billy's persona is evident from the opening catalogue, where Billy lists the slain and includes himself.[94] Gradually, however, Ondaatje dismantles the artifice of Billy speaking from beyond the grave. Several passages in which Billy shows an uncommon knowledge for a nineteenth-century cattle rustler strike an anachronistic chord, such as this reference to white dwarfs, which invokes Ondaatje's poem of the same name in *Rat Jelly*:[95]

> I have seen pictures of great stars,
> drawings which show them straining to the centre
> that would explode their white
> if temperature and the speed they moved at
> shifted one degree
>
> ...
>
> the one altered move that will make them maniac.[96]

Ondaatje wears a very thin mask while speaking in Billy's voice, but to a certain extent he strips away this mask at the conclusion of *Billy* by inserting a photograph of himself as a child into the empty picture frame that began the book. This portrait of Ondaatje the Kid does not fill the entire frame, and it remains unclear whether Ondaatje is juxtaposing his picture with Billy's portrait, or whether the snapshot is in fact the "picture of Billy" that has taken the length of the narrative to fix in a tray of developing solution. If the smaller photograph had been of Billy, it would have grounded the narrative by creating a bookend arrangement of portraits. As it is, the final photograph has a subversive, rather than stabilizing effect on the documentary framework.

Although T.D. MacLulich states that photography is a "controlling metaphor"[97] that creates stasis and stability in *The Collected Works of Billy the Kid*, I argue that Ondaatje uses the medium to unsettling ends. Only by questioning the media and perpetual conventions of portraiture may an artist undo his or her own rhetorical devices, as John Welchman asserts: "The frame is a virus in the machine of formalism, a sort of double agent functioning as a necessary part of the system but also as the gateway to its dissolution."[98] The very first photograph reproduced in *Billy* portrays three cavalrymen beside the skeleton of a large animal, even though "the law" in the story is a sheriff's posse, not a cavalry regiment.[99] This Huffman photograph thereby complements themes in the narrative (landscape, law, death) rather than illustrating its plot. It also calls attention to the style of Ondaatje's writing, as the soldier in the foreground steps out of the cropped picture while the soldier in the middle ground paints a sign. Manina Jones observes that all of the men "face the borders of the picture, creating the impression of what Roland Barthes calls a 'blind field' outside the frame beyond the access of the viewer."[100] As in the opening picture of Billy, Ondaatje here incorporates the conventional association of photography with the captive image into his authorial ruse and subverts its documentary authority. Ondaatje explains this Breavman-like framing practice in an anthology introduction to his poem "Peter": "I see my poems as I would a home-movie. I am still conscious of all the bits and pieces / relatives and friends that were just to the left of the camera and that never got into the picture."[101] Like Breavman, Ondaatje is tormented by the insufficiency of the frame to encapsulate experience.

Traditional portraiture fares little better than photography in capturing Billy's visage, as the outlaw observes: "a pencil / harnessing my face / goes stumbling into dots."[102] Other characters get caught in Billy's frames, but even then the writing gravitates toward formlessness. Billy frames a portrait of Sallie Chisum in a bright interior, but his narrative gaze directs the reader's eye toward a dark exterior: "Around us total blackness, nothing out there but a desert for seventy miles or more, and to the left, a few yards away, a house stuffed with yellow wet light where within the frame of a window we saw a woman move carrying fire in a glass funnel and container towards the window, towards the edge of the dark where we stood."[103] This passage supplies a perfect example of an aperture highlighting one aspect of a scene in contrast to the smudgy details of the surrounding landscape. It also rehearses the tenebristic contrast between light and dark that plays an important role in *The English Patient* and *In the Skin of a Lion* (hence the character Caravaggio).

Ondaatje explores the processual aspect of frames-within-frames in the actual photographs he selects as a visual complement to *The Collected*

Works of Billy the Kid. For example, one photograph depicts a conventional homestead in which a window frames the head of a woman and a doorway frames the body of a man. A later photograph seems to enter the open doorway and offer a shot of the homestead's interior. Yet another photograph reproduces a detail from this interior, showing a gun hanging in a holster by the bed.[104] Punning visually on the verb "to shoot," the lens narrows its focus from the formal portrait, to the rustic interior, to the bedroom detail with its suggestions of sex and violence. From panorama to close-up, the embedded series has the cinematic effect of a zoom, yet each frame unsettles the impression conveyed by the previous one.

By repeating images and performing variations in this way, Ondaatje encourages his reader to make the connection between pictures and moving pictures. In *Billy*, the empty frame begins as a photograph, but repetition of the motif creates the impression of a film being shown frame by frame. Indeed, as studies in motion, serial photography anticipated film. The photograph of man and horse on the original cover of *Billy* – which recalls the famous portrait of Ned Kelly as a centaur – comes from a motion study by the pioneer of serial photography, Eadweard Muybridge.[105] The photograph belongs to the second frame of Plate 79 in Muybridge's *Animal Locomotion* series, which bears the suggestive title, "Pandora jumping a hurdle."[106] In opening the cover of *Billy*, then, the reader opens a Pandora's box of framed images and authorial ruses. As in Muybridge's series, where, as James Sheldon observes, "framed dark space between the individual images produces a slow, careful cadence akin to the feeling of watching fast motion slowed down," Ondaatje uses black borders and white gaps to give each segment of his story the visual rhythm of poetry.[107] Ondaatje is not interested in arresting time completely; rather, as Spicer insisted, he is a "time mechanic" and his sequence of arrested images produces a sense of temporal continuity.[108]

In this context, it is perhaps worth noting that Muybridge's patron (and later adversary), Leland Stanford, was a railroad tycoon, because, both at the outset of *the man with seven toes* and at the conclusion of *Coming Through Slaughter*, the train functions as a symbol of the linearity that Ondaatje's narratives work with and against. Ondaatje creates an overall sense of narrative progression in *Billy*, but he reconfigures the individual segments of time's arrow – as did Muybridge, who went on to juxtapose photographs of one series of events taken from multiple angles, thereby producing an impression of simultaneity that Sheldon argues led directly to Cubism.[109] Thus, in writing a serial poem whose photographic imagery functions cinematically, Ondaatje reverses the artistic development of

Muybridge, who began his career as a bookseller and progressed to photography and film. Although Ondaatje does not overtly acknowledge Muybridge in his book credits, he plants a clue when he states that "the comment about taking photographs around 1870–80" is from the Huffman letter, which dates from 1885, as Barbour has demonstrated.[110] The 1870–80 dates point to Muybridge's experiments.

With Muybridge present, his double, Étienne-Jules Marey, cannot be far away. As Marta Braun observes in *Picturing Time*, her meticulous study of Marey, the two photographers were born within weeks of one another, used the same initials, and almost simultaneously devised similar methods for registering locomotion. However, the academic, French-speaking servant of public institutions (Marey/Garrett) was the behavioural opposite of the flamboyant, entrepreneurial, and murderous Westerner (Muybridge/ Billy). Without fanfare, Marey solved the problem of registering bird flight by switching from a row of cameras to a single camera with a revolving barrel of photographic plates that he called his "*fusil photographique*," his photographic gun.[111] Although *fusil* means rifle, this term alters the significance of the series of photographs of the revolver in *Billy*. It also casts a new light on the iconographic bird in "the gate in his head," since one of the first series of pictures Marey "shot" with his new apparatus was of a blurry gull in flight in 1882.[112] Drawing inspiration from these series, Ondaatje adds a temporal dimension to his sense of poetry-as-photography, such that in *Billy* poetry is a kind of chronophotography. Marey, who began his career designing writing machines and concluded it as a pioneer of cinema, is thus another photographer whose life story is encoded into the poem. Yet Ondaatje once again alters the artist's method, turning linear chronophotography into a non-linear design.

Braun champions Marey's rapid-fire images, which later overlapped on a single plate to produce the impression of staggered movement, because they broke with the post-Renaissance convention of making the frame of an image "enclose a temporal and spatial unity. We [conventionally] read what occurs within the frame as happening at a single instant in time and in a single space. Marey's photographs shattered that unity; viewers now had to unravel the successive parts of the work in order to understand that they were looking not at several men moving in single file, but a single figure successively occupying a series of positions in space."[113] Marey's sequences investigated the persistence of vision in the continuous gesture. The serial poem, on the other hand, explores the persistence of vision in the discontinuous gesture. Examining a recurring pun in Spicer's *A Book of Music*, Jed Rasula argues that the ear must substitute one word for the other in the same way that the eye makes substitutions while "watching a film in order to provide continuity between the frames. Serial poems are analogous to frames: the gap between each poem is the space through which the world arises spontaneously. If the world did not arise there, the poems would discontinuously go nowhere, one by one."[114] To make the discrete parts of the serial poem coherent, then, "persistence" must be as much an acoustic phenomenon as a visual one; hence Richard Cavell's interest in Marey in *McLuhan in Space*. Echoes are called up to link discrete segments of narrative together through multi-directional reverberations rather than linear causation.

Another means of segmenting the linear storyline is a cinematic technique that Ondaatje calls "banking." In his introduction to *The Conversations: Walter Murch and the Art of Editing Film*, Ondaatje describes watching the acclaimed editor Walter Murch work on a scene from the film adaptation of *The English Patient*. He praises the manner in which Murch would "remove one-fifth of the information and 'bank' it, so extending the hook of this scene's unspoken knowledge to a later point in the film."[115] He then contrasts this practice with the edit of the film *Washington Square*, in which "the edit was so competent, the scenes so articulate and so fully expressed, that every episode was complete in itself. The film progressed in a series of well-made, self-sufficient moments, and so it felt as if there was a wall between every perfectly articulated scene."[116] In *Billy* the recurring image of the outlaw crashing through a window to his death is not self-contained, but rather banked and extended across the length of the narrative.

Paying close attention to the cinematic aspects of *Billy*, MacLulich argues in his essay "Ondaatje's Mechanical Boy: Portrait of the Artist as Photographer" that repetition and fragmentation profoundly alter the narrative by enabling Ondaatje to reconfigure the segments of a linear storyline: "Ondaatje's images of Billy do not create a static portrait, but a shifting and elusive picture – like a film which contains discontinuities, flash-backs and slow motion segments. As we turn Ondaatje's pages, Billy's story dissolves into fragments of action, isolated moments of sensation, recollection or hallucination. Taken collectively, Ondaatje's snapshots of Billy lose their static qualities and map a world of flux and uncertainty."[117] MacLulich's interpretation of *Billy* here contradicts Nodelman's argument that the images are static, but even Nodelman observes that in one palindrome Billy "remembers putting his hand into a wounded stomach in order to retrieve a bullet, and the last six lines are the first six in reverse order – like a film run backwards."[118] Indeed, Ondaatje has claimed: "With *Billy the Kid* I was trying to make the film I couldn't afford to shoot, in the form of a book. All those B movies in which strange things that didn't happen but could and should have happened I explored in the book."[119] In this light, one could argue that the "picture of Billy" is in fact a film being projected onto the blank screen of the empty frame, just as Huffman's commentary projects images of his photographs onto the blank page. In any case, Ondaatje, Muybridge, Nodelman, and MacLulich may have set out to investigate photography, but their investigations, different as they were, led them to film.

Even as a filmmaker, Ondaatje is not content to work within the conventions of the genre. In discussing his film *The Clinton Special* (1972), Ondaatje says he "wanted that sense throughout the film that each shot would *almost* be a static photograph. Thus throughout the film the camera doesn't move very much at all … It's talking photography."[120] I have emphasized the adverb "almost" here because Ondaatje slows down film so that it is *almost* photography, and he blurs and serializes photography so that it is *almost* film. "Film" and "photograph" are not static nouns in Ondaatje's vocabulary; they are active verbs in the process of being modified. The author makes one genre approximate another by distinguishing the aims of "documentary poetry" from the Canadian tradition of documentary film in his introduction to *The Long Poem Anthology*: "In a country with an absurd history of film, real film goes underground. And it comes up often in strange clothes – sometimes as theater, sometimes as poetry."[121] In this game of disguises, the guiding generic format is not always the one designated on the cover, as Ondaatje explains: "You know, I wanted to call my new book of poems, *Secular Love*, 'a novel.' I structured it like one. For me its structure and plot are novelistic. Each section deals with a specific time period but the people in them are interrelated. But, of course, they are drawn in a lyric, perceived by a lyric eye."[122] Thus, whether writing, drawing, photographing, or filming, Ondaatje disguises one genre as another. His play of masks extends to his manipulation of generic conventions and expectations. Yet he consistently creates lyrical frames that combine to shape a non-linear narrative.

Ondaatje personifies the confrontation between lyrical and prosaic impulses in *The Collected Works of Billy the Kid* by staging a gunfight between Garrett (who communicates mostly in blocks of prose) and Billy (who speaks mostly in lyrics). Critics generally equate Billy with Ondaatje because of Billy's lyric eye, but the author also writes from Garrett's first-person perspective, and to ignore Garrett's prosaic role is to underestimate the complexity of Ondaatje's long poem. Barbour observes that in Garrett's voice, Ondaatje "finds Billy both attractive and undisciplined. The prosaic lawman dismisses out of hand the poetic outlaw – precisely for his poetry, the imagination confronting chaos."[123] According to the plot, Garrett overtakes Billy, but, formally, Billy exacts his revenge, by absorbing Garrett's voice and narrative strategies into his collected works. Their antagonism parallels Ondaatje's struggle to escape the perspectival confines of the lyric "I," as Ondaatje himself explains: "With *Billy* I began with a couple of poems I had written about Billy the Kid and moved from these to being dissatisfied with the limits of lyric; so I moved to prose and interviews and so on."[124] Writing prose poems and prose with line breaks, as well as having Billy speak increasingly in prose, and framing the comic book legend in the same black outline used for the photographs,[125] Ondaatje gradually breaks down genre distinctions until Sallie Chisum can offer these "FINAL THOUGHTS" on Billy and Garrett:

> *There was good mixed in with the bad*
> *in Billy the Kid*
> *and bad mixed in with the good*
> *in Pat Garrett.*
> ...
> *Both were worth knowing.*[126]

This near convergence of opposed personalities reflects the near convergence of poetry and prose in *Billy*.

Jones argues that by testing the univocal and synchronic limits of the lyric and photograph, Ondaatje calls attention to "the *fictional* nature of the frame and disrupts its coherence ... via the strategies of documentary-collage."[127] It is not surprising, she suggests, that he honed his literary technique by producing a "picture collage of Billy" as well as a concrete poem called "silver bullet," which incorporated the picture of Ondaatje the Kid.[128] Indeed, when Ondaatje revisits the Wild West in *Divisadero*, he states twice that "Everything is collage," including genetics and biography.[129] However, the intricate spacing and diachronic unfolding of Ondaatje's narrative limits the usefulness of Jones's term "documentary collage" because a collage depends upon simultaneous juxtapositions. Without abandoning the juxtapositional aesthetics of collage, it is possible to consider other artistic practices that shed light on Ondaatje's writing. For example, Ondaatje attributes his interest in visual strategies to being "surrounded by so many painters – my [ex-]wife Kim, and Greg Curnoe, Bob Fones, and Tony Urquhart."[130] Jewinski's biography of Ondaatje demonstrates the tireless mentoring and networking that Kim (an older, established visual artist) performed on behalf of the young poet. Curnoe also had a profound influence on Bowering, as I will demonstrate in the next chapter, and Fones stimulated Ondaatje's interest in the Bloor St Viaduct. However, the work of Tony Urquhart, husband of the poet-novelist Jane Urquhart, is the most compelling influence on Ondaatje's framing aesthetic.

Tony Urquhart taught in the Department of Visual Arts at the University of Western Ontario from 1967 to 1972, a period slightly longer than Ondaatje's tenure (or regrettable lack thereof) in London. Ondaatje took an interest in Urquhart's work, which switched in this period from the static, two-dimensional canvas to "mysterious, evocative, and shape-shifting boxes."[131] Inspired by medieval reliquaries, these boxes, typically set on pedestals, had irregularly shaped doors that could be opened from a number of sides to reveal hidden treasures. *Box With Six Landscape Shards* (1970), for example, is a sculpture whose walls resemble the unfinished frame of a house.[132] Through the gaps in these wooden walls, one sees the six irregular shards of landscape caged inside. Each of the four walls swings open such that the Euclidean forms of the house explode into a multiplanar space of landscape shards, attached to the doors and angled in various directions. This unframing strategy takes on a much gorier aspect in *The Roman Line*, another box from this period based on the story of Mrs Donnelly in the trilogy of Donnelly novels by James Reaney (also a professor at UWO at this time). Since Mrs Donnelly died in a house fire (north of the line in Southwestern Ontario that divided Protestants from Roman Catholics), the charred box opens up to reveal bright pink flesh, with all the sexual connotations that such a design infers. Ondaatje was particularly fascinated by this box and purchased it with a portion of the five thousand dollars he received for winning the Governor General's Award for Poetry in 1970 (a sum that co-winner bp Nichol notes was identical to the original ransom for Billy the Kid).[133] Ondaatje was not simply influenced by Canadian art in this period; like Bowering, he used the proceeds from his writing to collect it.

Ondaatje's enduring attachment to the London art scene was confirmed by the 1996 introduction he wrote for *Paterson Ewen*, in which he cites a special connection to that troubled artist: "There is a profound peace when you come into a gallery and see a work like *Portrait of Vincent* or *Rain Over Water* or *Halley's Comet as Seen by Giotto* after a gap of years. I'm not sure why this happens to me only with Paterson Ewen's work."[134] Ondaatje's affinity for Ewen's painting is easy to grasp if one reads the fascinating story of Ewen's personal and artistic maturation. The product of a line of alcoholic and suicidal men married to orderly yet romantic women,

Ewen was the type of emotionally scarred mongrel whom Ondaatje adores. He studied art in Montreal under Arthur Lismer. The Group of Seven artist spontaneously awarded Ewen a degree after he began exhibiting with Paul-Émile Borduas and the *Automatistes*. Although an anglophone, Ewen was drawn into the francophone avant-garde of Montreal when he met and married the dancer Françoise Sullivan, a signatory of the *Refus global* document that fuelled Quebec's Quiet Revolution.[135] Ewen later shared studio space with the minimalist Guido Molinari but refused to adopt the manifesto-driven dogmatism of his peers. Instead, he pursued an unfashionable interest in serial works of "lyrical abstraction" in his Montreal work of the late 1950s and early 1960s: "Each series" writes Matthew Teitelbaum, "had coherence and a sustained thrust, though no one idea carried him for very long. These series shared a denial of the gesturalism of automatic painting and the scale of the Plasticien aesthetic; they spoke for the lyrical over the epic."[136] As Teitelbaum demonstrates, Ewen attempted to bridge the most entrenched solitudes of Canadian culture and form.

After separating from Sullivan, Ewen received shock therapy treatments for depression in London, Ontario. Although older than Curnoe's circle, Ewen embraced the local art scene, which had acquired a reputation for "multidisciplinary and intergenerational conversation, and experimentation and risk."[137] Soon afterward, he abandoned the canvas in favour of giant, gouged, routered, and paint-rollered expanses of plywood that provided his artistic breakthrough. Like Ondaatje in his movement from poem to novel, Ewen elaborated on his lyrical skills until they achieved epic proportions in a new medium. As Teitelbaum explains: "However much Ewen breaks through the surface of the large scarred plywood sheets and makes the personal into an epic statement, he never loses the apparent direct relation to the image. The plywood reveals struggle, hard work, engagement, connectedness."[138] It is this union of epic technique and intimate force that Ondaatje stresses in his introduction to *Paterson Ewen* by citing Eudora Welty: "Virtuosity, unless it move the heart, goes at the head of the whole parade to dust."[139] One might look to the same quotation to explain why Ondaatje never fully abandons his romantic tendencies, no matter how fascinated he becomes by the cerebral dimensions of serial, concrete, or other poetic movements.

In keeping with the looser, mixed-media quality of Ewen's work, as well as Urquhart's three-dimensional approach to (un)framing, Ondaatje opens multiple entry points into *The Collected Works of Billy the Kid*. The importance of the initial picture frame should not be overlooked, because the individual sections of the long poem are not "modular" in the modernist

sense of "interchangeable," as Barbara Godard's terms (but not her examples) suggest.[140] Ondaatje stresses the connection between beginnings and
architectural strategies in one discussion of narrative form: "At the [York]
conference on the long poem, George Bowering was talking about the deri-
vation of the word 'order' as coming from 'to begin.' I don't know if that's
true or not but it's interesting that in writing *Running [in the Family]* and
Slaughter the two pieces I wrote to *order* the book were written last – but
went in at the beginning."[141] However, fifteen pages into *Billy*, there is a
second beginning that refutes the authority of photography in its opening
sentence: "Not a story about me through their eyes then. Find the beginning, the slight silver key to unlock it, to dig it out. Here then is a maze to
begin, be in."[142] This new beginning foregrounds the clash of interpretive
frameworks in *Billy*. It introduces the first reference to Canada and suggests, without historical basis, that Billy and his friends engage in border
crossings to the north as well as to the south: "Two years ago Charlie
Bowdre and I criss-crossed the Canadian border. Ten miles north of it ten
miles south. Our horses stepped from country to country, across low rivers,
through different colours of tree green. The two of us, our criss-cross like a
whip in slow motion, the ridge of action rising and falling, getting narrower
in radius till it ended and we drifted down to Mexico and old heat. That
there is nothing of depth, of significant accuracy, of wealth in the image, I
know. It is there for a beginning."[143] Despite the disclaimer of the penultimate sentence, beginnings are by definition significant for Ondaatje.

The ahistorical details in this passage suggest that the "key" to unlocking
Billy's maze involves close consideration of Billy's gang and its connection to
Canada. Researching the photograph of John and Sallie Chisum, Barbour
reveals that it is "a photo of two of the people the book is dedicated to, Stuart
and Sally Mackinnon" in pioneer dress.[144] Having inserted Stuart Mackinnon
– author of "The Intervals," collected in *The Long Poem Anthology* – into the
text in place of Tip McKinney, Ondaatje deputizes the Canadian poet to
accompany Garrett and Poe in their final pursuit of Billy.[145] Photography thus
functions both as an ordering impulse and as a force of disorder in *Billy*, as it
provides an entry point for Mackinnon's parodic interventions.

As the pretense of documentary realism in *Billy* gradually erodes, the
importance of the song cycle structure becomes clear. The dedication at the
end of *Billy* is in fact a list of the players – "Kim [Ondaatje], Stuart and
Sally Mackinnon, Ken Livingstone, Victor Coleman, and Barrie Nichol"[146]
– involved in the performance of this collective work. Ondaatje explains
this collective sesnsibility: "I *know* when I was writing both *Billy* and
Slaughter, I had a sense that it wasn't just my point of view that was writing

the book; it was people around me that I knew, the interests of people around me, being aware of certain things – certain questions – from the point of view of people around me as much as myself. It doesn't matter who writes the book; the book is for me a kind of funnelling of various people's ideas and emotions, between the years 1968 and 1973 or 1973 to 1976, who represent your age and your group and the book comes out that way."[147] The song cycle structure is thus attractive because it permits any voice, however minor and fragmentary, to enter and exit the narrative without disturbing the flow of the story.

As an editor of *Billy* and an artist in her own right, Kim Ondaatje had a behind-the-scenes influence on Ondaatje's writing that parallels the role of Victor Coleman, the poet and one-time curator of A Space Gallery in Toronto, who was involved with the production of *Billy* at Coach House Press, where the book was designed. Ken Livingstone, on the other hand, makes a direct appearance in *Billy*. A friend of Ondaatje from his under-graduate acting years at Bishop's University, who directed the first performance of *the man with seven toes* at the Vancouver Festival, Livingstone appears in *Billy* as a social outcast who breeds a race of mad spaniels.[148] Barbour also notes that Ondaatje is listed in the *Canadian Who's Who* for having "developed and bred [a] new strain of spaniel, 'The Sydenham Spaniel,' Candn. Kennel Club 1970, with Livingstone Animal Foundation Kennels"; however, this breed exists only in fiction.[149]

A reference to Barrie (bp) Nichol, a member of the sound poetry collective The Four Horsemen, also appears in *Billy*. Nichol's performances awakened Ondaatje's interest in the associative, aural dimension of poetry – for example the word play of "begin, be in" – and Nichol is the subject of Ondaatje's film *Sons of Captain Poetry* (1970).[150] The lives of these two poets further intersected in 1968, when they discovered that they were both writing poems on Billy the Kid. They exchanged manuscripts in 1969, published their works in 1970, and, much to the nationalist consternation of former prime minister John Diefenbaker, split the Governor General's Award in 1970 (for *The Collected Works of Billy the Kid* and four chapbooks by Nichol, including *The True Eventual Story of Billy the Kid*).[151]

Ondaatje's outlaw praises Nichol in an apocryphal statement toward the conclusion of his "Exclusive Jail Interview" with the *Texas Star*: "There's a Canadian group, a sort of orchestra, that is the best. Great. Heard them often when I was up there trying to get hold of a man who went by the name of Captain P——.* Never found him. But that group will be remembered a long time."[152] The asterisk lacks an explanatory note, but it emphasizes that the text is double-coded. The text can be read at the level of

American pop culture, whose influence stretches from contemporary Canada to the Ceylon of Ondaatje's childhood, and beyond. For audiences who recognize the clues, however, the text functions as a tribute to the stylistic experiments being conducted by a particular group of Canadian artists in the late 1960s. The name of Garrett's wife, Apolinaria Guitterrez, for instance, is probably an allusion to Nichol's beloved concrete poet Apollinaire, because the following sentence describes Garrett as a man with a "mind full of French he never used, everything equipped to be that rare thing – a sane assassin sane assassin sane assassin sane assassin sane assassin sane."[153] Read aloud, the repetitions in this phrase convert the sane assassin into an insane one, as the Four Horsemen recording of "Assassin" makes clear.[154]

Having put together his own gang of orchestral Horsemen in this *livre à clef*, Ondaatje summons them for a performance of the mock elegy that follows Billy's (possibly mistaken) shooting. The chorus performs Billy's ballad in a voice similar to, but more satirical than, the concluding ballad in *the man with seven toes*:

> Poor young William's dead
> with a fish stare, with a giggle
> with blood planets in his head.
>
> The blood came down like river ride
> long as Texas down his side.
> We cleaned him up when blood was drier
> his eyes looked up like turf on fire.[155]

"We" uses an "eight foot garden hose" to wash Billy down, then "I" sells the outlaw's bullets to the *Texas Star*, where "They weighed them, put them in a pile / took pictures with a camera."[156] Pushing this pronominal uncertainty one step further, the concluding verse repeats the opening verse, but invokes the authority of an ambiguous "he":

> Poor young William's dead
> with blood planets in his head
> with a fish stare, with a giggle
> like he said.[157]

The final line pays homage to Cohen by recalling a scene in *Beautiful Losers* where the historian describes the storytelling traditions of the Iroquois and explains the name given to them by the French: "[The Iroquois] developed a new dimension to conversation. They ended every speech with the word *hiro*, which means: like I said ... To *hiro* they added the word *koué*, a cry of joy or distress, according to whether it was sung or howled. Thus ... at the end of every utterance a man stepped back, so to speak, and attempted to interpret his words to the listener, attempted to subvert the beguiling intellect with the noise of true emotion."[158] Ondaatje thus transfers Billy's story from a cowboy to an Iroquois context, but the reader is left wondering who is responsible for the story.

The final entry in *Billy* further complicates the referent of "he" by blurring the distinction between author and protagonist. Having staged a gunfight between Billy (poetry) and Garrett (prose), Ondaatje clears away the smoke and remarks: "It is now early morning, was a bad night. The hotel room seems large. The morning sun has concentrated all the cigarette smoke so one can see it hanging in pillars or sliding along the roof like amoeba. In the bathroom, I wash the loose nicotine out of my mouth. I smell the smoke still in my shirt."[159] The death of Billy in the previous pages, combined with the picture of Ondaatje the Kid on the ensuing page, would seem to identify this speaker as Ondaatje. However, the passage repeats a description from an earlier scene in which Billy is the narrator, thereby maintaining the possibility that Billy speaks from beyond the grave.[160] On the other hand, the speaker is in a kind of garret, suggesting that he could be the lawman. These identities shift like the architectonic smoke and underscore the indeterminacy of the entire text. Kathleen Bethell goes so far as to argue that any "attempt to impose order on Ondaatje's disorderly text is a necessary, even inevitable, first step in a reading process that leads not only to the discovery of ultimate narrative absence, but of the reader's own complicity in constructing the narrative of that absence."[161] Bethell rejects the treatment of the text as a puzzle and argues that *Billy* anticipates the open form of the commonplace book in *The English Patient*.

In "Ondaatje Learning to Do," Bowering maps a different trajectory to Ondaatje's career. Bowering argues that Ondaatje's development – from its anecdotal and imagistic beginnings in *The Dainty Monsters* (1967) to the use of collage and serial techniques – epitomizes the course of Canadian writing in general:

The development of Ondaatje's poetry, from his early years in this country to the present, resembles the development of the main currents of Canadian verse over a period perhaps twice as long. Unlike the Vancouver poets with their advocacy of open-ended, process form,

Ondaatje emerged from the school that believes the poem to be an artifact, something well made and thus rescued from the chaos of contemporary world and mind. If the Vancouver poets might loosely be said to
descend from Robert Duncan, and Victor Coleman from Louis
Zukofsky, Ondaatje might be said to descend from Yeats and Stevens.

But over the course of his first fifteen years as a Canadian poet,
Ondaatje came to seek a less British and more American poetic.[162]

Although this summary greatly oversimplifies the history of Canadian
poetry, and although Bowering humorously stretches his point by baptizing
Coach House Press (Ondaatje's early publisher) as the "Toronto arm of the
West Coast movement," his observations are useful.[163] After all, *Billy* is a
Western, and Ondaatje wrote *the man with seven toes* for performance at
the Vancouver Poetry Festival. Jack Spicer's serial poem "Billy the Kid,"
which Ondaatje reviews as a "very good poem" in *Quarry*, may even have
been the catalyst for Ondaatje's book.[164] When one remembers that Yeats
was supposedly one of Bowering's "favourite predecessors," and that
Bowering sometimes claims (falsely) that the name *Tish* came from a marginal inscription beside a Yeats poem in Ross MacDonald's *The Chill*, it
becomes increasingly clear that, in his description of Canadian literary history, Bowering is outlining the course of his own career.[165] Ondaatje, on the
other hand, manifests an obsession throughout his career with unmaking
the well-made artifact. Like Stevens – who is American, as Bowering is well
aware – Ondaatje displays an abiding fascination with the dualities of
order and chaos.

Furthermore, the trick that Ondaatje is learning to do with myth and history in *Billy* is very different from the one Spicer performs. Spicer's serial
poem makes no attempt to tell the life story of Billy the Kid, but is rather a
lament for a failed gay romance: "*Billy the Kid* is apparently the only [serial
poem by Spicer] drawn directly and specifically from private emotion, 'the
big lie of the personal.' The work was written immediately after one of
Spicer's friends had left him, and he was desolate. But the poem argues that
erotic love is a kind of myth with the enduring powers that myths can
have."[166] An additional difference is pointed out by Ed Jewinski. Whereas
Spicer's serialism draws inspiration from the compositions of Berio and
Boulez, Jewinski proposes that Ondaatje draws inspiration from the more
eclectic compositions of Erik Satie: "In the signed edition of *Billy the Kid*
that [Ondaatje] gave to Kim [Ondaatje], Michael wrote that he had been
living 'in Billy's head,' and then, quoting the French composer Erik Satie, he
confessed: 'I am having a poor time dying of sorrow; everything I timidly

undertake fails with a boldness never before known.'"[167] Satie began his composing career in the early 1880s, the period that interests Ondaatje in *Billy*. But more significantly, Satie was the kind of quirky, anomalous figure that Ondaatje admires: a serious composer and a cabaret clown, a man absolutely devoted to his art who had a penchant for writing absurdly humorous commentary on his scores, a precursor to serialism and minimalism who wrote music inspired by furniture and dogs.

THE NOVEL AS SONG CYCLE

While the West Coast influences on the Toronto poet were crucial, particularly on his development of a serial poetics, the most important influence on Ondaatje at this stage in his career was the Montrealer Leonard Cohen. Ondaatje's only book of criticism, *Leonard Cohen* (1970), is a monograph on the Montreal poet's early career that reads like the draft of an artist statement for Ondaatje's writing in the late 1960s and early 1970s. Four things about Cohen particularly interest Ondaatje in his study: Cohen's transition from poet to novelist, the techniques that produce "a visual rather than literary style," the use of soundtracks in literature, and the aesthetics and politics of failing boldly in Cohen's *Beautiful Losers* (1966).[168] Ondaatje employs many of these techniques in *Coming Through Slaughter* to produce a portrait of an artist, Buddy Bolden, whose legendary cornet playing was, paradoxically, recorded on neither film nor phonograph.

Although Cohen took his ballads to the stage and abandoned the novel in the decades after the publication of Ondaatje's monograph, Cohen's technique for lyrical narrative, which cuts "into the natural progression of time like a movie frozen into a single image and then released to run again," lives on in *Coming Through Slaughter*.[169] For example, Cohen's birdsong conceit in *The Favourite Game*, where what sounds like a single note to the human ear proves to be two or more notes sung simultaneously, sets a precedent for the dolphin sonographs that frame *Coming Through Slaughter*. Stan Dragland makes the connection between Cohen's bird analogy and Ondaatje's dolphin sonographs in "F.ing Through *Beautiful Losers*." However, he misses the precedent established in *The Favourite Game* (see chapter 2). Ondaatje's sonographs substitute for the slow transistor machine that the historian in *Beautiful Losers* demands as a brain transplant:

Three sonographs – pictures of dolphin sounds made by a machine that is more sensitive than the human ear. The top left sonograph shows a "squawk." Squawks are common emotional expressions that have many frequencies or pitches, which are vocalized simultaneously. The top right sonograph is a whistle. Note that the number of frequencies is small and this gives a "pure" sound – not a squawk. Whistles are like personal signatures for dolphins and identify each dolphin as well as its location. The middle sonograph shows a dolphin making two kinds of signals simultaneously. The vertical stripes are echolocation clicks (sharp, multi-frequency sounds) and the dark, mountain-like humps are the signature whistles. No one knows how a dolphin makes both whistles and echolocation clicks simultaneously.[170]

Despite the obvious similarities between Cohen's birdsong passage and this one, Ondaatje's epigram contrasts with the Cohen excerpt in that Ondaatje takes great *pleasure* in the things that can happen between the beginning of a sentence and the end. Whereas Breavman aims to counteract dissolution through greater and greater discipline in his craft, Ondaatje's hero, Buddy Bolden, does "nothing but leap into the mass of changes and explore them and all the tiny facets so that eventually he [is] almost completely governed by fears of certainty."[171] Bolden's jazz scorns "the sure lanes of the probable" and delights in "showing all the possibilities in the middle of the story."[172] Hence the middle sonograph, the image of a miraculous aural hybrid, is the principal object of interest in the epigram.

Ondaatje uses the sonographs and commentary in *Coming Through Slaughter* to outline a poetics. The language in the novel, the author implies, will intermingle "common emotional expressions" in "many frequencies" (lyrics, prose poems, anecdotes) with "personal signatures" (of metaphor and symbol) while locating subjects within a matrix of echoes (that shapes the historical context). Like the triptych of sonographs, the structure of the novel will be triadic, depicting three stages of Bolden's career in separate books. As for characterization, the sonographs (photographs of sound) allude to the key artist figures in the text, the photographer Bellocq and the musician Bolden, and the way in which Ondaatje depicts them. The terms defining the dolphin language, for example, double as a vocabulary for describing Bolden's playing style. In the climactic moment when Bolden parades his finest jazz, he combines "squawks" with "slow pure notes" to create "squawk beats" on the cornet.[173] However, in order to achieve this synthesis, Bolden must first apprentice his understanding of art under Bellocq. The photographer teaches Bolden the usefulness of establishing a framework of the known and imbuing it with the inexplicable. Thus the sonographs represent an aural phenomenon that can be registered but not explained.

Likewise, Ondaatje's portraiture in *Coming Through Slaughter* pivots on a double axis of visual frame-making and aural frame-breaking. The novel is ekphrastic in the sense that the real Bellocq's *Storyville Portraits* were "an inspiration of mood and character," as Ondaatje acknowledges in his book credits.[174] Like Nolan's paintings, Bellocq's photographs function as a starting point for the author's investigation of his protagonist's environment and character. In addition, Ondaatje extrapolates much of Bolden's career from a black and white print of Bolden and his band, which Ondaatje fictitiously attributes to Bellocq and situates on the cover of the Anansi edition of *Slaughter* (and as the frontispiece to the Vintage edition). Ondaatje writes in a carefully worded statement that there "is only one photograph that exists today of Bolden and the band,"[175] and all the critics I have read take this statement to mean that "the picture on the title-page of Ondaatje's book is the only extant photograph of Bolden."[176] Bowering follows this interpretation when he raises the question of how a writer can "write a historical novel with no historical documents": "Having produced a book about Billy the Kid out of sources that were mainly frontier lies, Michael Ondaatje essayed *Coming Through Slaughter* about Buddy Bolden, 'born' at the dawn of the twentieth century, nothing saved from the multiplicity of chaos except one group photograph in which Bolden is holding a cornet in his left hand, as lots of people wish Billy had held his six-gun."[177] However, a careful look at the thumbnail portrait on the back cover of the Vintage edition of *Coming Through Slaughter* (1998) reveals that there are at least two extant photographs of Bolden. At first, the thumbnail portrait appears to be a detail from the band photograph. Bolden wears the same suit and stands in front of the same backdrop, but the picture is a solo portrait, probably taken at the same sitting. No part of Bolden's body is obscured by Brock Mumford, the guitarist, and Bolden holds his trumpet vertically in his right hand, not horizontally in his left hand. Ondaatje alludes to this second photograph when he writes that Bellocq "made one more print of the group and shelved it and then one of just Bolden this time, taking him out of the company."[178] As in *The Collected Works of Billy the Kid*, then, Ondaatje plants photographs like blueprints for the deconstruction of history's singular authority.

Although Bellocq and Bolden were of different generations and racial backgrounds, Ondaatje brings them together in his fictional version of the real Storyville (a section of New Orleans) in order to highlight their affinities. Ondaatje dips into the "pail of sub-history" and discovers two artists who, at least in the early 1970s, had been marginalized by the prevailing historical accounts.[179] (Bellocq has since become a principal character in Louis Malle's 1978 film *Pretty Baby*).[180]

However, Ondaatje's concern for questioning the form of historical narrative often distorts the factual evidence. For example, in his version of Bolden's life story, the cornetist works in a barbershop by day, publishes a scandal sheet called *The Cricket* in his spare time, goes insane while playing in a parade, and dies in an asylum in Jackson, Louisiana, leaving no written record of his life in New Orleans. However, except for the asylum detail, none of these key facts are valid, according to Donald Marquis's *In Search of Buddy Bolden: First Man of Jazz* (1978), which represents ten years of research into the subject. Although Marquis concedes that "unsubstantiated facts became part of the legend," and the stories of the barbershop and *The Cricket* were widely circulated, Bolden's wife and friends discredited these aspects of the legend in interviews.[181] Furthermore, Marquis demonstrates that Bolden became mentally ill six months before the parade, and he was not institutionalized until another nine months afterwards. If Ondaatje had researched his subject thoroughly, he would have discovered two newspaper articles from 1906 that report an incident in which Bolden, suffering from dementia that was later attributed to syphilis, lept out of bed and struck his mother-in-law in the head with a water pitcher because he believed she was poisoning him.[182]

The existence of these records undermines Ondaatje's portrait of a traceless Bolden, yet strengthens his argument about history. On the one hand, the articles demonstrate that Ondaatje did not research his subject extensively, or chose to withhold information that might prevent readers from empathizing with his romantic hero. On the other hand, the historical evidence bolsters Ondaatje's critique of the official record. Although Bolden was a pioneering black artist, a jazzman known as "King Bolden" in Storyville, he only warrants mention in the city newspapers by committing an act of violence. He achieves a place in what passes for history by conforming to a particular stereotype of black masculinity. Thus, while *Coming Through Slaughter* and the other novels studied here take great liberties with the historical record – in fact several of them make rumours the nucleus of the story – they are primarily interested in achieving redress for the omissions within that record. They aim to recuperate legacies that have been suppressed for one ideological reason or another, and although the new histories are also problematic, they counterbalance the gross inadequacies of the so-called official histories.

Ondaatje's fictional Bellocq is a social outcast whose only friend is Bolden. Like the heroes in "White Dwarfs" who "sail to that perfect edge /

where there is no social fuel," Bolden and Bellocq "tal[k] for hours moving gradually off the edge of the social world. As Bellocq lived at the edge in any case he was at ease there and as Buddy did not he moved on past him like a naive explorer looking for footholds."[183] Bolden explains that Bellocq fascinated him because of his dedication to making photographs that were "like ... windows. He was the first person I met who had absolutely no interest in my music."[184] Bolden, on the other hand, took an interest in the varieties of silence in Bellocq's portraits, which suggested something beyond the realist metaphor of the window. These qualities contrast the photographer with the (initially) loud and gregarious bandleader, as well as with "Mr Audubon," the naturalist whose photo-realistic paintings are the antithesis of Bellocq's art.[185] Audubon painstakingly renders every physical detail of the animals and birds he kills and then makes his subjects, whereas Bellocq seeks to record the dream states of nude or scantily dressed women. As an artist, Bellocq attempts to see beyond the body and incorporate something intangible into his portraiture. As a sexually frustrated individual, however, he degrades his subjects and his art by fetishizing the nudes and slashing the photographs with a knife in acts symbolic of sexual penetration.

Bellocq's strengths and weaknesses put him in the company of Ondaatje's other artist heroes, as Scobie observes: "Bellocq, the crippled artist who makes pictures of prostitutes, is strikingly reminiscent of Toulouse-Lautrec; and like another of Ondaatje's favourite artists, Henri Rousseau, 'he even talked to his photographs he was that lonely.'"[186] Toward the end of the novel, Ondaatje also inserts himself into this company of visual artists. The writer/historian stands on the street where Bolden lived seventy years earlier, and remarks: "The place of his music is totally silent. There is so little noise that I easily hear the click of my camera as I take fast bad photographs into the sun aiming at the barbershop he probably worked in."[187] Initiating his ekphrastic process, Ondaatje turns the street into "a black and white photograph, part of a history book."[188] The slippage between media also provokes slippage between the identities of the frame-makers. Ondaatje stares at Bolden's band photograph, and it "moves and becomes a mirror," as the author feels a surge of identification with his subject: "When I read he stood in front of mirrors and attacked himself, there was the shock of memory. For I had done that. Stood, and with a razor-blade cut into cheeks and forehead, shaved hair. Defiling people we did not wish to be."[189] This blurring of identities – in the novel Bolden defiles Pickett with a razor – leads to a merging of techniques, as the author emulates Bolden's assault on mirrors: "Why did my senses stop at you? There was the sentence, 'Buddy Bolden who became a legend when he went berserk in a parade ...' What was there in that, before I knew your nation your colour your age, that made me push my arm forward and spill it through the front of your mirror and clutch myself?"[190] Ondaatje the Artist thus passes through the looking-glass and enters the novel, just as Ondaatje the Kid inserted himself into the long poem through a photograph.

Annick Hillger's archival work reveals that Ondaatje practised this looking-glass trick in his small press publications, such as the serial version of "White Dwarfs":

> First published in 1971 in *Is*, a magazine edited by Victor Coleman, "White Dwarfs" appears not just once but several times: three large pages are each filled with one and the same poem. While the poem is presented once on the first page, we find two versions on the second and three on the third. With each reproduction the type gets smaller. We thus get the impression, as we follow from one printing to the next, that the text contracts. It is as if the poem were receding into itself. More importantly, though, the text is not printed on a white page but on a photograph showing part of a face: a pair of eyes framed by glasses and a nose, beneath which we see a faint hint of moustache. Maintaining the same size on all three pages, these eyes stare at us as we try to make out the text. While the text is still easy to read on the first page, it becomes more difficult on the second and almost impossible on the last. We therefore focus increasingly on the eyes, which protrude gradually as the text retreats into the background.[191]

Ezra Pound's *phanopoeia* (the power of image) and *melopoeia* (the music of poetry) are here fused and made concrete.

A shared technique also unites Bellocq and Bolden. Mixing the composure of Bellocq's photographic imagery with the ecstatic rhythms of Bolden's jazz, Ondaatje represents the friendship between the two artists as an exchange of ideas, a mutual apprenticeship in composition. Bolden plays his cornet through open windows, perhaps because Bellocq is Ondaatje's arch-typical frame-maker: "We were furnished rooms," Bolden states, "and Bellocq was a window looking out."[192] Bolden also has a propensity for breaking windows, and Bellocq unframes his creations when he slashes the portraits of prostitutes that he so carefully produces. Framing and unframing thus are united in Bellocq's aesthetic: "The making and destroying coming from the same source, same lust, same surgery his brain was capable of."[193]

This sublimated violence eventually turns upon its perpetrator, and Bellocq's suicide is yet another example of (un)framing. The photographer places chairs around the perimeter of his room, then walks along the chairs lighting fire to the walls, until he is boxed in by the blaze. He struggles to retain his composure amid the diminishing oxygen until his excessive self-control turns maniac.[194] In a move that recalls the mock suicide in *Beautiful Losers*, the suffocating photographer throws himself "into the wall, only there is no wall any more only a fire curtain and he disappears into and through it ... Then he falls, dissolving out of his pose. Everything has gone wrong. The wall is not there to catch or hide him. Nothing is there to clasp him into a certainty."[195] As with Billy in the barn, accidental and unforeseen events dissolve the pose of absolute self-control. Bellocq's making and destroying highlight the emphasis on what lies beyond self-control in Ondaatje's first novel, in contrast to the first novel by Cohen. As Michael Greenstein argues, Breavman's obsession with framing is an obsession with control: "If organizing lines into photographic frames orders the chaos surrounding Cohen's protagonist, so too do the story's other cameras – the rooms or partial homes Breavman inhabits."[196] Breavman feels the need to move beyond order; Ondaatje takes the impulse further and shows what this beyond might look and sound like.

The news of Bellocq's suicide foreshadows Bolden's self-destructive performance in the parade. When Bolden tells Nora about the suicide, she screams at him: "Look at you. *Look at what he did to you.*"[197] Bolden had earlier demonstrated this influence to Webb by instructing the detective to put his fist through a window.[198] This passage echoes the first thing Bolden says in *Coming Through Slaughter*, when he urges his bandmate to play louder: "Cornish, come on, put your hands through the window."[199] Two pages later, Bolden acts out the metaphor: "Furious at something he drew his right hand across his body and lashed out. Half way there at full speed he realized it was a window he would be hitting and braked. For a fraction of a second his open palm touched the glass, beginning simultaneously to draw back. The window starred and crumpled slowly two floors down. His hand miraculously uncut. It had acted exactly like a whip violating the target and still free, retreating from the outline of a star. [Nora] was delighted by the performance."[200] This passage was possibly inspired by the scene in *The Favourite Game* where Breavman argues with Tamara and then smashes his fist through a window. Although the episode is brief and of little importance to Cohen's plot, Ondaatje describes it as "the most powerful scene in the novel."[201] Bart Testa notes a similar motif in Ondaatje's *Sons of Captain Poetry*, "in which a set of broken windows fills the screen like a grid. Nichol passes through one of the windows, making his entrance, as if he were slipping through the grid of conventional language.[202] Derek Finkle has linked this stylized scene to the frame motif in *Billy*, but it also anticipates the window motif in *Coming Through Slaugher*.[203]

The (un)framing metaphors in *Coming Through Slaughter* accumulate until they reach an explosive density in the fight scene between Bolden and Pickett. The combatants throw fragments of shattered mirror at each other, break the barbershop window, pass through its "empty frame" and land in the street, where the rain falls "like so many little windows."[204] Chaos (Bolden) triumphs over the fence (Pickett), but at the same time Bolden passes through the liminal space between genius and madness. "Locked inside the frame, boiled down in love and anger into dynamo that cannot move except on itself," Bolden shines brilliantly in the parade and then goes silent.[205] The black jazzman becomes a white dwarf, one of "those burned out stars / who implode into silence / after parading in the sky."[206] In the interval between the fight and the parade, however, Bolden achieves his stylistic breakthrough.

Brock Mumford describes Bolden's breakthrough as he watches the cornetist play through the broken barbershop window. Mumford's peculiar vantage point and musical ear combine to shape an impression reminiscent of the middle sonograph of the dolphin triptych: "Thought I knew his blues before, and the hymns at funerals, but what he is playing now is real strange and I listen careful for he's playing something that sounds like both. I cannot make out the tune and then I catch on. He's mixing them up. He's playing the blues and the hymn sadder than the blues and then the blues sadder than the hymn. That is the first time I ever heard hymns and blues cooked up together."[207] This blues hymn is called a reel, a fusion of the secular and the spiritual that parallels the fusion of journalism and hagiography in Ondaatje's portrait of Bolden. The reel inspires Mumford to imagine himself dancing with prostitutes and then humming in church, because the "picture kept changing with the music."[208] The oscillation from image reel to musical reel and back is thus constant.

To underscore this sense of shift, Bolden contrasts his improvisational style with the waltzes of John Robichaux, who "dominated his audiences. He put his emotions into patterns which a listening crowd had to follow."[209] "Robichaux's arches" made every "note part of the large curve, so carefully patterned" that the "mind mov[ed] ahead of the instruments in time and wait[ed] with pleasure for them to catch up."[210] Although Bolden reluctantly admits that he sometimes enjoys listening to his arch-nemesis, the jazzman refuses to follow predictable temporal progressions and asserts that the "right ending is an open door you can't see too far out of."[211]

Despite its hybrid sensibility, the jazz of the early 1900s was not a "free-form music," as Linda Hutcheon describes it in her discussion of *Coming Through Slaughter*.[212] Rather, it was a loosely improvisational approach to the traditional patterns of blues and hymns. For example, Bolden's most famous song, "Funky Butt," which was popularized by Jelly Roll Morton as "Buddy Bolden's Blues," performs a slight variation on the traditional AAB pattern of the twelve-bar blues. The lyrics depict Bolden demanding that a window be opened to freshen the kind of stale room that confines Ondaatje's narrators at the conclusion of *Slaughter* and *Billy*. Given Ondaatje's enthusiasm for music history, it is likely that his window motif derives from Morton's lyrics.[213] These lyrics complement the legitimate testimony that Ondaatje cites from the chaplain of the East Louisiana State Hospital, who noted that Bolden had a "tendency to go to a window to play to [the] outside world."[214] Evidently, Ondaatje constructed his song cycle around this kernel of fact.

However, when Ondaatje states that the structure of Bolden's music is "never repeated" and that his "whole plot of song [is] covered with scandal and incident and change," he would seem to be describing the free jazz popular at the time he was composing the novel, not the jazz of Bolden's era.[215] All the songs that Ondaatje transcribes in *Slaughter* are experiments in word repetition but, given the stanzaic formulas of the lyrics in Bolden's era, one cannot say, with Barry Maxwell, that early jazz is "the enemy of plot, that square space, and is the limitless ground."[216] Ondaatje overestimates the variability of the music in the period in asserting that Bolden improves by learning "not craft but to play a mood of sound I would recognize and remember. Every note new and raw and chance."[217] Ondaatje's antagonism toward a preset rhythm also defines Bolden's relationship to Cornish, the trombone player in his band, "who played the same note the same way every time who was our frame our diving board that we leapt off, the one we sacrificed so he could remain the overlooked metronome."[218] Like Billy, Bolden incorporates frameworks into his art only to counter them, as his clarinet player explains: "But there was a discipline, it was just that we didn't understand. We thought he was formless, but I think now he was tormented by order, what was outside it. He tore apart the plot – see his music was immediately on top of his own life. Echoing. As if, when he was playing he was lost and hunting for the right accidental notes."[219] As this monologue progresses, it begins to paraphrase "the gate in his head."

The prose descriptions recall the poem's "sense of shift," its shapeless bird "moving to the clear," and its epistolary conversation with Coleman: "Listening to [Bolden] was like talking to Coleman. You were both changing direction with every sentence, sometimes in the middle, using each other as a springboard through the dark. You were moving so fast it was unimportant to finish and clear everything."[220] To demonstrate this point, *Coming Through Slaughter* concludes without clearing up all the questions surrounding Bolden's final years.

As in *The Collected Works of Billy the Kid*, the conclusion of *Coming Through Slaughter* portrays the writer ceasing to write. The scene is brief and haunting: "I sit with this room. With the grey walls that darken into corner. And one window with teeth in it. Sit so still you can hear your hair rustle in your shirt. Look away from the window when clouds and other things go by. Thirty-one years old. There are no prizes."[221] Locked inside these architectural frames, the author seems to follow Bolden into white-dwarf-like silence. However, Ondaatje stresses his connection to Bolden by rehearsing the final scene twice in Bolden's voice. Bolden first articulates the "cornered" theme while he is secluded in Webb's cabin: "Here. Where I am anonymous and alone in a white room with no history and no parading. So I can make something unknown in the shape of this room. Where I am King of Corners."[222] Later, Bolden improvises a lyric on this theme, in which the repetitions of "corner" produce mind-wandering associations with cornet (life) and coroner (death). The repetitions also force the rhyme scheme to depart from the AAB pattern of the twelve-bar blues:

> In the room there is the air
> > and there is the corner
> and there is the corner and there is the corner
> and there is the corner.
>
> If you don't shake, don't get no cake.[223]

The altered blues rhythms of this final line – also the title of the song – underscore the necessity of improvising exits from the labyrinth of pattern.[224] There is something pernicious about the way the corners impose their sense of order; indeed, it is by orderlies that Bolden is again and again raped in the asylum. However, just as Bolden submits wordlessly to these rapes, the author seems to be overwhelmed by the effort of constant improvisation in the final scene of the novel. The frames that he has manipulated throughout the story close in on him and he manages one final assertion of uncertainty – "There are no prizes" – before abruptly falling silent. This sudden silence does not achieve closure by tying up the various narrative threads in the novel and proffering the reader a neat package of resolutions. As in *Billy*, Ondaatje avoids closure by blurring the pronominal distinction between author and protagonist. He leaves the reader wondering whether the room with the window is Bolden's cell or Ondaatje's study. The suddenness of the ending recalls the mood of the serial poem, which, according to Blaser, "is often like a series of rooms where the lights go on and off. It is also a sequence of energies which burn out, and it may, by the path it takes, include the constellated."[225] But does a constellated series qualify as a novel?

Coming Through Slaughter was launched at A Space Gallery in 1976. Solecki notes that at the launch, which Ondaatje nearly missed because he was at a Cohen concert that went into multiple encores, Ondaatje described the book as "soup."[226] During the writing of *Coming Through Slaughter*, Ondaatje insisted that it is not a novel: "Right now I'm working on some prose but if I mention it people say that I'm working on a novel and I'm not. To me the novel is a 100 yard hurdles which you have to plan, prepare, etc. And what I'm doing doesn't have a preformed shape."[227] However, two decades later, Ondaatje changed his mind and declared *Slaughter* his first novel.[228] Perhaps Ondaatje's mind was changed by winning the *Books in Canada* award for the best first novel in 1976. But it is perhaps more likely that his opinion changed because he felt that in the intervening period there had been a broad reconsideration of what constitutes structure in a poem or novel. Like Bolden, Ondaatje aims "to overcome th[e] awful and stupid clarity" of generic convention, but once again it is a mistake to identify the author completely with his protagonist.[229] Despite the merging of artistic identities that Ondaatje imagines, important differences remain between writer and musician. The structure of Bolden's music is non-repetitive, whereas Ondaatje's text is carefully patterned with images of windows that get broken and mirrors that get shattered. Paradoxically, these symbols of disorder structure Ondaatje's text and give it continuity in place of a stable narrator, linear plot, or consistent tone.

From start to finish, the broken frame provides, in spite of itself, the formal coherence demanded by the designation "novel." As Bowering observes, *Slaughter* "works by recurrence rather than progression," and the frame motifs (like Cornish's trombone) function as vehicles of the order that the artist simultaneously challenges.[230] For the romantic artist, the imperative to create frames of reference is matched in force by the desire to transcend them: Bolden's character develops, but his development is a dissipation: the jazzman's portrait emerges out of a photograph, but that photograph is torn apart by the author's manipulation of history; descriptive prose is initially the dominant genre in the text, but it yields to lyrics, monologues, catalogues of research data, and oral interviews. For these and other reasons, Scobie remains "uneasy" about calling *Coming Through Slaughter* a novel: "Like Leonard Cohen's *Beautiful Losers* (a book to which it bears more than a passing resemblance), it is a 'novel' in which the real action takes place at the level of the poetic image. In Ondaatje's case, many of these images are extensions or parallels of images that he has used in his poetry, and it is impossible to discuss *Coming Through Slaughter* without reference to Ondaatje's other books, especially *Rat Jelly*."[231] However, like Cohen in *Beautiful Losers*, Ondaatje is also "dynamiting the delicate poetic imagery of his past" through his experiments in sonography, and the internal drama of Ondaatje's evolution as a writer acts as a unifying subplot within the overall narrative.[232]

The intermingling of poetry and prose in *Coming Through Slaughter*, as well as the relentlessly fragmented quality of the writing, compel Hutcheon to consider the novel a song cycle: "If *Billy* is more overtly a poetic song-cycle, *Coming Through Slaughter* (the story of a jazz musician whose unwritten and unrecorded music lives on ironically in Ondaatje's printed fragments) is also appropriately structured in this musical way."[233] Ondaatje indicates the musical value of the text by fashioning found poems out of song titles and band names, as well as devoting separate pages to the unrecorded lyrics of Bolden's songs.[234]

Ondaatje also embeds a song cycle within the novel by performing several variations on the phrase "Passing wet chicory that lies in the field like the sky."[235] The phrase initially appears in isolation on its own page, but as Heighton observes, "the use of the relatively uncommon dactylic foot and strong assonance (chicory/field, lie/like/sky) suggest the line's musical nature."[236] The emphatic first stress of the dactylic line is a feature of African percussive traditions in music such as calypso and funk, and Ondaatje builds on its driving rhythm to produce "Train Song."[237] This song reconfigures the original dactylic line through line breaks and converts "field" to the plural to underscore the variations being performed. The plural "fields," Kamboureli argues, designates both the "geographical field and the field of language."[238] She maintains that language creates its own terrain where "'lies' becomes highly ambiguous; 'like' can be read both as an adverb and as a verb; the simile is transformed into a metaphor, 'passing wet sky chicory,' finally to become something more than a metaphor, a riddle that brings into question the meaning of language."[240] This riddle grows more complicated toward the conclusion of the novel when Bolden takes the train through Slaughter and the phrase makes its final appearance.[234] At this point, the fields return to being a field and the dactylic line that became a song has been transformed into a prose fragment. These transformations of the refrain, as well as the title of the novel, raise the question of whether the entire book has been a series of variations on the emotional moment when Bolden takes the train through Slaughter. If so, the linearity of the train ride once again contrasts with the meanderings of the song cycle. The narrative does not derail: it is a derailment. Although the tracks from Storyville to the insane asylum are straight, the artist flourishes for as long as he can veer off, circle back, and forestall his unwelcome end. Such digressive and circumlocutionary narrative Robert Kroetsch describes as "a method, then, and then, and then, of composition; against the 'and then' of story."[241] Although Kroetsch intended these remarks for the long poem, Ondaatje has clearly transferred the narrative style he developed in his long poems to *Coming Through Slaughter*.

Solecki emphasizes the continuity of Ondaatje's endings in *Ragas of Longing*, where he locates the origin of the device of the deferred ending in the final ballad of *the man with seven toes*:

> Although the ballad summarizes or comprehends the book's dualities and tensions, it does not resolve them. This deliberate irresolution leaves the sequence with a sense of open-endedness reinforced by the grammar of the last sentence, whose verb ('God ... keep you'), in the optative mood, points to the future. Like the present-tense endings of *The Collected Works of Billy the Kid* ('I smell the smoke still in my shirt'), *Coming Through Slaughter* ('There are no prizes'), *Secular Love* ('He lies in bed'), and *Handwriting* ('I roam restless'), this gives the book an ending without narrative resolution, struggling against the closure inevitable in every work of art. The reader is left with a sense of the continuity of the story and its implications into present and future time. At the precise moment when the book is being finished and about to be put aside, it forces itself into the reader's real time.[242]

The present tense thus gives the story added presence, even as it moves towards absence.

To solidify the connection between the long poems and novel, Ondaatje gives a cameo role to a patient in the East Louisiana State Hospital named Antrim, which is one of Billy the Kid's aliases. Antrim, who receives a "weekly needle so he would detour his fits, forget to express them," causes a row when he disputes in which arm he should receive the shot according to his alternating schedule.[243] Siemerling, following Scobie, notes the use of Billy's alias and argues that the right-left debate in the cameo "alludes obliquely to ... the inverting potential of photographs in *The Collected Works of Billy the Kid*," which is subtitled "Left Handed Poems."[244] Yet this scene also precipitates the escape of a reaper-figure named Bertram Lord, who plots to kill Bolden upon his return, and Antrim's very presence in the text suggests that he did indeed escape death and capture at the conclusion of *The Collected Works of Billy the Kid*, to be reborn in prose.

Sally Bachner perceives a similar resurrection of Bolden in the names evoked by Ondaatje in the final third of the novel:

> The title of Ondaatje's novel refers, as we find out in the course of reading it, to Bolden's travels, first on the way to the East Louisiana State Hospital 'through Sunshine, Vachery and Slaughter' and then back again, on the way to being buried in Holtz cemetery in New Orleans, 'through Slaughter, Vachery, Sunshine.' The choice of town names to chart these movements is obviously important, as their entitling function implies. In fact, the sequence constructs Bolden as just another head of cattle, moving from the edenic freedom of sunshine, through the domesticated space of the vachery, or 'enclosure for cattle', to the inevitable slaughterhouse. In this sense, the title phrase nicely carries a sense of Bolden's double movement through historicity, first as a living artist trying to survive history in the form of fame, and second as a potential victim of posthumous historicization. But it also seems important that the way the phrase is isolated and framed as a title lends it a more hopeful air, since to come *through* slaughter is, in a sense, to survive it.[245]

For Bachner, the "rescuing intimacy of an identifying other" (both author and reader) offers hope for the isolated and seemingly tragic protagonists in Ondaatje's fiction.[246]

With the Booker Prize that followed the publication of *The English Patient* and the Academy Awards that followed its film adaptation, Ondaatje's fame as a novelist greatly overshadowed his reputation as a poet. However, the verse origins of his prose style are unmistakable. Even *Anil's Ghost* (2000), which Ondaatje claims he wrote "in a different kind of way than the way [he]'d written the earlier books," so that the language was "not too heightened," the effect not "too formal," and the narrative "full of [the] possibility of plot,"[247] has inspired an American reviewer to exclaim: "Michael Ondaatje breaks the rules. He forces the novel to do things it isn't supposed to do and he gets away with it ... The Sri Lankan-born Ondaatje is a poet, and he throws himself headlong at beautiful sentences, revelatory scenes, larger-than-life moments. He treats plot as if it were a line of verse: What's important is that it scan and swell, not that it ticktock along with the weary world."[248] Judging by the architecture of Ondaatje's narratives, the "great change in what 'structure' is in a poem or in a novel" has to do with serializing the lyric voice in order to vary its tone, expand its temporal scope, multiply its points of view, and produce what Bowering calls a "serial novel," which is the subject of the next chapter.

4

George Bowering: (Un)framing
the Serial Novel

Writing is not parallel it is serial.

George Bowering[1]

Bowering redefined the term "serial novel" in his trilogy, *Autobiology* (1972), *Curious* (1973), and *A Short Sad Book* (1977). While a wide variety of genres were serialized in the Victorian era, Bowering chose to define his conception of the serial against the nineteenth-century realist novel and its promise of a window onto a parallel world. Bowering was suspicious of what he perceived as an instrumental use of language in realism, as well as the causal momentum of the kind of plot produced by publication in installments. Instead of the plot-driven realist serial, Bowering developed a prose form based on the serial poem. He created continuity between discrete sections of narrative by developing them recursively around motifs, which in his work tend to be phrases and syntactic constructions (or other formal constraints), as much as visual images.

The serial poem is a key poetic form for Bowering, and it appears regularly in his oeuvre from the mid-1960s onward. It appeared first in *Baseball, a Poem in the Magic Number Nine* (1967), which is dedicated to Jack Spicer, and Bowering promoted the form as an antidote to the solipsism of the first person lyric.[2] However, his serial poems retained ties to his early lyricism, as Roy Miki explains in the afterword to *George Bowering Selected*: "In the midst of composing serial texts in the late 1960s and 1970s, Bowering announced many times that he had abandoned the lyric poem altogether, that he had gone post-lyric as it were, but the collections published in the 1970s belie that statement. The poems themselves reveal that the younger poet had learned to mistrust the conventional lyric stance which privileges the isolate self imposing order on the world, and had learned how to renew the lyric in complicated forms that maintain a vital

tension between order and process, craft and language, self and otherness
... lyric desire and serial composition."[3] Unlike Spicer and Blaser, Bowering
also adapted the techniques of serial composition to the novel. This chapter
explores how Bowering frames *Autobiology, Curious,* and *A Short Sad
Book* according to the logic of the serial poem, while at the same time dismantling the literary codes that he invokes through parody.

Like many avant-garde writers, Bowering has experimented with numerous literary genres and styles. The broad outline generally painted of his
career depicts him as a lyric poet in the 1960s, a serial poem writer in the
1970s, and a prose writer in the 1980s, although Eva-Marie Kröller notes
that such major works as *Kerrisdale Elegies* (1984) fall outside this paradigm.[4] In fact, Bowering published in all three genres in each decade, and
he continued in subsequent decades, as well as issuing a second edition of
Autobiology in 2007. Nonetheless, Bowering's prevailing interests map
important transitions in his development as a writer. At first, he embraced
the lyric, only to grow wary of its subjectivity; next he became interested in
the epic, but deplored its teleological treatment of history; several times he
tried his hand at the novel, but was dissatisfied with the language of his
early attempts at naturalism and realism. The serial novel thus presents
itself as a means of reconciling Bowering's attraction to, and rejection of,
these approaches to writing. The serial novel is a hybrid form, capable of
accommodating the linguistic and formal pyrotechnics of the lyric and the
long poem while sustaining the narrative dimension of the novel.

Unlike Ondaatje, Bowering did not move in a linear fashion from lyric to
long poem to novel. In his late teens, the "burning novelist from the
[Okanagan] Valley" was primarily interested in prose fiction, and his style
resembled the naturalism of James T. Farrell.[5] However, Bowering's early
novel, *Delsing,* was rejected by publishers.[6] His next novel, *Mirror on the
Floor,* was published in 1967, but by then he had already published four
volumes of lyric poetry: *Sticks & Stones* (1962), *Points on the Grid* (1964),
The Man in Yellow Boots (1965), and *The Silver Wire* (1966). The lyric
won Bowering his first success as a writer, and although he has spurned and
derided the form, it retains a central place in his repertoire. In addition,
Bowering's poetic affiliations in the 1960s aligned him with a group of
West Coast writers, many of whom would become friends and peers for the
rest of his career.

Along with Frank Davey, Fred Wah, James Reid, and David Dawson,
Bowering helped publish a poetry newsletter, *Tish,* from September 1961 to
March 1963. The monthly newsletter – which was later co-edited by
Daphne Buckle (Marlatt) – grew out of the Creative Writing and English

departments at the University of British Columbia, but it created a community of Vancouver writers by encouraging submissions from promising
local poets such as David Bromige and Roy Kiyooka. *Tish* offered the
young poets a forum for publishing new poems and debating poetics. It
also answered the demand for a Canadian journal receptive to the poetics
associated with the *Black Mountain Review* (1954–57), which published
avant-garde American poets such as William Carlos Williams, Denise
Levertov, and Allen Ginsberg. This review showcased the postmodernist
aesthetics emerging out of Black Mountain College in North Carolina,
where Charles Olson was rector and Robert Creeley and Robert Duncan
taught in the 1950s. The very name *Tish* bears the stamp of this influence,
because Duncan suggested it (as an anagram of "Shit").[7] The scatological
connotations of *Tish* underscore the collective's anti-establishment irrever-
ence, but they also suited the group's admiration for Charles Olson:
"Olsonites, we jokingly called ourselves. Olsonite was the brand name for
a toilet seat, but we were confident enough about where we stood." [8] Jokes
aside, the *Tish* poets were extremely serious about Olson's theory of poetry
as an energy discharge, and they formed a study group to discuss his 1950
essay "Projective Verse."

Bowering claims that Olson introduced the term "postmodern" to the
Tish poets as a guest lecturer at UBC in 1963.[9] He also credits Olson with
steering the young poets away from the Eurocentric bias of Eastern Canadian poetry: "Olson told us to dig exhaustively into our local concerns. We
began to do so, and the geography, history, and economics of Vancouver
became the grid of our poetry. In the late 1960s and the 1970s, xenophobic
critics and professors in Ontario accused us of selling out the 'Canadian
Tradition' to U.S. American interests ... They started calling us Black
Mountain poets. I dont know any Canadian poets who ever went to North
Carolina."[10] This east/west dichotomy does not quite work because, at the
same conference where Bowering pledged his allegiance to Olson, he was
so impressed with Ginsberg's reading of Percy Bysshe Shelley that he
resolved to "start poetry all over again, with Shelley on the first page."[11]
Moreover, the irony involved in students embracing the ideas of a visiting
American professor on counter-imperialism and adopting his theories of
the local has been noted. Many Canadian critics, including Keith Richardson, who wrote *Poetry and the Colonized Mind: Tish* (1976), and Robin
Mathews, who contributed a preface to Richardson's work and attacked
Bowering in his own articles, interpreted this supposed new allegiance as
treason.[12] Although Bowering now resents the identification of the *Tish*
group with the Black Mountain poets, the connection is well established –

and not only because Bowering discovered that there is a Black Mountain north of Vancouver. David Dawson wrote in an editorial for *Tish* 20 that the editors "print poems that work the way we think a poem should work. our debt, stated or otherwise, to the so-called Black Mountain group, is obvious."[13] Davey did his doctoral dissertation on the "Theory and Practice in the Black Mountain Poets" (1968) and, in other contexts, Bowering explicitly aligned himself with the figureheads of American modernism and postmodernism.[14] Although an Olsonite, he maintains in his recent *A Magpie Life* that his "personal model in the early sixties was H.D."[15] He also considers himself "the imaginary son of WCW and nephew of Denise Levertov and cousin of Ron Silliman," as well as being one of a group of "Vancouver poets [who] might loosely be said to descend from Robert Duncan."[16] Robin Blaser, Jack Spicer, and Robert Creeley (who lectured at UBC in 1962–63 and was Bowering's creative writing teacher) also occupy prominent positions on this family tree. Taken together, these poets are not a very compatible group, but Bowering picks and chooses his influences according to his purposes at a given moment. His dogmatic pronouncements on aesthetics are most profitably read as an extension of his constraint-based writing practices, for no sooner does he promote a style and prohibit another than he breaks his own taboos in a subsequent work.

Such a broad range of American mentors contrasts sharply with the limited influence of Canadian authors on Bowering's early poetics, as well as on that of the *Tish* group. However, Bowering claims that "when the whole *Tish* thing was happening, we were people who had been deracinated – we didn't get any Canadian writing at school in BC. Most of the people in *Tish* – Fred Wah and Frank Davey – didn't know anything about Canadian poetry. The only people that knew of Canadian poetry were Lionel Kearns and I, who got together before the *Tish* stuff happened anyway. Lionel had been an exchange student in Québec and he brought back the Contact Press books and I read them in one of those cabins in the dorms. Souster, Layton, Dudek, D.G. Jones, Milton Acorn and all those guys. I hadn't even thought about Canadian poetry. I didn't even think about thinking about Canadian poetry."[17] Bowering's commentary on the curriculum is not quite accurate, and he chooses to overlook the presence of Earle Birney, who founded the Creative Writing Programme at UBC (the Creative Writing Department from 1965 onward)," in the mid-1960s, and whose long narrative poem *David* (1942) was by then a canonical Canadian work.[18] Bowering's views on Canadian literary history are extremely selective and subject to change. For example, in a 1976 interview with Caroline Bayard and Jack David, Bowering praises Layton's "*Laughter in the Mind* – oh, a great book, and I was reading Dudek's *East of the City* – fantastic."[19] However, only three years earlier, he had ridiculed Layton and Dudek in *Curious* and portrayed Jones as too busy with family to write.[20] Generally, only Souster escapes Bowering's derision. Nonetheless, in the new millennium, Bowering has warmed to the idea of having Canadian predecessors and he now claims that Contact Press was "the signal of the new" for his generation of young Canadians.[21] The appointment of Bowering to the office of poet laureate (the first in Canadian history) has largely silenced Bowering's east-west polemics, because the appointment acknowledges the fact that authors such as Bowering and Davey (now an Ontarian) have become the establishment.

I have noted the influence of the *Tish*, Black Mountain, and Contact Press poets because they played an active role in Bowering's early publications. Bowering dedicated his first collection of poems, *Sticks & Stones* (1962), to Robert Duncan and had it printed as part of a larger series of chapbooks the *Tish* collective intended to produce.[22] However, fewer than thirty draft copies were circulated privately before Contact Press accepted Bowering's manuscript for *Points on the Grid* (1964), which included many of the poems from *Sticks & Stones*.[23]

The early poems are perhaps most notable for their use of polysyndeton. They layer image upon image using ampersands and record the metonymic correspondences of what Duncan calls "rime." Bowering tells Bayard and David that he is crazy about rime: "So what I'm paying attention to is not trying to render some other experience with the writing itself and seeing what happens from point to point."[24] Always contrasting a poetics of representation and a poetics of process, Bowering documents the interaction of his mind and body with his environment and favours techniques that promote a sense of movement, surprise, and becoming.

Bowering's second collection, *Points on the Grid,* expands on these preoccupations, as the title poem indicates:

> The man's life
> a series of points
> strung into a wavering line
> on the graph
> his grid of action.[25]

Bowering examines the strategies and media of observation throughout this collection, but the grid metaphor of the title poem suggests a Cartesian point of view that Bowering would later question. It also recalls Bowering's years as an RCAF aerial photographer, and Bowering would grow wary of this "god's eye" view for the same reason he rejected the military.

"Taking Pictures," a poem from the series "Four Jobs" in *West Window* (1982), expresses Bowering's reservations about the purpose of his military photographs and film footage. In this poem, Bowering describes shooting film footage through a portal in the wing of an airplane and remarks that "it was always a movie of one thing, / a target."[26] The cameraman's privileged vantage point here is analogous to that of poets such as Breavman, who aims his poems at (his bomb)Shell. In subsequent publications, Bowering steers away from this vantage point and strives to "edit out any verse that seem[s] to be peering thru a crenel at the passing show."[27] In "Brown Globe," Bowering criticizes the detached and aestheticized perspective that privileges such views:

> If this is confession it is crooked,
> it is not as valid as pure poetry, I once wrote
> pure poetry till the bombs fell on Asia,
> but that is an evasion, isnt it? Isnt it
> that I have to write letters to publishers instead of to
> angels?[28]

Bowering searches for an evasive poetics here, as opposed to an invasive one, even as he condemns (in a glancing fashion) the U.S. military and invokes Rilke's address to the angels in the first of the *Duino Elegies*.[29] Roy Miki demonstrates that Bowering was uncomfortable with the imperial stance "of a poetic self intent only on expressing its own centrality," and thus "did not simply go on honing a style and polishing a signature ... The singular lyric poem characteristic of his first volumes of poetry gave way to the extended form, to what Bowering would call (taking the term from Jack Spicer and Robin Blaser) the 'serial' poem."[30] The serial poem provided a means for the author to explore the complexity of phenomena because it registers how phenomena shift over a number of exposures and from a variety of vantage points. It also reconfigures the "wavering line" of temporal sequence such that it does not move across the "grid of action" in a linear fashion.

In 1964 Bowering established the journal *Imago* "expressly for long poems ... because at that time there werent (m)any magazines that printed long poems."[31] Although *Imago* grew out of Bowering's small magazine experience with *Tish*, it signalled his shift away from the lyric toward the long poem.[32] Bowering claims not to "recall having held any great theories about the long poem," but, like *Tish*, this journal was not entirely open.[33] He did not want "just anybody's long poems, but the long poems in our context" – that is, serial poems and proprioceptive writing.[34] Bowering published Duncan beside Davey in *Imago* 2 and Olson beside Kearns in *Imago* 7 while flatly rejecting any nationalist claims to the long poem. Indeed, Bowering maintains that he started *Imago* because he "noticed that in the United States all the good Modernist poets, all the Imagist poets, went ahead and made the long poem their main life's work."[35] However, what Bowering calls the "symphonic period" in his career also marked a broadening of his poetic interests.[36] The move to the long poem places him in a larger continuum than the legacy of American (post)modernism. Bowering observes that "in the eighteenth century the important verse [was] found in long poems. Among the Romantics and the Victorians the reputations were made on long poems of heroic visionary voyages."[37] The historical breadth of the long poem seems to have forced him to come to terms with the obvious: the Britishness of British Columbia and the Englishness of his language. In 1967 Bowering began a doctoral dissertation on Shelley at the University of Western Ontario in London. He abandoned this project a year later in order to accept a position at Sir George Williams University (now Concordia) in Montreal, but it influenced the Romantic theories of the imagination set forth in the nautical narratives of *George, Vancouver* and *Burning Water*.

Bowering's work as an editor preceded his output as a writer, and he would publish two more collections of short lyrics before producing his first serial poem in 1967. In 1965 he published *The Man in Yellow Boots*, a collection of lyrics preoccupied with the escalating military tensions of the Cold War. The title recalls the fact that Bowering spray painted his boots bright yellow while he was in the Canadian military, but in his poems he directs his irreverent wit primarily at the American military. Although Bowering retained his love of jazz and Hollywood Westerns, his growing disillusionment with American politics manifested itself here in poems such as "Vox Crapulous (alternative title: J. Edgar Hoover)" and in the reprinted letters to the book's editors:[38] "What are the Americans going to do now a country [China] they dont recognize has detonated the Bomb? They'll have to keep it a secret from America, or walk around wondering, where did that noise come from? It cdnt have come from that part of Asia because there aint no country there."[39] The publication of *The Man in Yellow Boots* coincided with increased American aggression toward Vietnam, and Bowering's youthful enthusiasm for the United States would steadily turn to disenchantment in subsequent publications. Although he would continue to side with counter-cultural figures such as Ginsberg, his disdain for American military ambitions became a standard theme in his writing from this point on: for example, in the serial poem *At War with the U.S.* (1974) and the "Vietnam & Other Wars" section of *Seventy-One Poems for People* (1985).[40] This disillusionment seems to have caused Bowering to reconsider the "openness" of serial writing as it was practised by his American mentors.

Intimations of Bowering's move to the serial poem are already present in *The Man with Yellow Boots*. Bowering gives the looming threat of nuclear holocaust poignancy by juxtaposing his lyrics with a series of collages by the Japanese Canadian artist Roy Kiyooka. Unlike the drawings by Gordon Payne in *Sticks & Stones*, which are interspersed between the poems and meant to complement or illustrate them,[41] Kiyooka insisted that his series be "included in the book in one solid block and not be scattered throughout the book."[42] The poems and photographic series represent two distinct meditations on the theme of war that are juxtaposed within the text. The split oval in Kiyooka's first collage juxtaposes a mushroom cloud with a headless torso, conjuring formal associations with the split atom and connecting thematically to such Bowering poems as "Her Act Was a Bomb" and "The Good Prospects," a poem "writ on the occasion of the Moscow test ban treaty meeting," which was reprinted in 2003 in an anthology of poetry to protest the American invasion of Iraq.[43] On a formal level, the collage series foreshadows the future direction of Bowering's poetry and underscores the importance of visual art to Bowering's craft.

In *George Bowering: Bright Circles of Colour*, Eva-Marie Kröller argues persuasively that Bowering's literary designs are heavily influenced by his friendships and collaborations with Canadian visual artists.[44] The starting point for Kröller's book is Bowering's dedication of *Another Mouth* (1979) to "three artists who have graced my life, illuminated my imagination, & talkt my year off: Greg Curnoe, Roy Kiyooka, & Brian Fisher."[45] Kröller goes beyond these three figures to examine Bowering's connections to Jack Chambers (who contributed the drawing of *Man and Dog* to the cover of Ondaatje's *the man with seven toes*) and others, but the three dedicatees played a particularly prominent role in shaping Bowering's poetics, as he acknowledged in the Bayard/David interview: "I hang out with painters in every city I go to, for some reason. Roy Kiyooka and Brian Fisher are two of my best friends in Vancouver. I think painters tend to talk more than poets do; poets tend not to talk about their art too much with each other, very seldom. But painters who have been quiet all day long, want to talk about serious things when they finish."[46] Among these artists, Kiyooka was the most influential because he was the oldest friend of the three.

THE SERIAL POEMS

Although Kiyooka puts a copy of Warren Tallman and Archibald Allen's *The Poetics of the New American Poetry* in his photoglyphic series "Pacific Windows," his background in the visual arts leads him to a different interpretation of the serial form.[47] He rejects the notion that serial poems are completely open in form and likes to establish certain parameters for his poems, which give them a recurring architecture. Bowering follows this example by working ekphrastically from the thirty-eight cards of the Geneva tarot deck in *Genève*, using the border of a single page to frame his literary portraits in *Curious*, and limiting his composition time to the duration of a Blaser lecture in *Allophanes*. In *A Short Sad Book*, to cite another variation on the trope of the train, the stops of the Yonge Street subway remind one character of a serial poem, because he sees radical difference framed by recurring architectural forms.[48] These forms establish a framework by which the reader may judge the differences among the discontinuous segments.

Such limiting practices are in place from Bowering's very first serial poem. *Baseball, a poem in the magic number 9*, responds to Spicer's opening injunction in "Seven Poems for the Vancouver Festival": "Start with a baseball diamond high / In the Runcible Mountain wilderness."[49] Acknowledging this literary debt, Bowering dedicates the poem to Spicer (who died shortly after lecturing at the Vancouver Poetry Festival in 1965) and celebrates their favourite game:

> I knew an old man in San Francisco
>   came to life
>   when the Dodgers were in town.
> Now he is dead, too,
>   & Jack is dead,
> & the soldiers play baseball
>   in Asia,
> where there is no season,
>   no season's end.[50]

On one hand, Bowering praises the exuberance of Spicer's serial technique by comparing it to the endless summer of America's favourite pastime. On the other hand, the spectre of American imperialism looms over this passage as the soldiers play baseball in Asia. Perhaps for this reason, Bowering signals his difference from Spicer by establishing limits to the reach of his poem. *Baseball* appears in nine sections, limiting its scope to nine innings of varying but not disproportionate length. Instead of creating a segmented form that is conducive to enlargement – the "to be continued" of Spicer's beloved radio serials – Bowering establishes a temporal or spatial limit ahead of time and plays against that limit.

At the same time, because he considers himself doubly colonized in B.C., Bowering resists the limitations that he feels are placed upon him by the Eastern Canadian literary establishment, as well as by the northern ethos of the Dominion:

the Mounties, nuts, they are Dominicans of the North,
dusky smiling on the lucky number souvenir program,
where I no longer write mystic scorekeeper numbers in the little squares,
sophisticate of baseball now, I've seen later famous players here.[51]

For Bowering, a product of the hot and dry Okanagan Valley, baseball has always represented his resistance to the cultural dictates of hockey-mad Eastern Canada. His views on baseball also allegorize his opinions on postmodernism, reading, and, in this case, his refusal to write short lyrics ("mystic scorekeeper numbers in the little squares") to please anthologists in the East.[52] Bowering thus embraces the American game and poetic genre in order to become more local. The situation is contradictory, but Bowering draws inspiration from conflict. It is therefore appropriate that he wrote a critique of Albertan culture in *Rocky Mountain Foot* (1968) while teaching in Calgary, and then started a serial poem on the colonial exploits of George Vancouver while beginning a PhD in London, Ontario.

Rocky Mountain Foot is less a serial poem than an experiment in collage. Bowering intermingles lyrics with quotations from Alberta road signs, newspapers, geological surveys, and other found materials in order to step out from behind his crenel and engage with the passing show. As he makes clear in his critique of Ondaatje's early lyrics, he desires "a world rather than a picture of one," an experience rather than an artifact.[53] Collage provides the means of creating a stereophonic impression in the reading, as well as a panoramic impression on the page. Clearly influenced by Kiyooka and their painter-poet friend bill bissett,[54] Bowering turns to collage in *Rocky Mountain Foot* as a means of addressing his dissatisfaction with the lyric as a mode, as he tells Bayard and David: "Now there's got to be some way of getting away from the danger of the lyric which is the personalism that's involved, the seeing things from that personal point of view. I don't know what the model might have been but I had a sense that the way to do

that was to inject or meet what you were writing with the other, so you can
somehow move it out of the lyric mode so it no longer is my opinion on
that or my response to that or my feeling on that, that there will be something like a collaboration perhaps."[55] Accordingly, Bowering juxtaposes
fragments from other Canadian poets with ordinary signage and non-liter-
ary texts in order to underscore that he is one voice in a larger dialogue.

In *George, Vancouver*, Bowering's lyric voice is interrupted by deadpan
historical reports on the state of King George's health and the English
Romantic movement, excerpts from journals by Vancouver and Menzies, a
catalogue of sailing vessels, nautical statistics, and other factual intrusions
into the subjective space of the lyric. *George, Vancouver* is subtitled "A
Discovery Poem" and it represents Bowering's exploration of this new
method of composition as well as his research into the history of Vancouver
– the place he continues to think of as home even while living in Calgary,
London, and Montreal.

Particularly in the revised version collected in *The Catch* (1976), *George,
Vancouver* follows *Rocky Mountain Foot* in offering visual analogies for
this diversification of voice. The use of interspersed italics, the repetition of
the pictographic symbol for Cancer, and the placement of stanzas across
the breadth of the page indicate that Bowering is beginning to think of the
page as a space to explore rather than as a transparent medium for tran-
scribing the voice. The juxtapositions of collage break down the singular
vantage point of Renaissance perspective as well as complicating
Bowering's already complicated politics.

There is probably no better illustration of Bowering's flair for controversy and contradiction than the public response to *The Gangs of Kosmos*
(1969). The book consists of short lyrics and a long poem that modernizes
the Haida myth of the cannibal "Hamatsa." Its title derives from a Whitman quotation, and its cover features a drawing of Margaret Atwood and
Angela Bowering. Miki notes that Atwood, who edited the collection, suggested the title *You Too*, but Bowering insisted on cannibalizing Whitman.[56] Despite the explicit Americanism of the title, *The Gangs of Kosmos*,
together with *Rocky Mountain Foot*, won the Governor General's Award
in 1969, to the dismay of nationalists such as Mathews. Seven years later,
Bowering ridicules Mathews and his ilk in *A Short Sad Book*, but he also
mocks the expansionist rhetoric of American transcendentalism:

I saw a stand of trees in London Ontario where Walt Whitman the
American had walkt & we lived a block away.
He said he had no ending.

Well, here I am Walt, & I dont see you around & you still havent annex'd Cuba & Kanada.[57]

In a similarly paradoxical manner, Bowering produced his greatest number of serial poems in the 1970s, but abandoned *Imago* in 1974 because "the long poem had become a fad."[58] Never content to run with the pack, Bowering started looking for ways to expand the form's generic vocabulary and his search led him back to the novel.

THE SERIAL NOVEL

In 1970, when Bowering began work on the serial novel *Autobiology* in London, England, he had already written two realist novels: *Delsing* (unpublished) and *Mirror on the Floor* (1967). The latter novel offers a Vancouver perspective on the late Beat Era and is, in many respects, a testament to Bowering's enthusiasm for "Jack Kerouac, the French-Canadian writer who happened to be born and raised in the United States."[59] Tallman recommended calling the novel "Vancouver Blues," thereby aligning it with Kerouac's *Mexico City Blues* (1959), but Bowering again insisted on his original title, perhaps because it engages explicitly with the definition of the realist novel as "a mirror held up to real life."[60] Set in diners, cars, and artists' houses, and populated with poets, painters, and other bohemian figures, *Mirror on the Floor* in many respects treads a well-blazed path. Stylistically, it approximates the speed and speech rhythms of Kerouac's shotgun prose through run-on sentences and hip, witty dialogue. It celebrates youthful exuberance and glamorizes the Beat aesthetic – except in the section where the Vancouver police beat up the narrator, Bob, after throwing him in jail.[61] In this respect, the novel emulates the accelerated realism of *On the Road* and reinforces Stendhal's statement that a "novel is a mirror walking down a road."[62]

However, *Mirror on the Floor* is also a romance, and in the passages where Andrea (Bob's love interest) appears, the writing frequently achieves a lyrical intensity that eclipses its realism. In the two-page chapter from which the title derives, for example, the mirror reflects a range of objects outside its field of reference: "She pulled the screws out and put the full-length mirror on the floor. The room seemed to tip without a lurch and the ceiling came into the mirror a little crooked. The edges of her eyes caught more yellow wall than before. Swimming season was over and white bodies lay waving back and forth in the long green weeds, long hair trailing wet with tendrils among little fish and fugitive underwater green sunshine.

Winter was ready with its cloud-bank out on the Pacific rainwaters and the cold air of fall was settling in over the city."[63] As this passage continues, the frame of the mirror fails to contain even the figures it reflects: "Poised over the mirror, she looked down ten feet to her face looking down to her from ten feet above. The figure in the glass was wavering, ready to fall, to sail, to come out and away, swaying on the edge of adhesion, out of the world in a second, it was herself seen from within the glass and out to the yellow walls."[64]

At the conclusion of this scene, Andrea strips naked and lies down on the mirror. The medium and the subject of representation intersect as Andrea's body spreads over the mirror and fills its frame. Bowering conveys the (auto)eroticism of this moment by emphasizing horizontal movement in the narrative:

> She stood over the mirror and looked down at the reflection. Somebody could have been standing at the rail of a bridge. Rain could be falling on bodies in the park. It could be summer in the world, somewhere. The quartet was in the middle of the blues.
>
> The glass was cold against her skin. She flattened herself more, pushing away the cold, and the fronts of her shoulders pressed against the glass. She lowered her open mouth to the open mouth.[65]

Andrea's kiss unites the composition's horizontal planes, bringing two parallel worlds into collision. The eroticism of Andrea's gesture challenges the supposed passivity of the mirror-image, blocks its gaze, and mocks its (in)ability to reproduce. The mirror becomes a figure in the story, not the unobtrusive ground. This rewriting of the Narcissus myth poses only a momentary challenge to realist prose and its symbols, but Andrea's gesture foreshadows Bowering's more aggressive challenge to realist convention in *Autobiology*.

When *Autobiology* was published in 1972, it signalled Bowering's most daring genre experiment to date. John Harris calls the "book-length lyric" Bowering's poetic "masterpiece," while the biographical blurb on the back cover of *A Short Sad Book* lists it as a novel.[66] The original York Street Commune edition of *Autobiology* facilitates the latter impression by using large type and double-spaced lines to create 48 chapters of two pages in length. However, subsequent reprintings of *Autobiology* in *The Catch* and *George Bowering Selected* present the work as poetry and condense its chapters onto single pages. The reprinted versions also have typographi-

cally unnecessary line breaks which suggest that Bowering came to think of
Autobiology as verse.

These changes reflect how editorial pressures can entrench genre boundaries. McClelland & Stewart editor Anna Porter accepted the original
manuscript of *The Catch*, but rejected Bowering's homage to Souster,
"Sousterre," for its middle section.[67] Bowering proposed *Autobiology* as a
replacement because, as a *Georgia Straight Writing Supplement*, it had had
a smaller print run than he felt it deserved: "I am also very high on it, and I
consider that I will stand on it in years to come."[68] Pooka Press in Vancouver published a second edition of *Autobiology* in 2007, but Porter's
response to Bowering's proposal triggered a debate on genre, as Miki's
annotated bibliography of Bowering demonstrates:

> Porter was hesitant because for her the work was prose, not poetry, so
> would create a mixed book that might be hard to market. GB
> responded 31 July 1975: "Recognize yr hesitation re *Autobiology*, but
> wd Instruct that the distinction is not really between prose and poetry
> but between prose and verse. Poetry can be in both prose or verse.
> Verse has to do with the making of lines, i.e. coming back to the margin
> at times, etc., while poetry has essentially to do with how one treats or
> is treated by the language regarding what he wants his reader to do.
> That is, prose directs one toward the world he presumably [is] already
> in, and poetry invites him into a world, a new one. Or as Hulme had it,
> prose is a train that tries to get you to a destination, and poetry is a
> pedestrian, who steps and sees every bit of the way. Well. In any case
> *Autobiology* is poetry.[69]

The serial structure of *Autobiology* is thus an elaboration of Bowering's
lyric impulse.

I have noted the poetic lineage informing the serial novel because Bowering claimed to have outgrown the lyric in the 1970s: "I started building on
the lyric into a larger mode and using an Olson sense of how you get into a
long poem, not very well. So I did that long Alberta sequence [*Rocky
Mountain Foot*] in which lyrics are mixed with non-poetical materials and
it was called [subtitled] 'A Lyric, A Memoir' and I did, after that, the Captain
Vancouver one in which there is a collection of lyrics taken from different
places, all on the same subject. Then I wrote some shorter long poems which
were a lot more interesting. Then I wrote *Genève* [1971] and from then I've
never written a lyric poem or a short poem."[70] This statement is useful, if

slightly misleading. The lyric is so fundamental to Bowering's practice that he apparently publishes whole collections despite himself. In addition to the "last lyrics" from *The Concrete Island: Montreal Poems 1967–71* (1977), Bowering produced two more collections of "Last Lyrics" in the 1970s: *In the Flesh* (1974) and *Another Mouth* (1979).[71] Bowering also writes lyrics under the pseudonyms Helmut Franz, E.E. Greengrass, Erich Blackhead, and Edward Pratoverde and offers this explanation of his trickery to Bayard and David: "I still publish lyric poems under a pseudonym because I'm not a lyric poet anymore."[72] Bowering's serial novels function as another disguise for this impulse, but they also extend his sense of selfhood.

Autobiology places a new emphasis on Bowering's family life. Bowering's only child, Thea, was born in 1972, and "a photograph of father and daughter appears on the back cover, complementing a picture of a three- or four-year-old Bowering with his mother [Pearl] on the front."[73] Framed by these portraits, Bowering's text explores new kinds of continuity in his writing by tracing his genealogy and translating it into a literary form. "Line is also lineage," as Wah says of the lengthening lines in Bowering's genealogical work.[74] In contrast to *Genève*, there is a discernible narrative in *Autobiology*. Bowering maps his progress from childhood to adulthood and thereby complies with the standard autobiographical technique hinted at in the title. However, as an auto*biology*, this piece of life-writing treats life and death in their biological contexts. The cover images position Bowering as a link in a chain of life extending from his mother, Pearl, to his daughter, Thea, and this sense of selfhood extending beyond the lyric "I" is part of the rationale behind the book's title, as Bowering explains in *Errata*: "I never wanted to write an autobiography. I think that certain works I have done with what looks like my life story should be called biotext ... Autobiography replaces the writer. Biotext is an extension of him."[75] The distinction between autobiography and autobiology is thus another example of the distinction Bowering makes between parallel writing (which mirrors a life) and serial writing (which multiplies versions of a life). The term "biotext" has become increasingly important to Canadian criticism because of the growing interest in life-writing practices that cross over into fiction and highlight the construction of multiple selves, identities, and bodies through writing. However, even Johanne Saul's reading of Ondaatje's *Running in the Family*, Marlatt's *Ghost Works*, Kiyooka's *Mothertalk*, and Wah's *Diamond Grill* as biotexts fails to acknowledge the importance of *Autobiology* as the basis of Bowering's autobiographical technique.[76] Saul briefly highlights the importance of the long poem as a genre from the 1960s onwards but like most critics she passes quickly over the authors' careers as poets to discuss their innovations in prose.

The concern with the self and its social nexus in *Autobiology* signals yet another departure from the impersonal serialism of Spicer and Blaser. The sense of familial extension and variation in *Autobiology* is particularly poignant when one considers that Thea Bowering is now a published poet, and that, prior to the death of his wife, Angela, in 2000, Bowering worked collaboratively with her on the novel *Piccolo Mondo* (1998), as well as on "a sequence of meditations on pictures" as yet unpublished.[77] The strong female presence in *Autobiology* also accentuates the author's growing enthusiasm for Gertrude Stein, who becomes his stylistic mentor in the 1970s. By modifying Stein's style of circumlocution, repetition, and comic inversion in *Autobiology*, Bowering establishes the stylistic basis for *Curious* and *A Short Sad Book*. *Curious* is a series of literary profiles akin to Stein's cubist portraits, while *A Short Sad Book* responds to Stein's *A Long Gay Book* by adapting its fragmented and incongruous style of juxtaposition. Bowering links these fragments with his beloved ampersand and builds poems out of an accumulation of objects and moments viewed from different angles. The effect is "something like a movie film, Gertrude Stein's analogy for her writing, 'discrete frames in / a continuous flow'" – an analogy that Bowering uses to describe bp Nichol's long poem *continental trance*, in which discrete images pass by like "picture windows in a moving train."[78]

In developing these continuities, Bowering also explores new kinds of discontinuity. The digressive, Steinian sentences are the most obvious example. However, one should also remember that Bowering writes *Autobiology* out of a sense of geographical displacement. This displacement affects the style and content of the text, as Bowering explains in his preface to his Montreal poems in *The Concrete Island*: "My sojourn in the east took me out of place & took place out of my poetry ... [In] Montreal I wrote my last lyrics, old habit, & my first books, or my first post-lyric books. I wrote *Genève* in Montreal, & most of *Autobiology*."[79] Although Bowering frequently equates the serial poem with the west coast, he finds the impetus to write many of his serial works while living away from it. As with *George, Vancouver*, Bowering produced *Autobiology* as a means of connecting to his roots. The dates of composition given in the back of *Autobiology* underscore this westward trajectory: "London, June 12, 1970 – Vancouver, June 12, 1971."[80] The way Bowering registers time is thus framed by his feelings of spatial dislocation, and the temporal shifts in the narrative have a vertiginous effect that communicates this displacement.

Although *Autobiology* documents Bowering's development as an artist, the novel largely shuns plot. On the level of the chapter, the text progresses in a roughly linear fashion from Bowering's childhood to his adulthood; but on the level of the sentence Kröller observes that it "introduces a complex superimposition of times, refusing to adopt a sequential ordering of time."[81] The narrative "rimes" rather than climaxes. It moves horizontally in a number of branching directions, developing a lateral technique that Bowering revisits in "Alphabiography" (a prose piece organized according to the twenty-six letters of the alphabet which constitutes the largest section of *A Magpie Life: Growing a Writer*). In *Autobiology*, time jumps forward and backward, but as with Cohen and his pin motif in "Lines from My Grandfather's Journal," Bowering creates a sense of duration through temporal overlay, not through extended description in any one tense.[82] The series of forty-eight (twice twenty-four) chapters is thus both chronological and achronological. The number of chapters in *Autobiology* also gently parodies the conventional divisions of the Homeric corpus into forty-eight books, a convention Carson also parodies in her verse romance "Autobiography of Red."

Although the serial novel abandons the ticking chronometer of naturalistic pace, it is no less preoccupied with the passage of time. The importance of family history to *Autobiology* is a symptom, Bowering explains, of entering a new phase in his life: "Especially for somebody who has been deracinated, it makes sense, in your twenties, to write lyric poems in which the configuration of the place is so important to your finding out who you are in the twenties. I think in the thirties you tend to get out of place and more into time."[83] Of course, Bowering's new interest in time does not cause him to abandon his old enthusiasm for narratives of place. Instead, he maintains that the "next place is really a series of places so that the next place is really time, that is, a series, not as on the railroad, though that is certainly, there."[84] Bowering's biographical technique is to consider time as a series of places and place as a series of times.

Times and places intertwine from the very first chapter of *Autobiology*, which begins in a circuitous fashion: "When I was thirty I had free raspberries in the backyard & I loved them. In the back yard & I ate them. & I ate them in the kitchen out of an aluminum pot. When I was thirty I loved raspberries, I loved to eat them."[85] Bowering immediately contrasts this recollection with its negative: "I could not eat raspberries when I was three years old when we had free raspberries in the front yard."[86] This juxtaposition enacts a series of inversions similar to the inverted parent/child roles in the cover photographs: front yard becomes backyard, 30 becomes 03, a love of raspberries becomes a fear of raspberries. The parallel worlds intersect in the iconic image of the raspberry because, as Kröller points out, "Bowering's prose insistently repeats and varies key phrases. These repetitions blur temporal and spatial distinctions between individual sentences, which are looped together with the melodious playfulness of the *terza rima*."[87] The raspberry motif recurs in chapter 6, where it continues to blur distinctions between times and places (Montreal, Peachland, Greenwood): "I lookt up when I was five & when I was twenty & when I was thirty when I had raspberries in my backyard across Canada while the yard in Greenwood grew not berries but sweet peas."[88] The looping tangle of the raspberry canes thus sets a precedent for the shape of the narrative.

Although Bowering rejects the classical demand for clarity of image, he evidently does not reject the concept of mimesis entirely, because his syntax imitates the convoluted shape of the raspberry canes. Instead of holding up a mirror to nature, he strives to imitate organic processes of growth, as he explains in an essay on William Carlos Williams: "The plant, the city, the human being, any kind of organism, the poem, undergoes perpetual change; yet at the same time it is characterized by a unique shape. For the organism, order is process – the search for form IS form, the form. It is the poem, searching for language, that manages to imitate nature, the only palpable universal. An Aristotelean desire suggests that poetic form implies a beginning, a middle, and an end, and that this is the base for all that can be said about form in nature or in its imitation. But a humble eye looking at the water sees nothing ending."[89] Thus, Bowering cannot conclude chapter 1 of *Autobiology* with the static contrast of the thirty-year-old and three-year-old. To imitate nature as a process in motion, he introduces the story of himself as a three-and-a-half-year-old who eats the raspberry but suspects there is a bug in it.[90] Years later, the child sees a man's face "at a girl's window" and this juxtaposition transforms the raspberry into the Biblical forbidden fruit.[91] In the next two chapters, Bowering amplifies these allusions to Genesis by having the young narrator perform the Adamic task of naming. Both chapters begin, "Sometimes they are called ..." but Bowering dispels any impression of him being the first man by making the act of naming an act of choosing between regional lexicons: "Sometimes they are called see-saws, but that is in a school-book or back east, & we always called them teeter-totters."[92] Instead of sanctioning the definitive, referential Word, Bowering distinguishes between parallel and serial by offering (at least) two linguistic perspectives on the same object. Such bifurcations are his means of maintaining movement in the text, rather than letting it achieve the static state that, in organic terms, signifies death.

To complicate matters further, Bowering explains his ideas of movement in terms of pictorial art. One might assume that pictorial art is synonymous with a frozen image and stable composition, but Bowering disagrees. Paraphrasing Olson in the Bayard/David interview, Bowering offers an opinion of what he considers the great formal shift for his stylistic mentors:

The main twentieth century change from nineteenth century esthetic is that in the nineteenth century all art aimed at rest, finally. When you looked at a painting, you were led by the structure of the painting to having your eyes rest on some area of the painting. And when you taught painting in the academy, you taught where to put the most important material of that painting. And similarly with poetry. You were finally to come to rest. And the main thing that happened in the twentieth century art was that you weren't allowed to do that. So Cézanne came along, and your eye doesn't rest anywhere in that painting. And the same thing started to happen with William Carlos Williams. There's one guy who finally cracked through and showed you that where Williams was coming from was from French painting. Not from Whitman or wherever. Gertrude Stein was another one. And that's why I've come back to her. It seems to me that that's the main message of the twentieth century. You can't come to rest – your eye or ear or whatever. So what do you do? You say, OK, very clear articulation of the muscle rather than a golden bird on a golden bough.[93]

Translating this rest/restlessness distinction into a Canadian context, Bowering contrasts his poetics with those of the Quebec poet Ralph Gustafson, who had strongly criticized Bowering's early poetry: "[Gustafson is] interested in structure and I'm interested in form. I ran across the structure argument all the time when I first came East to go to the University of Western Ontario, and people were talking about structure and they never said anything about form. If you look at a human being physically, structure is bones but form is what you can see. Form is the way the wrist moves. And that's the argument between us. He's an artifact man."[94] While it is certainly true that Bowering's compositions record form in motion, the limiting conditions he places on his writing must, according to this definition, be seen as structural. Movement occurs within a well-defined frame of reference. Bowering thus gives his serial poems a structural skeleton, but he also shows how the individual parts can dance.

Bowering's theory of art has interesting consequences for the photographs in *Autobiology*. If "Bowering's work is restless," as Blaser asserts, then how does one explain the presence of an art form that is not inherently cubist or abstract?[95] Bowering agrees with Ondaatje's views on photography and places emphasis on the way that snapshots evoke transience. Bowering does not consider art an act of touching up the blemishes and stains of experience, and photography exhibits the immediacy he seeks. For Bowering, snapshots suggest the ephemeral and absent more than the eternal and present. Thus, in chapter 9 of *Autobiology*, a photograph substitutes for a memory instead of preserving one: "My aunt Dorothy died when I was a baby so I saw her but mainly in the photograph."[96] In chapter 11, Bowering recalls a photograph for what it does not depict: "There is a picture of me wearing a large black hobo hat in the front yard. I am wearing it with no smile on my face & big round eyes. I am not carrying it upside down."[97] In chapter 37, Bowering turns a photograph into the negative of memory: "In the photograph of the group I am the only one without a smile with closed mouth an hour before I fainted & I cant remember the pain. That is the reason for fainting."[98] In chapter 7, Bowering even questions photography's ability to capture the present moment by underscoring the complexity of the instant caught by the shutter: "I took [Pearl's] photograph & was careful with the f-stop, aiming the camera to catch the present forever. Now the photograph is a reminder of my past but I look forward every time for the present."[99] This statement is even more complex in the lineated version, where a line break registers the final word as "pre- / sent" and implies that the present exists as a fragment of the past that Bowering looks forward to in the future.[100] In his habitually contradictory way, Bowering thus demonstrates that photography is and is not an agent of the eternal.

Perhaps this doubleness is what Bowering aims to capture by juxtaposing the mother and child photograph on the cover of *Autobiology* with a hand-drawn outline of its silhouette on the title page.[101] Kröller observes that the silhouette "is both an abstraction of the potentially sentimental photograph and an elaborate enactment of the entry into the 'composition' and the 'code' with which the book is concerned."[102] Pictorially, the silhouette enacts the iconography of madonna and child. In the text, however, "The Code" is the title of chapter 17 and refers to the Steinian mantra, "Consciousness is how it is composed," which Bowering repeats in *Autobiology*, *A Short Sad Book*, and *Harry's Fragments*.[103] Just as the position of the cover photographs implies the transmission of genetic code from mother to granddaughter, Bowering's compositional technique implies the continuation of Stein's literary code. Following Stein in her rejection of the subconscious, Bowering humorously interjects, "I may be romantic but I am no dream," in both *Autobiology* and *A Short Sad Book*.[104] However, genetic and literary codes do not pass onto the next generation unmodified. Codes, like skeletons, are not inviolable, and both chapters 8 and 20 of *Autobiology* thus bear the title "The Breaks," while chapter 47 shares Cohen's fascination with "The Scars." Structures decompose over time and the "code is broken article by article, as teeth are, as confidence is, & once it was triumphant to break the mystery but now it is sad because one loses confidence."[105] Five years after *Autobiology*, Stein's *A Long Gay Book* becomes Bowering's *A Short Sad Book*, but the latter's unmaking of Canadians is a far cry from the former's *The Making of Americans*.[106] Bowering summarizes this (de)composing process with an aphorism: "It is not so much composing as the imposing & breaking the code to break the imposing."[107] This aphorism eloquently expresses what I have been calling (un)framing.

Because Bowering adopts the Heraclitean idea that life is flux, he perceives composition and decomposition as two parts of the same process, as he acknowledges in *Allophanes*:

> When you've finisht with them words
> throw the skins on the compost, will ya?
>
> That is composition,
> autobiologist.[108]

In *Autobiology*, Bowering identifies the body as "the basis for composition," but he also recognizes that the body decomposes: "The body of the work gets tired as the body gets tired & that is your own biology & it is not disaster."[109] This decomposing process can be clearly seen in the conclusion to *Autobiology*, where the poet defies closure by joining his narrative to the Heraclitean stream: "I am in the middle of a stream & my body is the stream & what is the boat. The body is not muddy it is mostly water & so was my mother, she was the first stream the primal stream I floated out on to the land I landed on making a bit of mud with my water."[110] For all its photographic imagery and stylized syntax, Bowering's text is finally dispersive. The reader "sees nothing ending" as Bowering's autobiology extends beyond his own body, through amniotic fluid to his mother and through semen to his daughter. The narrative also goes beyond these gestative and seminal metaphors to incorporate feces and urine because, in an ever-changing universe, even birth is accompanied by decomposition. Such refuse is a substance of creation, and although Bowering rejects the lyric as an old habit, the conclusion of his autobiological novel alludes to his origins as a lyric poet publishing in *Tish*. Bowering's creative process thus recycles his lyrical "mud" and transforms it into the clay of his autobiological Genesis.

The processes of recirculation also shape the works that follow *Autobiology*. In 1973 Bowering published *Curious*, a series of literary and photographic portraits of authors (from Olson to bissett) who had influenced his development as a poet. While Bowering continues to use Stein's portraits as his stylistic model in this collection, many of the poems alter the Steinian voice by responding to the literary style of their subject – by, for example, satirizing the braggadocio of Irving Layton. This diversification of Bowering's voice reflects his renewed curiosity about other writing styles: "*Autobiology* tends to be the same form of prose in every place, whereas this one [*Curious*] plays around. It goes into what could be verse, other times it's straight prose, and other times a mixture, but it takes certain key phrases that were still running through my head when I was writing *Autobiology* and they show up somewhere in *Curious*."[111] Thus, literary echoes create a feed-back loop in *Curious* that distorts the Steinian voice.

At the same time, although Bowering maintains that *Autobiology* is poetry, he claims that it "was [his] way back into writing fiction, this book, which really got going again in *A Short Sad Book*."[112] The serial form of *Autobiology* thus lays the groundwork for *Curious* and *A Short Sad Book*, as Bowering explains in the Bayard/David interview: "So in *Autobiology*, I began to understand, after a while, that the subject of that was, as the title suggests, things that happened to me biologically that changed my head around ... And the one I'm working on now [*A Short Sad Book*] is a book about taking that form and turning it into what I now call a novel."[113] However, in order to determine what sort of novel interests Bowering in this period, it would be useful to examine an essay in which he articulates his formal concerns in the 1970s.

POST-REALIST FICTION

Bowering published "The Painted Window: Notes on Post-Realist Fiction" in 1978, but the essay begins by discussing a quotation that he claims to have been pondering for nearly a decade. The citation comes from John Hawkes, a leading figure of American postmodernism in the 1970s: "My novels are not highly plotted, but certainly they're elaborately structured. I began to write fiction on the assumption that the true enemies of the novel were plot, character, setting, and theme, and having once abandoned these familiar ways of thinking about fiction, totality of vision or structure was really all that remained ... Related or corresponding event, recurring image and recurring action, these constitute the essential substance or meaningful density of my writing."[114] Bowering maintains that "the whole quotation from Hawkes illustrates a major shift in attention," and he illustrates this shift through an architectural metaphor: "Whereas the realist had seen his writing as a window, the post-realist presents something opaque. Notice that Hawkes spoke of meaningful density, where a realist might have striven for clarity."[115] Rejecting the ideal of transparency in the realist novel, Bowering elsewhere insists that "the art in fiction, as in poetry, is that part of language that is not communication."[116] Bowering paints over the realist window that Cohen and Ondaatje chose to smash.

Bowering pursues this analogy further by drawing connections between literature and the fine arts:

> The representational painting whose condition as serious art Henry James claimed for fiction, would begin to disappear from the scene during his lifetime. By the first decade of the twentieth century western art had insisted that it be looked upon as paint & collage materials, not as window-like reference to the real world.
>
> Even after poetry had been captured by the printers & referred to as one of the writing arts, poetry always had that distinction from prose, that one should be reminded continuously of its construction.[117]

Searching for an example of a novel that shares the formal concerns of twentieth-century painting and poetry, Bowering chooses Hawkes's *The Beetle Leg*, because the "time in the book is not sequential & linear, but repetitive":

> The imagery is not explanative but eruptive, connected by visual rime rather than realist representation. The characters act not according to how they treat each other, but metaphorically, as in a fable.
>
> In other words, Hawkes demands for his fiction what readers have earlier in this century accorded to poems by T.S. Eliot & Ezra Pound.[118]

The mention of Eliot, Pound, and fables gestures toward the mythic and underscores the distance that Bowering has come from the naturalistic technique he used at the outset of his career.

In this mythic context, it is fitting that the only Canadian examples of post-realist fiction that Bowering cites are Sheila Watson's *The Double*

Hook, bp Nichol's comic strips, and Ondaatje's *Coming Through Slaughter*.[119] The shift in attention that Bowering discusses in the "The Painted Window" is akin to the "great change in what 'structure' is in a poem or in a novel" that Ondaatje mentions in the passage that prefaces my third chapter. Both authors maintain that the change is architectural, but Bowering's essay opposes the spatial arts of sculpture and architecture to the temporal arts of music and cinema, a distinction that Ondaatje does not make.[120] Although Bowering does not cite Joseph Frank (see chapter 1), he essentially follows Frank's argument for spatial form by insisting that "space, & the inter-relationships of smaller spaces, is the ordering principle" informing post-realist fiction.[121] He also divides space from time, but this segregation does not hold up even for the duration of his essay. At the conclusion of "The Painted Window," Bowering's emphasis on spatial technique transforms into an endorsement of oral performance and ritualized time: "If the reader is directed now to the surface it is to a verbal surface, a linguistically interesting surface. So, far from being a window on a world, today's fiction is a voice in one's ear, & at the best of times a whisper on one's lips. One is advised to read a lot of the new novels aloud. In that way one is engaged as one's ancestors may have been, in a ritualized narrative."[122] As this fusion of the visual/spatial and the aural/temporal is more consistent with the rest of Bowering's writings than his earlier assertion, I can only surmise that Bowering wants to stress the ritualistic properties he admires in painting and poetry, as well as the self-reflexive construction of books such as *Coming Through Slaughter*.

Many of the ideas that Bowering outlines in "The Painted Window" are put into practice in *A Short Sad Book*. Part detective story, part poetry, and part literary criticism, Blaser observes that *A Short Sad Book* is "without innocence or realism of plot, character and action. Thus, it enters concernedly the long modern meditation on anti-forms – the anti-novel and anti-poem – which by a paradox becomes a renewal of form in consciousness."[123] Bowering reminds his reader continuously of the constructedness of his novel, even as he writes against his conception of what the novel is.

Unlike Ondaatje, however, Bowering focuses specifically on the Canadian novel in *A Short Sad Book* and he associates it with realism:

It is all around us, writing that makes it appear as if it is there. That is writing about or writing of or what is it it is writing as if it is there. The reader loves Canadian literature because he can just about see it it is as if it is there.
But if you hear it you have the right to speak.

In the best writing it is there.
In the best writing it is there & now it is not it it is writing.
If you are lucky you are reading writing.[124]

Although early Canadian literature is more romantic than realist, Bowering is addressing canonical works such as Hugh MacLennan's *Two Solitudes* (1945), as well as the work of certain eastern peers. Atwood's novel *Surfacing* (1972) and her book of criticism *Survival* (1972) are his most visible targets, and thus he mocks the conclusion of the former:

Put it another way, [writing] is not a clear lake with a body on the bottom.
It is a body & who needs a lake.
This is the real body of literature.[125]

However, even in his polemical mode, Bowering admits that realist prose is not merely an eastern phenomenon. As I mentioned in chapter 3, in regard to Bowering's attempts to read the development of Canadian literature through Ondaatje's writing, it is clear that in his criticisms of his peers Bowering is, at least in part, talking about his own career. Bowering also implicates the realist qualities of his first published novel in *A Short Sad Book*: "It is so easy to write something & make it appear as if it is there. We all like to read about something as if it is there. This is not writing it is thinking, I mean this, yes a mirror on the floor."[126] In this way, Bowering paints over the realist mirror that Andrea had covered in *The Mirror on the Floor*.

However, by arguing that the "real body of literature" is an extension of the larger literary corpus (which is predominantly myth and poetry), Bowering comes close to the position of Northrop Frye, one of the pillars of the eastern Canadian literary culture that he had set out to topple. Bowering seems to refer to the mythopoeic poets (MacEwen, Macpherson, early Atwood) and the Contact Press poets when he observes that critics "have been pretending that there is a succession in Canadian literature. One of them said there are two main lines in Canadian poetry & I noticed that I'm not in either. This is happening around the Great Lakes & down the St Lawrence River, the same place Canadian history happened."[127] To counteract this exclusion, Bowering deconstructs a number of national myths and sacrifices the sacred cows cherished by his friends, publishers, and critics. He claims to be trying "to turn this short story into a roman-à-clef," but he barely manages to disguise the characters by using their first names and caricaturing them.[128] He turns the poet "Al" (Purdy) into a detective hunting for the killer of "Tom Thomson" (whose name he spells two ways), while arguing that "Canadian literature is a lot like a bank. It has Group of Seven paintings all over the wall & it is always lockt up at night."[129] From chapter 6 onward, he makes frequent reference to "Peggy" (Atwood) and in one infamous passage he has Sir John A. Macdonald and Longfellow's Evangeline (who has returned from Acadian Louisiana) convert the psychological "victim positions" from *Survival* into sexual positions.[130] The concluding scene in *A Short Sad Book* also features the writer conversing with the vision of Evangeline, who, before departing for "the paradise [she] ha[s] found in women's heaven," first lectures the writer on Frygian theories of myth:[131]

Myth is a truth of repetitive time. It is a blot that bleeds thru all time.
    I bowed my head beneath her point. You are right, I said. This has all been a waste of time.[132]

Satirical to the end, Bowering nonetheless acknowledges the value of myths as long as they do not automatically exclude westerners. His unframing of national myths leads to a renewal and enlargement of these myths, not to their dismissal.

    Indeed, for the most part, Bowering treats history, even recent history, as myth in his novels. In his 1984 essay "A Great Northward Darkness: The Attack on History in Recent Canadian Fiction," he situates the Canadian debate over history and myth (see my discussion of Stephen Henighan in chapter 7) in an international context: "Novelists who believe that history is a force or a law tend toward realism and naturalism – Zola, Dreiser, Hugh MacLennan. They believe that history speaks and teaches. Fiction writers who believe that history is someone's act of narrative tend toward myth and invention – Conrad, Borges, Robert Kroetsch. History comes from an old European word meaning possession of knowledge. Fiction comes from an old European word meaning the act of shaping. Our artists and critics are engaged in a dispute regarding which comes first."[133]

    Bowering deploys an idea of myth different from that of Northrop Frye. He follows Olson in defining myth as a performance, rather than a narrative structure: "The word 'myth' gets tossed around a lot, by people who may have forgotten for a while that it comes to us from Greek *muthos*, meaning mouth and speech, and is related to Old Slavic *mudh*, meaning to think imaginatively, and even Lithuanian *mausti*, to yearn for, to desire. Myth is not a story about desire (for salvation, e.g.), but is the expression, the body of desire itself. The desire of the author is in the text itself, and if it is to mean anything, the reader too must experience his own."[134] Although Bowering uses archetypal figures such as the trickster, he does not accept narrative templates as given, but rather foregrounds the imaginative part of the shaping process. Instead of relating certain knowledge about a person or event, Bowering maintains that "if you dont understand the story you better tell it," a phrase that becomes an epigraph to Marlatt's *What Matters*.[135] He considers storytelling a creative act of shaping and cites Paul Ricoeur's definition of narrative as the act of "extract[ing] a configuration from a succession."[136] Of course, Ricoeur argues that all narrative, including realist narrative, configures time. Bowering does not deny this fact, but he criticizes realists for disguising their hand in the configuring process. His critique is rather ineffectual when applied to the latter half of Atwood's *Surfacing*, which departs from any sense of the quotidian and foregrounds the mythic configuration – life (journey), death (descent into the underworld), rebirth (surfacing) – of the narrative. However, despite the gerund of the title, Bowering would likely reject Atwood's use of myth in *Surfacing* because she does not call enough attention to her role in shaping it.

To underscore the constructedness of history and myth in *A Short Sad Book*, Bowering foregrounds the presence of the writer writing and makes his literary persona part of the story:

> Canada is the country in which writing about history is history.
> Let me try again.
> I meant to say that Canada is the country in which writing history is history.
> In some countries killing natives is history & some countries killing kings is history but in Canada writing history is history.
> Every historian writing history knows this.
> Every historian is aware of this, he is at his desk writing history & he is the history of Canada. He is the history of Canada in many volumes.[137]

This passage foregrounds both the strengths and weaknesses of Bowering's ludic style. On the one hand, his wordplay illustrates the constructedness of history by focusing attention on minute differences in the construction of the first and third sentences. On the other hand, in making his point, Bowering insinuates that the killing of natives is not history because "He" – the white, male historian – chooses not to write about it in his "Tercentenary History of Canada" in many volumes.[138] This omission does not mean that Bowering is indifferent to the historical sufferings of native Canadians. Indeed, the execution of the Métis McLean gang and the situation of natives in the B.C. Interior in the late nineteenth century is the subject of his historical novel, *Shoot!* (1994). However, Bowering likes to overstate the formal positions he holds at a given moment and in so doing he minimizes some enduring social conflicts.

Having foregrounded the capriciousness of the writer and of language in *A Short Sad Book*, Bowering demands that readers acknowledge their own role in shaping the story:

> Shove over, I want to talk to the reader. I want to say something to the reader reading. Reader reading, dont imagine any more that you can put on your invisibility suit & watch what [the characters] are doing ...
>
> Either admit that what I report of the matter is the truth of the matter or face the truth, that if you can see them they can see you. Literature is not a one-way mirror ... Writing is not transparent writing is not a window people dont live in three-sided houses like a play by Arthur Miller.[139]

To prevent his audience from feigning passivity, Bowering filters *A Short Sad Book* through two introductory frameworks that emphasize the readers' role in the construction of the text. The first such framework is an epigraph from Alain Robbe-Grillet: "Under our gaze, the simple gesture of holding out our hand becomes bizarre, clumsy; the words we hear ourselves speaking suddenly sound false; the time of our minds is no longer that of the clocks; & the style of a novel, in its turn, can no longer be innocent."[140] Bowering then addresses the active reader in an author's note that follows the epigraph. This framework offers some tips for reading that turn the reading process into a scavenger hunt:

> Dear Reader Reading:
> 1. Please take your time.
> 2. Also there is one dream in the following pages. You should be able to find it.[141]

Bowering thus invites the reader to play detective. However, this detective story has as much to do with the crimes of the author as with the crimes of the characters.

There are multiple dreams in *A Short Sad Book*: the national dream of Macdonald's railroad, the final vision of Evangeline, the "curious dream"

from which the author awakes to declare "I love this country," and so
on.[142] Like *the man with seven toes*, *A Short Sad Book* presents history as a
kind of dream, except that Bowering calls attention to the way in which he
consciously invents it. The Purdy detective story and the Evangeline-
Macdonald romance supply two sketchy plot lines, but the actual writing
of the book is a story within the story. Chapter 1 begins by introducing the
writer's romance with the *roman* and establishing a phrase that recurs
throughout the novel: "I was going to write a book about love, & one time
I woke up & said I love this country."[143] Bowering immediately qualifies
this opening statement: "I love this country, I didnt then, thirty years
ago."[144] Baiting the critics who have publicly questioned his love of country, Bowering describes his youthful enthusiasm for the United States:

> When I grew up I was going to be an American boy. I loved that coun-
> try. That was human nature not my mind.
>   I didnt say hello to my mind till I came back to Vancouver from the
> east fifteen years later.[145]

In the ensuing chapters, Bowering periodically names the reasons for this
enthusiasm, but he explains his preferences in the present tense, giving the
impression that his mind has not changed:

> Let me introduce myself.
>   I am eight years old & my name is George Bowering & I will change
> that & the name of my country when I grow up.
>   I will shoot the guns out of their hands the way all us Americans
> do.[146]

The autobiographical dimension of the novel thus splits into an older persona and a younger one, as it did in *Autobiology*. Bowering accentuates this
duality by allowing repetition to generate difference: "I love the country, I
didnt thirty years ago but am I I."[147] Kröller demonstrates that this sentence problematizes the continuity of the lyric "I" because "the first-person
pronoun suddenly looks like the Roman numeral for the number 'two.'"[148]
Only two pages earlier, Bowering had rejected the "I" altogether: "To hell
with the first person he was definitely he."[149] Furthermore, according to
the index, George Bowering is an individual who appears on pages 16,
101–3, 108, and 126, while "Wunder, George" is a person who emerges
from the interjection:

No Wunder.
I'm probably not hiding anything from you at all.[150]

George Delsing and George Vancouver also make appearances in *A Short Sad Book*, as they will in *Burning Water*. By serializing pronouns, pseudonyms, and namesakes in this way, Bowering invites readers to read the self through multiple frames of reference and thereby creates the ambiguity he cherishes.

In "Part Four: The Black Mountain Influence," however, Bowering is unambiguous about his antagonism toward critics such as Richardson and Mathews who villainized him as a traitor. In the same year that *Poetry and the Colonized Mind* accused the *Tish* poets of a "lack of interest in Canadian culture," Bowering was putting the finishing touches on a book "full of Canadian content, it's all about me and Canada."[151] Using *A Short Sad Book* as a vehicle of counter-critique, Bowering gives Robin Mathews a pseudonym and mocks "the Canadian nationalist professor from Ottawa name of Sparrow ... paid by the CIA to give Canadian nationalism a bad name":[152]

> Sparrow said we got to stop them Americans from getting the beautiful Okanagan Valley but he wrote it the way the Americans do in Washington, Okanogan, with an O.
>   It was a dead give away. He went to college in the U.S. That's where he was recruited by the CIA.[153]

As in Atwood's *Surfacing*, where the imperial "Americans" prove to be Canadians, the voice of Canadian nationalism in *A Short Sad Book* ends up espousing the protectionist and monocultural "American" values that it purports to deplore. In contrast, Bowering stands by his record of commitment to Canada as a student and teacher: "I think it is obvious, I love this country. Once I got a grant to spend two years in England but I went to London Ontario instead. Another time I got a grant to spend a year in Austria but I went to Vancouver, British Columbia instead."[154] Although he is an ardent regionalist, few Canadian novelists have written as much about Canada, championed as many new Canadian writers, or dramatized the process of becoming (as opposed to conforming to a definition of) Canadian as Bowering has. As if to dispel the controversy once and for all, Bowering reinvented himself as a popular historian of his province and country, a kind of irascible Pierre Berton, in the 1990s.[155]

However, I make this judgment with the benefit of hindsight, viewing Bowering's literary output over a forty-year period. At first glance, the title and style of *A Short Sad Book* certainly do suggest a colonized imagination. Bowering makes this anxiety part of the story: "& people say why are you doing archaic avant-garde writing. This is warmed over Gertrude Stein there I said her name why are you doing it."[156] Bowering's question is rhetorical, but a brief consideration of *A Long Gay Book* suggests at least one answer.

Stein finished *A Long Gay Book* in 1913, but it was not published until 1933, when it appeared in GMP, a collection that included two other early Stein works, GMP (*Gertrude Stein, Matisse, and Picasso*) and *Many Many Women*. The long prose piece begins with a discussion of why people procreate. At a certain age, Stein argues, people "lose their everlasting feeling" and counteract this sense of mortality by having babies.[157] However, on a vacation in Spain in 1912, Stein fell in love with Alice Toklas, committed herself to a lifelong lesbian relationship, and rejected the vocation of motherhood for herself. Instead, she, as writer, partakes of the "everlasting" by developing a new way of seeing that is intimately related to the art of Picasso and Matisse (dubbed Paul and Claudel in *A Long Gay Book*).[158] Ulla Dydo explains that, the last third of *A Long Gay Book*, in particular, responds to the radical reorientation of the planar surface in the paintings of Picasso and Matisse: "[It] confronts a world of magnificent, joyous chaos where no connections are given, no relations taken for granted, and everything is perceived anew every day in all its heterogeneity. There is no need for a totalizing system to explain the world."[159] Examining the impact of these disruptive techniques on Bowering's writing, Blaser notes that *A Long Gay Book* is "fundamental to an understanding of [Stein's] 'incongruous' and 'discontinuous' method. It was to be about her sexuality, that is to say, about her identity. It is a record of the famous change of style that leads to the later work."[160] Bowering's interest in these changes offer clues to his own development.

Autobiology echoes, but does not parallel, the first part of *A Long Gay Book* – that is, Bowering embraces fatherhood. The series of portraits in the middle of *A Long Gay Book* sets a precedent for the portraits of poets in *Curious*. The "world of magnificent, joyous chaos" in the latter half of *A Long Gay Book*, finally, presages the outrageous and digressive narrative in *A Short Sad Book*. Taken together, *Autobiology*, *Curious*, and *A Short Sad Book* record two important changes of style that affect Bowering's later work: the development of the serial novel and the use of large-scale parody.

Just as Williams and Stein adopted the grammar of French painting to develop their "American" poetics, Bowering borrows from Stein's cubist syntax to deconstruct a Canadian literary tradition he considers Eurocentric and biased toward realism and the east. He develops a form of syntax that dispels the realist illusion of the mirror image, yet he breaks this imposed code through parody, both in Linda Hutcheon's sense of repetition with a difference and in the popular sense of satire.[161] For example, *A Short Sad Book* is longer than *A Long Gay Book*. It is also decidedly heterosexual and much more lighthearted than Stein's work. Bowering is reluctant to situate the sexual politics of his novel, but the inversion is plainly a consequence of his parodic technique.[162] Parody demands inversion, as Bowering explains in a discussion of his novel *Caprice* (1987), a western featuring a woman poet-outlaw: "In order to create a Canadian western you have had to do something that was not an American western. I had to have all the signs of an American western but there had to be irony – you had to turn them upside down. Put it this way: you had to have (a) sign and (b) difference."[163] In *A Short Sad Book* the American signs are in the chapter titles: "The Exile of Evangeline," "The Black Mountain Influence," and "The Pretty Good Canadian Novel" (a reference to Williams's *Great American Novel*). Bowering articulates the differences in the body of the chapters: Evangeline returns to Canada and falls in love; Al Purdy determines that the Black Mountain Influence did not kill Tom Thomson or Canadian literature; the Canadian novel shirks the modernist demand for all-encompassing greatness and gets published by a small independent press run by "Stan" (Bevington of Coach House Press), an Edmonton Doukhobor turned Toronto avantgardist. Thus, Bowering breaks the American codes he invokes and the disruption of these continental connections energizes the narrative.

(Un)framing also occurs at the syntactic level in these pieces. Like Picasso, Stein rejected most realist conventions with the aim of developing a unique style. In this endeavour she was so successful that, given only a few lines of *Autobiology*, one can immediately identify Stein's trademark voice. However, over the course of his trilogy, Bowering gradually moves beyond the Steinian echoes and explores new avenues in his style. Whereas Stein rarely modulates her tone in *A Long Gay Book*, Bowering experiments with a variety of tones: academic, satiric, burlesque, hard-boiled, lyrical, and so on. This mixture of tones corresponds to Bowering's mix of genres in *A Short Sad Book*. Whereas *A Long Gay Book* is a long prose poem composed of portraits interspersed with wordplay – a technique of lyrical narrative know as "arabesque" – *A Short Sad Book* is a serial novel that dabbles in the essay, satire, romance, detective story, lyric, and other forms. Bowering continues to employ Stein's looping patterns of repetition, but he does not use repetition to produce mind-wandering monotony as much as Stein does. Stein takes a set of words and repeats them in all their possible syntactic combinations before moving on to the next set, while Bowering maintains an equilibrium between narrative progression and digression. He follows Stein in playing with syntax but he does not entirely derail the narrative. Thus he initiates "the untying / that frees the mind" by diversifying Stein's medium.[164] Stein is still a presence in *A Short Sad Book*, but as an echo within a chorus of echoes.

Bowering's diversified approach is partly due to the influence of Greg Curnoe, to whom Bowering dedicates the poetry collections *Layers* and *Another Mouth*. Kröller observes in her chapter on Bowering and "The London Scene" that *A Short Sad Book* "is ostentatiously connected to Curnoe's convictions," which she characterizes as eclectic and "aggressively local": "he refuses to show his work in New York ... he is co-founder of the Association for the Documentation of Neglected Aspects of Culture in Canada, and he objected to the University of Western Ontario's acquisition of manuscripts by Milton for a quarter of a million dollars, while the historic core of Curnoe's home town was in danger of being replaced by parking lots and office buildings."[165] Although Bowering spent only a year in London, he claims that he learned "a lot about art from Greg Curnoe" while living in the east.[166] For example, Bowering's Montreal poem "No Solitudes" credits Curnoe with teaching him to see in a cubist fashion, which is ironic given Curnoe's rejection of Picasso as a figurehead of cultural imperialism, as well as Stein's quest for a new way of seeing.[167] Kröller notes that Curnoe also created the collage *Bowering Westmount No. 4* "after a visit to Expo '67" in which "Curnoe stayed in the Bowerings' Montreal apartment, [and] collect[ed] trivia picked up on the site of the exhibition, much as Kiyooka's series *StoneDgloves* recorded workers' gloves trampled underfoot at the World Fair in Osaka."[168] During this visit Bowering helped Curnoe install a mural for Expo at Montreal's Dorval airport. Authorities eventually ordered Curnoe to take down this mural because critics read it as an anti-Vietnam War statement. It featured a figure resembling President Johnson, a quotation from Mohammed Ali, and a fighter plane, despite commission guidelines prohibiting the depiction of airplanes. Curnoe installed the mural alongside an escalator, implying that the viewers themselves were caught up in the machinery of war.[169] Furthermore, Curnoe pasted pictures of his family and friends (including painters Jack Chambers and Tony Urquhart) into the composition so as to underscore the personal impact of a public war.[170] This is a theme that Bowering takes up in *At War with the U.S.*, to which Curnoe contributed the cover illustration.

The cover of *A Short Sad Book* also features a drawing by Curnoe. It depicts Okanagan MLA and British Columbia premier W.A.C. Bennett reading Bowering's novel and laughing heartily. The portrait is a caricature, of course, and it establishes the tone for the novel. Formally, however, the book "resembles Curnoe's mixed media approach and presents a series of possible openings and endings, offers a random selection of styles, and tries out various genres."[171] Just as Bowering responds to "Greg Curnoe's serigraph" in the poem "Uncle Louis,"[172] he writes *A Short Sad Book* using the techniques of muralism that he learned from Curnoe: "I was trying to get the sense of spreading the whole thing out on one big flat surface and then you might see something in the top right-hand corner that connects with something down at the bottom left-hand corner ironically or simply in order to rhyme with it."[173] Given the linear direction of reading and the limitations of the conventional page, however, Bowering cannot present the novel as an image that can be viewed at a glance and then analysed in detail. Instead, he creates a mural of sorts by linking one fragment with another in a serial fashion and emphasizing the interrelations of each unit.

Blaser notes the serial architectonics of *A Short Sad Book* in his introduction to *Particular Accidents*, where he explains why he chooses to include sections of *Autobiology* and *A Short Sad Book* in his selection of Bowering's poems: "*Autobiology* and *A Short Sad Book* appear to be prose. They are, however, anti-prosaic and are written against the unconsciousness or innocence of ordinary prose. The style of them – and style is a great pleasure in this work, presenting a distance moved in the depth of the language and a freed verbal imagination – stands in extreme contrast to the 'straight' prose of Bowering's novel, *Mirror on the Floor* (1967) and the short stories in *Flycatcher* (1974). Both *Autobiology* and *A Short Sad Book* have to do with transformations of self and place into imaginative structures, which derive from the discovery poem, *George, Vancouver*. For these reasons, I have considered them poems in prose."[174]

In fact, the interrogation of genre in *A Short Sad Book* is much more extensive than the prose/verse question in *Autobiology*. The first section of *A Short Sad Book*, "Canadian Geography," follows Stein in connecting New World geography to a non-Aristotelean style of narrative: "What do you mean, this is no novel. / Novels have a beginning a middle & an end. But scenery doesnt."[175] Having complicated the passive role of setting in the novel, Bowering satirizes the pose of the objective narrator: "This is getting so personal, it has to be a short story, novels arent that personal."[176] Continuing to blur genre boundaries, Bowering places the power struggle between the author and language under scrutiny:

(I mean I said it was a novel but did it say it was a novel. & if it didnt say so it can hardly be a novel because then it would have been something else calling itself a novel & I would have disagreed.)

It may get to be a short sad book.[177]

In place of block paragraphs of prose, the single-line paragraphs that emphasize the important passages in *A Short Sad Book* suggest that "this is poem containing history, not a bloody romance."[178]

In addition to the visual clues that suggest poetry, Bowering attributes the liberties he takes with historical fact to poetic licence:

He sat at his desk & wrote history. What he wrote was George Bowering sat at his desk writing history. He didnt make the mistake, so something is playing games with history here.

Maybe it is poetry.[179]

Bowering gives rein to this power struggle, much as Ondaatje let Billy (poetry) and Garrett (prose) have their shoot out. Bowering asserts that "history is filled with mistakes & most of them are written by poetry. The novel can only sit back & try to understand."[180] Yet Bowering stresses that this dynamic is a struggle between the push and pull of genre, as much as between authorial will and narrative whimsy:

A poet is not a dealer in a card game. Not even a poet writing a novel.

They all do in this country.[181]

The designation "novel" persists in the story, but these meditations on the poetic dimensions of the novel clearly redefine the term.

Finally, in the opening section of "The Pretty Good Canadian Novel," Bowering declares unequivocally: "This is a serial novel."[182] The declaration comes as a surprise, but in fact Bowering has prepared the reader for it all along. In chapter 1, he announces that he "was going to write a curious book about love," and although he implies that he is writing something different from *Curious*, he establishes a theme that he later repeats: "I woke up out of a curious dream & said I love this country."[183] The allusions to the preceding serial poem are made explicit in the middle of chapter 49 when Bowering interjects in the third person: "Forty-nine, he thought, this is longer than Autobiology or Curious," which both have forty-eight chapters.[184] The similar style and structure of these three works is not coincidental. In a letter to Dennis Lee dated 16 June 1971, Bowering states that

Autobiology is "the first book in a (at least) 3 book work."[185] Thus *Autobiology* narrates Bowering's growth in its biological and familial context, while *Curious* builds on this narrative base by tracing Bowering's growth as a poet through more experimental portraits of writers who have influenced him. *A Short Sad Book* combines these two modes by intermingling prosaic paragraphs and poetic stanzas, and by situating Bowering in his national context. In case readers have not followed this development closely enough to recognize the pattern, Bowering states baldly: "You learn it in writing poetry you tell it in writing prose."[186] It is therefore possible to consider each book in Bowering's trilogy as an installment of a larger serial novel, particularly when one takes into consideration the structure and publication history of Stein's *A Long Gay Book*.

There are also more oblique and humorous references to serial forms in *A Short Sad Book*. As in the section "Cereals for Roughage" in *The Catch* (1976), Bowering puns on the phonetic similarity of serial and cereal by making "Flacons de blé!" Louis Riel's battle cry in *A Short Sad Book* – a nod to the bilingual packaging laws of the Trudeau era.[187] The pun recurs in Bowering's discussion of a computer:

> The small electronic box works in series. It is a serial box. That is how literature works, I mean that, not seeming to put that in front of your eyes but putting this next to your ear.
> It's in speaking that ideas come to us.[188]

Bowering is in phonocentric mode here, but in *A Magpie Life* he claims to have been influenced by a different kind of serial box: "An earlier invention of mine was the shoebox theatre: I would get a few months' worth of some comic strip such as 'Steve Canyon,' and glue them end to end, and make a reel to crank through a slot at one end of a shoebox. There would be a skylight right over the strip and a peephole at the other end of the shoebox. Most of the movies I saw when I was in grade three were showing in my shoebox theatre."[189] These two examples underscore the segmented quality of Bowering's serial technique, as well as echoing Cohen's obsession with Blue Beetle comics in *Beautiful Losers* and Ondaatje's admiration for Muybridge.

I propose, then, that the serial novel is Bowering's new answer to Olson's old question in "Projective Verse" of how to construct the poem as an energy discharge. In this 1950 essay, which greatly influenced Bowering's early poetics, Olson discusses ways of constructing "the sentence as first act of nature, as lightning, as passage of force from subject to object, quick, in

the case ... in every case, from me to you, the VERB, between two nouns."[190]
Olson places particular emphasis on the spatiality of modern poetry as he
proposes that "the poem itself must, at all points, be a high energy-con-
struct and, at all points, an energy-discharge."[191] In trying to sustain this
energy and keep objects in "their proper confusions," Olson runs up,
"immediately, bang, against tenses, in fact against syntax, in fact against
grammar generally, that is, as we have inherited it. Do not tenses, must they
not also be kicked around anew, in order that time, that other governing
absolute may be kept, as must the space-tensions of a poem, immediate,
contemporary to the acting-on-you of the poem?"[192] The energy of Olson's
prose in this essay (which also influences Marlatt's prose style in *Zócalo*
and *Ana Historic*) derives from its peculiar syntax. Olson uses commas to
fragment the sentence and facilitate sudden shifts in tense by juxtaposing
phrases in space. These shifts create tension by accelerating and then interrupting the "passage of force from subject to object," as well as building
anaphoric rhythms. In his poetry, Olson attempts to shape poems that
mimic the "inertial structure of the world," and Bowering's early poetry
follows Olson's lead in this regard.[193] However, in *Autobiology, Curious*,
and *A Short Sad Book*, Bowering abandons Olson's nebulous concept of
energy structures in favour of a more concrete engagement with established
forms of myth and syntax. In so doing, Bowering responds to the style of
"Projective Verse," but does not necessarily adhere to the principles outlined in it.

Bowering's work from *Autobiology* onward is less concerned with
proprioceptive principles, although in *A Short Sad Book* Bowering mischievously equates Olson with Van Horne, the American who engineered the
Canadian Pacific Railway and helped to bring British Columbia into Confederation.[194] Until (at least) *Kerrisdale Elegies* (1984), Bowering turns his
attention to serial forms that (un)frame other literary models. Trent
Keough observes that in "the years 1968–69 Bowering became intrigued
with the possibility that his interest in the writer's relationship with physical place could be exchanged or translated into an exploration of the metaphorical space constructed by language."[195] Bowering generates the energy
he seeks by disrupting syntactic patterns, defying genre conventions, and
playing on the tensions of parody, in which one reads both the original text
and the adaptation.

Although I have traced, in a chronological fashion, Bowering's evolution
from lyric poet to novelist, it would be misleading to read this movement as
a climactic progression. Bowering's "post-realist" novel is only one in a
series of genre experiments that he performs. In fact, *Burning Water* serves

as a departure point for several other important projects. It begins a trilogy of historical novels set primarily in western Canada that includes *Caprice* and *Harry's Fragments* (which bears the dedication "for Mike Ondaatje in flux").[196] It also leads directly to the long poem *Smoking Mirror* (1982), which is a series of ten lyrical meditations on the metaphor of the smoke-framed mirror. Although the name of the series recalls *Mirror on the Floor,* Bowering states in the title poem: "This moment was brought to me / on the burning water," and titles such as "The water flame" make it plain that the series indulges the impulse to perform lyrical variations on the central metaphor of *Burning Water.* In addition, Kröller observes that the original manuscript version of *Burning Water* included numerous quotations in German from Rilke's *Duino Elegies* and "may be called an *étude* for the *Kerrisdale Elegies.*"[197] It would be a mistake, therefore, to view the serial poems as merely an apprenticeship for the novel, because the novel can equally be read as a study for the later long poems. Rather than a formal perfection – a trademark formula or definitive voice – one sees, in Bowering's writing, recurring symmetries in continual flux. Like the Heraclitean river to which Bowering so often refers, the forms in this continuum evolve, devolve, and spawn new variations – one cannot step into the same river twice. The serial novel is a large vortex in this river that absorbed all the neighbouring whirlpools in the 1970s and released them in new directions.

Many of the directions Bowering takes in his writing are problematic, however. For example, Bowering is fond of a form of humour called "tapinosis," which he defines as "a sneaky kind of rhetoric – it means the saying of very serious things in offhand language, in vernacular, even in slang."[198] Tapinosis works better in a burlesque such as *A Short Sad Book* than it does in a historical fiction such as *Burning Water.* For example, the First and Second Indian in *Burning Water* perform comic functions as they act out romantic stereotypes of the Indian brave and elder. However, they do not alternate between allegorical and realist roles in the way that their counterparts Vancouver and Menzies do. The Indians go without names and are trapped in their allegorical context as mouthpieces for the Romantic worldview. Although Ondaatje praises "Bowering's outrageous version of the explorer George Vancouver – who in his travels is surrounded by Indians who speak like eighteenth-century Englishmen" – the manner in which Bowering's comic tone denies the Native characters the right to tell their stories is often disturbing.[199]

Some critics praise Bowering's flippancy for its antiauthoritarianism,[200] but Glenn Deer observes that his treatment of history does not, finally, undermine its own authority:

Bowering's "heracliteanism" and serendipity-approach to history is rendered problematic by his deliberate focus on certain types of male competition and power conflicts. Bowering's interest in exposing certain types of power conflicts, by targetting the male will-to-power, is teleological, argumentative, and didactic; and this is an interest that fits uncomfortably with the postmodern aesthetics of *ludism*.

Rhetorical scrutiny of *Burning Water* shows how shot through with power this work is, how it really mobilizes a serious critique while posing as ingenuous play. The postmodern rhetoric of liberation and open-endedness here does involve the inscription of new authority and new belief.[201]

Compounding this gender bias is the fact that ludic approaches to writing work best when the author deals with known personages, events, and myths. As I shall demonstrate in the next chapter, this strategy is not necessarily effective for women whose stories have been suppressed. However, Marlatt claims that Bowering's voice and sense of play in his serial novels influenced her own efforts to develop a lyrical prose form. Russell Brown also praises the impact Bowering's lyrical pose has had on his criticism. Brown adds line breaks to some of Bowering's essays and notes their literary complexity: "Providing puns, introducing allusions, turning metaphors, and generally keeping things moving, sometimes in several directions at once, this speaker does have a way with words."[202] Bowering's contribution to Canadian literature as a stylist, critic, and provocateur should not be underestimated.[203]

5

Daphne Marlatt: (Un)framing the Quest Narrative

(f) act. the f stop of act. a still photo in the ongoing cinerama.

Daphne Marlatt[1]

In the ongoing cinerama of Marlatt's poetry and prose, her first book, the long poem *Frames of a Story* (1968), establishes a narrative framework that reappears in her novella *Zócalo* (1977) and her novel *Ana Historic* (1988). These works perform variations on the heterosexual quest narrative that Marlatt finds in the source text for *Frames of a Story*, Hans Christian Andersen's *The Snow Queen* (1884). Taken together, the erotic plots of *Frames of a Story, Zócalo,* and *Ana Historic* map a lesbian quest narrative, departing from a scene of heterosexual dissatisfaction and moving towards one of lesbian fulfillment. Although not strictly autobiographical, these narratives fictionalize Marlatt's own development of a lesbian identity – and her relationships with Alan Marlatt, Roy Kiyooka, and Betsy Warland – in order to critique the sexual roles available to women in traditional quest narratives. Her development of a lesbian identity is full of detours and setbacks, but it evolves toward an ecstatic state that overcomes social constraint and homophobic fear. In order to track Marlatt's efforts to integrate her sexuality and feminist scholarship with "a largely male-mentored postmodernist poetic," I offer some biographical context to Marlatt's works while examining the way she dismantles the heterosexual bias of the quest narrative.[2]

From her beginnings in the *Tish* movement, Marlatt has emerged as one of the leading voices in Canadian women's writing. In "Language Women: Post-anecdotal Writing in Canada" (1987), Bowering celebrates her position at the forefront of "the avant-garde in English Canadian writing" and praises her practice of "feminist difference" in place of "feminist equivalence."[3] However, his enthusiasm for her writing in this essay glosses over the controversy that surrounded Marlatt's work during the *Tish* years. Marlatt was among the "second wave of writers who continued *TISH*" after four of the original editors left Vancouver, but her writing did not entirely meet the standards established by the original group.[4] As Marlatt reminds Bowering in the 1979 interview "Given This Body," she clashed with Frank Davey, who refused to publish some of her early work:

> [Davey] accused me of falling into my imagination & failing to sort of live up to the Williams criteria of literalism, & precision, & accuracy to geography & place.
> GB: He thought you were being sort of smarmy or ...
> DM: ... yeah, romantic.[5]

In the charge of romanticism one also hears the charge of being too effeminate, of writing what Bowering calls in this interview "lady poems."[6] Marlatt retained the more distinctive elements of her writing in spite of the prevailing editorial mandate at *Tish*, but she recalls that her status as a woman within the group initially hampered her literary ambitions: "I wanted to be taken seriously as a poet (o that passive voice!) but was taken more seriously as a woman, the object of a few love poems, one or two about my deficiencies as a 'beauty' – 'belle' in its conventional sense."[7] Marlatt's gender and sexuality were thus inextricably tied to her writing from the start, whether she wanted them to be or not.

However, in order to chart her own literary course, Marlatt's post-*Tish* writings stressed sexual difference, first in terms of gender and later in terms of sexual persuasion. Marlatt's acclaimed long poem *Steveston* (1974) bears a strong resemblance to Olson's *The Maximus Poems* (1960). However, according to Sabrina Reed, "Olson's poetics ... are a result of his equation of the body with freedom, openness, and insight" and, as Marlatt "illustrates in *Steveston*, a woman's experience of her body is not always as optimistic or as open as Olson's."[8] To distinguish herself from her male mentors, therefore, Marlatt focuses on the ways in which language and social relations restrict her speech and bodily freedom, as she tells Bowering: "I have to be in my body. And I have to be in the inarticulate. The inarticulate is ground."[9] Over the years, Marlatt has made it her life's work to fashion an idiom that speaks through her body and articulates "the unsaid, the yet-to-be-spoken, even the unspeakable."[10]

At the same time, Marlatt's own statements on poetics are frequently contradictory – although her poetry is richer for the contradictions. For example, meditating on Creeley's slogan, "form is never more than an extension of content" in a 1968 journal entry, Marlatt embraces open form poetics: "poetics then consists of attention to extension (implication unfolded) – no more the notion of filling up a form – but the *act*, out in the open."[11] Marlatt rejects the notion of poetic form as a pre-cast container here, but elsewhere she stresses her abiding interest in architectonic forms. In 1979 she tells Bowering that she consistently feels a need to "go back to a very early sense of what the poem is, & that [i]s a house that one constructs, with doors & windows & different rooms & perspectives inside it ... But the reader has to be able to move around inside it, & the solidity of that structure is the work of the imagination."[12] Oscillating between her attraction to mythic structure and her desire to allow language to flow uninhibited, Marlatt works to reconcile the linguistic features of open-form poetics – tone leading, metonymy, wordplay – with myths and conceits that give her narratives an overarching structure. Several of Marlatt's early works are open-ended syntactically but structured thematically according to the Kwakiutl myth of the end of the world, in which the ocean descends into a hole in the earth that generates the rebirth of the world.[13] To balance the rival imperatives of structure and improvisation, Marlatt employs a complicated syntax that dismantles the conceits she employs. A typical Marlatt poem such as "Mokelumne Hill" concludes by unframing its own rhetoric: "The whole set, false front, the frame, go up in flames."[14] Marlatt's poetry, says Christina Cole, is "pervaded by images of entrapment and containment," but she undermines this rigidity through wordplay.[15] As in Ondaatje's work, the interplay between the preformed and performed is fundamental to her poetics.

According to Miriam Nichols, Marlatt achieves a balance between structure and indeterminacy through a process poetics in which "form unfolds *behind* the poet as s/he moves through a poem or a life, rather than before her as a thesis to be explicated."[16] However, I am skeptical of the assertion that there is no thesis to be explicated in fiction-theory such as *Ana Historic*, where argument plays a vital role in structuring the text. Nichols observes correctly that in *Ana Historic* "the narrative line is complicated through an excess of connectives, to the point where it begins to change form," but in my view the author's wordplays work these transformations back into the line of argument in a perpetual feedback loop.[17]

On closer inspection, Marlatt's preoccupation with framing reflects a concern for situating subjects and language in a liminal space. Deborah O advocates such positioning because the "lesbian body signifies in space through a defiance of the sexual economy of gender. It does this through a proliferation of gender configurations that lie outside the restrictions of a

compulsory heterosexuality."[18] Marlatt's first book, *Frames of a Story*
(1968), is a fine example of how the author negotiates these different configurations. This book-length poem articulates her burgeoning feminism by
rewriting Hans Christian Andersen's *The Snow Queen* in a lyric voice that
works against the thrust of the heterosexual plot. Like many feminist
authors, Marlatt seeks to reconfigure the power dynamic between girls and
boys in fairytales. However, Marlatt goes beyond balancing power relations in *Frames of a Story* and, at least briefly, derails the heterosexual plot
in favour of a lesbian one. The dense and allusive qualities of Marlatt's lyricism are particularly important to this task because they all but conceal the
lesbian encounter that jeopardizes the telos of heterosexual union in the
fairytale.

FRAMES OF A STORY: RESHAPING THE ROMANTIC PLOT

Andersen tells his tale in a series of seven linked stories, but Marlatt signals
the different outcome of *Frames* by dividing her tale into seven sections and
a preface. The preface to *Frames* rewrites the first section of *The Snow
Queen*, while Andersen's last story, "What Happened in the Snow Queen's
Palace and Afterward," is split into a Snow Queen episode and a very different afterword. Marlatt's preface also summarizes the events of
Andersen's tale in a short synopsis that, like the MacInnes quotation in *the
man with seven toes*, gives provisional form to a plot that is otherwise
difficult to discern:

> Once there was a girl & boy who lived, with their families, in attic
> apartments whose window boxes were full of roses. They were play-
> mates, & often Gerda would go to Kay's place to hear stories his
> grandmother told. One winter she told them about the Snow Queen.
> Soon after, Kay's heart & eye were pierced by slivers from a mirror, so
> that he grew cold towards Gerda, & wanted only to be outdoors racing
> his sled in the square. He would hitch it to big sleighs that went by, &
> one day he never came back.
>   Gerda was lonesome. Finally she decided to leave home & search for
> him.[19]

The rest of Marlatt's preface highlights the major events in Gerda's quest.
The heroine leaves home in search of Kay, is mesmerized by the storytelling
of an old woman, and then escapes. She discovers a prince who "seems sus-
piciously like Kay"; gets kidnapped and almost murdered by robbers;

escapes with the help of a young robber girl who mistakes Gerda for a princess; finds the Snow Queen's palace with the help of two women; discovers
Kay "black with frost & absorbed in his puzzle"; and brings him back to
consciousness through the warmth of her tears.[20] This is the narrative template against which Marlatt works in several of her early narratives, and
hence I examine it in detail below.

A major difference, however, is that in *Frames* Marlatt fails to explain
the origins of the cursed mirror, an omission that effectively razes the outer
framework of *The Snow Queen*. Andersen's prologue explains that the
devil once fashioned "a mirror which had the strange power of being able
to make anything good or beautiful that it reflected appear horrid; and all
that was evil and worthless seem attractive and worth while."[21] When this
mirror was held up to heaven it shattered into more than a billion pieces,
the majority of which lodged like sand in people's eyes. The fantasy element
of Andersen's story thus stems from a dystopian premise. Only Gerda's love
and perseverance can restore the proper appearance of the Good. In
Marlatt's version, on the other hand, the narrator is not so quick to reproduce the Christian allegory of the Fall and the Resurrection that is fundamental to Andersen's story. Instead, Marlatt splinters and fragments her
narrative even further. This splintering distinguishes the early work of
Cohen, Ondaatje, Bowering, Marlatt, and Carson from that of Klein,
Michaels, and Ondaatje after *In the Skin of a Lion*, where greater emphasis
is placed on reconstituting a world that is already shattered. And even
grouped with the former writers, Marlatt interrupts, interrogates, and
explores the dissonance of speech more than any other.[22]

Bowering argues that there are "at least three strands" braided together
in *Frames*: "There's the Snow Queen story of Gerda & Kay; there's
[Marlatt's] personal, or getting to be personal, love story; & [Marlatt's]
growth or fall from a fairytale sense of love to that adult sense of love that
includes the possibility of death. Plus all the contradictions. It is an elaborate structure."[23] The last two strands are really just two ends of the same
thread, as the story initially shifts between sections of lineated poetry,
which sustain Gerda's story, and stanzas of poetic prose, which primarily
relate Marlatt's own. To a certain extent, these two strands alternate, with
Marlatt's prose meta-commentary interrupting the lyrics she fashions out
of Andersen's prose. Thus *Frames* begins with a lyric passage about Gerda
in her room and then Marlatt interrupts: "which names my state of containment (not content –) where doors are lockt ... or more precisely, this
room has none."[24] However, this alternating pattern is full of contradictions, as Bowering observed, and Marlatt weaves the strands together such

that they are often indistinguishable. A merging of characters results from this interweaving, because Marlatt was trying to read herself into – and write herself out of – Gerda's story: "I'd been reading Jung's analysis of fairytales. I was convinced about the reality of myth. I was trying to interpret what the reality of that fairytale [*The Snow Queen*] was for me in terms of my own daily life."[25] The weaving technique that Marlatt develops in *Frames* becomes typical of her narrative writings, and several critics have compared her to another mythic weaver, Penelope.[26] This comparison works well if one considers weaving in its historical context as a pictorial medium developed primarily by women. However, unlike Penelope, Marlatt's women characters work their way out of marital relations with men and embark on their own quests. Thus Marlatt breaks down the distinction between paragraphs and stanzas because, as Bowering points out, "'stanza' comes from a root meaning 'room'" and Marlatt refuses to confine herself to a room whose syntactic and symbolic doors are locked.[27]

Marlatt derails the plot of *The Snow Queen* by inserting her own story into the tale of Gerda and Kay such that the fairytale appears in glimpses, serialized moments of import, as if Marlatt were working from illustrations of Andersen's story and not from the text. In order to connect her craft to the visual arts, Marlatt invokes all the visual media conventionally associated with the lyric sequence: camera obscura, photograph, photographic series, tableau.[28] Furthermore, the titles that she gives to the seven sections of her long poem create a serial commentary on the gradual development of her literary canvas. Robert Lecker, a keen collector of Canadian art, observes that Marlatt's speaker "is found, static, in (I) 'white as of the white room,' moving cautiously through (II) 'shadows doors are' into colour and sunlight, where she experiments with poetry as painting in (III) 'primarily colours,' gradually employing (IV) 'light effects,' and realizing (V) 'visual purple.' In (VI) 'eye lights,' the eye is defined in a play upon the painter's word 'highlight.' But in the last section, 'Out a rose window,' Marlatt renounces all claims to what she herself saw as progress, admitting that her art, which depended largely upon a voice at second remove, never managed to progress beyond a semi-real word encounter with experience. So the image of the window and 'containment (not content –)' is reinstated as Marlatt confesses to a lingering predilection for rose-coloured vision."[29] Lecker's sense that Marlatt's technique is not fully developed here is valid, but her conclusion is not as romantic as this quotation implies. Nor is Marlatt uncritical of visual media, in particular photography, which Lecker contrasts to painting and valorizes for its verisimilitude. For Marlatt, in *Frames*, a photograph is "a flat remembrance" and the one of her husband strikes her as "false."[30] Elsewhere, Marlatt argues that photographs are "unreal because the real is the constant streaming of time, & they try to take a fix on it."[31] Even when individual photographs are placed in a series, Marlatt is suspicious of the emotions invested in them: "And when you find yourself thus salted, when the photographer strokes his moustache satisfied at capturing you, do you feel luminescent? Or do you disappear at the outer edges of the negative?"[32] Rather than elide the problems of photography and the arrested image, Marlatt incorporates them into her critique of gender relations. She deconstructs visual media even as she offers a less idealized vision of heterosexual union than the fairytale romance. That Ondaatje and Bowering have received comparatively less critical attention for the ways in which they use visual media to facilitate this fairytale union edifies her argument about the normative status of the heterosexual quest narrative.

The writing of *Frames* followed a period of writer's block for Marlatt that lasted from the summer until the winter of 1966. Her inability to write arose from her feelings of dislocation in the United States, her lack of occupation there, and the resulting strain on her marriage:

> I was there on no particular visa. I mean my category there was basically as [Alan's] wife – I couldn't study, I couldn't get a job – and again it was ideal for writing and I couldn't write. That Christmas we came up to Canada, to Montreal, and I felt so good about coming back: I'd never realized until that point that I did identify very strongly as a Canadian. And so when I went back to Indiana, I said, "O.K., I'm going to forget everything I learned in '63 and '62 [at UBC] and I'm going to go back to my own sources" and the earliest sources I had were fairytales. Of course reading [Robert] Duncan allowed me to go back, I mean right back to childhood, because he is constantly stressing the importance of that. So I went to Hans Christian Andersen's fairytale of the Snow Queen and just started from there. This gave me a structure, a story line I didn't have to worry about because it was already "told," so I could then move into the writing out of what was simply coming up each day in the act of writing.[33]

Marlatt considers the interjection of her first person voice into *Frames* to be a personal revolution that ended her writer's block and affirmed her vocation as a writer. This intrusive voice is an assertion of authorial presence, an act out in the open that enabled her to give expression to her domestic discontent. She uses this active voice to articulate her resentment at having to play the role of the passive female: "*here's* the lie. Here where I sit waiting, forced, the female, to abide."[34] To counteract this passivity, Marlatt uses her personal experience to alter Andersen's storyline. Barbour notes that her autobiographical intrusions are surprising because "the poets from whom she learned so much at the beginning of her career wrote against the 'confessional' mode."[35] Whereas Olson vowed to get "rid of the lyrical interference of the individual as ego," Marlatt restores the lyric "I" and interferes with the momentum of the narrative by using her personal voice to disrupt Andersen's storyline.[36] Her interventions thus set a precedent for *Ana Historic*, where the metafictional author, Annie, decides to write her own story instead of researching history for her husband, Richard Anderson. As Caroline Rosenthal observes of *Ana Historic*, Marlatt's wordplays and "textual devices ... sho[w] that heterosexuality is a *regulatory fiction*, which 'frames' men and women into one story by ruling out more complex constructions of gender and sexual identity."[37]

In *Frames*, Marlatt scrutinizes the sexual underpinnings of children's stories in the grandmother section. The husband's grandmother sees Marlatt "as part of her story" and she teaches the young woman "history" – that is, family history and the dominant place of men in it.[38] The grandmother's narrative line is a family lineage in which the men are the agents and the women are the media. For Marlatt, narrative is a performance of gender, and as she listens to the grandmother's stories she reflects on how women become complicit in their own oppression: "Who doesn't know [men] knit a thicket of thorns about you? Don't move, for fear of skin pricks. Thus interred, mummified, like bodies found in bogs, certain women grow old in the tea service trot daily from kitchen to bedroom where she waits for the accustomed cup."[39] Uncomfortable with this role, Marlatt receives the old woman's story as "a ball of / dead string" and remarks that she is "stuck with it / here at the end or / entrance, where / ever entranced [Kay and Gerda] sit."[40] This thread leads Marlatt into a labyrinth of generational and gender differences. To convey her sense of confinement in this labyrinth, Marlatt stresses the architectural images of rooms, doors, and stages that frame the plot she yearns to escape: "Out? I can't imagine it, left here holding the thread of our story, knotted in remembrance, not ... seeing. Is flat as this room with its kitchen chair, table, a cardboard place whose exits never go far. Doors? lead off to a blind alley of dreams. & the white lights onstage (do you know what it's like being always onstage?) invent shadows for depth, in a false frame of reality."[41] Unwilling to further the grandmother's lineage, the speaker "beats a hasty exit, allowed at last, having broken through walls of her trance."[42] However, as Marlatt's pun indicates, every exit is an entrance, and having unframed the inherited story-line, Marlatt embarks on a quest for her own story.

Several critics have noted Marlatt's preoccupation with quest narratives, which typically pair a romantic quest with an artistic one.[43] A decade before Marlatt published the story of Annie Torrent in *Ana Historic*, Lecker identified the formal dimension of her quest narrative in *Frames*: "Marlatt is involved in a quest for words which will give access to the truth of sight, reflecting not only the moment, but also the dynamic nature of experience and cognition. She arrives at a torrent, but not overnight."[44] The "truth of sight," for Marlatt, has to do with process and not a particular perception. Like Bowering, she sees the universe in Heraclitean flux and aims to register images "in a serial light, a series of other takes," as she later states in a love poem for Kiyooka.[45] However, both the successes and failings of Marlatt's early poetry derive from what Lecker describes as "the tension between a tentative, frightened spontaneity, and an ambitious, robust control. So in her first book, *Frames*, we find her hesitant about the plunge into this riverine experience, content at first to watch this movement called Life from the sidelines, as if it were a show."[46] Like Bowering in his early work, where he "peer[s] thru a crenel at the passing show," Marlatt's tone is initially disengaged as she contemplates her domestic situation.[47] However, as Susan Knutson suggests, Marlatt's increasingly critical appraisal of her sexual identity enables her to "rewrite the traditional quest structure while foregrounding the gender of the fundamental plot positions."[48] Her version of *The Snow Queen* thus tailors the original narrative structure to fit her changing sense of the erotic, and thereby brings to the fore the contributions of gay and lesbian authors to the rethinking of the narrative forms of Marlatt's heterosexual peers.

In a 1988 journal entry, Marlatt is still mulling over questions she first raised in *Frames* about plot, heroism, sexuality, and gender roles in fairytales:

so why do i still balk at the notion of action? the hero?

early forms of story: adventures for children – i read them avidly, but except for the *Swallows & Amazons* series they were all boys adventuring – Jim Hawkins, Tom Sawyer. Alice, yes, but look what happened to her – those distortions of body-size, distressing transformations – she suffered her way back home, & all because she was curious.[49]

While this is a fair appraisal of children's stories in general, the fact that it does not apply to *The Snow Queen* beyond the first few pages perhaps explains Marlatt's attraction to the story. Although Kay ventures into the public square, he gets abducted by the Snow Queen and thenceforth plays a passive role in the story (which includes a distressing bodily transformation). He is the prize in a contest between two women and the principles they represent: the domestic warmth of Gerda and the icy seductiveness of the Queen. Males are largely absent from the original story (except for Kay, his double, and the animals), and the main human characters (Gerda, the Snow Queen, the robber wife, the robber girl, the Lapp woman, the Finn woman) are women.

Although Gerda's quest operates within the confines of patriarchal codes of femininity (the virgin and the whore), it is a quest narrative nonetheless. As such, it is useful to read her quest in relation to Teresa de Lauretis's essay "Desire in Narrative" (1984) because the essay formulates many of the issues that Marlatt engaged with intuitively in *Frames*, and Marlatt uses this essay as the basis of her 1998 meditation "Old Scripts and New Narrative Strategies." De Lauretis argues that a major function of narrative is to produce differences between identity groups, in particular between men and women. She asserts that the role of the male in the quest narrative is to be the hero, to act, to create momentum in the story, to anchor its point of view. In contrast, the female represents "what is not susceptible to transformation, to life or death; she (it) is an element of plot-space, a topos, a resistance, matrix and matter."[50] The edges of this plot-space are, furthermore, marked by monstrosities, such as Medusa and the Sphinx, who are closely linked to women and/or sexual deviance. Looking forward to the portrait of the hero and monster in Carson's *Autobiography of Red,* one should remember that, as de Lauretis insists, the "stark Platonic opposition of man/non-man" conceals a "painstakingly rich articulation of sexual difference" in the ancient texts.[51] However, at least for the ancient quest narratives that have attained canonical status in the present, these monsters delineate "the symbolic boundary between nature and culture, the limit and the test imposed on man."[52] In considering the fairytale narrative in *Frames*, one must therefore ask: What happens when a heroine crosses the plot-space of female characters who aid and/or delay the attainment of her prize? How do Gerda's quest and Marlatt's adaptation of it map sexual difference?

The chapter about "The Robber Girl" in *The Snow Queen* – "visual purple" in *Frames* – provides an example of a type of Heroine-Woman encounter that becomes increasingly important in Marlatt's later prose narratives. In *The Snow Queen*, Gerda fears for her life when she is kidnapped by robbers. A young robber girl rescues Gerda because she believes Gerda is a princess, but this rescue from physical harm brings with it a sexual threat. (Marlatt spells the appellation "robbergirl." Say it fast: robbergirl, rob-a-girl, rub-a-girl). Andersen's robber girl demands that Gerda yield up her dress and muff, and then forces Gerda to kiss her pet bird and sleep in her bed. The narrative tension thrives on homophobic fear, as Gerda dares not move in bed lest the robber girl stab her with a knife for being restless. When the frightened heroine finally departs, the robber girl keeps Gerda's muff (the symbolic counterpart of the robber girl's knife) as a token of remembrance.

In *Frames*, Marlatt makes the sexual undertones of the fairytale explicit and Gerda's encounter with the robber girl plays a crucial role in the narrative. In Marlatt's version, the robbers threaten Gerda with rape, not murder. They demand "some hair some thigh / some eyes some breast" and Gerda is rescued only because Marlatt shifts to her personal narrative.[53] Here, Marlatt's tentative encounter with a woman transforms the sexual tension of the moment into a power that she can either accept or refuse: "You wanted power. All this time calling for it. Well I'm here, she said, what more? Called up the black depths of an embittered eye. In the light how you bleach to white (rods, cups, cones), but night comes black with purple – of flesh, of a feast long interred."[54] The unusual chapter title "visual purple" thus indicates an intimate glimpse of female flesh. This erotic encounter offers Marlatt the possibility of committing an act out in the open in place of the thought: "You see what doors are for now? Come, offer yourself. (Steady furtive odour reducing me to earth.) But no, but what for? Out of love."[55] Marlatt is frightened to open this door, just as Annie is frightened to open the door of the wardrobe in *Ana Historic*. In both cases, the heroine encounters what Marlatt calls "fears that are crystallizations of space, because they erect walls which are not only enclosures for the sake of comfort, home, say, but barricades against what lies beyond them."[56] And in both cases, the narrative tension thrives on a mixture of desire and homophobia. Like the historian in *Beautiful Losers*, the married protagonist is torn between her queer yearnings and her heteronormative status. But Marlatt's protagonists eventually move beyond the "IF" of nostalgic and hypothetical musings and commit themselves to a course of action.

More than anywhere else in *Frames*, the contemporary and fairytale narratives overlap in "visual purple," as do dreams and consciousness. The sexual scenes are veiled in innuendo, obscured by pronominal uncertainty, and rendered in a kind of dream state in which Marlatt, or possibly Gerda, asks herself:

> lie to my
> eye's dead eye
> this
> is my love?[57]

Marlatt does not inform the reader whether this eye/I is dreaming of Kay or dreamily eyeing the woman beside her. In any case, the dreamer immediately "comes back down through light to ground" and resumes the socially approved heterosexual quest.[58] Marlatt/Gerda feels compelled to continue Andersen's line because she is unsure how to channel the power of the torrent welling inside her:

> Taps run, water. To tap again, at the still centre of the story, power that is conjuring – but who of who? Who tells letters to fall by the wayside? Or way-houses to merely swing their doors?

> I can see, in the woods, a pair of doors through which I lept as the trap of the story. Shut of her, I thought, to a new place.[59]

Discussing the many meanings of this "trap" with Bowering, Marlatt names one that is particularly suggestive: "My fear is that I'm being seduced. I'm being seduced by something that is not giving me the information but is seeming to."[60] Marlatt does not give any more information about what this "something" is, but for the moment it is more important to note that she thinks of narrative in terms of forces of attraction. Although *Frames* is full of erotic detours, the pull of linear narrative initially overcomes the other forces of attraction: "And all these fragments spun from every direction freely oppose her who moves, can move, only in one – forward, to lodestone."[61] However, the power of this masculine lodestone diminishes steadily as Marlatt strays further from the course of Andersen's plot.

In *The Snow Queen*, Gerda and Kay reunite and miraculously transform into an adult couple who live happily ever after. However, in Marlatt's version, the couple's reunion lacks this fairytale ending. Marlatt's final section, "Out a rose window," gently satirizes the formulaic elements of the heterosexual quest: "Once there was a girl & boy etc. Once roses exfoliate surrounded them. Thus unpeeled, they stand nude in the luminous centre of themselves. Back to back to the room. Where windowboxes with roses border their image of the world."[62] The couple's situation is tense, as they "transfix each other, in each, see the room & themselves contained."[63]

Their rapt gaze is a painterly conceit, because the attention that the couple pays to each other mimics the attention that the viewer pays to the literary portrait. This triangular state of affairs is disrupted by the return of the robbergirl, who confirms their union before setting out on her solo journey into the wide world: "Only one interesting event occurs on their return: they meet the robbergirl, who has freed herself at last. Was out to see, so she said, the wide world. Signpost, had sped Gerda on her way. And this (with only a shadow of you see!) is Kay. Ah! She is happy for them, she smiles over their joined hands & utters the word: 'Snip-snap-snurre-basselure.' Sound of connexion breaking (its bas allure). Progressively Kay & Gerda drift further into summer."[64] Other translators render the robber girl's words as "snip, snap, snout, your tale is out," but Marlatt changes the rhyme in order to underscore the forces of attraction that are drawing the couple apart.[65] In Marlatt's copy of *The Snow Queen*, a child has printed "firmly in red, they lived happily ever afterwards comma to the end of their summer,"[66] but the adult speaker cannot reach the same idealized conclusion: "Here we must step back from the frame, the delicate tracing of willow. Not to see through glass shades distort."[67] The reason for unframing Andersen's mirror conceit becomes apparent in this scene. Whereas pieces of the devil's glass are fashioned into windowpanes and spectacles in *The Snow Queen*, in *Frames* the rose-coloured glass distorts the actual status of the couple by making a bad situation look good. Dedicated to Alan Marlatt, *Frames* in fact documents the beginning of the end of the Marlatts' marriage.

Having pursued the narrative line to its terminus alongside the railway tracks, Marlatt finds that her story does not fit Andersen's narrative template: "Doors hang askew in their frames & will not close."[68] Marlatt responds to this crisis of order by abandoning his-story: "Time to give up, history as his or theirs & even knowing – where they came from, why they did, who do you love ... Long hoot of a train echoes into the walls pursuit. Is crackt already."[69] In a slightly ambiguous conclusion, the couple step out of this cracked matrimonial room: "And some minutes after: You're sitting on the back steps in the dark with cigarette, absorbed, watching the shapes of boxcars travel night. Or I think you do & don't ask, Stars or boxcars? Step out of the doorway too, step out & sit, down."[70] These lines might indicate that the couple are taking the necessary steps to break out of their routine and have reunited as they sit together. On the other hand, their dejection colours this scene in anything but an optimistic hue. With the benefit of hindsight, one could argue that "Out a rose window" hints at Marlatt's coming out as a lesbian – Stein's motto "a rose is a rose," which recurs at the conclusion of *Ana Historic*.[71] This allusion would explain the strange capitalization of "Out" in the otherwise uncapitalized chapter titles. However, with the exception of the scenes centring on the robbergirl, a lesbian reading of Marlatt's poem remains largely conjectural.

While the fate of the couple in *Frames* is uncertain, Marlatt's own marriage foundered soon after publication of the long poem, as she explains in the preface to *What Matters: Writing 1968–70*:

> In 1968, my husband Al & i were living in the Napa Valley in California, each of us having finished several years of graduate work at Indiana University & supposedly heading for home, Vancouver, BC ... In the fall of that year a job came through for him from the Psychiatry & Psychology Departments at UBC. We returned home as we always knew or imagined we would. Our child was born there but the job didn't fit & by the fall of 1969 we were back in the States, in Wisconsin, where he was teaching in the Psychology Department at UW. I was writing about Vancouver, watching our son grow, & wondering what i was doing on a tobacco farm in the American Midwest. By the end of 1970 i had come home to Vancouver with Kit for good (as it has since been).[72]

This period of Marlatt's life is documented in *Rings* (1971), a sequence of poems which is also full of images of matrimonial containment. However, in voicing her marital discontent, Marlatt transfers the ring symbolism, which shapes the narrative structure, from the wedding band to the birth canal – a theme to which she returns in a birthing scene in *Ana Historic*, where the "mouth speaking flesh" is characterized as an "angry powerful o."[73]

Marlatt also wrote shortline poems in the late 1960s – for example, *Leaf leaf/s* (1969) – but the complex syntax of *Rings* and *Our Lives* (1975) appealed to her more. She recalls that she consciously built her poetic line into a prose form: "it was the [longline poems], which i thought of as 'prose poems,' that engaged me most, most gave me room to play around. I wanted to build syntactic structures that i could sustain far longer than i could in verse, & i wanted to build looser & more complicated rhythms. It wasn't just a case of extending my line, i had to really believe i was writing prose, tho with a poet's ear on the pulse of language."[74] Marlatt's poetry thus directly shapes her prose style. In contrast, Marlatt wrote a short novel, *The Sea Haven*, for a creative writing course with Earle Birney at UBC in 1962, but she "never did anything with the novel" because she felt it "wasnt very good."[75] On Birney's recommendation, *The Sea Haven* was published in the journal *Evidence*, but it was never submitted to a publishing house. The early novel anticipates Marlatt's later work in the respect that "it was a serial story with two central characters, a girl & a boy. They went thru all these adventures, & every night it would be the next installment of the story."[76] However, *The Sea Haven* followed realist conventions in its descriptions, and Marlatt was not satisfied. Her longline experiments in the 1970s, on the other hand, generated an enthusiasm for prose that laid the groundwork for her later novels.

FROM SERIAL POEM TO PROSE

The boundary between poetry and prose becomes particularly obscure as Marlatt moves into the territory of the novel. In 1975 Marlatt published *How Hug a Stone*, which her publisher advertised as a novel, but which she maintains is "a cycle of prose poems."[77] The quest theme driving this narrative is Marlatt's wish to reconnect with her dead mother, who is identified with the circles of standing stones in her mother's beloved England – hence the titular question, "how hug a stone (mother)."[78] However, as Marlatt tells Bowering, a serial poem "has certain obsessions" that "reappear in motion within the poems as you're reading them," and one of the obsessions in *How Hug a Stone* is the function of narrative itself.[79] In the early poem "departure," Marlatt asks a question that recurs throughout the collection in various forms: "without narrative how can we see where we're going? or that – for long moments now, we happen."[80] As co-editor of *Periodics* (1977–81), a journal dedicated to experimental prose, the question of narrative's function is foremost in Marlatt's thoughts. In the poem entitled "narrative continuity" in *How Hug a Stone*, for instance, Marlatt shifts her initial focus from the future to the past: "without narrative how can we see where we've been? or, unable to leave it altogether, what we come from?"[81] Toward the conclusion of the sequence, as Marlatt approaches the "limit of the old story, its ruined circle,"[82] she offers one answer to the questions she has raised: *narrative is a strategy for survival. so it goes – transformative sinuous sentence emerging even circular, cyclic.*"[83] Her inquiry into generational cycles thus furthers her interest in recursive prose, as well as laying the groundwork for her treatment of mother-daughter relationships in the influential essay "Musing with Mothertongue" (1982–83), where she asks: "how can the standard sentence structure of English with its linear authority, subject through verb to object, convey the wisdom of endlessly repeating and not exactly repeated cycles [a woman's] body knows?"[84] Applying this logic to the constraints of "English lady plots" in *How Hug a Stone*, Marlatt responds by obeying another imperative: "so as not to be lost, invent: one clear act in all that jazz."[85] The alternative format she devises is a cycle of prose pieces whose serial format hybridizes the travel journal and photographic sequence.

How Hug a Stone is a photograph album of a lost family, snapshots of the "hereditary home" that existed more in the language and imagination of Marlatt's mother than in the fact of Marlatt's childhood in Australia, Malaysia, and Canada.[86] The narrative Marlatt uses to tell the story of her visit to England thus reflects her established interest in photography and the photographic sequence. Her collaboration with the photographer Robert Minden in *Steveston* is celebrated. In addition, many of her books feature photographic inserts and covers by artists such as Cheryl Sourkes, to whom *Ana Historic* is dedicated. Indeed, Marlatt's poetry books "are progressively characterized by an application of photographic principles," as Lecker observes, but her most extensive meditation on photography is found in her novella, *Zócalo*, where desire for a mother-figure takes on more sexual connotations.[87]

Zócalo relates the experiences of a Canadian couple vacationing in Mexico. The work is dedicated to the photographer and poet Roy Kiyooka, with whom Marlatt lived from 1975 to 1981. Although Marlatt and Kiyooka "forsook the rites of marriage," they sustained a caring relationship that lasted even after Marlatt came out as a lesbian in the early 1980s.[88] Kiyooka's *Pear Tree Pomes* (1985), which is dedicated to "Daphne & [her son] Kit," documents the artist's acceptance of Marlatt's decision, as well as his profound sense of loss.[89] Marlatt, in turn, published "A Lost Book" of love poems that date from 1974 to 1999 in *This Tremor Love Is* (2001), which is dedicated to Kiyooka. When Kiyooka died suddenly in 1994, Marlatt also took on the editing of his biography of his mother.

Although critics frequently read *Zócalo* as autobiography because of its dedication and identifiable characters, Marlatt explains that, in contrast to *Frames*, she found it liberating to write the novella in the third person: "What intrigued me about writing [*Zócalo*] was how much more easily i could remember in the third person. As if this Yucatan journey had not only occurred in another place but to another person ... As if this she, through whose eyes and nerves and skin everything filtered, could open onto the streets of Merida or the pathways of Uxmal like a camera lens, a performing eye/she whose active perception brought alive the feel and texture of these places populated by strangers walking and talking there on the brightly lit stage of the text."[90] The woman in *Zócalo* goes unnamed, which complicates the first name of her photographer companion, Yo, which Marlatt notes elsewhere is "a combination of first and third persons (*yo* meaning 'i' in Spanish as well as a shortened form of Yoshio, a Japanese given name)."[91] The absent autobiographical "I" is thus othered in the perceptions of the woman and the identity of the male companion. This pronominal split blurs the boundary between the narrative eye/she and the camera eye/he, fostering a kind of gender confusion that recurs throughout the text.

Zócalo begins with an epigram from *Visions of the Night* (a work of dream interpretation) that establishes the mood and setting of the novella: "Among the Aztecs, dream interpretation and divination by dreams were the prerogative of the priestly class *teopexqui*, the Masters of the Secret Things; and among the Maya of *cocome*, the Listeners."[92] Marlatt's divination theme endorses the Freudian tenet that "every dream reveals itself as a psychical structure which has a meaning," as well as supporting Warren Tallman's view that reading is a process of divining.[93] The epigram encourages readers to seek out the latent Secret Things concealed by the manifest content of the dreams and the Mayan prophecies. Although Marlatt stresses the potentially damaging effects of psychiatric therapy on women in *Ana Historic*, *Zócalo* is heavily influenced by psychoanalytic theories of dream interpretation. Marlatt regularly attended a Jungian dream analysis group in the early 1970s because she was having "recurrent dreams about the sea."[94] She kept a dream diary during this period, which undoubtedly influenced the writing of *Zócalo*, where the sea plays a symbolic role in a Mayan prophecy.

The narrative in *Zócalo* begins with a traffic jam at the U.S.A.-Mexico border, where the woman and Yo are lined up in separate vehicles. Impatient, the woman follows an official-looking truck that pulls out of the line ahead of her, thinking it will lead her to another border crossing. She follows the truck into the countryside, absorbed by her love of speed, and she loses Yo, who was following her in a different vehicle. The woman thereby enacts Marlatt's whimsical desire, expressed elsewhere, to be a race car driver: "For me it's a solitary pleasure, loving the way the road unfolds, and writing prose approximates it as i lean into the sentence, feeling it slant in unexpected ways, take me in its momentum towards the next tilt, pushing thought-in-syntax to the limit of its stretch."[95] On one level, the opening chapter allegorizes Marlatt's impatience with conventional prose, even as she yearns to cross the border into that genre. The excursion also introduces the prophetic theme that gives the novella an overarching structure. When the protagonist gets lost and stops to ask a native family for directions, an elderly woman replies cryptically: "I will tell you now is the time, now, when man's powers are coming to the full ... The power of the sea and the power of dwarfs are acting together – that's what my mother would say."[96] Here, as elsewhere in the first chapter, the text is vague to the point of inscrutability. In fact, one could almost read the young woman's flight from the traffic jam as a day-dream, because the Mayan family behaves in a symbolic manner and the woman circles back to the line-up where she started.

However, on the woman's return, an important event occurs that grounds the narrative and suggests that the subtext of chapter 1 is a "Jour-ney" that is intimately tied to her sexuality. Confused by the Mayan's prophecy, the young woman turns her car around and, realizing that she has lost Yo, drives back toward the border crossing. Along the way, she sees Yo's truck pulled over at an abandoned garage. The prophecy acquires another cryptic symbol when the woman approaches the truck and finds Yo in the passenger seat with a parcel:

> He says quietly, I can't drive, and indicates the seat beside him. On it, a parcel trussed up in rope sits in front of the driver's wheel, bulkily in front, leaving no room for him.
> I followed you when you first left the line, he says, I trusted your sense of direction. I thought you were following the sea.[97]

Yo's comments cause her to remember the old woman's prophecy and for some reason she is haunted by the mysterious package:

> The parcel sits there, malevolent and unmoving. It almost emanates its own presence, not a sign but, more inexplicably, a knowledge of itself in front of them. She doesn't ask him how it got there.
> We must go back. Now.[98]

Where did the package come from? Why can Yo no longer drive? And why is this incapacity so significant that his phrase "I can't drive" echoes in the woman's mind? The answers to these questions are not immediately forth-coming. As Fred Wah observes, *Zócalo* "is a sensuous journal-novel which, like *Frames*, charts perception after perception, looking to find a way," and what answers Marlatt supplies are communicated through strategic juxta-positions within the narrative, rather than by what the characters say directly.[99]

The woman's journey gets underway again in Progreso, the Mexican town whose name appears as the title of chapter 2. In Progreso the couple pass through their first *zócalo*, or central square.[100] The *zócalo,* in Mexico, is at once the hub of social activity and the place where "the stone cathedral looms" alongside the major government buildings.[101] In the original Spanish, *zócalo* means "pedestal stand," thereby confirming the phallic authority of the place. As a tourist, the woman admires the square and the buildings, but she struggles with the moral exigencies of church and state in her personal life. A part of her yearns to maintain her straight relationship with her male lover, but her physical desires begin to lead her elsewhere. Thus, in the slang of the period, she must decide whether or not to be "square."

Like the dictated image in a serial poem, the *zócalo* is the given around which Marlatt's narrative orbits. Over the course of their vacation, the couple sit in many different public squares because Yo isn't "as romantic as [the woman], nor as young" and the "square is just about [his] speed (i can't drive, he said[)]."[102] Although Yo likes the atmosphere of the square, it "isn't her way, she is running back to this island in the dark of the sea, to the sea running yes to a limitless horizon."[103] Marlatt's prose in *Zócalo* attempts to reconcile these opposing aesthetic principles, as her longlines did in *Steveston*, where the constraints of the town and cannery contrast with the flow of the Fraser River and the ocean. Reflecting on this tension in her prose from the 1970s, Marlatt writes in "The Measure of the Sentence" (1982): "I had definitely abandoned the textbook notion of sentence as the container for a completed thought, just as writing open form poetry had taught me the line was no box for a certain measure of words, but a moving step in the process of thought ... Our word 'sentence' comes from L. *sentire*, to feel, think – the muscularity, the play of thought that feels its way, flexive and reflexive, inside the body of language. In short, a proprioceptive (receiving itself) prose."[104] Part of the spectacle of the narrative is thus to watch Marlatt open the "box" of grammatical usage even as her heroine struggles against the moral limitations represented by the *zócalo*.

Like the photograph/empty frame in *Billy* and the canvas/white room in *Frames*, the public square in *Zócalo* is a tropological space in which the woman develops her photographic narrative over a number of exposures. Each visit to a *zócalo* provides the couple with a means of measuring change in their deteriorating romance. As they discuss their visit to the *zócalo* in Mérida, the woman senses that their relationship is falling apart: "she won't let them harden onto separate benches (we have to get out of here, she said) & in despair reaches toward him, her hand encountering his shoulder's bony firmness in the dark, persisting."[105] The conversation amplifies the feeling of separation that the woman had experienced on a beach earlier, when she went swimming and communed with the sea while Yo remained in the shade to photograph: "are we really as different as that? you love water, he laughs shortly, i like earth, isn't that what our signs say? it's true, she had told him that, but she didn't want to play with their signs, she didn't want to play."[106] Marlatt, in contrast, plays with their signs throughout the novella as she mixes their respective media and gender markers. If, as I will argue in the next chapter, Carson's novel in verse is a novel inverse, Marlatt's novella is her first attempt to write a novel in which the "elle" is not simply "Bella" – the idealized female of *Fugitive Pieces* who is memorialized by male writers.

The woman in *Zócalo* attempts to bridge the emotional divide between herself and Yo by studying his preferred medium: photography. Like Kay, who enjoys playing in the square, Yo enjoys photographing people in the *zócalo*. Like Gerda, who followed her male companion on his adventure, the woman accompanies Yo on his artistic quest. Also like Gerda, she encounters impediments to her liberty that stem from her status as a woman. Staring through Yo's camera, the woman experiences the male gaze of the camera as liberating, until this gaze is returned and she is reminded of her own sexual identity: "she fingers the camera with its tele-photo lens she wants to move into the street, through an eye that is an extension & even impertinent accessory to the act of her seeing, she wants, not to see but to be – him? impossible. The young man on the seawall knows she is aiming at him though she pretends to follow the wavering movement of the orange vendor, & she focuses, carefully, his dark glance which is both *for* her & *at* her."[107] The woman's use of the telescopic lens stresses the artistic potential of photography in a scene that, as Nichols puts it, "opens and closes like a camera shutter in a text where one micro-event flows into the next, pushed by paragraph length, run-on sentences that move incrementally through a global experience of sight, sound, and intellect."[108] However, Nichols also observes that the young man's "dark glance" makes her acutely aware of the politics of the gaze: "the female tourist finds herself shut out from a culture that is not hers and is forced to see herself as a foreigner in the eyes of locals."[109] Yo also admonishes the woman for her use of the lens, on the grounds that "people who don't know cameras think you're taking their soul": "[Yo] says, you're snooping, that's what you like about that lens isn't it, that's what it allows you to do. & she says yes, laughing, almost joyously, yes, she wants to see, into them, into their hearts as if that might let her know them but he persists, half-jok-ing, it's like looking into people's windows at night, you're spying."[110] However, Yo shows no restraint in taking his own pictures of Mexicans, and he also has a tendency to see the world as "a moving movie lens."[111] The woman confronts a double standard because of her gender both verbally and visually in this scene. Despite these discouragements, the woman covets the male gaze and boldly "continues to peer through the camera, focusing, shifting as the people's movements shift, but now they are only elements of a visual image, they have closed down into visual integers, hermetic & hidden as perhaps, they have always been."[112] The woman even risks becoming sealed in this mode of perception when she arrives in Puerto Jaurez and declares: "this, this is a picture, here is the bluegreen they'd seen on paper."[113] Her photographic mindset impedes her ability to connect with her environment and she briefly acquires what she later describes as the masculine "distancing eye."[114]

Although Marlatt genders photography as male in *Zócalo*, she elsewhere defines the "aperture" as feminine and uses the language of photography to distinguish herself from an earlier generation of Canadian writers preoccupied with myth and symbol: "i'm more interested in focussing the immediate, shifting the experience of distance and dislocation through the use of montage, juxtaposition, superimposing disparate and specific images from several times and places. I want to see the world as multidimensional as possible and ourselves present within it."[115] While the photographic principles guiding Marlatt's pen perhaps distinguish her style, it would nevertheless be a false distinction to say that myth and symbol do not interest Marlatt. Throughout *Zócalo*, the woman reads aloud to Yo from her guidebook, and the myths she relates frame her perceptions in the same manner that the telescopic lens frames Yo's gaze.[116] For example, in a crucial scene at Uxmal, the speaker recounts to Yo the myth behind the construction of the Pyramid of the Magician: "[The myth] begins with a dwarf whose mother was a witch & hatched him out of an egg (so far back in time it can't even be told with any probity). She sent him off to challenge the king & the king said build a palace overnight or I'll kill you. His mother helped of course with magic ... So the dwarf got to be king of Uxmal & she went off to live with a serpent in a waterhole."[117] This quest narrative puzzles the woman because she cannot understand why the Mayans would "name the pyramid after a woman" when "they didn't even have a goddess creator & destroyer."[118] However, when the couple enter "the bodily cavity of [the] huge stone being" and the woman sees "the oval stone body of this giant," she becomes convinced that "its contours [are] surely female."[119] Whereas the speaker in *Frames* finds the manufactured rooms of the grandmother threatening, the protagonist in *Zócalo* finds (rather naively) the ancient and mythologized spaces of the pyramid empowering.

The way in which the narrator genders the pyramid's interior is important because it shapes the context that she will use to interpret a crucial
dream of her own toward the end of the novella. According to Freud,
"rooms in dreams are usually women," as are window-sills and balconies,
and "boxes, cases, chests, cupboards ... ovens ... hollow objects, ships, and
vessels of all kinds."[120] The woman is not dreaming in this scene, but the
two women she meets in the Pyramid of the Magician will, I suggest, reappear in her final dream and shed light on the significance of the strange parcel encountered in the first chapter.

On a staircase near the top of the pyramid, the woman meets two female
tourists who "smile at her, the smile of outsiders who recognize their shared
alienness."[121] The two women prove to be from Calgary, but there is the
suggestion that they share something more than nationality. The
Vancouverite and the "Prairie girls" engage in a discussion about caves and
the woman "feels a drop, a slight tremor" that is both fear and attraction.[122] The Prairie girls are travelling Mexico without guidebooks or
chaperones and they ask the woman to explain some Mayan masks. The
woman informs them that the masks are the faces of Chac, the male rain
god, although she notes to herself that "somehow the witch persists, chaotic mother, though all the images are male."[123] The woman suddenly
notices that Yo is well ahead of her on the staircase, however, and she "hur-
ries to catch up" and eventually announces: "I met two Calgary girls, she
laughs, jubilant now, they said there were caves. You climbed to the top of
a pyramid to find out about caves? She grins, abashed, where else?"[124] The
encounter on the stairs is brief, but significant from a psychoanalytic standpoint. According to Freud, dreams of climbing or descending stairwells represent fantasies of sexual encounters because of "the rhythmical character
of both activities."[125] Marlatt expands on the stairwell symbolism later in
Zócalo, but for the moment the encounter with the Prairie girls functions as
a double of the robbergirl encounter in Frames. Both scenes supply a
moment of lesbian intrigue that is broken off when the woman feels compelled to resume her heterosexual journey. Much as the comma splice, caesura, and line break perform a vital interruptive function in Marlatt's syntax,
this interlude plays a disproportionately important role in her narrative.

The Prairie girls return later to confirm the narrator's choice of mate, but
for the moment the woman sublimates her lesbian desires. The Vancouver
couple enter a windowless vault near the top of the pyramid and Yo proposes that the vault is a "burial chamber," but the woman disagrees: "The
door's too big. She's seeing him framed there, one hand cradling his camera

(what he will *make* of it), the other in a back pocket twists his body, single & resistant in the doorway there, the better to see. Man, she thinks, men with their distancing eye. She feels a pang of envy for that clarity, & leaning forward, you're standing in the light you know, bites his ear."[126] This scene enacts a number of gender reversals. Yo is clearly identified as a man, with his "distancing eye" and suggestively positioned camera. However, implicitly, the narrator recovers the etymology of "camera" in the word "chamber" and frames Yo as an object of desire. This framing of Yo resembles Billy's "photograph" of Angela D in *The Collected Works of Billy the Kid*, as well as Bowering's portrait of a lover in his poem "Frame," from *In the Flesh*:

> Her frame in the doorway
> replaces the door; he can never leave
> thru her, he may only enter by her leave.[127]

Having framed Yo as a love object, the woman toys with the focus of her desire. The woman projects her desire for the Calgary girls onto Yo, which causes Yo to make jokes about her wanting to become a nun: "As his hands disengage themselves to enclose her, she sees over his shoulder the grassy courtyard their cave looks out on & the small figures of all the others. So you've found a use for it (his teasing tries to meet her), & in The Nunnery too. She wants to say they didn't have nuns, but doesn't. His body feels warm & resilient against her skin already chill from the mould. Do you think these rooms were here for their doorways? she murmurs into his neck. Are we in one? he asks, withdrawing, & she thinks he feels framed. I'm trying to seduce you. You're playing with the idea of being a nun. But there weren't nuns here! Nevertheless – he grins, you're irrevocably christian."[128] Yo's sarcasm ends the romantic moment and the couple walk "down the steps into the heart of the quadrangle"[129] where they briefly separate: "Having drained his visual curiosity, [Yo] lays the camera aside & lies down in the grass. Aren't you going to walk through that arch? vaulted like the rooms below, but leading onto bush, a genuine passageway. No, I've had enough. I'm just going to see where it goes. He nods."[130] Despite her denial, the woman explores the passageway and stumbles upon "an ancient square" and a "path [that] leads into a hollow."[131] In place of the phallic pedestal at the centre of the modern *zócalo*, the woman discovers a vaginal hollow in the ancient square – another example of Marlatt's equation of the prehistoric with the feminine and the genuine.

In a deeply sexualized passage, the speaker explores the Freudian land-scape and momentarily overcomes her fears:

> she feels very visible walking down the path, she shuffles her feet, she makes a noise for the snakes to hear, so they can get out of her way – although she knows it isn't her way but theirs. The ruin, in all its mon-umental silence, says nothing to her, only stands, stands at the edge of an earth she descends, she chooses, between two paths, she keeps her eye on the mound as best she can, through the increasing foliage. And then as the path turns at the bottom of the hollow, across & to one side she sees a hole. Powdery white limestone opens on the dark, mouth – enough room for one person to slip into, lowering herself down.
> She thinks of the Calgary girls.[132]

The speaker seems to make a choice here in favour of caves over serpents – that is, for female genitalia over male, the Calgary girls over Yo – but she is immediately stricken with guilt: "The end of the story, she thinks, I didn't tell him how the witch exchanges water for children she feeds to the ser-pent. That is a sacrifice she can't understand & struggles away from. Per-haps he is right, she wants her individual soul – 'irrevocably christian' after all."[133] As in the lesbian scene in *Frames*, where the seduced narrator thinks "Noster. Nostra. Dame. Help us," the narrator in *Zócalo* grapples with her inherited sense of ethics and continues to repress her sexuality.[134] This repression also has consequences for the woman's creativity. Marlatt's "out" lesbian characters and speakers create in a collaborative, transla-tional, and dialogic fashion, but the woman in *Zócalo* continues to write and appropriate in a secretive manner.

After her experience in the ancient square, the woman finds it difficult to return to her heterosexual relationship. Restless in bed, she lies awake and contemplates the meaning of hell: "hell, is the square, 'in the middle of,'"; "hell is having to be here, she thinks, suddenly seeing him"; "hell is this / constraint."[135] Her restlessness wakes Yo and they discuss the shoeshine man they had seen in the *zócalo* in Mérida. The shoeshine man is another of the woman's quixotic obsessions. He fascinates the woman because he is "letting himself go," as Yo suggestively observes: "the shoeshine man's busy dreaming himself. she knows what he intends – you too, likewise – but does he know what the words imply, in that one dreamily decisive com-ment, you mean, we only *dream* ourselves? & she is frightened because it is there, the absence she wants to stay this side of, but how does he know? & how can it be?"[136] Neither Yo nor the reader possesses the telescopic lens that will allow them to see directly into the woman's heart, but, as she suspects, both can glean from her language what this "absence" refers to. Marlatt resists clarifying the woman's fear/desire and, instead, superimposes one example of it on top of another.

When the couple travel to Chichen-Itza, Marlatt replays a variation of the Prairie girls encounter. The couple visit a limestone sinkhole, which is a "word [that] keeps echoing" throughout the novella because it provides an analogy for the woman's emotional state: "the water just drips & drips & the cave gets bigger & bigger & then one day, boom, there's a hole – you can see how they'd think it was magic. Not magic, she wants to say, no, not magic."[137] While contemplating this torrent, the woman overhears a Mexican guide explain that young maidens "dressed in fine clothes like brides" sacrificed themselves by jumping into the sinkhole and bearing messages "down to the house of Chac."[138] "Two girls in shorts," who are not the Prairie girls but doubles of them, protest that no woman would jump in voluntarily.[139] "All legend," Yo concurs, but his partner, who thinks of Chac as a woman and who has the memory of sinking in the hole at Uxmal fresh in her mind, can only agree with him in part.[140] Here Marlatt foregrounds the difference between myth as received and reproduced, instead of performed and transformed. This difference inspires all the poet-novelists, but Marlatt is the first among her peers to rethink and reposition the gender roles of mythic plots.

The woman's thoughts and coded language find another architectural analogy at El Caracol, a "shellcoiled observatory" where the priests "watched the movements of the moon, of Venus."[141] A guide leads them through the building and "point[s] upward to a hole she had missed" which was "covered by a cloth & reached by a small ladder."[142] Unfortunately for the tourists, they cannot climb the ladder because "it was forbidden to all but the priests to enter this most sacred heart."[143] Listening carefully to these words, the woman "feels suddenly trapped in the peopled air, the containment of this stone."[144] She runs outside to gain a different vantage point:

& looking back, [she] sees suddenly that the four outer doors must face the cardinal points, & the inner ones some points between, while what is left of doors or starholes at the top look also north east south west – the outer sphere of the building keyed one way, the way the world lies, the inner keyed another.

       Those inner doorways form, not a cross then but an x, x marks the spot, that point, points outward on the horizon, sunrise,

sunset, summer zenith, winter descent, converge: four zones of the
earth turn green at their meeting, that fifth point, visible only as a hidden stairwell.[145]

This passage clearly associates the town Mérida with its echo in the English
word "meridian," which means "a great circle on the surface of the earth
passing through the poles" or a similar circle in the celestial realm.[146]
Marlatt draws this circle in her chapter titles once the couple arrive in
Mérida in chapter 3: 1-NIGHT (MERIDA; ISLA MUJERES; 2-NIGHT (ISLA
MUJERES; UXMAL; 3-NIGHT (MERIDA; CHICHEN-ITZA; 4-NIGHT (MERIDA;
MERIDA. Whereas Laurie Ricou observed that in *Steveston* the "key technique [...] is the labyrinth of unclosed parentheses," in *Zócalo* Marlatt closes
the circle by joining the four quarter-circles in the chapter titles.[147] She thus
converts the numbered corners of the masculine square into a feminine circle.
Moreover, each numbered section in the chapter titles is followed by an
unnumbered subsection, marking an inner series of coordinates within the
outer series, like the inner doors concealed by the outer ones at the observatory. All this geometry converges on a point, a fifth point or hidden stairwell,
where the "Secret Things" of the priestly class are marked by the chromo-
some signature "x,x." Whereas, in the traditional *roman à clef*, one outs the
name of the person behind the character (as in *The Collected Works of Billy
the Kid*), the key in Marlatt's novella is used to out the sexuality of a character who makes little effort to conceal her resemblance to the author.

The penultimate chapter of *Zócalo*, "4-NIGHT (MERIDA," begins to close
the narrative circle by replaying the cryptic passages from the opening
chapter and interpreting them through the woman's experiences in Mexico.
The couple recall the Mayan frieze of the four *bacabs* (dwarfs) who stand
at the corners of the earth, and "something slid[es] quietly into place" as
she "begins to remember ... (i can't drive)."[148] Marlatt also embeds these
parenthetical echoes of the package scene into Yo's dialogue when the discussion turns to the shoeshine man: "he's not *my* fascination you know (a
package wrapt & tied on the driver's seat), he's yours, you're the one who
remembers him (a package in her lap)."[149] The curved walls of the parentheses here are the feminine room of pause and reflection within the linear
syntax that Marlatt genders as masculine.

The woman's thoughts next turn to the strange road by the border and
she decodes the old woman's prophecy: "she'd thought they simply marked
the ground of her dream, that native family who said she'd better go – the
power of the sea & the power of dwarfs, they said, are working together –
now she knows who they are, how they preside over the sun's going & initi-

ate her in her own departure, lords of the turning of light to dark who live where absence is, at the mouth."[150] The woman does not explain exactly where she is going, but over the course of the narrative she characterizes Yo and the Mexican boys as dwarfs and identifies the sea as her element.[151] These forces work together in the woman's imagination to "initiate her in her own departure."[152] But here Marlatt encounters the difficulty of reconciling feminism with tourism, as well as the pitfall that had previously distinguished her proprioceptive writing from that of Olson. Whereas Sabrina Reed criticized Olson for aestheticizing a sense of bodily freedom that women cannot share, the woman – as a tourist in Mexico with Canadian money, rented cars, and bus tickets – enjoys a mobility and lifestyle the Mexicans cannot share. Vendors such as the hammock salesman pander to her in the hope of making a sale, and she responds to her elevated status by positing herself as the locus of all action and perception. Strangers, lovers, and the elements all conspire to initiate her symbolic journey. Like Olson, she creates what Jeff Derksen calls a "scopic regime" in which the "locus of perception" is anchored in a privileged body, "a regime that creates a world from a central and exclusive subject."[153] She converts Yo and the Mexican boys to dwarfs and harnesses the power of the sea for her own purposes. As she reads her desires into the Mayan ruins, she becomes the zenith (another meaning of meridian) of all actions and energies. She even feels at liberty to change the gender of Chac to suit her symbolic purposes.

However, even with all the energies of Mexico pressuring her, the woman still resists departure. She fears the "absence" and the "mouth" because "she isn't ready, no not yet, she will cling to numbers, to any evidence of their presence to each other, she will not be tricked, she will stay where the world is & they are all together."[154] Her departure is inevitable, however, which Yo realizes: "he laughs at her need to be here, laughs to make her realize the impossibility of what they nevertheless give their otherwhere up to: the laughing insistency of skin, warm to each other, the only reply she might make, wordless, is in the weight their bodies do press against the dark."[155] They consummate their union, but the narrator is haunted soon afterward by a nightmare that she characterizes as a descent:

> into the night. fall (apart) into that flesh self creeps from. no, NOT to feel it, run, run straight through (home?) to get away from
>
> i am running, running, it runs behind me, that horror (it will touch) get home, get home, through, the door & into, humming, house (no house i recognize) is full of relations – mother! – & the place is dark,

they come out to meet me, twins in yellow dresses, so
you've come, cousins, smiling, you've come to the party after all – they
thought i wouldn't, they thought i would stay up where they haven't –
just, fresh, raw with it (don't touch me) pushing by to reach her,
mother, who is busy with them all who come, i see from the doorway,
who stay here, the dead, she queens it over them, this is her house & i
have come in error –
            turning to steal away, i hear her voice move out of
that cavern to stay me, warning "I don't want to lose that one too."[156]

This dream operates on a number of semantic levels. On one level, the
woman later tells Yo, she dreamed of a party at her mother's house where
twins of her cousin came to greet her. In this family context, sex is taboo
and the raw touching in the dream contravenes the extreme propriety of the
queenly mother. On another level, the dream enacts a descent into the sinkhole of the house of Chac, "chaotic mother," where the woman encounters
maidens who substitute for the Calgary girls/tourist girls.[157] On both levels, the dream is fraught with sexual tension as the twins in fine dresses
offer the flesh that the woman shuns. Both the puritanical and the lesbian
elements claim a part of the woman's psyche and one fuels her homophobia
("that horror") even as the other arouses ("it will touch"). The next morning the woman resolves that "she must not, step into that house again," but
the comma preserves the dream's semantic doubleness.[158] As in the conclusion to *Frames*, Marlatt will end her narrative by holding two possibilities
in suspension.

The morning after the dream, the couple sit in the *zócalo* and attempt to
interpret the dream's content. As in the conclusion to *Frames*, the couple
have reunited and broken out of their routine. The day is auspicious
because they sit "on the side of the square [they] never sit on."[159] Like the
Roman augurs who sat in sacred squares to judge the flight of birds, the
couple interpret the dream that signals the woman's departure. However, a
sadness and desperation colour the scene, as the woman explains: "it seemed
to take an extraordinary effort to get back into myself, to get back beside
you & wake up."[160] Yo seems unaware of the significance of the dream and
simply replies, "so you went to visit your mother."[161] He then revises this
assessment by stating that her "descent" was a "voluntary" return to
"mother earth."[162] To a certain extent, a cosmology centring on mother
earth does develop over the course of the narrative, as the *Norteamericanos*
leave behind the cars and buses of the early chapters and try to get in touch
with the land and its inhabitants. However, the woman insists that the

mother was a specific person. When Yo suggests, in Freudian fashion, that the mother represents someone she had just met, "the falling begins": "o the horror of falling into, earth, in that we are alone – she had wanted him to pave it over, into nothing more than leaf play on paving stone, a surface she or anyone might walk across – she hadn't wanted to be alone."[163] Here Marlatt reiterates her early and somewhat paradoxical association of lesbianism with solitude and alienation. Carson's red monster feels a similar alienation because of his gay desires in *Autobiography of Red* but, as the heterosexual bedroom scenes in *Zócalo* and *Ana Historic* demonstrate, remaining in a dysfunctional relationship is no solution. Rather, Marlatt interrogates homophobic fear itself until she arrives at the place where lesbianism signifies community.

The woman's revelatory moment at the conclusion of *Zócalo* is interrupted by a young man selling hammocks who gives the woman an opportunity to exercise the transformative, translational powers that become central to Marlatt's writing in the 1980s. The vendor teaches the woman the word for "house" in Spanish, but he misspells it as "donmicilio," which the woman interprets as "'don,' gift, house ... this house you fight up through, at centre, dark, hole at the heart of the field."[164] The handwritten word reproduced in the text, like Ana's handwritten signature in *Ana Historic*, is a sign that anchors a long semiotic chain attached to the theme of the house of Chac. The man selling beds is a messenger bearing a gift that, like the package in the truck, or the Kiyooka photograph of the shoeshine block on the cover of the original Coach House edition, emanates a certain knowledge. Rather than reveal the contents of this package, however, Marlatt invokes another sign that displaces a determinate conclusion. She disappears into the absence at the "Mérida" point of her narrative circle. Form is left to speak in place of the demonstrative utterance.

Marlatt frames the final paragraph in *Zócalo* with the words of a Spanish road sign that the woman had seen earlier and translated: "El Mayab (something to do with the Mayans) is the earth ... mysterious & ancient ... in which (I think) ... everything speaks in the silence."[165] Marlatt inserts these words into the beginning, middle, and end of the novella's final paragraph in parenthetical echoes:

Or their day (*El Mayab*) out in the square (*es la tierra*) the men with xmas tree lights have got them down & left, the others stay, much as they have done, slumped on benches or halfturned watching passersby. Sun falls silently all around them. From a sky advanced to noon the whitewashed trunks of indian laurel bear up masses of glossy leaves

against – four corners light & shadowy, these trunks make of themselves, among, light bearing down (*mysterioso y antigua*), she sees Yo
coming from across the square, she sees him walk, quick & almost
light, almost disappearing into the ones he walks among, this man with
whom she shares the day, whose face, alight with question, singular in
that field that lights all ways – she takes her eyes from his, embarrassed
by the distance – not them, the dark against its lighting – eyes slide
back to, making of them in the way dark lights them, shining, showing
forth what each one is, each of them in the night they also rise up from,
in which everything speaks – well? he will say, did you learn any
Mayan? – *into the ... (silence).*[166]

The Christian façade (the Christmas tree lights) comes down in this passage
and the woman follows a different "light bearing down" into the ancient
earth. Yo's dark eyes have somehow guided the woman along this path, but
she is now embarrassed to look at him because of the distance between the
couple. The woman leaves Yo's final question unanswered. However, in
Ana Historic, Annie resolves to "break the parentheses and let it all surface," such that everything speaks, unbracketed.[167]

ANA HISTORIC: TOWARD A LESBIAN QUEST NARRATIVE

Ana Historic documents the process of a woman "writing her desire to
be, in the present tense, retrieved from silence."[168] In this full-length
novel, Marlatt weaves together the stories of several women of different
generations in Vancouver. The sense of history in the novel adheres to the
body-centred definition of the "(f)actual" alluded to in the epigram from
Susan Griffin: "The assemblage of facts in a tangle of hair."[169] Annie, the
metafictive author of the book, tangles these (f)actual strands together into
a personal and political history of lesbian desire. Annie describes herself as
"a middle-aged woman who hasn't held a job for twelve years" because she
ended her "graduate career by getting pregnant and marrying Richard
[Anderson]," her history professor.[170] While doing research for her husband, Annie becomes fascinated by a nineteenth-century schoolteacher,
Mrs Richards, whom Annie calls "Ana" because the annals of history have
not recorded her first name. Mrs Richards is remembered only because of
the history that she wrote herself: a journal that "years later would be
stored in the dustfree atmosphere of [the Vancouver] city archives."[171]
Although "there is no image of Mrs Richards" extant, Annie fashions an
imaginative portrait of her from the scant details available.[172] According to

the archival record, Mrs Richards travels from England to colonial British Columbia in 1873, gets a teaching job, "buys a piano and afterwards marries Ben Springer, as if they were cause and effect, these acts."[173] Like the grandmother in *The Snow Queen*, who captivates Gerda but whose storyline Gerda must resist, Ana fascinates Annie, but Annie does not want her life to follow the same path because Ana disappears from the record after she marries Springer. One of Marlatt's strategies for transforming the fear of absence in *Zócalo* is thus to associate absence with the non-identity of the conformist in *Ana Historic*.

The disappearance of Ana also compels Annie to reconsider the history of her own mother, Ina. Frustrated by her marriage and the provincial atmosphere of Vancouver in the 1950s and 1960s, Ina descends into madness, which is presented as the only alternative to conformity, and disappears into a lobotomized silence. Marlatt explains in *Readings from the Labyrinth*, a collection of essays and journal entries, that *Ana Historic* is composed of Annie's attempts "to find a way of speaking her reality without going mad, as her mother does, or fading into silence as Ana Richards does."[174] Annie is the centre of this novel, which, as Keith Green and Jill LeBihan describe it, "contains mental dialogues between Annie and long-dead Ana, Annie and recently dead Ina, Annie and her new lover Zoe; it sets out to represent these women either as speaking subjects themselves or as speaking through the subject (Annie)."[175] In reading her own desires through these women, Annie takes liberty with the brief historical record and imagines a lesbian affair for Ana, as well as speculating on the relation of Ina's madness to the mother's stifled sexuality. The resulting narrative contravenes Richard's historiographic method, but Annie justifies her speculations on the grounds that Richard's method has edited out women, and in particular lesbians, from history.

Marlatt calls *Ana Historic* "a fictional autobiography."[176] She marvels that in the writing of the novel "whole phrases came back to [her] that were [her] mother's," and there are echoes of Marlatt's marriage as well in the relations of Annie and the professor.[177] In a 1968 journal entry, Marlatt expresses her fear of becoming the sort of "faculty wife" that Annie is: "not 'struggling students' anymore, as Al said. now he's a faculty member & I'm a 'faculty wife' (part-time English teacher too). it doesn't fit & yet it's what we've worked for, or he has, to return successful – home town boy makes good."[178] Both Alan Marlatt and Kiyooka were UBC professors, but the avant-garde Kiyooka bears little resemblance to the conservative Anderson, and Marlatt cautions that "Annie isn't me though she may be one of the selves i could be."[179] Furthermore, as Annette Lönnecke's work on

Marlatt's *How Hug a Stone* and Ondaatje's *Running in the Family* demonstrates, "a postmodern version of autobiography calls for an autobiographical concept which allows an autobiography to criticize its own generic
limits [and it] forges the link between self and world anew."[180] *Ana His-*
toric is thus a fiction that performs a variation on the autobiographical faculty novel, which is rarely told from the perspective of the "faculty wife,"
especially one who abandons her husband for a woman.[181]

In this fiction, Marlatt establishes distance between herself and her characters through Annie's metafictive role. Yet, at the same time, Annie's editor, Zoe, rejects this distancing practice. In discussing the book that Annie
is writing, Zoe criticizes Annie's use of personae: "'characters.' you talk as
if they were strangers. who are they if they aren't you?"[182] As in *Zócalo*,
Marlatt's novel invites and inhibits an autobiographical reading. I am not
concerned to establish the autobiographical veracity of these works, but I
do want to stress the continuity of the authorial process that shapes the
interpretive framework for the facts.

I am interested in the way narrative events in *Ana Historic* stand in a
serial relation to her earlier works and participate in an ongoing reconfigu-
ration of the narrative paradigm articulated in *Frames of a Story*. Marlatt
defines a fact as "the f stop of act[,] a still photo in the ongoing cinerama,"
and she insists that the facts be interpreted as significant points in a larger
process.[183] Each frame in this literary cinerama depicts a new set of fictional circumstances, but draws from a common set of narrative motifs. In
Frames and *Zócalo*, the male protagonist embarks on a physical and intellectual journey from which the female protagonist is excluded. The woman
tries to follow the man but she encounters a number of impediments that
make her feel physically restricted and emotionally confined. To combat
this sense of containment, the woman embarks on a quest of her own that
is literary in nature. On this separate journey, the woman has a lesbian
encounter in which she grapples with the conflicting impulses of fear and
attraction. Fear gets the better of her and she resumes her heterosexual relationship, only to find that the emotional divide between herself and her
male lover has widened. In *Frames* and *Zócalo*, the woman feels compelled
to abandon the heterosexual relationship, but the stories end by suspending
her decision. In *Ana Historic*, however, the heroine overcomes this state of
inaction. Instead of remaining in a relationship in which she plays a subordinate role as a research assistant, Annie decides to write her own book and
consummate her desire for her lesbian friend and editor, Zoe.

Ana Historic begins with a bedroom scene that echoes the "hell" episode
in *Zócalo*. It depicts Annie trapped in a marriage bed that feels to her like a

prison: "Who's There? she was whispering. knock knock. in the dark. only it wasn't dark had woken her to her solitude, conscious alone in the night of his snoring more like snuffling dreaming elsewhere, burrowed into it, under the covers against her in animal sleep. he was dreaming without her in some place she had no access to and she was awake. now she would have to move, shift, legs aware of themselves and wanting out."[184] Annie whispers to herself in the dark, exploring the mouth of some nameless potential that the woman in *Zócalo* had submerged in silence. She reproduces the question and answer dynamic that concluded *Zócalo*, but in posing this question aloud to herself, Annie stands a better chance of evoking a response than her predecessor did:

> it was the sound of her own voice had woken her, heard like an echo asking,
>> who's there?
>>> echoes from further back, her fear-defiant child voice carried still in her chest, stealing at night into the basement with the carving knife toward those wardrobes at the bottom of the staircase. wardrobes. wordrobes. warding off what?[185]

Whereas, after Ovid, the Echo of Graeco-Roman myth pined for Narcissus (who loved only himself) and could only repeat the last syllables of his words, Annie responds to a loveless marriage (and a husband enamoured of his own projects) by listening closely to the child's voice within the adult one. As in *Frames*, the narrator in *Ana Historic* searches for an explanation to her present condition in her childhood and the manner of speaking that she learned in those formative years. The answers Annie seeks come from the sound of this voice, not from the man beside her.

The wardrobe/wordrobe that the narrator is afraid to open/articulate resembles the malevolent parcel that the woman in *Zócalo* is afraid to unwrap. Annie repeatedly descends the staircase and opens the door, but she recoils every time at the absence she finds:

> Who's There?
>> empty. it always was. though every time she believed it might not be. relief, adrenalin shaking her legs. she had chosen the darkest first and must go to each in turn, confronting her fear.[186]

Annie's quest in *Ana Historic* is to confront and transform this fear from a negative absence into a positive presence. In the process, she must revise the

Freudian/Lacanian association of female genitalia with lack and develop a body-centred idiom that is capable of donning these wordrobes and bringing them out of the closet.

The first step in achieving this conversion is, for Marlatt, to reconsider the storytelling paradigms that shape desire in narrative. As in *Frames*, Marlatt returns to fairytales in *Ana Historic* to explore the formative influence of children's literature on adult sexuality. Robin Hood, Lancelot, Little Lulu, and the Lost Girls in Never-Never Land all make an appearance in the opening chapter, as does Bluebeard, whose nasty reputation emphasizes the taboo act of the young girl opening the closet door. However, as Heather Zwicker observes, the most important among these fairytale figures is Frankenstein, because Annie's castrating knife discovers, not a phallus, nor even Gerda's muff, but a crystallization of her fears:

> The empty closet – initially a puzzling trope – stages Marlatt's complicated vision. Whereas conventions of the coming-out narrative posit a stable closet out of which emerges a homosexual Self, Marlatt turns the closet inside out around homophobic fear. The figure of Frankenstein the monster is crucial here – but inverted. Instead of using Frankenstein in the most transparent sense as outlaw and inassimilable Other, in order to revalorize conventional representations of lesbianism as monstrosity, Marlatt shows the ways in which homophobia at once creates and exceeds the carceral dimensions of the closet as a trope.
>
> Instead of Frankenstein, what Annie confronts when she flings open the dark wardrobe door is the fear that she will "end up as girls were meant to be." The monster is not, then, a presence in the closet, but a free-floating signifier for the terror that keeps women inside the bounds of propriety.[187]

Initially, Annie stays within these bounds, even when she believes she is being transgressive. When Annie informs Ina that she is pregnant and planning to marry her history professor, she realizes that even her rebellion has been scripted: "i ended up doing what i was meant to, i followed the plotline through, the story you had me enact."[188] In marrying a conservative historian known for his well-supported research, Annie weds herself to "history[,] the story ... of dominance. mastery. the bold line of it."[189] Separating herself from Richard pushes Annie to reconsider the method and moral of this story.

Although Richard's perception of Annie as his assistant at first appears to be the cause of her sorrow, the problem is much larger, more systemic,

and reaches back to her childhood. Annie argues that the male gaze in general converts all action by women into the passive, and her description of
the pick-up scene at the Princess Pool provides ample support for her
claim.[190] Annie summarizes the mood of her teenage years by stressing the
passivity and absence associated with the vaginal "o": "(o the luck, to be
looked at. o the lack, if you weren't. o the look. looking as if it all depended
on it)."[191] Analysing this "look," she argues that the male gaze is part of an
incestuous practice in which mother and daughter compete for the father's
approving gaze. When Ina accuses Annie of playing the "Perfect Little
Mother" and trying to replace her[192] – as Richard's star student will try to
replace Annie[193] – the daughter replies: "the truth is (your truth, my truth,
if you would admit it) incest is always present, it's there in the way we're
trained to solicit the look, and first of all the father's, Our Father's. framed
by a phrase that judges (virgin / tramp), sized-up in a glance, objectified.
that's what history offers, that's its allure, its pretence. 'history says of her
...' but when you're so framed, caught in the act, the (f) stop of act, fact –
what recourse? step inside the picture and open it up."[194] Thus, for Annie,
unframing history necessitates unframing the Freudian family drama.

Yet Annie also courts her mother's attention, and the incestuous quality
of desire in *Ana Historic* extends to Ina's "soft breast under blue wool
dressing gown, tea breath, warm touch."[195] Marlatt equates loving with
birthing in her later writings, and incest is always present in the language
she uses to describe lesbian relationships, from "Musing with Mothertongue" through *Ana Historic* to *Two Women in a Birth* (1994), a collaboration with her lover in the 1980s, Betsy Warland.

The scene in which Annie discusses *Frankenstein* demonstrates how
Marlatt doubles Ina and Zoe as mother-figures to Annie within *Ana Historic*. During one of their editorial sessions, Zoe grows impatient with
Annie's need to fictionalize her desire instead of acting on it, and she challenges Annie: "and you? do you really exist?"[196] Annie recognizes "Ina in
that phrase" and her thoughts turn to her mother, whom she also characterizes as "[her] fear, [her] critic."[197] Just as the mother in *Zócalo* doubled
as the voice of heterosexual propriety and of lesbian eroticism, Annie oscil-
lates between two mother-figures in *Ana Historic* who represent opposite
poles of behaviour. Annie's erotically charged dialogue with Zoe in the cafe
switches to an internal dialogue with her mother in which Ina admonishes
Annie for not telling a story properly, and Annie replies: "if i'm telling a
story i'm untelling it. untelling the real. trying to get back the child who
went too far, got lost in the woods, walked into the arms of Frankenstein."[198] At the mention of Frankenstein, Ina thinks of "that Spanish

movie about a child's fantasy" in which Frankenstein is a monster, but Annie reminds her that in the book "Frankenstein was the man who created [the monster]."[199] The contrast between the original story by Mary Shelley and its film adaptations is crucial because Shelley wrote *Frankenstein* in 1818, shortly after her marriage to Percy Bysshe Shelley and while she was pregnant with her first child. Hers is a horror story (composed during a ghost-story competition between Percy Bysshe and his friends) about a creation that returns to destroy its creator, part of the fear of a male child that Zoe and Annie discuss shortly before the conversation about Frankenstein.[200] The film versions of *Frankenstein*, on the other hand, represent "a man's name for man's fear of the wild, the uncontrolled. that's where *she* lives."[201]

In Cohen's *Beautiful Losers*, the historian exhibits this fear of the uncontrolled when, in a moment of "fake universal comprehension," he imagines sewing the fragmented world together with his phallus turned needle.[202] However, when F. instructs the historian to call him "Dr Frankenstein with a deadline," he demonstrates the entropic consequences of this rage for order.[203] F. imagines waking up "in the middle of a car accident, limbs strewn everywhere, detached voices screaming for comfort," and sewing the fragments together: "My needle going so madly, sometimes I found I'd run the thread right through my own flesh and I was joined to one of my own grotesque creations – I'd rip us apart – and then I heard my own voice howling with the others, and I knew that I was also truly part of the disaster. But I also realized that I was not the only one on my knees sewing frantically. There were others like me, making the same monstrous mistakes, driven by the same impure urgency, stitching themselves into the ruined heap, painfully extracting themselves."[204] Annie aims to find a method of sewing lives together without sacrificing identity, and she tries to convert grotesque fear into a positive vision.

In *Ana Historic* the uninhibited "*she*" is Zoe, the robbergirl-figure, so there remains a transparent sense in which Frankenstein is the outlaw. However, Annie recognizes that the monstrosity is her fear of her own desire, not Zoe. Therefore, Annie works to transform her behavioural patterns such that she and Zoe can "giv[e] birth, to each other" at the conclusion of the novel without disastrous consequences.[205] Annie does not want to write the story of heterosexual conquest, as she asserts on one of the nearly blank pages that interrupt the narrative: "this is not a roman / ce, it doesn't deal with heroes."[206] Instead of conquering a feared Other, Annie seeks to conquer the fear of alterity in herself and offer a feminist vision of the heroine.

To break the causal chain of the heterosexual quest narrative and fashion a lesbian one, then, demands that Annie reconsider the relation of women to *eros* and power. As Carson explains in *Eros the Bittersweet*, the "Greek word *eros* denotes 'want,' 'lack,' 'desire for that which is missing'": "The lover wants what he does not have. It is by definition impossible for him to have what he wants if, as soon as it is had, it is no longer wanting. This is more than wordplay."[207] In *Ana Historic* this desire for something missing guides the narrative voice as well as the wordplay, and Annie rejects the objective tone that Richard urges her to adopt: "i don't want history's voice. i want ... something is wanting in me. and it all goes blank on a word. want. what does it mean, to be lacking? empty. wanton. vanish. vacant, vacuum, evacuate. all these empty words except for wanton (lacking discipline, lewd). a word for the wild. for the gap i keep coming to."[208] Through wordplay, Annie converts the etymology of "eros" from a passive lack to an aggressive presence or wantonness.[209] Annie uses this wanton voice to rewrite history because erotic attraction challenges the causal logic that undergirds conventional historiography. One cannot "speak or write rationally of the erotic," says Marlatt, because the erotic "is raw power, a current surging through my body surging beyond the limits of self-containment, beyond the limits of syntax and logic."[210] In the anti-authorian power of the erotic, Annie finds the force to challenge the codes of rationality that she blames for Ina's madness: "it occurs to me you died of reason ... i mean explanation, justification, normal mental state – that old standard."[211]

Of course, in Greek mythology Eros is a meddling boy who creates sensations of longing in men and women alike. Marlatt seeks a specifically feminist version of this power. Hence Annie's experiments in body-conscious "scribbling" coincide with her learning to express her desire for women.[212] "Meaning-slippage, seductive by-play, wet labia, 'labyl mynde' and labial phonetics all find a place in a joyous slide of meaning in rhythmic lines across the page[s]" of *Ana Historic*, and the absence of longing reasserts itself as a presence through Marlatt's poetic word associations.[213] The sentence, for Marlatt, is an expression of sensuality, and with this etymology in mind she fashions an erotic narrative that reclaims the sensual in the sensible: "in poetry, which has evolved out of chant and song, in rhyming and tone-leading, whether they occur in prose or poetry, sound will initiate thought by a process of association. words call each other up, evoke each other, provoke each other, nudge each other into utterance. we know from dreams and schizophrenic speech how deeply association works in our psyches, a form of thought that is not rational but erotic because it works by attraction."[214] By reconsidering the function of desire in the quest

narrative and structuring her narrative around "concept constellations" –
or what chaos theory calls strange attractors – Marlatt devises a serial
alternative to the single lodestone of linear prose.[215] The recursive
symmetries of the serial poem can efficiently be transformed into prose.

TRANSFORMING ECHO: MARLATT'S RECURSIVE NARRATIVE

As Marlatt explains in "Eratic/Erotic Narrative: Syntax and Mortality in
Robin Blaser's 'Image Nations,'" the logic of serial narrative can generate a
different style of prose from one that follows time's arrow: "When a poet
engages prose, prose, that 'straightforward discourse,' is not single-track. It
leaps like verse, returns circuitous, doubles over, duplicit and incantatory,
resists the sentence that wants to come to a full stop. Endings: the problem
of syntax like the problem of narrative in the serial poem: mortality. 'Its
unrest and proses.'"[216] Marlatt's serial novel is thus a kind of anti-novel, as
Annie declares on one of the nearly blank pages interspersed throughout
Ana Historic: "a book of interruptions is not a novel."[217] Writing out of a
medial position between poetry and prose, Marlatt strives to reconcile theoretical discourse with "that strong pull to narrative, even the loosest kind,
& a lyrically charged language coincident with it."[218] Like Ondaatje,
Marlatt employs echoes to create continuity across the segmented narrative, with its juxtaposed genres, times, and places.

  Echoes give the novel a recursive structure akin to the anaphoristic repetitions of poetry, as the repetition of "who's there?" in the opening chapter
of *Ana Historic* demonstrates. Marlatt's journal entries catalogue "knock-
knock jokes for Ana" that resemble bp Nichol's saints' names in *The
Martyrology*: "Ana Colutha / Ana M. Nesis / Ana Chronistic."[219] The latter knock-knock (Who's there? Ana. Ana who?) jokes outline two of the
novel's major themes, time and reminiscence, while the former denotes
"syntactical inconsistency or incoherence within a sentence; *esp*: the shift
from one construction to another."[220] Thus, the "ana" in anaphora is part
of the wordplay that structures the text. Caroline Rosenthal also sees a
number of anagrams in the names of Marlatt's characters. Following
Scheel, she notes that "'Zoe' means 'living'"; she also notes that "Birdie
contains two possibilities as the word can be reconfigured to mean 'bride,'
woman situated within the patriarchal system, or 'bird,' free to step outside
of those conventions."[221] Anagrams create multiplicitous echoes within the
seeming unity of words and non-linear possibilities within the linear
movement of reading.

In addition to disrupting chronology, Marlatt shifts the syntactic frame-work from the linear pattern of subject-verb-object to what she considers a less masculine format, as she suggests in another knock-knock joke: "Ana Strophe: inversion of the normal (syntactic) order."[222] Given the baptismal theme of water, white robes, and rebirth in *Ana Historic*, the reader also perceives a playful reformulation of "Anabaptist," which means "one who baptizes again" and refers to the practice of adult baptism.[223] In place of a patriarchal cosmology ordered by the unitary, masculine *Logos*, Annie for-mulates a lesbian world view based on ana-logies between women's lives, variations on keywords, and an adult baptism into a new belief system.

Peter Dickinson examines Marlatt's analogical practice in "Towards a Transnational, Translational Feminist Poetics: Lesbian Fiction/Theory in Canada and Quebec" and demonstrates that the trope of translation ani-mates her novels.[224] Marlatt graduated from Indiana University in 1968 with a degree in comparative literature, and she has tried to bridge the divide between Anglo-Canadian and Québécoise writing by co-organizing the 1983 *Women and Words / Les femmes et les mots* conference and co-founding the bilingual journal *Tessera*. *Tessera* seeks to facilitate the exchange of women-centred theories of literature, but its principal impact seems to have been to motivate anglophone writers to engage with the kinds of *écriture féminine* being practised in Quebec by the likes of Marlatt's collaborator, Nicole Brossard. In his chapter on Marlatt and Brossard, Dickinson surveys the theories of composition that configure les-bian writing as a practice of translation through which the lesbian articu-lates selfhood and desire in an alien code (a language geared toward patriarchal expression). He shows how this translational sensibility influ-ences everything from Marlatt's rethinking of the relation between the female body and the nation to her unorthodox syntax and punctuation. Jun Ling Khoo also examines Marlatt's collaborations with Brossard and demonstrates that the authors bring translation out of the literary closet and turn it into a collaborative performance that contests patriarchal codes of sexuality and cultural belonging.[225] However, Dickinson cautions that "such a poetics need not automatically imply an end point of transcen-dence," and he concludes by arguing that Marlatt's achievement in the novel is to establish a viable "*counter*-narrative" to standard discourses of settlement and nationhood.[226] This point is worth keeping in mind when one considers the emancipatory rhetoric toward the conclusion of *Ana Historic*.

Annie thinks of writing as "knocking on paper, not wood, tapping like someone blind along the wall of her solitude."[227] However, Marlatt's writing is not as directionless and blind as she would have the reader believe. In place of an Aristotelean beginning, middle, and end, the "knock knock" echoes in *Ana Historic* map the major transformative points of Annie's story. After the sequence of echoes in the opening paragraphs, the echo resurfaces when Annie resolves to abandon research on Richard's book and get serious about writing her own story, "tapping there, looking for a way out of the blank that faced her."[228] Exploring "the unspoken urge of a body insisting itself in the words," Annie hears the refrain: "who's there? (knock, knock). who else *is* there in this disappearing act when you keep leaving yourself behind the next bend. given that 'yourself' is everything you've been, the trail leading backwards and away from you."[229] As Annie ponders her past selves and the sexual politics that fuelled her rivalry with Ina for her father's attention, she hears the knocking once more: "trying. a trying child. trying it on for size. the role. all that she had been told would make her a woman. (knock, knock). would she ever be one?"[230] However, Ina's descent into madness warns Annie against accepting this conventional role, which she blames for her mother's eventual lobotomization: "when Harald brought you home, he brought home a new fear (who's there?) that no one was there at all. Mum: mum. wandering around in some lost place, incapable of saying what it was they'd done to you. under the role or robe was no one."[231] Thus the recurring phrase is no joke: it awakens Annie's fear of lesbian desire at the same time as it augments her fear of becoming her mother. This indeterminacy creates suspense for the reader in terms of the passage of events, but it also unsettles the reader-protagonist relationship. Carson notes that "the Greek verb 'to read' is *anagignōskein*, a compound of the verb 'to know' (*gignōskein*) and the prefix *ana*, meaning 'again.' If you are reading, you are not at the beginning."[232] By the same token, the answer to the question "Who's there?" is always in part "the reader," and the story the reader weaves into Marlatt's tale through empathy precedes the beginning of the book and plays a role in its conclusion.

The final knock-knock sequence occurs when Annie breaks her long silence by responding to Zoe in word and deed: "Annie – she said, as if it were fiction, as if there were quotation marks around it – Annie Richards. the sound of a door closing."[233] The painful memory of Ina's silence gives Annie the courage to open this taboo door and declare herself to her would-be lover:

> i want to knock: can you hear? i want to answer her who's there? not
> Ana or Ina, those transparent covers. Ana Richards Richard's Anna.
> fooling myself on the other side of history as if it were a line dividing

the real from the unreal. Annie / Ana – arose by any other name, whole wardrobes of names guarding the limitations – we rise above them. Annie isn't Richard's or even Springer's.

Annie Torrent, i said. (she looked up from the water she was floating something on in the dark, white robes or words, silver boats.)[234]

Whereas Gerda floats helplessly down a river in a boat to begin her journey, Annie and Zoe take control of the words and metaphors that are the "silver boats" conveying the story of Annie's initiation.

In *Frames*, Marlatt expresses a desire to "tap again, at the still centre of the story, power that is conjuring," but she is perplexed by the question, "who of who?"[235] In *Ana Historic*, Annie answers this question by renaming herself and identifying her true love. However, she still must summon the wantonness to act on Zoe's question, "what is it you want?": "she asks me to present myself, to take the leap, as the blood rushes into my face and i can speak: you. i want you. *and* me. together."[236] This passage replays an ambiguous stanza from *Frames*. Shortly after the robbergirl scene, an indented and bracketed stanza disrupts the lineation of a larger lyric:

> your face, it's familiar
> what do you want?
> you to be there[237]

The "you" in this passage could be a flash-forward to Gerda's meeting with Kay or a flashback to Marlatt's encounter with her female lover. However, in *Ana Historic*, Annie clearly designates Zoe as her choice. Finally, one of Marlatt's heroines achieves "one clear act." The erotic force of the concluding scenes derive its energy from the breakdown of the social and narratological restrictions that had previously obscured a clear expression of this desire in Annie and her predecessors.

Marlatt employs pronominal uncertainty to a different end at the conclusion of *Ana Historic*. Whereas Marlatt uses the second-person pronoun in *Frames* to conceal the object of her desire, in *Ana Historic* she employs the second person to confound the identity of the desiring subject. Marlatt "gives voice to the relationships between women by creating a nonexclusive pronominal system" as Green and LeBihan argue in "The Speaking Object: Daphne Marlatt's Pronouns and Lesbian Poetics."[238] Green and LeBihan build their argument around the pronominal indeterminacy of a lyric that appears on one of the "interruption" pages in *Ana Historic*:

                    worlds apart she says
                    the world is

                    a-historic
                    she who is you
                    or me
                       "i"
                    address this to[239]

Reversing the "Great Man" approach to historiography, in which the
events of an age are interpreted through the life of a prominent man,
Marlatt opens the a-historic subject position to a variety of women from
diverse historical periods. Green and LeBihan explain that the lyric "i" is
not exclusive in this case:

> Although other poems in the novel refer explicitly to 'ana,' this poem
> more readily participates in the discourse of lyric poetry because of its
> pronominal reference and lack of antecedent or cataphoric full forms.
> The poem is thus a deictic center whose references form a large and
> significant paradigm of participants. The pronouns could be attached
> to any of the women in the narrative (Annie, Zoe, Ina, Ana
> Richards) since these characters are directly addressed in dialogic
> exchange elsewhere in the novel. The "you" and "me" could plausibly
> be directed towards women outside the text too (the reader, the writer).
> Locating a speaking subject in the poem proves astonishingly
> difficult."[240]

In this manner, Marlatt complicates the apostrophic mode of the lyric and
returns to a question that she first articulated in *Vancouver Poems* (1972):
"How far do 'I' go & where do 'you' begin."[241] She also embeds this question into the coda to *Ana Historic*.
     The "you" in the concluding prose poem confuses second-person refer-
ents and thereby draws the reader into the narrative:

                    we give place, giving words, giving birth, to
                    each other – she and me. you. hot skin writing
                    skin. fluid edge, wick, wick. she draws me
                    out. you she breathes, is where we meet.
                    breeze from the window reaching you now, trees
                    out there, streets you might walk down, will,

soon. it isn't dark but the luxury of being
has woken you, the reach of your desire, reading
us into the page ahead.[242]

Whereas the second line of the coda distinguishes first, second, and third persons, the "you" in the fourth line refers to either the narrator or the reader, depending on whether the passage is dialogue or not. This indeterminacy displaces the centrality of Annie in the story and opens up a space for readers to become the focus of the narrative. The accusative coaxes readers to take off what Bowering calls their "invisibility suit[s]" even as it dispels the "dark" of Annie's homophobic fear.[243] Together, reader, author, and protagonist come out of their respective closets.

The bedroom scenes that frame *Ana Historic* thus shape the narrative as a space of transformation for Annie as a desiring subject – a series of closets to enter and exit. Moving from Richard's bed to Zoe's, and from the stairs to her childhood basement to the stairs to Zoe's bedroom, Annie breaks the mold of Andersen's quest narrative, as well as disrupting "a feminism anchored to a single axis of gender as heterosexual difference", as Gillian Whitlock observes.[244] Annie's character develops, but she narrates her development on her own terms. Thus, as Green and LeBihan argue, in "reproducing a mother-daughter dialogue, in presenting a narrator with both lesbian and heterosexual relationships, in using extracts from historical and scientific documentaries as part of a fiction, and by creating psychological fantasy, *ana historic* both claims and rejects reassuring points of reference."[245] This collaging of reference points also informs the cover image on the Anansi edition of *Ana Historic* (1997), which presents a portrait of a young woman (held in the palm of what appears to be the photographer) and raised against a backdrop of maps and archival photographs. The image's overlapping frames of reference disallow a fixed vantage point and the presence of the mysterious hand raises questions of self-reflexivity and the role of the perceiver in (self-)portraiture.

The convolutions of Marlatt's "Eratic/Erotic" narrative in *Ana Historic* also confound the psychoanalytic templates that influenced her early prose works. After exploring the Freudian notion of absence and lack in women, Annie converts it to the plenitude of her new world view. Thus *Ana Historic* "resists easy assimilation into a pattern provided by any one psychoanalytic metanarrative," but this fact does not mean that Marlatt rejects all metanarratives per se.[246] In an interview with Brenda Carr, Marlatt explains that the feminist dimension of her writing derives from her choice of a political metanarrative:

Working for change is what makes feminism different from the postmodernism I learned from the *Tish* days. Even though there's a continuity with some of those strategies, I'm using them for different ends now ... Postmodernism, although it critiques the master narratives of our culture, the institutions and the codes, still ends up being complicit with them because it has no program for change. A program for change means valorizing a difference, and as soon as you valorize a difference you're moving out of postmodernist deconstruction into a position of ... belief or trust in a certain meta-narrative. It's a difference at such a basic level that I think it's often been overlooked, but it's a difference that leads to a radical shift in world-view.[247]

Marlatt tends to attract a different readership from Ondaatje and Bowering precisely because of what Glen Lowry has characterized as her "ability to tie formal innovation to political purpose."[248]

RETHINKING UTOPIA

But is it possible to have a metanarrative that is not a master narrative? There are certainly traces of the old master narratives in Marlatt's new metanarrative. Knutson observes that although the "refusal of the patriarchal logos opens into the endless multiplicity of women's experiences," Marlatt's "often utopian projection of a postpatriarchal epistemology is a feminist vision of the metanarrative of the liberation of the people."[249] Thus Marlatt has not entirely done away with linearity in *Ana Historic* because A and Z come together in an alphabetical and orgasmic completion that creates a progressive story arc from the heterosexual bedroom to the lesbian one.

Of course, Annie maintains that the coda is not the end of the story. She writes "the period that arrives at no full stop" and directs the reader to the page ahead.[250] This gesture inhibits closure but it encourages eschatology by pointing toward a utopian future. On the other hand, Annie informs the reader that the "story is 'only a story' insofar as it ends ... in life we go on."[251] In her own life Marlatt goes on to write a more openly autobiographical novel, *Taken* (1996), in which the emancipatory rhetoric of *Ana Historic* is notably absent. *Taken* fictionalizes the end of Marlatt's relationship with Betsy Warland and thereby follows the elegiac pattern that seems to inspire her prose. The novel dispels the utopian fervour of *Ana Historic* by illustrating how the breakdown of a lesbian relationship during the Persian Gulf War (1990–91) mirrors a crisis in Marlatt's parents' marriage during the Second World War. As in *Frames*, the narrator is abandoned by her lover and turns to writing "to fix an image so it won't fade over time."[252] Returning to the labyrinth, she "hang[s] onto that slight thread in the darkness of [her lover] gone" and acknowledges that the legacy of the past is difficult to escape because old narratives resurface in new guises.[253] By way of conclusion, the narrator asserts that everyone in society is "complicit, yes. Folded into the wreckage of grief and power" created by the past.[254] However, she resolves to allow her serial narratives to "go on spinning out of eyeshot, snapshot, beyond the reach of evidence. The stories we invent and refuse to invent ourselves by, all unfinished ..."[255]

Given this admission of complicity, it is appropriate that one of the scripts Marlatt breaks in *Taken* is that of *Ana Historic*. She tells Sue Kossew that "there is a conscious connection between [the novels] because when I finished writing *Ana Historic* I realized that I wanted to go back and talk about the mother figure. I felt that she was too much a victim figure in *Ana Historic* and that there wasn't enough of her past to explain why she was like that. So I thought I needed to write a book about *her* young adulthood and the war. I was very interested in talking about how war impacts on civilian women and it just so happened that the Gulf War started at the same time so, of course, it got written in."[256] Marlatt's practice of rewriting master-texts thus extends to her own most successful publication.

Another ambivalence can be found in *Ana Historic* if one ignores the tone of the coda and examines the narrative on an abstract level. *Ana Historic* experiments at the level of the sentence, but conforms to certain genre conventions at the level of the chapter. In comic plots such as the one that shapes *The Snow Queen*, the narrative crisis produced by a period of misrule is generally resolved by a marriage at the conclusion. Heather Zwicker observes that *Ana Historic* "parodically reproduces the comic plot of marriage and childbirth by rendering both lesbian."[257] Thus, in the same way that Marlatt reconfigures the linear values of standard syntax, she reconfigures the comic model such that men no longer play the dominant role in the plot's libidinal economy. For Annie, "the lure of absence" is initially "self-effacing," a desire to submerge her personality in the role of the conventional housewife.[258] Later, the lure of absence is precisely the opposite: Annie's desire to develop a life outside the framework of heterosexual norms. *Taken* indicates, however, that these frameworks overlap and that behavioural patterns identified with heterosexuality and patriarchy also manifest themselves in lesbian relationships.

While *Frames of a Story*, *Zócalo*, and *Ana Historic* do not usher in a utopian era, their accomplishment is to transform a mythic paradigm that the

author once believed governed her life. Marlatt's new variations of the
quest narrative do not ossify into static paradigms; nor should they, as
Teresa de Lauretis maintains in her introduction to *Feminist Studies/Criti-
cal Studies*: "An all-purpose feminist frame of reference does not exist, nor
should it ever come prepackaged and ready-made. We need to keep building one, absolutely flexible and readjustable, from women's own experience of difference, of our difference from Woman and of the differences
among women; differences which ... are perceived as having as much (or
more) to do with race, class, or ethnicity as with gender or sexuality per
se."[259] Marlatt employs the recursive symmetries of the serial poem in her
prose to record the "endlessly repeating and not exactly repeated cycles [a
woman's] body knows" and to fashion a narrative structure that accommo-
dates this body consciousness and sense of flux.[260] However, there are
other revisionist strategies besides Marlatt's proprioceptive method, as
Anne Carson demonstrates in *Autobiography of Red*, where she rewrites a
quest narrative and its erotic subtext from the perspective of a male
monster.

6

Anne Carson: (Un)framing Myth

MDM: *Plainwater* is described or "packaged" as an anthology of essays and poetry yet I found it in the critical anthologies section of a large bookstore. Some works need sections entirely on their own. Is this a problem for you? For reviewers? For publishers? For bookstore clerks?
AC: Not a problem but a question: What do "shelves" accomplish, in stores or in the mind?[1]

As in this interview with Mary di Michele, Anne Carson repeatedly tells interviewers that she defies genre conventions because her favourite means of stimulating her imagination "is to break rules or change categories or go outside where they say the line is."[2] The subtitle of Carson's *Autobiography of Red: A Novel in Verse* only hints at the variety of genres that the Montreal poet employs.[3] In *Autobiography of Red* Carson brings together a preface on the Greek poet Stesichoros, translated fragments of Stesichoros's long poem *Geryoneis*, three appendices on the blinding of Stesichoros by Helen, a romance in verse recasting Stesichoros's *Geryoneis* as a contemporary gay love affair, and a mock interview with the "choir-master." Each section has its own style and story to tell. Although the romance in verse forms the core of *Autobiography of Red,* this narrative sequence is surrounded by an elaborate series of scholarly frameworks whose epigrams come to play a central role in the conclusion of the story. Men appear to be the subject of both the romance and the academic apparatus, but Carson sets the stories of Stesichoros, Geryon, and Herakles within a framework of citations from Gertrude Stein and Emily Dickinson that, far from being subordinate, assumes equal importance with the male-centred narrative when Stein supplants Stesichoros as the "choir-master" in the concluding interview.

At the same time, Carson's allusions to the myth of Isis emphasize her (un)framing of mythic forms. Her retelling of the *Geryoneis* (itself a lyrical revision of an epic myth) draws inspiration from Stesichoros's portrait of

Helen of Troy in the *Palinode* (a recantation of the poet's earlier, Homeric portrait), as well as from the mythic scenes in which Isis reconstitutes the fragmented body of Osiris. Negotiating this complex arrangement of literary allusions, Carson uses shifts in gender and genre to foreground her extensive alterations to the myths that underlie *Autobiography of Red*. She performs a chiasmus on the power relations within these myths such that the novel in verse becomes a novel inverse – that is, an overturning of expectations in both form and content.

Because *Autobiography of Red* employs fragmentation and "radical recontextualization" to "overturn the conventional distinction between a framing 'master-text' and a cited text that exists in supplementary relation to it," the novel in verse could be situated in the Canadian tradition of "documentary-*collage*" that Manina Jones traces in works such as *The Collected Works of Billy the Kid* and *Ana Historic*.[4] Indeed, Daphne Marlatt has written a favourable review of *Autobiography of Red,* and its cover bears a strong endorsement from Ondaatje: "Anne Carson is, for me, the most exciting poet writing in English today."[5] The connection to Ondaatje is particularly intriguing because, in a 1984 interview with Sam Solecki, Ondaatje denounced the segregating mentality of literary criticism and then made this prophetic statement: "We really need a Guy Davenport around us. Instead we get a lot of self-serving essays on all these forms. I think it's very dangerous for a writer to be living in a community obsessed with all these categories."[6] Two years later, Carson published a condensed version of her doctoral dissertation from the University of Toronto entitled *Eros the Bittersweet*. A lyrical meditation on classical philosophy, this book anticipates Carson's later work in the lyric essay, as well as her sequence of prose poems, *Short Talks* (1992), which she describes as a series of "one-minute lectures."[7] *Short Talks* was published by Brick Books, a small press edited by Don McKay, which is affiliated with the literary magazine *Brick*, where Ondaatje is an associate editor. Although Ondaatje had no part in soliciting or editing the manuscript, his comments illustrate that there was a niche in Canadian literature waiting to be filled by someone who could combine classical and modern forms in eclectic ways that defied Cohen's caricature of the constipated academic.[8] Carson's theory of myth as duplicity has inspired comparisons to Ondaatje's work from Solecki and other critics.[9] But whereas editors such as Dennis Lee had pressured Ondaatje to abandon his early interest in classical myth in favour of New World mythologies, Carson (who attended the University of Toronto in the heyday of Canadian nationalism) persisted with her classical studies in a fashion that pushed her writing underground for the next two decades.

In 1995 Carson published two collections that combined long poems and essays: *Plainwater* (Vintage) and *Glass, Irony and God* (New Directions). The latter featured an introduction by Guy Davenport in which the innovative American classicist marvels that Carson "writes philosophy and critical essays that are as beautiful and charming as good poetry," and he affiliates Carson with a group of poets (including Joyce, Pound, and Stein) who "dare new forms."[10] However, the strong Hellenic influence on Carson's writing also prompts Davenport to situate Carson's poetry within a revived classicism: "She is among those who are returning poetry to good strong narrative (as we might expect of a classicist). She shifts attention from repeating stanzaic form (which came about when all poems were songs) to well-contoured blocks of phrases: analogues of paragraphs in prose. Prose will not accommodate Carson's syncopations, her terseness, her deft changes of scene."[11] Marlatt has adopted the term "stanzagraph" to describe her dense poetic paragraphs, where non-standard punctuation divides her lyrical phrases in place of line breaks.[12] But Carson takes a different approach to amalgamating poetry and prose. The romance at the centre of *Autobiography of Red* alternates between long and short line lengths to approximate the feel of the heroic metre of epic, without ever abandoning the lyric voice or attempting to scan.

THE "MIMNERMOS" PRECEDENT

The romance in *Autobiography of Red* upholds Davenport's argument for "good strong narrative," and hence the storytelling dimension of classical verse, which established the basis for modern prose and the novel, is foregrounded. But the scholarly framework surrounding Carson's romance is modelled on her non-narrative experiments in the long poem "Mimnermos: The Brainsex Paintings," collected in *Plainwater*.[13] "Mimnermos: The Brainsex Paintings" is the stylistic prototype of the essay, interview, and translation that frame *Autobiography of Red*. The translations in "Mimnermos" combine fragments from the Greek lyric poet Mimnermos (also Mimnermus, c. 630 BCE) with contemporary details such that poet and translator seem to be engaged in a kind of cerebral copulation, or "brainsex." Like Bowering's *A Short Sad Book*, "Mimnermos" is what Jeff Hamilton calls an "intellectual burlesque" that takes perverse liberties with its subject material, but there is much more rigorous scholarship undergird-

ing Carson's piece.[14] To her unorthodox translation of the Greek fragments, Carson adds an essay and three mock interviews with Mimnermos.
In "The *Matrix* Interview" she explains the function of these sections to
Mary di Michele: "When I was working on ["Mimnermos"], I started from
a translation of a body of fragments, then added to the translation an essay,
in some degree historical, explaining the background of the poet and how
the fragments have come down to us. And in dealing with that historical
material, I found a whole lot of what they call, in Classics, 'testimonia,'
which means anecdotal stories about the poet or about the poem, that are
passed down and aren't really regarded as credible history. But they shape
our notion of who the poet was as a person ... So the interviews are about
this interstitial matter that comes down to us in semi-historical sources."[15]
Elaborating on this model in *Autobiography of Red*, Carson plays on the
double-meaning of "body of fragments" by titling the first two sections
"Red Meat." She then inserts the "body" of Gertrude Stein into the fragments of Stesichoros, at first via a quotation about red meat and later as a
character. In "Mimnermos," however, Stein is present only as an echo in
the voice of the interviewer. Although Hamilton remarks in one review of
Plainwater that Carson is "surprisingly candid about presenting herself as
an heir to Gertrude Stein," the echo of Stein in the translations is only
strong if one considers literary treatments of collage.[16]

Each one of the "brainsex" paintings extrapolates from a fragmentary
line of Mimnermos, adds an explanatory caption, and then creates a lyric
that intermingles the speaker's world with that of Mimnermos, in the manner of a collage. When asked by John D'Agata if the juxtapositions of
ancient Greek and contemporary material in her long poems are meant to
function as collage, Carson agreed and acknowledged that she has "always
thought of [writing] as painting. Painting with thoughts and facts."[17] She
then explained that her "painting notion comes out of dealing with classical texts which are, like Sappho, in bits of papyrus with that enchanting
white space around them, in which we can imagine all of the experience of
antiquity floating but which we can't quite reach. I like that kind of surface."[18] Thus, in "*fr. 2*" of "The Brainsex Paintings," Carson begins with
the Mimnermos fragment "All We As Leaves"; notes that the lyric poet follows Homer in "compar[ing] man's life with the leaves"; introduces
Mimnermos's favourite image ("You see the sun? – I built that"); and then
shifts the focus of the poem to a contemporary setting:

> But (let me think) wasn't it a hotel in Chicago
> where I had the first of those – *my body walking out of the*

room
> *bent on some deadly errand*
and me up on the ceiling just sort of fading out –
> brainsex paintings I used to call them?
In the days when I (so to speak) painted.[19]

The final line alludes to Carson's early ambition to be a painter, which was temporarily abandoned when the poems in *Short Talks* garnered more interest than the paintings they were supposed to complement. However, the introduction of the term "brainsex" – a more ethereal version of the "Skull Coition" in *Beautiful Losers*[20] – suggests that writing and painting continue to interpenetrate in Carson's work. Like Ondaatje, Carson takes a mixed-media approach to writing in which the defining genre (in this case painting) is absent except as a trace in the writing.

The opening paragraphs of the essay that constitutes the second section of "Mimnermos" identify painting as the model for the form of the translations. Pondering the collected fragments of Mimnermos, Carson notes their serial qualities: "it is true we see the windows glow in turn with boys and flesh and dawn and women and the blue lips of ocean. It is true he likes to get the sun into every poem."[21] More important than the recurring motif of the sun, however, is Carson's interest in the mechanics of time: "the poet's task, Kafka says, is to lead the isolated human being into the infinite life, the contingent into the lawful. What streams out of Mimnermos's suns are the laws that attach us to all luminous things. Of which the first is time."[22] As in Ondaatje's *The Collected Works of Billy the Kid*, Carson here presents a series of framed images that combine to map the passage of time. However, Mimnermos's interest in time is not readily apparent in the fragments. "What is time made of?" is Geryon's favourite question in *Autobiography of Red*, and Carson frames the poems in *Men in the Off Hours* (2000) with meditations on the nature of "Ordinary Time"; but in "Mimnermos" the preoccupation with time seems to be the projection of Carson's own preferred theme.[23] She concedes that the Greek poet "scarcely uses the word," but then asserts that "everything in his verse bristles with it."[24] She maintains that time manifests itself in the form of the poetry, not the diction: "Time goes whorling through landscapes and human lives bent on its agenda, endlessly making an end of things. You have seen this vibration of time in van Gogh, moving inside color energy."[25] However, van Gogh differs from Muybridge – who used "Helios" as a pseudonym – in that the painter's technique is more expressive and less linear.[26] Van Gogh's brushstrokes and colour patterns move "in circles (not lines) that expand with a kind of biological inevitability, like Mimnermos's recurrent metaphor of the youth of humans as a flowering plant or fruit."[27] In Carson, these expressive forms expand beyond the boundaries of "Mimnermos: The Brainsex Paintings" and into *Autobiography of Red*, as at least one reviewer has noted.[28]

The final section of "Mimnermos" consists of three interviews between Mimnermos and an interviewing "I." The pair discuss a range of subjects concerning Mimnermos's writing and the *testimonia* about his life. Of particular interest is the long poem *Nanno*, which Archibald Allen notes was allegedly named after Mimnermos's "*aulos*-playing lover, [although] there is not a trace of her in the fragments. In fact there is not much trace of love at all in the fragments."[29] The interviewer observes that "Kallimachos talks about Nanno or 'the big woman' as if it were an epic poem on the founding of Kolophon," but then despairs that "no one understands this reference."[30] Mimnermos does not respond to the interviewer's request for clarification and thereby compounds the absence at the heart of interviewer's desire to know Mimnermos as a person and to grasp the history of the text.[31] Carson transforms the fragments into a story of unrequited desire between poet and scholar, and thus foreshadows her transformation of the *Geryoneis* into a story of unrequited gay love that bears the mysterious designation "autobiography." Indeed, the following exchange between the interviewer and Mimnermos might allude to *Autobiography of Red*, which was published by Knopf in New York:

> I: I understand the text as we have it is merely the proemium to a much longer work
> M: Well I don't know what you're reading over there nowadays those American distributors get some crazy ideas[32]

Mimnermos compounds this open-endedness in the third interview when he asks: "who are the storytellers who can put an end to stories"?[33] Here, Carson is perhaps playing on the etymological connection between Mimnermos's city and the colophon, a printer's insignia that is typically inserted at the end of a book in order to authenticate its contents. No authentication is possible in the cases of the *Nanno* and "Mimnermos," because the definitive story exists in the white space bordering the fragments. This is the space onto which Carson projects her desire and imagination in "Mimnermos," and it was the desire to honour this space that caused Carson to transform her first draft of *Autobiography of Red* into a novel in verse.

THE NOVEL IN VERSE

In the *Brick* interview with D'Agata, Carson is asked if she sometimes begins an essay and then reworks it as a poem. Likely thinking of the essay that begins *Autobiography of Red*, Carson responds by explaining the evolution of the form of her novel in verse: "Well, there's a novel I've written that was all prose at first and very thick. Then I thought, 'What if I break these lines up a bit? Maybe they'd move along more smartly.' So now the novel's in verse. But when I'm writing, usually I mush around first with the form, and if I don't get it in a few days then I don't try to write the thing because I can't begin without a form."[34] Carson ultimately borrowed the form of "Mimnermos" to shape the academic apparatus in *Autobiography of Red*, but as concerns the romance in verse one must ask how breaking up a line can make it move along smartly. The answer, for Carson, is that narrative can emerge from a rapid succession of images and insights that resonate thematically but do not connect in a continuous manner. She therefore contrasts poetic narrative with "straight narrative" and explains her preference for the former: "in a straight narrative you'd have too many other words, too many other words that aren't just the facts. You're too busy trying to get from one fact to another by standard methods: *and; but; oh, no; then I was in this room; because; that's Patti.* These aren't facts; they're hard to paint."[35] Note that Carson has no interest in connective words and phrases, but in the poem "By God" she wakes up at night "thinking of prepositions" that situate something in relation to something else without conflating the two things.[36] Although Carson claims not to know why prepositions intrigue her in this poem, Chris Jennings argues that she displays a fascination with "liminal syntactic position[s]" because prepositions facilitate the triangulation of desire that Carson outlines in *Eros the Bittersweet* – that is, a preposition mediates between two things in the way that Eros mediates between lover and beloved.[37]

A more recent example of this preoccupation with the syntax of juxtaposition appears in the "Note on Method" in *Economy of the Unlost*, where Carson contemplates the sentence "And The Word was with God" from the Gospel of John and asks: "What kind of withness is it?"[38] There is not a single answer to this question because the Greek preposition has at least fourteen meanings. Indeed, for Carson, the answer seems to be to perform as many variations on this "withness" as possible. Like Bolden on the train to Slaughter, Carson writes her "Note on Method" on the train to Milan, where the passengers "flash past towers and factories, stations, yards, then a field where a herd of black horses is just turning to race uphill."[39] Capturing the movement of the herd in a moment of change, Carson records the serial transformations of the landscape but avoids continuous description of it. She suggests that there is a relation between windows and "aesthetic structure" and rejects expansive description in favour of a lyric sense of narrative in which "one may encounter a fragment of unexhausted time."[40]

The field that Carson views from the train can be usefully compared to the field that Bolden sees from the train in *Coming Through Slaughter* and the field of blue-green flowers in Carson's introduction to *Short Talks*.[41] Standing in the latter field, the speaker in *Short Talks* listens to the conversation of three wise women and copies down everything that they say. The snippets of their conversation suggest to her a style of narrative that works against the convention of continuous emplotment: "The marks construct an instant of nature gradually, without the boredom of a story. I emphasize this. I will do anything to avoid boredom. It is the task of a lifetime. You can never know enough, never work enough, never use the infinitives and participles oddly enough, never impede the movement harshly enough, never leave the mind quickly enough."[42] To avoid the unsatisfactory movement of the narrative in her early draft of *Autobiography of Red*, Carson fragmented its prose, toyed with its syntax, and juxtaposed the literary legacies of Stein and Dickinson with the myths of Isis and Helen of Troy to create a novel that is "wise" in its canny subversion of narrative expectations.

THE RECEPTION OF *AUTOBIOGRAPHY OF RED*

The reception of *Autobiography of Red* highlights the diversity of readings made possible by what Melanie Rehak calls Carson's "dazzling hybrids" in a feature-length article on the poet in the *New York Times Magazine*.[43] However, one should note the media dazzle that accompanies the discussion of Carson's hybrids when Rehak's article includes a full-page fashion shot of Carson in red.[44] The success of *Autobiography of Red* has rocketed Carson from cult status in small literary magazines to international prominence, creating a mystique summed up by the opening question of an article in the *Boston Phoenix*: "What if a Canadian professor of classics turned out to be a greater poet than any living American?"[45] Assessing *Men in the Off Hours*, the *New York Times Book Review* calls Carson the "most instantly penetrating of contemporary poets," *Time Magazine* declares that Carson "fulfills poetry's highest calling," and the *Globe and Mail* (scrambling to respond to the feature in the *New York Times Magazine*) proclaims that "Carson is where the action is in contemporary poetry."[46] However, while Carson can mix and match with the best postmodernists, she distinguishes herself by writing essays, lyrics, narrative, and non-narrative poetry with equal facility.

Many critics have praised Carson's versatility, but this ability also creates contradictory appraisals of her talent. In a review of *Autobiography of Red* for the *London Times Literary Supplement* (3 December 1999), poet Oliver Reynolds praises Carson's attempt to blend intellect with emotion, but laments that the romance at the heart of her novel in verse could not "sustain the expectations created by its extraordinary first half."[47] In the same issue of the *TLS*, critic Karl Miller chooses *Autobiography of Red* as his book of the year on the strength of its "single magnificent and perplexing poem [the romance]," while suggesting that it "might have shed the gnomic appendices which both precede and round off the romance proper."[48] The reception of *Autobiography of Red* has been overwhelmingly positive (among reviewers such as Marlatt, Jed Rasula, Karl Miller, Kate Moses, Richard Siken, Elizabeth Macklin, and Jefferey Beam), but some critics of the novel in verse find it either "top-heavy with its absurd apparatus" or "so devoted to the emotional fluctuations of [the] protagonist" of the romance that it "ends up feeling like a lyric poem fanatically extended."[49] However, a closer look at the treatment of myth in *Autobiography of Red* reveals that the academic apparatus surrounding the romance is neither absurd nor subordinate to the lyric sequence.

Section 1: Essay

The first section of *Autobiography of Red*, a proem entitled "Red Meat: What Difference Did Stesichoros Make?" introduces the reader to the ancient Greek lyricist. Stesichoros (also Stesichorus) was born in Himera, on the coast of Sicily, between 650 and 628 BCE.[50] Of the "dozen or so titles and several collections of fragments" remaining from Stesichoros's works, Carson is particularly interested in a "long lyric poem in dactylo-epitrite meter and triadic structure" called the *Geryoneis*.[51] The eighty-four surviving papyrus fragments and half-dozen citations of the *Geryoneis* expand on the story of Geryon from the tenth labour of Herakles (also Heracles or Hercules). The fragments "tell of a strange winged red monster who lived on an island called Erytheia (which is an adjective meaning simply 'The Red Place') quietly tending a herd of magical red cattle, until one day the hero Herakles came across the sea and killed him to get the cattle."[52] Instead of adopting the "conventional ... point of view of Herakles and fram[ing] a thrilling account of the victory of culture over monstrosity,"

Stesichoros offers a "tantalizing cross section of scenes, both proud and pitiful, from Geryon's own experience."[53] Malcolm Davies notes that Stesichoros gives Geryon an "unexpectedly noble" character and marks the transition from epic deed to lyric encounter as a shift from heroic conquest to subjective engagement.[54] In the lyric sequence "Autobiography of Red: A Romance," Carson furthers this evolution by transforming the *Geryoneis* into a contemporary gay love affair between a leather-jacketed Herakles and his little red admirer. However, as the introductory position of the essay in *Autobiography of Red* (as opposed to the secondary position of the essay in "Mimnermos") implies, it is necessary to understand Stesichoros's deviations from the epic tradition before engaging with Carson's romance.

Willis Barnstone points out that Stesichoros was "ranked with Homer by some of the ancients," and achieved considerable fame by reframing the epic narratives of Homer and Hesiod, as well as by reconsidering the targets of their abuse, such as Geryon and Helen of Troy.[55] Although Quintilian remarks that Stesichoros "sustained on the lyre the weight of epic song" and Carson has Longinus – in a slight manipulation of Longinus 13 – call Stesichoros the "most Homeric of the lyric poets," Stesichoros's primary contribution to literary history lies in his alteration of epic for lyric purposes.[56] Alison Dale Maingon observes that Stesichoros was probably the first to combine elements of lyric monody (solo song), epic narrative, and dance in order to recast the ancient myths as choral performance: "Although he may well have been preceded by Terpander (and others unknown) in the invention of musical settings for the traditional epics, his poems on epic themes appear to have been distinctive in their completely 'lyrical' form, composed as they were in a triadic structure and adapted to *nomoi* for the lyre."[57] Davies cautions that Stesichoros's compositions may not have been strictly choral but his verse differs from the monody of Sappho, Alcaeus and Anacreon in its preference for "an artificial language with a strong Doric flavour" and its triadic structure – in which "a strophe is followed by an antistrophe in the same metrical pattern, the antistrophe by an epode in a related but different rhythm."[58] Instead of relying solely on the conventions of either lyric or epic, Stesichoros – like Carson – creates his own hybrid form.

In "Stesichorus and the Epic Tradition," Maingon examines Stesichoros's treatment of Homeric form and diction and offers these conclusions: "Retaining the heroic theme, he amalgamated traditional and original material in narrative poems of about 1500 lines in length to be performed to the accompaniment of the lyre, either by solo voice or by chorus, or even both. Held within the bounds of this structure the poems were far more narrowly defined as far as content was concerned and less digressive than epic. The musical accompaniment in itself, the *nomos* which was traditionally divided into seven parts, imposed a finite structure on the theme."[59] Toying with these numerological conventions, Carson divides *Autobiography of Red: A Novel in Verse* into seven sections (in the manner of lyric performance) and the lyric sequence "Autobiography of Red: A Romance" into forty-seven numbered sections (one short of the Homeric corpus). This kind of generic play becomes increasingly important toward the conclusion of *Autobiography of Red*, where the lyric/epic evolves into a "photographic essay" that gives way to an interview which appears to be part of a "concealment drama."[60] In Western literature, this manipulation of genres begins, according to Carson's proem, with Stesichoros.

Carson explains Stesichoros's achievement in terms of adjectives, which she calls "the latches of being."[61] "Homer's epithets," Carson writes in her proem, "are a fixed diction with which Homer fastens every substance in the world to its aptest attribute and holds them in place for epic consumption."[62] In Homer "blood is *black*," "God's laughter is *unquenchable*," and the name Helen of Troy is attached to "an adjectival tradition of whoredom already old by the time Homer used it."[63] As a young man, Stesichoros followed Homer in making "the most of Helen's matrimonial misadventures" in his lost *Helen*, as J.A. Davison observes.[64] However, for "no reason that anyone can name, Stesichoros began to undo the latches" in mid-career, according to Carson: "Suddenly there was nothing to interfere with horses being *hollow hooved*. Or a river being *root silver*."[65] This change affected the fixed characterization of Helen as a whore. Whereas Homer has Helen qualify her speech in the *Iliad* with disclaimers such as "slut that I am," Stesichoros reconsiders the denigrating effects of these insults.[66] By rejecting the presentation of Helen as a (self-described) "nasty bitch evil-intriguing," Stesichoros implicated the men who made her both the prize and scapegoat of the Trojan War.[67]

Legend has it that Stesichoros changed his attitude toward Helen after she blinded him. Newly deified, Helen revenged herself on the epic tradition by blinding Stesichoros when he engaged in the standard Homeric slander of her name. To regain his sight, Stesichoros spontaneously composed a *palinode* or counter-song, and performed a kind of public retraction. The *Palinode* parallels other innovations by Stesichoros in its unconventional diction and use of inversions. To cite one example of relevance to *Autobiography of Red*, Stesichoros assigns Helen her husband's distinctive hair colour, ξανθos or reddish-brown, in fragment 2619 14.5

(probably from the *Iliou Persis*).[68] By Maingon's count, the epithet "ξανθός belongs primarily to Menelaus (16 times in the *Iliad* and 15 in the *Odyssey*) while it is used in the feminine of Demeter (twice), of Agamede (once) and Ariadne (once, in the *Theogony*)."[69] In contrast, Homer leaves Helen's exalted beauty unspecified, enabling her to stand in more easily as a synecdoche for all women of treacherous beauty. Undoing this particular latch, "Stesichorus probably intended the relationship between Menelaus and Helen to be accentuated (perhaps ironically) by th[e] transference of the epithet regularly expected with Menelaus to his misguided wife."[70] This simple verbal transgression not only speeds Helen's conversion from archetype to individual but it also sets a precedent for Carson's manipulation of epithets and proper nouns in her final interview, where Gertrude Stein answers questions in place of the "choir-master," Stesichoros.

Stein maintains a strong presence in the academic frame of Carson's novel in verse. Carson begins her proem with an epigram from Stein, "I like the feeling of words doing / as they want to do and as they have to do," and then immediately situates Stesichoros "after Homer and before Gertrude Stein, a difficult interval for a poet."[71] Between the epigraph and the interview, Carson develops the connection between Stein and Stesichoros as a shared talent for fragmentation. Just as Stesichoros's adjectives broke with the standard diction of Homeric epic, Stein's experiments in sentence structure changed the face of twentieth-century narrative by "repudiat[ing] the conventions of syntactical causality," according to Richard Kostelanetz.[72] In Stein's cubist treatment of the verbal surface, "nouns ... are used in ways that obscure their traditional functions within the structure of a sentence," adverbs that "customarily come before a verb now follow it, and what might normally be the object of a sentence either becomes its subject or precedes it ... Instead of saying 'someone is alive,' Stein writes, 'Anyone can be a living one.'"[73] For Stein as for Stesichoros, fragmentation serves as a means to destabilize fixed modes of representation and perception. Thus, when Carson returns to the proem's titular question – "What difference did Stesichoros make?" – she offers a comparison that links early Greek lyric to high modernist portraiture: "When Gertrude Stein had to sum up Picasso she said, 'This one was working.' So say of Stesichoros, 'This one was making adjectives.'"[74] The theme of working – as in working with, belabouring, modifying – fragments serves as a bridge to the essay's conclusion, where Carson invites her readers to create their own work: "the fragments of the *Geryoneis* itself read as if Stesichoros had composed a substantial narrative poem then ripped it to pieces and buried the pieces in a box with some song lyrics and lecture notes and scraps of meat. The fragment numbers tell you roughly how the pieces fell out of the box. You can of course keep shaking the box. 'Believe me for meat and for myself,' as Gertrude Stein says. Here. Shake."[75] The interjection of Stein's voice here completes her framing of the proem and provides a clue to the meaning of "Red Meat" in the first two chapter titles.

Stein's disturbing conflation of meat and self in a paragraph about the fragments of Stesichoros jars the reader momentarily, but the interjected quotation points back to "The Gender of Sound," the final essay in Carson's *Glass, Irony, and God*, where Carson contemplates sexual *double-entendres* in antiquity and asserts that "putting a door on the female mouth [mouth/vagina] has been an important project of patriarchal culture from antiquity to the present day. Its chief tactic is an ideological association of female sound with monstrosity, disorder and death."[76] In the midst of discussing epithets attached to the voices/mouths of Helen, Aphrodite, and Echo, Carson asks her reader to consider this description of the sound of Gertrude Stein by the biographer M.D. Luhan:

> Gertrude was hearty. She used to roar with laughter, out loud. She
> had a laugh like a beefsteak. She loved beef.
> These sentences, with their artful confusion of factual and metaphorical
> levels ... projec[t] Gertrude Stein across the boundary of woman and
> human and animal kind into monstrosity. The simile 'she had a laugh
> like a beefsteak' which identifies Gertrude Stein with cattle is followed
> at once by the statement 'she loved beef' indicating that Gertrude Stein
> ate cattle.[77]

When compounded with details of Stein's "large physical size and lesbianism," Carson argues, Luhan's allusion to cannibalism completes the "marginalization of [Stein's] personality" as a "way to deflect her writing from literary centrality. If she is fat, funny-looking and sexually deviant she must be a marginal talent, is the assumption."[78] Likewise, Carson argues in the essay "Dirt and Desire," the "women of [Greek] mythology regularly lose their form in monstrosity. Io turns into a heifer ... Medusa sprouts snakes from her head."[79] *Autobiography of Red* redresses this slight by giving Stein's voice increasing prominence in the story of a monster who tends a herd of mythical red cattle and whose name means "roarer" or "speaker." Stein's voice in the epigraph of the first page resurfaces as reported speech in the body of the proem, as a stylistic echo in "Appendix C," and eventually as an active voice in the final interview. Yet, because women in Greek myth are also "notorious adaptors of the forms and boundaries of others" who "repeatedly open containers which they are told not to open (e.g. Pandora, the daughters of Krekops, Danaë)," Carson equates her text with a box of fragments.[80] Like the parcel at the outset of *Zócalo*, this mysterious box entices the reader to turn the page and look inside.

Section 2: *Translation*

In the novel's second section, "Red Meat: Fragments of Stesichoros," Carson offers her own experimental translation of the *Geryoneis*. Carson does not simply render the Greek into English; she blends details from the *Geryoneis* and her upcoming adaptation of it to create a hybrid translation. Her translations exaggerate the "strangeness ... of language" by incorporating foreign elements into fixed narratives and refusing the smooth transition of Greek into English.[81] To alert the reader that scenes where, say, Geryon's mother takes him to his first day of school are not features of Stesichoros's text, Carson inserts anachronistic details such as "the ticking red taxi of the incubus" into the gaps of Stesichoros's narrative.[82] Painting fragments in the manner of the cubists, Carson combines glimpses of ancient and modern narratives in a style that foreshadows the perspectival shifts of the concluding interview. Translation, in this way, becomes an act of composing elements from different epochs and speech genres, rather than an exercise in maintaining a uniform identity for the text across languages and periods.

Even Carson's direct translations are highly unconventional. For example, Carson translates only the latter half of fragment 15 (which she numbers 14), focusing on the moment of penetration in the conquest of Geryon by Herakles. The clipped diction in Carson's translation contrasts sharply with the heroic tone in Andrew Miller's version:

(Fr. S15)   xiv. Herakles' Arrow

[T]he arrow held its course straight through   Arrow means kill It parted Geryon's skull like a comb Made
  to the top of his head   The boy neck lean At an odd slow angle sideways as when a
and stained with crimson blood   Poppy shames itself in a whip of Nude breeze[83]
  his breastplate and his gory limbs.

Then Geryon's neck drooped
  to one side, like a poppy
which, disfiguring its tender beauty,
  suddenly sheds its petals ... [84]

Traditionally, the three-bodied grandson of Poseidon posed a formidable threat to Herakles. The Greek folk hero, as Carson notes sardonically, "got the idea that Geryon was Death."[85] Although Herakles and Geryon are descended from immortals, both suspect they are mortal. Davies therefore speculates that "the labours involving Cerberus and the Hesperides are recent in origin" and he reads the tenth labour of Herakles as a "heroic journey to the land of the dead" in which the hero must attain "immortality and triumph over death."[86] Carson's translation, on the other hand, makes Geryon a "boy" and sexualizes his encounter with Herakles by limiting the imagery to penetration, nudity, and shame. Carson's version of the *Geryoneis* remains a "matter" of life and death, but the contemporary poet explicitly eroticizes the border between mortality and immortality. As translator and author of the romance, Carson foregrounds the homoerotic subtext in the *Geryoneis* (which would have been obvious to the Greek audience of Stesichoros) but under the generic title of autobiography Carson's work as a whole suggests a heterosexual subtext in Geryon's romance.

On the level of the book as a whole, the fragments of "Red Meat" begin to cohere only when Carson works the myth of Isis (conventionally represented with cattle horns) into the story of Geryon. While Carson's use of the Isis myth is not conventional, she insists that "conventions exist to be re-negotiated."[87] Instead of modifying the story of Geryon to match the Egyptian myth, Carson appropriates formal elements of the myth and uses them to shape her narrative framework.

Numerous elements of the Isis myth resonate with the *Geryoneis* – the characters, the fetishization of red, the goddess' journey and triumph over death – but one story does not transpose onto the other. With her husband/ brother Osiris, Isis ruled Egypt in its earliest epoch, introducing magical incantation, justice, and weaving in the company of the "watchdog of the gods," Anubis, with his "dog's head and spotted dog's coat."[88] Osiris taught writing, astronomy, poetry, and "traveled throughout the world with his kinsman Heracles, spreading the science of agriculture."[89] Periodically, the siblings' peaceful kingdom suffered droughts brought on by their evil brother Seth (Typhon), father of "Orthos the hound of Geryones."[90] Seth "haunted the delta region, his red hair flaming," and consequently Egyptians "abhorred the color red, considering it a manifestation of all the forces of treachery, murder, and jealousy."[91] According to Plutarch, the inhabitants of Coptos hurled asses off cliffs because of their red coats and Egyptians generally "sacrifice[d] red cattle."[92] Turning Egypt into a "Red Place," Seth trapped Osiris in a coffin and sent him floating down the Nile. Isis recovered her husband's coffin in Syria and revived him through a kind of necrophilic magic, only to have Seth chop him into fourteen fragments and cast them into the Nile. Isis retrieved the fragments of Osiris, but "did not find ... his male member ... In its place Isis fashioned a likeness of it and consecrated the phallus, in honour of which the Egyptians even today hold festival."[93] Revived, Osiris ascended to the sky and left his wife to rule in his absence, her power confirmed by the symbolic phallus entrusted to her priestesses.

This theme of a reconstituted "body of fragments" provides the most important link to the structure of *Autobiography of Red*. The ordeal of Isis pertains to "Red Meat: Fragments of Stesichoros" because Carson's chapter title makes an explicit connection between authorial corpse and literary corpus. These terms are similarly interchangeable in Plutarch's *De Osiride et Iside*, where the historian writes that Typhon (Seth) "scatters and destroys the sacred Word which the goddess [Isis] collects and puts together and delivers to those undergoing initiation ... of which the end is the knowledge of the First and the Lord."[94] In this context, Carson's brainsex is a kind of necrophilia. "Words after all are dead," Carson tells di Michele, "they impersonate life vividly but remain dead."[95] Lacking the presence of Stesichoros's original text, Carson must work – Isis-like – with likeness (that is, citations, testimonia) and absence (textual gaps). "No passage longer than thirty lines is quoted from [Stesichoros]," Carson explains, "and papyrus scraps (still being found: the most recent fragments were recovered from cartonnage in Egypt in 1977) withhold as much as they tell."[96] The fragments of the *Geryoneis* – like the fragments of the story of the house of Oedipus by Stesichoros, recovered from a mummy case in 1974 – are pieces of the Stesichorean/Osirian body that Carson summons all her poetic and academic craft to revive. However, Carson does not follow Isis in using the power of inscription entrusted to her to uphold patriarchal codes. Rather, like Marlatt, she pieces together a textual Frankenstein that will subvert these codes by redefining the gender codes attached to the authorial body.

Carson's translations are not simply a re-membering of the Greek poets in English. In choosing to work with fragments of Mimnermos and Stesichoros, Carson deliberately chooses texts that have been dis-membered – as the missing book in Carson's "epic" underscores. While Carson's scholarly work resuscitates these nearly forgotten poems, the fictional elements of her writing actively resist any attempt to restore the authority of "the First and the Lord." Thus, the Mimnermos interviews are complicated by the Greek's insistently phallic language. In the first interview, Mimnermos corrects the interviewer's use of the word "mystical": "M: Mystical I don't think we had a word mystical we had gods we had words for gods 'hidden in the scrutum [sic] of Zeus' we used to say for instance, proverbially."[97] Similarly, the second interview terminates when Mimnermos (named for his grandfather) objects to the interviewer's question on disguises:

> M: Well eventually someone has to call a boat a boat you can't dismember everything
> I: Dismember
> M: Sorry I meant remember
> I: Freud was named for his grandfather too[98]

In *Autobiography of Red*, Stesichoros and Helen engage in a similar linguistic power struggle, but one that suggests another paradigm for Carson's inversions. The red-headed Helen of the *Palinode* offers Carson a second role model for reconstituting the male corpse/corpus with a difference.

Section 3: Citations

Carson's "Appendix A: Testimonia on the Question of Stesichoros' Blinding by Helen" uses citations such as Isokrates's *Helen* 64 to demonstrate how Helen goes from being the object of language to being an active agent informing it: "Looking to demonstrate her own power Helen made an object lesson of the poet Stesichoros. For the fact is he began his poem 'Helen' with a bit of blasphemy. Then when he stood up he found he'd been robbed of his eyes. Straightaway realizing why, he composed the so-called 'Palinode' and Helen restored him to his own nature."[99] Carson offers no commentary here, but it is clear that in her appendices and "Red Meat" fragments she is also making "an object lesson of the poet Stesichoros" by subjecting his master-text to the same kind of overhaul to which the lyricist subjected his epic predecessors. Carson restores the "vision" of Stesichoros by reconstituting his literary corpus and presenting it to the eye of the modern reader. But just as Helen's magic altered Stesichoros's impression of her, Carson's translation of the *Geryoneis* creates a new portrait of the ancient Greek lyricist.

Section 4: The Palinode

"Appendix B" consists solely of a translated fragment from Stesichoros's famous retraction. The thrice-repeated "No" in the left column of the palinode is unique to Carson's translation. It recalls the use of "(no)" as a caesura in the first brainsex painting and "measures out the area of the given and the possible" along a margin of negatives:[100]

> No it is not the true story.
> No you never went on the benched ships.
> No you never came to the towers of Troy.[101]

Such fragments withhold as much as they tell, as Carson observed earlier. Although Carson does not state it explicitly, Maingon points out that Stesichoros's revised story of Helen amounts to "a revolutionary version of the legend of Helen ... Such an innovation called into question the entire mythical basis for the legend of the Trojan War."[102] Contradicting Homer, Stesichoros argues in his *Palinode* that the *eidolon* (image, phantom) of Helen goes to Troy with Paris, while the real Helen waits out the war in Egypt, where Euripides finds her in *Electra*: "Helen, in fact, / Never saw Troy; she has just come from Proteus' palace / In Egypt. Zeus sent off to Troy a phantom Helen / To stir up strife and slaughter in the human race."[103] Carson, too, follows Stesichoros's version of the Helen story in her uncollected poem about the daughter of Tyndareus. Carson's "Helen" begins with the statement, "Nights of a marriage are like an Egypt in a woods," and she proceeds to imagine Troy vanishing, "murmuring, stain / is a puzzle you do not want / the answer to."[104] Although there is some debate in the matter, A.M. Dale argues – in a view corroborated by Maingon – that there can be "no serious doubt that, as all antiquity believed, the [*eidolon*]-story was the bold invention of Stesichorus, a volte-face in mid-career, possibly the outcome of a visit to Sparta" where Helen was worshipped as a goddess.[105] Stesichoros's Helen story never supplanted Homer's version, but it created a rival interpretation well known throughout antiquity. Thus, in *The Republic*, Plato can remark without embellishment that "as Stesichoros says the wraith of Helen was fought for at Troy through ignorance of the truth."[106] Using absence to define presence, the *eidolon* story stresses the fact that the Trojan war was fought, not over a woman, but over the way a woman was imagined.

In *Helen: Myth, Legend and the Culture of Misogyny*, Robert Meagher explains the crucial and codified role Helen played in the mythological foundations of Greece: "Helen – goddess, wife, consort, whore – [figured as] the epitome of woman to the Greek eye. In ancient Greek poetry and art, Helen was indeed always more than *a* woman who brought on *a* war. The Trojan War, whatever its actual insignificance may have been, stood as the paradigm for all war and Helen, its reputed cause, was the avatar of the feminine, the provocatrice of all mischief and pain, the original *femme fatale*. This synecdoche by which Helen was seen as all women and by which all women were seen as 'Helens' was a simple liberty taken by the ancient tradition and operative, in one guise or another, ever since."[107] Stesichoros's challenge to the truth about Helen – the paragon of that "deadly race and tribe of women who live amongst mortal men to their great trouble," according to Hesiod – called her vilification into question.[108] He severs the possessive epithet "of Troy" from her name and removes its bloody connotations. However, Carson is not content with a simple reversal of value judgements. Having apprenticed in "No," Carson attempts to go beyond the rigid opposition of truth and falsehood in "Appendix C: Clearing Up the Question of Stesichoros' Blinding by Helen."

Section 5: Mock Syllogisms

In fact, the twenty-one syllogisms in "Appendix C" clear up nothing at all. On the contrary, Rasula argues that the mock syllogisms "induce a narcosis of logic" by manipulating the binary movement of statement and counterstatement.[109] Pressuring the gaps created by language, Carson begins with the simple syllogism, "1. Either Stesichoros was a blind man or he was not" and proceeds to more vertiginous and Steinian statements: "10. If we are now in reverse and by continuing to reason in this way are likely to arrive back at the beginning of the question of the blinding of Stesichoros either we will go along without incident or we will meet Stesichoros on our way back."[110] Reversing, circling, and supplementing, Carson draws out the phantom of doubt in deduction's linear movement toward truth.

Section 6: The Romance in Verse

Welcoming this spirit of doubleness, Carson then launches her reader into "Autobiography of Red: A Romance," the principal narrative in *Autobio-*

graphy of Red: A Novel in Verse. The romance within the *roman* suggests a duplicity befitting the novel's second version of the Geryon myth. Likewise, the multiple potential meanings of "autobiography" – of red, of Geryon, of a concealed "I" – make a fitting introduction to the story of a three-headed monster whose "triplicity makes him a natural symbol of deceit" and whose spirit presides "over the second of the three lowest regions of Dante's Hell, the circles of those who sinned by fraud."[111] Carson's duplication of Geryon makes little attempt to be true to the classical version. Gone are two of Geryon's three conjoined torsos, his blue hair and his yellow skin, familiar to classicists from his sculpture (c. 560 BCE) at the Athenian Acropolis.[112] The red cattle and the "little red dog" of the fragments also disappear. Instead, Carson makes red a symbol of sexual drought in the romance and colours her anti-hero in the ochre of desire. By reducing details and narrowing the narrative focus to a lyric subjectivity that frequently approximates the first person, Carson makes Geryon the representative of passion *in extremis* in "Autobiography of Red" and concentrates the reader's empathy on her little red misfit.

Although Carson sometimes claims not to "fee[l] easy talking about blood or desire," Eros is in fact the subject of her first collection of essays and the principal theme of her poetry.[113] "The vocation of anger is not mine," Carson writes in "The Glass Essay":

> I know my source.
> It is stunning, it is a moment like no other,
> when one's lover comes in and says I do not love you anymore.[114]

By translating the power struggle between Herakles and Geryon in the *Geryoneis* into a story of sexual conquest and unrequited love, Carson once again addresses "that custom, the human custom / of wrong love."[115] Geryon's love is not wrong because he is gay. On the contrary, Carson offers sensitive renderings of same-sex desire in several of her long poems, most strikingly in "Irony Is Not Enough: Essay on My Life as Catherine Deneuve" (about a professor of ancient Greek who falls in love with one of her female students).[116] Geryon's sexuality serves instead to complete his alienation. His desire pushes him away from his otherwise supportive mother, and makes him dependent on Herakles at the very moment that Herakles terminates their love affair. It is from this perspective of powerful desire and disempowering attachment that Carson prefers to explore "How people get power over one another, / this mystery."[117] Dominant-subordinate relations – particularly their inversion – fascinate Carson,

whether the relations be between men, between women, between men and
women, or between a master-text and its adaptation.

Carson's genre-mixing is appropriate in this erotic context because, as
she explains in *Eros the Bittersweet*, the "terms 'novel' and 'romance' do
not reflect an ancient name for the genre. Chariton refers to his work as
erotika pathemata, or 'erotic sufferings': these are love stories in which it is
generically required that love be painful."[118] Most of Geryon's erotic suffering takes place in Erytheia, a combination of Stesichoros's mythic "Red
Place" and contemporary Montreal. Geryon endures a difficult adolescence
in this setting, surviving his brother's sexual abuse and the humiliation that
a public school would hold for a winged red child. Then, in "one of those
moments that is the opposite of blindness," Herakles gets off the bus from
New Mexico and Geryon falls in love.[119] The term "wrong love" acquires a
double-meaning in this scene because of the echo in Carson's metaphor of
blind Stesichoros "restored to his nature." In Geryon's visionary moment
of sexual awakening, he sees that gay love is right for him, yet he is blind to
his choice of lover. It takes Geryon the entire course of the narrative to
admit that his unrequited desire, his "wrong love" for Herakles, is
"degrading."[120]

There is a hint of national allegory here as Herakles makes a quick conquest of Geryon and, tiring of him, moves on to more exotic challenges in
South America. Carson's Erytheia is a North American island where older
brothers play hockey, where baby-sitters read from "the loon book," where
an American dollar bill is a novelty, and where schoolchildren examine
"beluga whales newly captured / from the upper rapids of the Churchill
River."[121] Since Carson wrote the novel in the mid-nineties, the notion of
Montreal as Erytheia would have particular resonance, because the elec-
toral maps leading up to 1995 referendum depicted Montreal as an island
of federalist red in an ocean of separatist blue. Arriving in Erytheia,
Herakles instantly makes Geryon his love slave and on one level he plays
the role of the unitary subject who subdues hybrid monsters at the edges of
empire; but, in Montreal, the definition of empire is manifold.

The Herakles of the *Geryoneis* epitomizes the masculine ideal described
by Teresa de Lauretis in her discussion of the quest narrative,[122] and Carson's portrait of him matches his traditional profile as "the heroic individual, performing incredible feats, single-handed, in remote corners of the
earth."[123] With a club and arrows dipped in the gall of the many-headed
Hydra (slain in the second labour), Herakles kills the two-headed guard
dog Orthos and then destroys (the fragments suggest) each of Geryon's
three heads individually. Similarly, in *Autobiography of Red*, Herakles

"slays" the man-dragon of the north and then assumes control over his Quechua-Peruvian lover, Ancash, whose name suggests both economic and cultural currency (Ancash's name occurs in a Quechua folk song that Herakles sings against Ancash's wishes). As if to confirm Herakles's covetousness, the "master of monsters" enlists Geryon and Ancash to help him steal a statue of Tezca, the tiger god, when Geryon runs into the couple in Buenos Aires years later.[124] However, Carson confirms Dante's association of Geryon with fraud, because she tells one interviewer that she invented the name Ancash – which means "blue" and is the name of a region in Peru – so that she "couldn't settle on a meaning."[125] The name in fact completes the triumvirate of the primary colours associated with the characters in the love triangle: red (Geryon), yellow (Herakles), and blue (Ancash). Since the autobiography adopts Geryon's point of view, one should not trust its information to be reliable.

Although Carson states in an interview that Geryon's accent is Canadian, one should not push the national allegory too far.[126] In addition to teaching at McGill, Carson has held posts at Princeton, Emory, Berkeley, and the University of Michigan, and her books, with the exception of *Short Talks*, have been published in the United States. A recipient of the Lannan Award (1996), the Pushcart Prize (1997), a Guggenheim Fellowship (1998), and a MacArthur Foundation Fellowship (2000) in the United States, Carson has so far been honoured with only one national award in her native country, the inaugural Griffin Poetry Prize (2001). Her border-crossing reputation is such that one American poetry editor calls Carson, without qualification, "our new Emerson."[127] While this is a high compliment in some circles, little in Carson's work suggests an interest in nation building, either Canadian or American. As the contemporary North American setting for her Geryon story indicates, Carson uses myth to span the borders of time and space, not to entrench national boundaries.

The novel's dedication, "For Will," which almost certainly refers to Carson's friend Will Aitken, emphasizes this cross-border perspective. Aitken was born in Indiana and moved to Montreal in 1972 to attend McGill. Two years later, he co-founded Montreal's first gay and lesbian bookstore, Librarie L'Androgyne, and has lived in Canada ever since. His portrait of a Canadian giantess wreaking havoc in refined Japanese settings in the novel *Realia* (2000) makes a fine counterpart to Carson's American Herakles. Perhaps taking a cue from Ondaatje's endorsement of her novel, Carson contributes this glowing blurb to the cover of *Realia*: "Will Aitken is my favourite novelist writing in English today."[128] Aitken has reciprocated by conducting a very insightful interview with Carson for the *Paris Review*.[129]

Carson's topography also remains resolutely mythic. "Herakles' home-town of Hades" lies "at the other end of the island [Erytheia] about four hours by car, a town / of moderate size and little importance / except for one thing," it has an active volcano.[130] On an early visit to this volcano, Herakles breaks up with Geryon, and the molten, volatile volcano immedi-ately becomes a metaphor for Geryon's emotional life. Years later, when Geryon runs into Herakles and Ancash in South America, they are record-ing the sound of volcanoes for a documentary on Emily Dickinson. The couple take Geryon with them to record the volcano Icchantikas in Peru, where Geryon finally frees himself from Herakles. Along the way, however, Ancash discovers Geryon's wings and tells him the Quechua myth of the Yazcol Yazcamac, eyewitnesses who descend into the volcano and "return as red people with wings, / all their weaknesses burned away – / and their mortality."[131] This mythic frame transforms Geryon's status as an outsider to that of a liminal figure – "On[e] Who Went and Saw and Came Back" – whose role is to transgress boundaries that others cannot cross.[132]

The association of Geryon with volcanoes, Lava Man, and the Yazcol Yazcamac is not coincidental. In *Hercules' Labours*, Jan Schoo argues that Geryon personifies the volcano El Tiede on the Canary Island of Tenerife. Schoo cites as evidence the meaning of Geryon's name ("roarer"), the winged images of the volcano Talos on Crete, and the fact that Geryon's dog Orthos is the "brother of Kerberos, the hellhound, one of the most out-standing representatives of the underworld."[133] Orthos's father, Typhon, is also identified with Mount Etna. Maingon furthers the equation of Geryon with volcanoes by pointing out that in fragment 4 of the *Geryoneis*, Stesichoros uses the epithet κορυφη in its "less common sense of 'head' ... [Retaining] the epithet most frequently associated with the word in its sense 'mountain[,]' he has deliberately suggested both potential meanings, mag-nifying the dimensions of the monster."[134] This monster occupies a critical position between nature and culture, disorder and order, inhuman and human.

However, if one tries to determine the gender of this volcanic monster, an important fissure emerges in the narrative. The first reference to a volcano in the romance occurs in the opening stanza of its epigraph, a heavily alle-gorical poem about speech and immortality by Emily Dickinson, #1748. The first stanza of #1748 offers a surprising variation on Dickinson's "often reiterated analogy of the self as a dormant volcano":[135]

> The reticent volcano keeps
> His never slumbering plan –

> Confided are his projects pink
> To no precarious man.[136]

While the masculine adjectives in this stanza may refer to the "Jehovah" of
the second stanza, I choose to apply them to the volcano because Dickinson
usually capitalizes adjectives and pronouns referring to God.[137] In either
case, as an epigraph, "his projects pink" alludes to Geryon's "autobiography," which begins as a "sculpture" when the reticent monster is five years
old.[138] Ultimately, Geryon's autobiography takes "the form / of a photographic essay" and helps Geryon to get over the fickle Herakles.[139] However, the fact that Geryon's photographic essay is a thinly veiled metaphor
for Carson's lyric sequence (which culminates in a series of eight "photographs") undermines Geryon's masculinity. The final two stanzas in
Dickinson's poem compound this ambiguity. Like the antistrophe and
epode in Stesichoros's verse, Dickinson's second stanza introduces a female
counterpart to the male volcano, while the third stanza changes the mood
with an abstract aphorism that reconciles male and female figures as
"people" with a shared secret:

> If nature will not tell the tale
> Jehovah told to her
> Can human nature not survive
> Without a listener?
>
> Admonished by her buckled lips
> Let every babbler be
> The only secret people keep
> Is Immortality.[140]

The prize of immortality for which Geryon and Herakles struggle is, in
Dickinson's hymn, a secret divulged by neither the reticent volcano nor the
woman with "buckled lips." While this secret is not directly verbalized,
Dickinson nonetheless conveys it as a property of what Sharon Cameron
calls "lyric time"[141] – that sudden eruption of past and future into the
poem's present tense that Carson calls "*Volcano Time.*"[142] Both Dickinson
and Carson prefer these lyric flashes of eternity to the plodding flow of continuous narrative: "Much truer / is the time that strays into photographs
and stops."[143] One of these moments occurs in photograph "#1748," the
synchronic and synaesthetic climax of Geryon's erotic suffering, where
Geryon takes Ancash's tape recorder to the summit of Icchantikas to record

an instant that blurs the borders between acoustic and visual, female and male, nature and culture.

Photograph "#1748" stands out because, in addition to sharing the numbered title of Dickinson's epigram, it "is a photograph he [Geryon] never took, no one here took it."[144] The poem depicts an event that is the inverse of Bowering's experience as an aerial photographer, because in this case the photographer becomes the target. Following a preamble in which Carson once again casts doubt on the identity of the autobiographical subject, the "eyewitness" descends into the eye/I of the volcano:

He peers down
at the earth heart of Icchantikas dumping all its photons out her ancient eye and he smiles for
the camera: "The Only Secret People Keep"[145]

The picture taken of the eyewitness by "her ancient eye" in this scene is a kind of mirror image – a self-portrait that borrows its title from the final lines of Dickinson's poem. Dickinson's interjected fragment, like the Stein quotation earlier, enters the narrative abruptly, yet comes close enough to the end of the romance to frame it. The once-reticent male volcano thus concludes the romance using a feminine adjective and speaking in Dickinson's voice. Carson completes this transition from phallic to labial imagery in the concluding lyric where the three men stare at "the hole of fire" in the side of the volcano and Carson explicitly distinguishes between the men and the fire to which they are "neighbors."[146]

Such "lateral fissures" – "called fire lips by volcanologists" – permeate Carson's romance.[147] The most obvious example occurs in the poem "She," where Geryon finds himself in the bedroom of Herakles's mother and asks, "Who am I?"[148] Surveying the mother's pearls and slips, Geryon is shocked to see himself "in the mirror cruel as a slash of lipstick": "He had been here before, dangling / inside the word *she* like a trinket at a belt."[149] While this simile seems to disparage femininity as passive and ornamental, the pronoun "she" carries extra weight coming from a poet who tells di Michele: "I cannot stand reading reviews of my work (I skim) or in general sentences in which I appear as 'she.'"[150] Di Michele pursues the question of why Carson presents herself as a "person of no particular gender" in *Plainwater*:[151]

MDM: In "The Anthropology of Water" you write: "I am not a person who feels easy talking about blood or desire. I rarely use the word

woman myself ... The truth is, I lived out my adolescence mainly in
default of my father's favour. But I perceived I could trouble him less if
I had no gender ... I made my body hard and flat as the armour of
Athena. No secrets under my skin, no telltale drops on the threshold."
What is the relationship of your writing to this word "woman"? To
being a woman?
AC: A relationship of dis-ease as is suggested in the passage you quote.
MDM: Are "feminisms" of interest to you?
AC: Not currently. Particular females are of interest to me.[152]

Although Carson names Stein and Dickinson among the writers of interest
to her, she clearly does not (like Marlatt) present herself as a proponent of
an *écriture féminine*.

It is important to note, however, that Carson's relationship to patriarchy
in "The Anthropology of Water" is also one of "dis-ease." This long poem
begins with Carson struggling to understand the "word salad" of her ailing
father, who suffers from dementia, and concludes with Carson writing
from the perspective of her estranged brother.[153] As in *Autobiography of
Red*, Carson treats gender here as a phenomenon to be explored through
fictional guises. If Carson presents herself as a person "of no particular gender" in her writing, it is because she refuses to restrict herself to the perspective of a woman. Similarly, if Carson's novel in verse is of no particular
genre, it is because Carson wants to explore the potential of different
approaches to the Geryon myth.

A fundamental question raised by *Autobiography of Red* is not whether
Geryon is a "he" or a "she," but rather how this "monster" can negotiate
the conflicts entailed by loving and existing in a world more complex than
its social, linguistic, and literary conventions would suggest. "Gay, red and
winged," Marlatt observes, Geryon "wants to know how to survive in a
world where difference equals pain."[154] Herakles's photographer grandmother suggests one solution to this dilemma by redefining Geryon's question during a conversation on women and art: "Question is / how they use
it – given / the limits of form."[155] Nowhere is Carson's formulation of gender as a question of genre more explicit.

Section 7: The Interview

The final section of *Autobiography of Red* tests the limits of gender and genre.
Titled simply "Interview" – with "(Stesichoros)" set below the title and
divided from it by a double line – it unfolds as a dialogue about literature:

I: One critic speaks of a sort of concealment drama going on in your work some special interest in finding out what or how people act when they know that important information is being withheld this might have to do with an aesthetic of blindness or even a will to blindness if that is not a tautology
s: I will tell about blindness
I: Yes do
s: First I must tell about seeing[156]

Carson sets up the reader to expect that Stesichoros will describe his blinding by Helen. However, the conversation makes a sudden chronological leap:

s: Up to 1907 I was seriously interested in seeing I studied and practiced it I enjoyed it
I: 1907
s: I will tell about 1907
...
s: Paintings completely covered the walls right up to the ceiling at the time the atelier was lit by gas fixtures and it glowed like a dogma but this is not what I saw[157]

This shift in time-frame alerts the reader that returning to Carson's scholarly apparatus entails entering "a wickedly parodistic parallel universe to the novel inside it."[158] The proem and interview surrounding Carson's romance prove not to be merely a passive frame, but rather active agents in determining the course of the larger story. As Jacques Derrida argues in "Parergon," those elements marked as extrinsic to the *ergon*, or principal artwork, in fact perform an intrinsic function in mediating the borders of that artwork.[159] Carson employs this mediating power to shift the focus of the story and resituate Stein, Helen, and Dickinson – women marked as extrinsic to the history of Stesichoros, Geryon and Herakles – in more intrinsic positions. This manipulation of frames is a question of self-definition for experimental writers because, as Derrida notes, "*Parergon* also means the exceptional, the strange, the extraordinary," revealing how easy it is for writers such as Stein and Dickinson to be dismissed as merely strange.[160]

With the temporal frame destabilized, the reader's eye turns toward the left margin of the interview transcript for several reasons. First of all, the references to a gas-lit atelier, paintings, and 1907 make it clear that the "S" in the column stands for Stein, not Stesichoros. Secondly, *Autobiography of Red* has been, thus far, an autobiography without an "I." Suddenly the reader is confronted with an interviewing "I" speaking in the first person and asserting his or her presence in the story: "It is I who thank you."[161] Remembering that Stesichoros often spoke "in his own *persona* in the introduction and conclusion of his poems" without "intru[ding] within the framework of the narrative itself," one presumes that the interviewing "I" is Carson's academic persona returning from the proem.[162] Thus the women's voices framing the male narrative have moved from the extrinsic positions of epigram and proem to occupy more intrinsic positions in a story they actively create as direct speakers.

Carson achieves this subversive manoeuvre within the limits of literary form. Schoo notes that according to myth, each of Herakles's twelve *athloi* or *erga*, labours or works, included minor deeds called *parerga* or side-works.[163] Thus, the *ergon* of stealing the red cattle included the *parerga* of killing Geryon and Orthos. Stesichoros transforms the myth of Herakles into the *Geryoneis* by moving the parergonal figure of Geryon from the myth's periphery to its centre. Carson duplicates this parergonal movement by having Stein supplant Stesichoros in the mock interview. Just as Carson's opening section on Stesichoros begins with an epigram from Stein, the final section on Stein begins with the proper noun "(Stesichoros)" suspended in parentheses. The choir master unmastered figures as the starting point in a word play between Stein and Carson where the contemporary poet accentuates the epithetic origins of the Greek proper noun. Once famous for his unconventional adjectives, Stesichoros looks on from the wings as the women's concealment drama takes centre stage. The reputed inventor of the choral hymn (a form of performance involving several singers and dance, and a precursor of drama) finds himself listening silently to a duet of female voices, neither of which appears to command control. This *hymn*-become-*her* casts an ironic pall over the title of the romance's final lyric, "XLVII. The Flashes in Which a Man Possesses Himself." Clearly, women's voices have taken possession of the narrative at this point.

Carson parodies autobiography's pretense to objective self-expression by using the genre as a means of fictional disembodiment. She thereby follows Stein's example in *The Autobiography of Alice B. Toklas*, where Stein tells the story of her life through the fictional voice of her lover, Alice Toklas. Only on the final page of Toklas's autobiography does Stein concede her authorial ruse. Stein's originality – as Shirley Neuman argues in *Gertrude Stein: Autobiography and the Problem of Narration* – lies in her "repudiation for literary purposes of the continuity of the self": "Once [Stein] reconceptualizes narrative as that written as though by someone else, as analogous to translation, she begins to free herself to write about the 'self' without concern for its duration and consequent identity."[164] Enacting similar translations, Carson dons several literary disguises – Athena, Stesichoros, Geryon, Stein – in search of "another human essence than self."[165] Like the Helen who waits out the Trojan War in Egypt, Carson explores the pleasures and horrors of a multiplicitous identity. Each of the distinct voices in her identity collage offer a kind of testimony that, while it cannot be "regarded as credible history," nonetheless shapes "our notion of who the poet [i]s as a person."

And Carson's concealment drama has a final act. Reading the interview's marginal inscription vertically, one finds that the Steinian "ISISISISISISISISISIS" transforms – through the difference generated by repetition – from an assertion of being, "*Is* is," to an ontological question, "Is *is*?" (A similar question is raised if one reads the marginal inscription of the Mimnermos interviews, "IMIMIMIMIM," as "I am" and "Am I?"). And who could the subject hiding behind these verbs be but Isis, "she of the thousand titles[?]"[166] As a clue to this encryption, the Montrealer disguises her voice in vintage Montmartre and shifts "Isis" from the left margin to the main narrative:

I: Description can we talk about description
s: What is the difference between a volcano and a guinea pig is not a description why is it like it *is is* a description (my emphasis)[167]

Isis is not directly named here, she is de-scribed, her name fragmentarily en-crypted in a passage that stresses the difference between surface appearance and a dynamic understanding of form. Such concealment pays homage to the goddess, as Plutarch explains: "At Saïs the seated statue of Athena, whom they consider to be Isis also, bore the following inscription: 'I am all that has been and is and will be; and no mortal has ever lifted my mantle.'"[168] The secret Isis keeps, having struggled hard to win it for Osiris and herself, is immortality.

CONTEXTUALIZING *AUTOBIOGRAPHY OF RED*

While the secret of immortality remains intact in *Autobiography of Red*, Carson claims in an interview with the *Globe and Mail* to have discovered it:

"The secret of immortality," she explains after a pregnant pause, "is simply to regard all time as infinite. Whatever time you're in, think of it as going on forever. The time you're in suddenly becomes huge and you do a huge thing very fast."[169]

Carson writes across this temporal expanse, from antiquity to the twentieth century, in *Autobiography of Red*. Yet she also creates a sense of temporal continuity across her oeuvre by serializing key phrases and performing variations on certain forms from book to book. For example, *The Beauty of the Husband: A Fictional Essay in 29 Tangos* (2001) is a meditation on the Keatsean adage that beauty is truth. While Carson endorses this aphorism to a certain extent, she also creates a palinode from Keats fragments which implies the opposite:

> {Not for the glance itse}
> {Not for the fiery glance itelf perhaps}
> {Nor at the glance itsef}[170]

The husband in this poem, whose fiery glance is as cruel as it is beautiful, creates another echo of *Autobiography of Red* by reiterating one of the questions that perplexes Geryon: "How do people get power over one another"?[171] The woman in *The Beauty of the Husband*, who resembles Geryon more than the man, takes up Geryon's question later in the story.[172] Thus, as Daphne Merkin observes in a review of *The Beauty of the Husband*, "a story line in any conventional sense is not what fuels Carson's writing – or what she cares about, except as it may enable her to ask the questions that interest her."[173] Although *The Beauty of the Husband* reprises the trope of the tango from *Autobiography of Red*, however, Carson confounds any easy transposition of an early narrative onto a later one by also assigning the autobiographical "I" to the husband in poems such as "XXVII. HUSBAND: I AM."[174] Indeed, it is the husband who "write[s] paintings" in this book, although the woman also writes.[175] Thus, while *The Beauty of the Husband* might seem to be Carson's autobiographical take on her failed eight-year marriage – which would establish a master-narrative for the subtext of her previous books – the concealment drama continues. This fact is particularly evident in the final poem, where the husband gets the last word and suggests that readers have been gulled by a sleight of hand into believing they were reading the wife's account.

The wife's comments on her husband, who is a serial adulterer, also reflect on Carson's compositional process. In discussing the husband's mistress with Ray, the couple's gay friend advises the wife: "don't waste your tears on this one." The wife interjects: "This one. It's a series?" Ray replies: "It's a gap in a series the series is you."[176] Playing with repetitions and gaps even within this short passage, Carson opens an intertextual link to her earlier long poems through a carefully orchestrated use of echoes. Yet she also unframes each installment of the myth in her series on marital heartbreak.

The Beauty of the Husband thus reduces to its barest elements the theory of the lyric novel presented by Carson in *Eros the Bittersweet* and put into practice in *Autobiography of Red*. Carson founds this theory of the novel on Sappho's epithet for Eros the "sweetbitter." The conjunction of opposing emotions in this neologism epitomizes for Carson the ambivalence of love, and she identifies the sweetness of desire and the bitterness of erotic lack in a variety of classical and modern authors. Carson sees the I-You address in Sappho's poetry as "the radical constitution of desire. For, where eros is lack, its activation calls for three structural components – lover, beloved and that which comes between them."[177] The lyric thus contracts and intensifies certain tensions within epic through the "systematic breakup of the huge floes of Homer's poetic system."[178] According to Carson, the lyric distillation of the love triangle reduces the narrative sweep of epic to its erotic underpinnings. Correspondingly, Carson sees the novel, which is conventionally identified with the epic tradition, as in fact an elaboration of the erotic paradoxes of the lyric: "Tactics of triangulation are the main business of the novel. These tactics are the ones familiar to us from the archaic poets, now employed prosaically and *in extenso*. The novelists play out as dilemmas of plot and character all those facets of erotic contradiction and difficulty that were first brought to light in lyric poetry."[179] Moreover, when the writer triangulates desire on the page, it mirrors the reading process because reader and character are separated by the paradoxical boundary between fiction and reality, as Carson demonstrates in a chapter of *Eros the Bittersweet* beginning with an epigram from Keats's "Ode on a Grecian Urn." Like the figures on the urn, the character may "touch" the reader emotionally, but not physically.

A similar tension between metonymic contiguity and metaphorical connection influences the arrangement of the generically distinct, but thematically related, sections of *Autobiography of Red*. Monique Tschoffen has argued that Stesichoros's principal achievement was to shift narrative connections from the horizontal axis of metonymic contiguity to the vertical axis of metaphorical association.[180] However, Line Henrikson challenges this argument in "The Verse Novel as a Hybrid Genre: Monstrous Bodies in Anne Carson's *Autobiography of Red* and Les Murray's *Freddy Neptune*"

by insisting that "the actual lines of the romance about Geryon are dominated by metonymy."[181] Furthermore, Henrikson argues that verse novels
differ from traditional lyric or epic genres because they incorporate devices
most closely associated with the novel: "To Bakhtin the novel differs from
the so-called high poetic genres in its use of irony, polyphony, free indirect
discourse and parody: modes that the high poetic genres ignore."[182] By
reconfiguring the power dynamics of the Geryon myth through parody, or
incorporating the palinode into a larger narrative, Carson embraces the
subversive potential of parody and irony. However, Henrikson argues that
Carson's hybrid text is ultimately "sterile" in the biological sense that
hybrid organisms are unable to reproduce. She believes that the verse novel
is overly preoccupied with its subversive agenda, and is thus incapable of
emerging from this wreckage as a new and "pure" genre (although Henrikson acknowledges the problematic quality of the latter term). She believes
that Murray's *Freddy Neptune* achieves a more balanced and productive
balance between verse and novel and thus heralds the possible emergence
of a new genre, the novel in verse.

Henrikson's argument is well formed, but I see three problems with it.
First, Carson is fascinated by the anomalous, the erratic, the inimitable. If
Autobiography of Red is an anomalous text, an outsider's production, and
not the foundation of a reproducible genre, then I believe Carson would
consider the text a success within her own frame of reference. Second, the
sexual metaphor that undergirds Henrikson's essay, whereby the success of
the hybrid is determined by its ability to reproduce biologically, strikes me
as inappropriate to a story about gay lovers that queers the Herakles myth
– particularly since the story is written by a childless woman whose feminist enquiries devote attention to the lives of childless female intellectuals
(Dickinson, Stein, Woolf), or married women whose behaviour departs
from normative maternal roles (Sappho).

Finally, Henrikson's study of genre needs to acknowledge the long tradition of novels in verse, in particular the work of Alexander Pushkin
(1799–1837). Initially an admirer of Byron, Pushkin broke with the deca-
dent voice of late Romanticism in his novel in verse, *Eugene Oneigin*
(1831), and depicted quotidian settings from a realistic narrative perspective that greatly influenced Tolstoy. Pushkin's psychological portraiture of
Onegin also laid the groundwork for Turgenev's character studies, and
Bakhtin identifies *Eugene Onegin* – with its deft perspectival shifts, under-
scored by alternating masculine and feminine rhymes – as a precursor to
the polyphonic discourse in Dostoyevsky's novels.[183] In this respect, not

only is Pushkin one of Russia's most beloved poets but he is widely considered to be the founder of modern Russian fiction.

In Canada, authors have set out to write novels in verse since at least Archibald Lampman's *The Story of an Affinity* (1894), which the author describes in a letter as a "short novel in blank verse."[184] Nonetheless, Lampman's heroic narrative employs a straightforward plot and a mostly linear temporal arc, and thus conforms to the realist standards of nineteenth-century prose. An example of an *erotika pathemata* more relevant to Carson's style of writing is Elizabeth Smart's *By Grand Central Station I Sat Down and Wept* (1945), which Marta Dvorak describes as a "meditative and plotless prose poem on illegitimate passion."[185] (Critics often point to this work in their discussion of precedents for Ondaatje's work, as does Ondaatje himself in the private canon he delineates in an afterword to *Tay John*). However, if one returns to the question of metonymy and metaphor, a comparison of Carson's technique to that of Marlatt is useful once again.

Pauline Butling in an interview invites Marlatt to comment on the proposition that her "use of the prose poem forces more attention to the horizontal language axis and puts words into metonymic relation, in contrast to the lyric form which torques the line in interesting ways but mostly on a vertical (metaphoric) axis."[186] Marlatt responds by explaining the evolution of her prose poem sentences and their "run-on effect":

> Well the tension in a short-line poem is between the torquing of the line and the continuation of the discursive. In a prose poem you're working with a sentence, and it's a sentence that's very loose, it can gather all kinds of stuff into it, because in English we're not so driven by the Latinate declinations to indicate grammatical connections. English rests much more on position. You can put things side by side and they have a very loose connection with a capacity for meaning-play and that's how I like to build my sentences; that's why I play around with the resources of punctuation like commas, dashes and brackets. Those are the ones I principally use. An English sentence has a tremendous capacity for detour, and that's what's pulled me further and further into prose.[187]

Marlatt's experience as a translator of French poetry and prose thus alerts her to a different set of productive lacunae than those that preoccupy Carson. What is lost or difficult to reproduce in translation from French to English becomes an opening for Marlatt's explorations. Carson, for her part, searches for a means of approximating the aorist (timeless or eternal) tense of ancient Greek in *Autobiography of Red*.

Carson's emphasis on triangulation also creates an intriguing resonance between *Autobiography of Red* and *Beautiful Losers*. Like the *Geryoneis* and *Coming Through Slaughter*, *Beautiful Losers* is triadic in structure. And like *Autobiography of Red*, it combines an introductory history of the principal characters with a long lyrical section and "An Epilogue in the Third Person" that in fact reverts to the first person and what appears to be a cameo appearance by the author. Furthermore, both Montreal novels feature a crucial excursion to Argentina where a taboo dimension of the love triangle is explored and the characters grapple with the destructive and insightful aspects of twentieth-century German history and thought. The connections between the monstrous protagonists in these books are enticing if one considers that Sylvia Söderlind tracks the numbers and dates mentioned in *Beautiful Losers* and observes that the repetition of "6" recalls "the name of the beast in the Book of Revelation."[188] Thus one might count Geryon among Cohen's balancing monsters of love, except that Geryon balances between a revolutionary American and an Indigenous Peruvian. Furthermore, Carson maintains that triangulation is a basic feature of most novels, and one must refrain from pushing analogies too far in the name of national unity, as Cohen warns in *Beautiful Losers*: "Science begins in coarse naming, a willingness to disregard the particular shape and destiny of each red life, and call them all Rose."[189]

Carson composes her text from a different set of fragments than Cohen does, but the use of Isis in contemporary Montreal underscores that for Carson, as for Cohen, the present is mythic. The cult of Isis appears to thrive in Montreal, for Scobie recalls that when the "Rolling Thunder Revue visited Montreal in 1975, [Bob Dylan] dedicated one song to Cohen, introducing 'Isis' (an interesting choice, considering the importance of Isis in *Beautiful Losers*) with the words 'This is for Leonard, if he's still here!'"[190] Furthermore, when one considers that Cohen wrote *Beautiful Losers* on the island of Hydra, the mythological home of the many-headed monster in whose gall the arrows of Herakles were dipped, the seemingly eclectic assemblage of myths in *Autobiography of Red* appears less random. Like her Montreal predecessors, Carson chooses myths that give physical expression to a multifaceted identity, and she develops a multipartite narrative that raises the question of formal unity even within the space of the text. Cohen has an Isis-figure make her famous claim to timelessness in Greek toward the end of *Beautiful Losers*, but Carson finds different ways of encrypting the Isis myth in her novel.

Although Carson is loath to acknowledge debts or affinities to any contemporary Canadian writers – indeed, to any living writers – it is possible that Carson, Klein, and Cohen share more than a cultural geography as anglophone Montrealers, living just off the Main. Consider, for example, the scene in *The Favourite Game* where Breavman and Krantz watch women pass by on a summer evening on rue Stanley and the narrator remarks: "The strolling girls had their bare arms on."[191] This interjection strikes a chord with the oft-cited passage in *Autobiography of Red* where Geryon watches "his mother / rhinestoning past on her way to the door. She had all her breasts on this evening."[192] Carson's version strikes with greater force, but perhaps she riffs on passages of Cohen in the same way that Andre Furlani has demonstrated she improvises from passages of Paul Celan.[193] If this is the case, the resemblance to Ondaatje's writing that critics have noted in Carson may in fact be an oblique acknowledgement of Cohen's influence, a case I will argue more strenuously in my discussion of Anne Michaels's *Fugitive Pieces*. At the very least, one should keep in mind while reading *Autobiography of Red* that, as Michael Greenstein observes, Breavman's supratemporal flights of imagination in *The Favourite Game* are stimulated by his interest in archaeology, geology, and astronomy, and by his sense of living on the slope of "Mount Royal's ancient crater."[194] This intertext is even more poignant when one considers that the popular depiction of Mount Royal as an extinct volcano is an urban myth.

As a hybrid novel, *Autobiography of Red* also has much in common with Klein's *The Second Scroll*. Both novels combine an academic apparatus with lyricism and narrative. Both double the reader's frames of reference and explore the interplay between lyric and epic. But *Autobiography of Red* is designed to unhinge the epic epithets that Melech's nephew had hoped to fix. Carson's affinities reside with the subplot of *The Second Scroll* (where the anthologist compiles translations that will bridge two cultures), rather than with the main plot (to glorify a race, nation, and epic hero). Carson thus stresses the ongoing and irresolvable aspects of signification and social formation, and here we can draw an important conclusion. If there is a hero in the Canadian poet's novel, it is not the conqueror, founder, or transcendent male. It is the translator, bridge builder, or monster. Beverly Curran, for instance, focuses on the hero as translator in order to position the adulterous, cross-cultural experiences in Ondaatje's *the man with seven toes* as the precursor to the desert scenes and marital politics of "*The English Patient*, which uses sex, drugs, and translation to derange both time and space in an extreme complication of the captivity narrative, and to reconfigure the role of the artist as a translator."[195] Revisiting

Carson's obsession with emotional captivity, translation, and photography in this context helps to locate the artist in her international travels. Her Canadian background is revealed, not by particular signs, but by the way she relates (to) them.

Carson also takes a unique approach to the "spinner" motif that Klein and Cohen employ. Although her first published work, *Eros the Bittersweet*, is a study of ancient Greek literature, she prefaces it with a brief meditation on Kafka's "The Top."[196] This short story describes the peculiar habit of a philosopher who spends his free time watching the spinning toys of young children. Although Kafka hails from the same Jewish, Eastern European environment that spawned Klein's "The Chanukah Dreidel," the passion of Kafka's philosopher for the top contrasts diametrically with that of Klein's rabbi. Kafka's protagonist is in love with the vertiginous poise of spinning tops (which he periodically steals), but he is always disappointed when he arrests the actual object. His situation is paradoxical, because, as with the lovers on Keats's Grecian urn, it is the impossibility of grasping the love-object, of arresting the spin, that attracts him.

Carson argues that Kafka's story is really "about the delight we take in metaphor. A meaning spins, remaining upright on an axis of normalcy aligned with the conventions of connotation and denotation, and yet: to spin is not normal, and to dissemble normal uprightness by means of this fantastic motion is impertinent ... To catch beauty would be to understand how that impertinent stability in vertigo is possible. But no, delight need not reach so far. To be running breathlessly, but not yet arrived, is itself delightful, a suspended moment of living hope."[197] Carson spends the rest of this book, and much of her subsequent career, investigating this lover's reach and the beloved's vertiginous balance. Her preferred subject of inquiry is thus a centripetal force whose centre cannot be reached. Her characters move "several times through a cycle of remarks" without reaching definitive conclusions, as the questions spin into subsequent volumes.[198] She writes a series of poems about failed love affairs, each one echoing the other, but she enucleates the master narrative that would supply the interpretive centre and stabilize the hermeneutic axis.

Thus, Carson does not use the *Geryoneis*, the myth of Isis, Canadian literature, or even her own autobiographical material as a fixed template, but rather sets in motion a series of literary allusions that intertwine ancient and modern, masculine and feminine, Greek and Quechua, Egyptian and Canadian. These surprising juxtapositions are the hallmark of Carson's style, whether in long poems such as "The Glass Essay," where she "weaves and conflates one theme with another ... tell[ing] two strong stories with

Tolstoyan skill,"[199] or in academic works such as *Economy of the Unlost: (Reading Simonides of Keos with Paul Celan)*, where Carson explains her technique in a "Note on Method": "To keep attention strong means to keep it from settling. Partly for this reason I have chosen to talk about two men at once. They keep each other from settling. Moving and not settling, they are side by side in a conversation and yet no conversation takes place ... With and against, aligned and adverse, each is placed like a surface on which the other may come into focus."[200] In *Autobiography of Red*, Carson draws female and male literary figures into closer focus through a series of alternating frames of reference. She combines the Osirian art of writing with the Isian art of weaving to create "good strong narrative" through constant fragmentation and displacement. These shifting frames of reference are far from settled, as the reappearance of the "little red dog" in the final lines of the interview underscores.[201] *Autobiography of Red* thus demonstrates that the frameworks of myth, genre, and gender are volatile and constantly subject to revision.

However, while Carson has put volatility to use, she has also been its victim. The praise that was initially heaped on Carson for producing her dazzling hybrids has prompted a backlash. When Carson was awarded the T.S. Eliot Prize for *The Beauty of the Husband* in January, 2002, Canadian national newspapers responded with articles entitled "Poet or 'Prize-Reaping Machine'?" and "Who's Afraid of Anne Carson?"[202] Carson's most virulent critic, David Solway, who is cited in both articles, condemns *The Beauty of the Husband* for blurring the lines between poetry and prose: "Decently compressed and tucked into the featureless prose that is its natural medium, *Husband* would make a tidy little article on marital infidelity in *Chatelaine*."[203] His sentiments are echoed by the poetry editor for *The Guardian* (U.K.), who reacted to the awarding of the Eliot Prize by complaining that Carson's poetics exhibit "Neither Rhyme nor Reason": "[*Husband*] fails as poetry, simply because it shows either crashing inability or an unbecoming contempt for the medium. Its materials – the narrative, its details and a dry wit are engaging enough – would have made for a compelling short story."[204] These are isolated voices, of course, and they do not reflect the general appraisal of Carson's work.[205] Nor can the critics agree on the particulars of their judgments. For example, the simile "He could fill structures of / threat with a light like the earliest olive oil" in *The Beauty of the Husband* has been cited by critics as an example of both Carson's brilliance and her shortcomings as a poet.[206]

However, what is certain is that Carson has challenged her critics to reconsider their notion of what structure is in poetry and the novel. Thus, in a largely enthusiastic review of *The Beauty of the Husband* in *The New York Times*, Daphne Merkin hails Carson as "one of the great pasticheurs" and recommends that what Carson's "fellow poets would do well to ask themselves is not whether what Carson is writing can or cannot be called poetry, but how has she succeeded in making it – whatever label you give it – so thrillingly new?"[207] Carson's hybrids are certainly fascinating, and she deserves credit for bridging the gap between antiquity and (post)modernity at a time when Classics departments across North America, including Carson's former one at McGill, were being dismantled. She has a flair for startling images and psychological insights, as well as a quirky sense of humour that makes her tone unique. However, at least in a Canadian context, it is rather overstated to say that the forms of Carson's long poems and novels in verse are brand new. Given Klein's scholarly apparatus, Cohen's love triangles, Ondaatje's use of collage, Bowering's Steinian wordplays, and Marlatt's questioning of the relation between Eros and expectation in the quest narrative, it is simply not the case that "Carson's writing is without precedent in Canada."[208] I return to Carson's reputedly incongruous relation to Canadian literature in the discussion of Lynn Crosbie in my conclusion.

7

The English Patient, Fugitive Pieces, and the Poet's Novel

Sometimes one must try to invent a form which expresses the limitations of form, which takes as its point of departure the terror of formlessness.[1]

Glenn Gould

I began this study by suggesting one response to the question of why so many of Canada's acclaimed novelists begin and continue as poets. For Cohen, Ondaatje, Bowering, Marlatt, and Carson, the long poem facilitated the transition from the lyric to the novel by allowing them to develop serial forms of narrative that can convey a sense of duration without sacrificing the intensity and concision of the lyric. The authors apply these serial techniques differently in their novels and address particular regional, political, and aesthetic concerns, which has garnered them acclaim in diverse quarters.

The poet's novel is the subject of strenuous criticism, however, even among fans of poetry. At the conclusion of *The Idea of Lyric: Lyric Modes in Ancient and Modern Poetry*, W.R. Johnson argues that with the exception of "the ballad, which is an extremely successful lyric hybrid, narrative tends to be fairly secure against lyrical aggression. So-called lyrical novels, which often thrive on the sentimental, that is, on the inchoate impressions and frustrations of their readers and so make them complicit in the illusion of composition, tend to be bad novels."[2] Johnson makes an exception for Virginia Woolf because her novels are still firmly grounded in the concerns of nineteenth century realism, but in general he feels that lyrical novels lack formal integrity and fail to address broad social issues. Similar complaints are made by Canadian critics, and I hope to overturn both these objections.

The most outspoken critic of the poet's novel in Canada is Stephen Henighan. He devotes a long essay in *When Words Deny the World: The Reshaping of Canadian Writing* (2002) to an attack on Ondaatje's *The*

English Patient (1992) and Anne Michaels's *Fugitive Pieces* (1996). Henighan's conclusion makes his position emphatic: "Most of the world's literatures preserve a pocket for the 'poet's novel,' a book governed by metaphor rather than the vital interlinking of character and story. Such works generally attract a few appreciative readers who then pay more attention to the poet's next book of poems. A literature dominated by 'poet's novels' is an anomaly. A culture whose reading public requires this sort of fiction – self-consciously 'artistic' without posing the challenges of authentic art – is ill."[3] Although this bold condemnation was not received warmly by Canada's literary press, it seems to have articulated the sentiments of many Canadian readers, as the book sold well and received a nomination for the 2002 Governor General's Award in the non-fiction category.

When Words Deny the World was issued as part of a series of critical reappraisals published by Porcupine's Quill Press under the iconoclastic editorship of John Metcalf.[4] It builds on the criticisms of Philip Marchand's *Ripostes* (1998) and finds support in David Solway's *Director's Cut* (2003), both published by Porcupine's Quill. Henighan and Solway have used their polemics as a platform for promoting their own material and they propose to replace the poet-novelists with a short list of their own preferences and peers. Cohen escapes this erasure, but by an act of negative definition the Porcupine's Quill authors reinforce the affinities between Ondaatje, Bowering, Marlatt, Carson, and Michaels that I have traced in this study. On the Porcupine's Quill website, Bowering responded to his denunciation in *Director's Cut* with the quip: "I am sure glad that Soilway [sic] put me on the list he put me on and not the other one."[5] While both *When Words Deny the World* and *Director's Cut* are riddled with inconsistencies of argument, I have demonstrated elsewhere that the criteria according to which Solway condemns Carson invalidate his own poetry, so I concentrate here on *When Words Deny the World*.[6]

Although I challenge Henighan's broad arguments, I do not wish to dismiss all his observations. Henighan's lampooning of the stagey dialogue in *The English Patient* exposes certain passages as indefensibly bad writing (and makes one pine for the editorial rigour that the poet Dennis Lee brought to *The Collected Works of Billy the Kid* and *Coming Through Slaughter*). I agree with Henighan that Ondaatje is at his best in his early books, where he "animate[s] his poet's gift for image with a quick sluice of narrative."[7] I also agree with Henighan's accusation that Toronto writers receive a disproportionate amount of press coverage in Canada. And since, a year after the publication of *When Words Deny the World*, the books editor of the *Globe and Mail* was still worrying about Henighan's charges of

Toronto-centrism and felt compelled to write a column about the vibrant literary scene in Vancouver, Henighan has done something worthwhile.[8]

However, Henighan's attack on the poet's novel is too haphazard to escape rebuttal. The centrepiece essay in *When Words Deny the World,* "Free Trade Fiction, or the Victory of Metaphor over History," proposes that the fragmented and metaphor-laden forms of *The English Patient* and *Fugitive Pieces* were largely by-products of the economic climate of the 1990s in Canada and the signing of the NAFTA free-trade deal with Mexico and the United States. The weak historical basis of this argument should now be clear, as I have demonstrated that the kind of novel Henighan abhors has been written in Canada since at least the 1950s. Even if one wished to assess the broader impact of Ondaatje's writing, as Henighan does by linking *Fugitive Pieces* to *The English Patient,* the dates would have to be pushed back to the 1970s, according to Sam Solecki: "It's arguable that Ondaatje's critical success with *The Collected Works of Billy the Kid, Rat Jelly,* and *Coming Through Slaughter* was the moment when the definition of the Canadian canon became problematic. Almost single-handedly, he introduced postmodernism, post-colonialism, and multiculturalism into the discussion. I'm not suggesting that there were no other writers whose work was considered 'pomo' or 'poco' in the late sixties and through the seventies. I'm simply saying that none had produced a body of work of sufficient originality and stature to cause a seismic shift in the Canadian field."[9] Solecki overstates his case here, because such movements do not emerge by the efforts of one man alone, as my chapters 2 and 3 have shown. However, there is no doubt that Ondaatje's work helped to popularize these shifts in the production and definition of Canadian literature.

Henighan compounds the flaws in his economic analysis by arguing that, "in Canada, globalization means Americanization."[10] He then proceeds to support this argument by discussing books set partly (*Fugitive Pieces*) and almost entirely (*The English Patient*) in Europe, and in which Americans are portrayed unfavourably. On the other hand, a quick check of the MLA bibliography of publications on Ondaatje, most of them on *The English Patient,* leaves no doubt that Ondaatje's book profited from the debate over globalization in the 1990s and the Hollywood film of his novel. If Henighan had built his argument around the film version of *The English Patient,* which establishes Almásy as the central protagonist, turns Kirpal Singh into an ornament, cuts Hana's connection to Toronto by giving her a French accent that betrays her European origins even in English, and echoes *Casablanca* more than it revises it, he might have had a case.[11]

Although Henighan concedes that he has set much of his own fiction outside Canada, he maintains that novels such as *The English Patient* offend Canadians because they fail to test Canadian values "against the contours of other cultures."[12] Henighan's spatial terminology intrigues me because I take this sort of comparative test to be a core theme of *The English Patient*, which is about shifting cultural, political, and physical topographies. *The English Patient* depicts the experiences of three characters from the Toronto novel *In the Skin of a Lion* – Hana, Patrick, and Caravaggio – in Europe at the end of the Second World War. (A fourth, Clara, remains in Canada as a dissenter.) Over the course of the novel, the reader discovers that Patrick has died in combat after being abandoned by his unit in a French dovecote. In her sorrow, Hana latches onto the burned English patient as a surrogate father-figure and forsakes her medical unit to nurse the ailing man in a bomb-ravaged Italian villa. As in *Fugitive Pieces*, the penitent child must grapple with the question of how best to live in the aftermath of clashing superpowers and mass devastation. Patrick's friend Caravaggio, who served in the Allied intelligence services and lost his thumbs for the cause, hears of Hana's endeavours and arrives at the villa to campaign for her return to Canada. In her traumatized state, however, Hana refuses to abandon the burned man, whose wounds she sees as emblematic of Patrick's emotional state in his dying hour. Hana thus becomes the seeker, the empathetic figure who draws most of the characters in the novel together, and she helps to recreate in Italy the multicultural dynamism of her hometown by attracting the soldier Kirpal (Kip) Singh into the microcosm.

Almásy's love story suggests that such a juxtaposition of cultures might work in Old World settings. Almásy recalls that a pan-European crew of archaeologists and translators worked to recover and contextualize fragments of an ancient African civilization in the shifting sands of a North African desert. This tale begins idyllically but ends tragically, once Katharine transfers her love for the aerial photographer Geoffrey Clifton to the explorer Almásy. Hana, like Katharine, is charmed by Almásy's meandering stories and his copy of Herodotus's *Histories*, in which he pastes maps, word lists, and anecdotes about the desert. Caravaggio, on the other hand, knows about Almásy's collaboration with the Nazis and is wise to the guilty secrets behind his aristocratic air. Caravaggio also divines the repressed feelings of mourning for Patrick that are the real wellspring of Hana's attachment to Almásy, and he attempts to talk her out of this transference. The cultural contours of the Canadian group are thereby tested against Almásy's African past and the European present.

Ultimately, Hana realizes that the English patient is not the noble figure she wants him to be, and Patrick's circle is not interchangeable with the group forming around the English patient's bed. In short, European patterns of social cohesion are being tested against Canadian ones, and Hana decides that the Europe of the 1940s fails the test (although the novel is full of allusions to successfully cosmopolitan periods in European history). Whereas a climactic bombing had been averted in *In the Skin of a Lion* and a social unit formed through negotiation, the social unit at the villa is shattered by the nuclear Holocaust at Hiroshima. Kip blames the American bombing on the legacy of English imperialism and departs for India. The English patient loses his will to live. Hana resolves to return to Canada, and only the Italian Canadian Caravaggio seems unsurprised by the cataclysmic turn of events. The gradual ruin of a desert civilization stands in sharp contrast to the instantaneous and large-scale destruction produced by modernity, and none of Almásy's romantic stories can heal the rift. However, Ondaatje seems to gesture toward new paradigms for understanding this cross-cultural condition at the end to the novel, where the emotional bond between Kirpal and Hana allows them to retain a synchrony in the global village, symbolized by the concluding image of Hana knocking a glass off a shelf at the same time that Kirpal catches his daughter's fallen fork. Whereas Kirpal spends the war cutting the wires of bomb fuses to protect the Europeans from themselves, and whereas he cuts his ties to caucasians after Hiroshima, his fate remains wired to that of Hana in a world where electronic connectivity, shared nuclear and ecological concerns, and his own memory triggers link their emotional lives.

Ondaatje's treatment of the poetry of Anne Wilkinson (1910–61), a lesser-known Canadian modernist, also provides a clue to his perception of Canada's place on the international stage. Wilkinson first appears as a character in the later portion of *In the Skin of a Lion*, where the thief Caravaggio escapes from prison and encounters "Anne" writing at her cottage north of Toronto. In "Anne Wilkinson in Michael Ondaatje's *In the Skin of a Lion*: Writing and Reading Class," Katherine Acheson argues that the fact that Anne is "the only writer character in the novel suggests that she has a metafictional role."[13] Acheson then demonstrates that large portions of this section paraphrase Wilkinson's poetry and her biography of the Osler family, *Lions in the Way*. Anne's wealth and ancestral pedigree as a member of an illustrious family grant her a sense of rootedness and security in cottage country that the fugitive Caravaggio both envies and resents. She exercises her command over the English language (as a writer), over the northern landscape (as an expert canoeist), and over Toronto (as an Osler).

The Osler family "were not just rich and powerful; they were deeply involved in laying the foundations of the official culture of Toronto in the nineteenth and early twentieth centuries. Edmund Osler [Wilkinson's grandfather] was a founding member of the Royal Ontario Museum, the Art Gallery of Ontario and one of the Chancellors of the University of Toronto."[14] In shifting the status of the lion from Edmund Osler to Patrick Lewis, Ondaatje shifts the narrative focus from financier to labourer. And, as Anne discovers her literary prowess, the wealthy woman moves from patron of the arts to producer of art. Although Ondaatje, like Cohen, practises a decidedly "phallic art," Lorraine York insists that one should not overlook the creative roles played by Ondaatje's female characters, particularly in the later works.[15]

Acheson's essay on Wilkinson sheds a fascinating light on *In the Skin of a Lion*, but Dean Irvine's introduction to *Heresies: The Complete Poems of Anne Wilkinson (1924–1961)* demonstrates that Acheson misses an important detail.[16] Wilkinson's writing also makes an appearance toward the end of *The English Patient*, where Hana recalls: "The Englishman once read me something, from a book: 'Love is so small it can tear itself through the eye of a needle.'"[17] This aphorism, attributed by Ondaatje to one of Wilkinson's journal entries, is not flagged as Canadian. It impresses itself on Hana's memory by virtue of its own force and takes its place among the many quotations, from Herodotus to Wallace Stevens, that the Englishman summons from Western literature. Yet, as Irvine demonstrates, the aphorism has a precipitous effect on Hana: "These are Hana's final words to Kip, an attempt at reconciliation after his violent reaction to the news of the bombings at Nagasaki and Hiroshima, for which he holds every 'white' nation and person responsible."[18] The quotation deepens the significance of Hana's gift to Kirpal of the maple syrup spile, a needle-like instrument that drips syrup and which Kirpal leaves behind, like their love. The quotation prompts Hana to tear herself away from the English patient, whom she has solaced with injections of morphine (tears from a needle). Rather than signalling Hana's dissipation into a nebulous world order, the aphorism immediately precedes her decision to return to Canada and her adoptive mother, Clara. Clara's silhouette, paddling the shoreline of Georgian Bay, resembles the figure cut by Anne in *In the Skin of a Lion*. The conclusion of Hana's portion of the novel thus clearly is shaped, not by NAFTA, but by allusions to much older Canadian texts and artistic movements, such as the Group of Seven painters. Far from being Americanized, the vision of Canada in Hana's final letter is syrupy with Canadiana. The sense of continuity with the past is particularly acute when one considers that the maple spile was originally given to Patrick by Caravaggio prior to his assault on the Waterworks in *In the Skin of a Lion,* and it was given to Caravaggio as a memento from the boy Al in Trenton. Annick Hillger identifies this boy as a youthful version of that area's most celebrated poet, Al Purdy, and she demonstrates that Ondaatje bases the scene on a Purdy memoir.[19]

Wilkinson interests Ondaatje because she represents the kind of liminal figure he admires: a woman in the male-dominated milieu of Canadian modernism; a Toronto poet with close ties to the Montreal intelligentsia; a modernist in form, diction, and allusion who remained suspicious of ideological and aesthetic systems; a wealthy writer who lamented that her publications lacked "social significance" in the class wars of her day, yet whose "engagement with political, social, and gender issues has retained its efficacy and, in fact," according to Irvine, "is gaining relevance to the concerns of poets writing at the present time."[20]

Perhaps Ondaatje also chooses a fragment from Wilkinson's 1951 journals because it is in this year that she records her decision to move from the short lyric to the modernist series: "Plan a long poem. Keep notebook of ideas and lines. Decide on theme then play the variations, each thing going a step farther from the original; conclude by bringing the whole thing *home* ... Write a connected series of poems. BUT DO IT – *Write a longish poem.*"[21] Wilkinson's battle with cancer prevented this series from being completed, but Irvine cites the entry above in his conviction that either the short cycle "Nature Be Damned" or the entire unpublished collection which this cycle began, *Heresies and Other Poems,* represents the rudiments of a long poem.[22] Since 1951 marked the year that the modernist tradition in Canadian poetry made a successful leap to prose through Klein's *The Second Scroll,* it is appropriate that Ondaatje highlights the generic ambiguity of Wilkinson's writing at this stage in her career – an ambiguity matched by Almásy's commonplace book.

By repeatedly citing Wilkinson, Ondaatje enables critics to situate his writing more precisely within the Canadian canon. Henighan regards Ondaatje's novels as misguided departures from the emergent tradition of modern realism in Canadian fiction, which Henighan traces from 1945 onward through Hugh MacLennan, Mordecai Richler, and Alice Munro. However, in both *The English Patient* and *In the Skin of a Lion,* Ondaatje signals that his writing draws inspiration from a cosmopolitan tradition of modern writing in Canada, which one can trace back to the 1920s through Wilkinson to poets such as A.M. Klein, F.R. Scott and A.J.M. Smith. Scott and Smith were friends and lovers of Wilkinson, who founded the *McGill Fortnightly Review* (1925–27) and the literary journal *Preview* (1942–45) to foster the development of modern writing in Canada. Their European understanding of modernism was challenged by the journal *First Statement* (1942–45), which favoured a more vernacular and North American poetics, exemplified by the work of Irving Layton. However, when Wilkinson entered the literary scene, in the wake of the ideology-sanctioned violence of the Second World War, there was an aesthetic of *rapprochement* in Canadian writing. The modernist journals had merged under the banner of *Northern Review* (1945–56), where Wilkinson published many of her early poems. Indeed, Brian Trehearne has demonstrated that critics have always exaggerated the ideological differences between *Preview* and *First Statement*.[23] Wilkinson, a *Preview* poet in tone and taste, published her first collection, *Counterpoint to Sleep*, with First Statement Press in 1951. She later co-edited and funded the launch of *Tamarack Review* in 1956, the year that *Northern Review* disbanded. If Wilkinson's ancestors helped to found key Toronto cultural institutions, Wilkinson and her peers established many of the textual foundations of modern Canadian writing that Ondaatje's generation would inherit. Smith, for example, edited the first bilingual edition of the *Oxford Book of Canadian Verse* (1960), as well as *The Collected Poems of Anne Wilkinson and a Prose Memoir* (1968). This shift in Canadian modernism from contest to crossover – a movement that mirrored larger attempts to bridge social divides in the late 1940s and 1950s – is a movement that Ondaatje's narratives extend in form, plot, and symbolism. Thus Ondaatje manages to invoke both the vernacular Al Purdy and the patrician Anne Wilkinson through the maple syrup spile.

Cohen merged the rival Montreal modernisms in the late 1950s and 1960s through his interest in Klein and Layton, and the influence of Cohen, as well as American and Australian artists, shaped Ondaatje's early narratives (see chapter 3). But in writing a novel about Canadian expatriates in Italy, Ondaatje points back to *Preview* efforts to bridge North American and European sensibilities. In *The English Patient*, he recuperates a cosmopolitanism that fell into disrepute during the nationalist euphoria of the late 1960s, a movement in which both Ondaatje and his critics had trouble situating his work. The cultural and political achievements of the *Preview* group – in particular Scott's brazen legal challenges, Smith's bilingual anthologizing, Klein's cross-cultural mediation, Page's writing in Brazil, Anderson's status as a gay poet and editor – remain undervalued today, even though the poets' works could be seen as contributions to Canadian diversity rather than being subsumed by the stereotype of Anglo-Montreal stodginess. Canada's European connections are also ripe for reconsideration in *The English Patient* because the novel is set in the era when "colonialism," the charge made against the *Preview* poets, begins to denote American, and no longer British, power in Canada.

Ondaatje seems to have come to his appreciation of the *Preview* poets gradually, and it is only in the context of an older Ondaatje reconsidering his Canadian predecessors that one can fully appreciate his "quotation" of Wilkinson. Hillger's chapter on "The Young Poet and the Fathers of Can.lit" demonstrates that Ondaatje, living with the poet D.G. Jones and immersed in the same Anglo-Quebec milieu that nurtured Cohen, oscillated between reverence for and rebellion against the older poets in the 1960s.[24] Like Cohen, the young Ondaatje embraced American popular culture as an antidote to the lingering elements of a British colonial mentality in the *Preview* poets. Ondaatje's "Song to Alfred Hitchcock and Wilkinson," which he identifies in the *Manna* interview as the first or second poem he wrote for *The Dainty Monsters*, illustrates this tension.[25] Solecki remarks, too hesitantly, that the poem "contains a comic *hommage* to Hitchcock's *The Birds* and perhaps to Anne Wilkinson," and that it "may owe something to D.G. Jones's 'For the Birds.'"[26] The comedy of this short "Song" arises from the fact that Ondaatje esteems the sound effects of an American horror film, *The Birds*, above the elevated diction of Canadian modernism:

> Flif flif flif flif very fast
> is the noise the birds make
> running over us.
> A poet would say 'fluttering,'
> or
> 'see-sawing with the sun on their wings.'
> But all it is
> is flif flif flif flif very fast.[27]

To the young Ondaatje, American film and music suggest a model of dynamism, immediacy, and explosive (or implosive) energy (see chapter 3). In the early poetry, Hitchcock (emblematic of the U.S.A.) corrects Wilkinson (emblematic of Canada), but this pattern is reversed in the later novels.

The real source of Ondaatje's Wilkinson quotation is the first stanza of "White Dwarfs," which critics agree is the finest distillation of Ondaatje's early, implosive world view:

> This is for people who disappear
> for those who descend into the code
> and make their room a fridge for Superman

– who exhaust costume and bones that could perform flight,
who shave their moral so raw
they can tear themselves through the eye of a needle[28]

This stanza combines biblical (Matthew) and Greek (Icarus) allusions with pop cultural references to Hollywood film to create a composite portrait of the hero as a monster of energy who is at once dazzling and self-destructive. However, the mature Ondaatje concentrates on the destructive consequences of this energy for society at large. When Ondaatje turns his attention to Canada in *In the Skin of a Lion*, he rejects the violence of charismatic but dangerous loners. The explosive violence of Potter, Billy, Bolden, and Small gives way to characters who defuse explosions (Patrick, Kirpal, Anil). The new bond between characters in the later works is not the spectacle of the death drive, but rather the "small" love that counteracts this force. Hence, Ondaatje's homage to Wilkinson in *The English Patient* is less a quotation of Wilkinson than a rewriting of his own poetics in a manner that honours her empathetic world view.

As Irvine points out, the Wilkinson passage that Ondaatje cites is very different from the original journal entry: "We should never lose sight of the glorious, untouchable sun that is love ... Never let me write a word about love that is not in praise of love. It is only its perversions that sting in my poetry and on my skinny skin. The hare that circles, a vulture beaked and taloned about the dove, poor thing – but beautiful because it is, in the New Testament sense, always poor and therefore able to pass through the eye of a needle."[29] Irvine notes that Ondaatje's paraphrase pays homage to the sense of Wilkinson's journal entry, as both Hana and Kirpal come to praise their interracial love with age. Alice Brittan also demonstrates that Hana imitates Almásy's practice of writing in (and therefore personalizing) printed books, so perhaps one could attribute her quotation to the imaginative engagement of one Canadian woman with the writing of another.[30] In any case, by citing the journal entry as if it were a line of free verse, Ondaatje secularizes Wilkinson's terms and situates her writing in the ambiguous zone between poetry and prose, where she resided in her final decade. His treatment of Wilkinson is both true in spirit and perverse in form.

FUGITIVE PIECES

Homage and transformation are also key elements of the treatment of history by Anne Michaels in *Fugitive Pieces*. *Fugitive Pieces* relates the life of poet Jakob Beer, a Jew who fled the Nazi occupation of Poland and hid on the Greek island of Zakynthos before moving to Toronto. His memories and poetry live on in the mind of a young Canadian professor, Ben, whose name is "the Hebrew word for son," and who acquires Beer's fragmentary memoirs after the poet dies in Athens.[31] The book is framed with an unpaginated epilogue that explains how "countless manuscripts – diaries, memoirs, eyewitness accounts" were kept or destroyed during the Second World War. Once again, the poet-novelist constructs a story in which there is "no energy of a narrative," only suppressed details and historical fragments.[32] The scholar Ben has a particular interest in Beer's memoir because of the devastating impact of the Second World War on his own father. The theme of generational recurrence takes on an added significance in this Jewish context because, as Michaels explains, it is "Hebrew tradition that forefathers are referred to as 'we,' not 'they.' 'When we were delivered from Egypt ...' This encourages empathy and a responsibility to the past but, more important, it collapses time. The Jew is forever leaving Egypt."[33] This is precisely the voice that Cohen reacted against in his library speech when he complained that Klein's poems disturbed him "because at certain crucial moments in them he used the word 'we' instead of the word 'I.'"[34] Whereas Cohen embraced the power of language to instigate revolutionary change in the 1960s, Michaels sides with Klein and defines poetry as "the power of language to restore."[35] Michaels thus reclaims the priestly voice that Cohen had tried to banish from Jewish Canadian literature and makes sacred the family bond that Cohen had blasphemed.

On the other hand, as in Cohen's *The Favourite Game*, "always" is the word that must be used to describe Michaels's manner of recording perceptions in *Fugitive Pieces*. Collapsed time and "Vertical Time" shape her sense of Jewish history, and she treats language as a "core sample" and history as a vertical section of archaeological strata.[36] She speaks of "lyric geology," lyric meteorology, and applies the synchronic properties of the lyric to a variety of other discourses because she believes that memory is "heightened by relation," as she demonstrates in her short essay "Cleopatra's Love."[37] For Jakob Beer, this emphasis on the arrested moment stems from a history of trauma: "I couldn't turn my anguish from the precise moment of death. I was focused on that historical split second: the tableau of the haunting trinity – perpetrator, victim, witness."[38] Whereas Cohen has Breavman seize on the arrested instant as a means of transcending the world of events, Michaels considers synchrony a "good way to teach ethics" because she believes it promotes a sense of interconnection.[39] Although Ben struggles as a child to master the connections of his electrical circuit board, the narrative only resolves itself when the adult Ben learns to manage interpersonal connections through the examples of his lovers, his parents, and Jakob Beer. This power is augmented by a particular apprehension of time: "The past is desperate energy, live, an electric field. It chooses a single moment, a chance so domestic we don't know we've missed it, a moment that crashes into us from behind and changes all that follows."[40] Ironically, the wired world view, for which McLuhan was often criticized on moral grounds in the 1960s, becomes an ethical paradigm in the 1990s. Michaels's writing is full of circuits and tactile metaphors for emotional connection which she converts into narrative paradigms.

In her poetry, Michaels's penchant for metaphorical and temporal conjunctions often prompts comparisons to Ondaatje's work. For example, commenting on the third poem in Ondaatje's sequence "The Nine Sentiments," Solecki remarks: "With the exception of Anne Michaels, I can't think of another contemporary Canadian poet capable of risking the shift from the strong and musically evoked simile of the second verse to the equally striking visual simile in the third."[41] However, key differences emerge between the writers if one compares the authors' inspiration for the social networks and temporal conjunctions in their novels.

In "Chronology, Time, Tense and Experientiality in Narrative," Monika Fludernik identifies *The English Patient* as a prime example of the "dissolution of the concept of narrative tense" in the contemporary novel. She demonstrates that Ondaatje uses a variety of devices inspired by the visual arts to create a sense of present tense immediacy.[42] Ondaatje makes frequent use of the "*pictorial* or *tabular present tense*," describing scenes as if they were friezes and occasionally adding titles to his word portraits.[43] As in *Beautiful Losers*, the "use of *now* in *The English Patient* does not necessarily disambiguate between the punctual and habitual," but rather draws us into the immediacy of the author's sensual freeze frames or a character's recollections.[44] Fludernik points out that this aesthetic of *ut pictura poesis* makes the narrative easy to translate into film:

> What *The English Patient* does is ... to struggle free from the regular use of tense in narrative texts and to treat all narrative tenses as differential, using different kinds of morphemic difference for the same functions. Only the *past perfect tense* and the *future tense* in Ondaatje's novel retain their regular functions of shift into the past (memory) and shift into the future. The present and past tenses of the text constitute both deictic and adeictic instances of tense usage. The patterning provided by this technique gives the novel a very static, pictorial atmosphere. It also foregrounds the experientiality of the narrative, allowing

the reader easy access to the characters' psyches. As a consequence, much of the text appears to be a dream sequence rather than a narrative controlled by the shaping will of a narratorial consciousness. Perhaps this also explains why *The English Patient* became such a success in its film version. The text, not least on account of its use of tenses, superbly lends itself to filming. The stasis evoked by the verbal fiction translates beautifully into slow-motion camera angles.[45]

Kirpal's physical and cultural vantage point toward the end of the novel identifies this framing technique explicitly: "The naive Catholic images from those hillside shrines that he has seen are with him in the half-darkness, as he counts the seconds between lightning and thunder. Perhaps this villa is a similar tableau, the four of them in private movement, momentarily lit up, flung ironically against this war."[46]

Unlike Henighan, Fludernik does not perceive Ondaatje's alterations of conventional chronology as an attack on historical consciousness: "The loss of sequentiality does not ... elide history from the text; the novel is in fact glutted with history, and this is equally true of the film, despite its more chronological design. In my view, therefore, the novel thematizes the hazards of historical reconstruction, especially in the memory of participants. Its nostalgia for the past, by the blurring of consistent temporality, emphasizes the irreality of past and present in view of the nightmare of the war."[47]
The bulk of the criticism on *The English Patient* offers a variation on this theme of the dangers and necessity of historical reconstruction. To cite a few examples, Vernon Provencal argues that Ondaatje "abuses *historia* for the sake of *poetica*"; yet, by using Herodotus as an intertext and investigating his subordination of myth to history, Ondaatje highlights the shortcomings of the Western historiographic tradition.[48] Although Ondaatje is usually viewed as an apolitical writer, Lisa Pace Vetter asserts that Ondaatje critiques end-of-history liberalism through his depiction of the failed rationalism and imperfect autonomy of characters such as Almásy and Anil.[49] Troy Jollimore and Sharon Barrios maintain that *The English Patient* performs an important ethical function by portraying a Nazi collaborator who is motivated by genuine passion for another human being, thereby contesting the flatness of character in the banality of evil argument and risking a fuller historical engagement.[50]

Fugitive Pieces shares many of these preoccupations. Like Ondaatje, Michaels begins her history of the Second World War with a description of textual and social ruins, and she gradually constructs a narrative and social unit across racial and national divides. Whereas Ondaatje's novel establishes a rural idyll that is ultimately shattered by the nuclear Holocaust in Japan, Michaels begins with the calamity of a pogrom in Poland and works toward the formation of intergenerational bonds. Michaels shares Ondaatje's cosmopolitan world view and she resists binaries between Jews and anti-Semites or masculine oppressors and female victims. Yet the Judaic elements of Michaels's narrative make the identity politics of *Fugitive Pieces* different from the radical uncertainties of *The English Patient*. Whereas Almásy dreams of a life unmarked by racial or national identity, Jakob Beer and the other Jewish characters in *Fugitive Pieces* seek a way to retain their Jewish identity and reconcile it with their non-Jewish surroundings. The fundamental questions driving the writers differ, but Michaels's response to her conundrum resembles Ondaatje's response to his own transnational upbringing. Michaels shares with Ondaatje the notion that the construction of plot in the poet's novel is the construction of a social and historical web, and not an exercise in linear causality. Froma Zeitlin enlarges on the use of this strategy in *Fugitive Pieces*: "It is the transfer of affection to others not related by blood that can bring some closure to the act of mourning and authorize the sense of an individual identity. If adoption counts more than biology, then Ben can overcome his fatalistic conviction that 'my parents' past is mine molecularly.' Marriage, too, introduces an other into the family circle to disrupt or mediate between kin. Even more, it is the intertwining of stories and destinies – Athos and Jakob, Jakob with Ben – that enlarges the field of sympathy and endows these relationships with restorative power."[51]

Michaels also makes use of specifically Jewish notions of simultaneity. According to Hillger's reading of *Fugitive Pieces*:

[Phrases such as] "it is your future you are remembering" ... immediately call to mind Walter Benjamin's conception of *Jetztzeit*, "the time of the now," put forth in his "Theses on the Philosophy of History": "[T]he present ... as a model of Messianic time, comprises the entire history of mankind in an enormous abridgement." Like his friend and contemporary, the Marxist philosopher Ernst Bloch, Benjamin writes within a specifically Jewish tradition of remembrance. Like Bloch, he revises the Marxist dialectical conception of history by departing from a linear, continuous concept of time and introducing a notion of the present which brings the dialectics of historical materialism to a standstill. While Marx's emancipatory project is concerned with looking toward the future as delivering the fullness of liberation, Bloch insists that the present contains moments of *utopia,* and if it is blind to these moments it turns into a past containing our present as already lost."[52]

Influenced by this Jewish tradition, Michaels is not interested in dissolving narrative tense simply for pictorial effect. The time of the now is, for the Jewish writer, an assertion of enduring cultural presence in all its ecstatic and tragic dimensions. As Marlatt's feminist work illustrates (see chapter 5), the present is not simply a tense but an ontological condition in which one refuses to relegate being to the past or future, and in the process silence oneself.

Yet messianic time and a pictorial sensibility are not incompatible, as Klein's development of the "double-exposure" motif in *The Second Scroll* underscores. Critics such as Nicola King have emphasized the use of this motif in *Fugitive Pieces*, in terms of the juxtaposition of both times and places:

> Throughout [Jakob's] narrative the image of double exposure recurs: the present exists as an echo of the past, the past is a shadow always just behind the present moment. Watching the candles of the Easter procession on Zakynthos
>> I watched and was in my own village, winter evenings, my teacher lighting the wicks of our lanterns and releasing us into the street like toy boats bobbing down a flooded gutter ... I ... placed this parallel image, like other ghostly double exposures, carefully into orbit ... Even now, half a century later, writing this on a different Greek island, I look down to the remote lights of the town and feel the heat of a flame spreading up my sleeve.[53]

Likewise, Zeitlin perceives "'a surplus of memory' underlying present experience, ready to resurface into uncanny repetition or painful contrast" in "the poetic density of Jakob Beer's (or Ben's) layered recollections."[54] Dalia Kandiyoti also emphasizes the "disturbing, spectral bifocality (with the gaze on past *and* present), which permeates every aspect of Holocaust memory work. Doubles, ghosts, and phantoms populate *Fugitive Pieces* as they do much fiction about survivors, in which time-places and generational memories blur into one another."[55] Yet it is important to note that Michaels does not simply layer tragedy upon tragedy for bathetic effect. In her cross-cultural juxtapositions, she also searches for the warmth of good will (even if it is haunted by the sensation of fire approaching skin). As Kandiyoti suggests, "it is not accidental that Jakob survives on Zakynthos. In a country 80 percent of whose Jewish population was murdered, this was one island where most of the community survived. Michaels thus describes the Zakynthos Jews able to go into hiding, thanks to Bishop Chrysostomos, who refused to turn in their names."[56] Whereas Easter processions inspire only terror in Breavman's mother, Jakob momentarily overcomes the trauma of his pogrom experience by fixating on a small commonality that is also the light of hope.

In "Empathetic Identification in Anne Michaels's *Fugitive Pieces*: Masculinity and Poetry after Auschwitz," Susan Gubar proposes that lyrical fiction differs from realist fiction in its means of fostering empathy between characters and readers:

> Fiction: since the eighteenth century, the novel has emotionally drawn readers into identifications with characters in a process that "involves a kind of virtual experience through which one puts oneself in the other's position while recognizing the difference of that position and hence not taking the other's place," to quote LaCapra's definition of "empathic unsettlement" again. Lyrical fiction: if, as it is impossible not to suspect, the fugitive pieces of a subjectivity based on empathic identification can only be fleetingly experienced, and if the intangible, the invisible, the unseen of grievous suffering remains a primary responsibility for the living imagination, then the sounds of intimate voices that stop and start in fragmentary bits and parts may be best suited for such an undertaking. The discontinuities and stutters of repetition, the cutting of connectives found in ordinary prose, the blank spaces between stanzalike chapters, the recurrence of mystic maxims, the clustering of rhythmic image patterns, the elaboration on extended metaphors – all testify to an otherness that can neither be fully incorporated nor externalized.[57]

Seen in this light, *Fugitive Pieces* generates different strategies of human and narrative bonding than those employed by realist fiction. To a certain extent, the great emphasis on the family unit in *Fugitive Pieces* also distinguishes it from the novels discussed in my earlier chapters, where the erotic and artistic connections between characters were paramount.

However, if Carson is correct in saying that "novelists play out as dilemmas of plot and character all those facets of erotic contradiction and difficulty that were first brought to light in lyric poetry," then Michaels's intermingling of love stories and survivor stories in *Fugitive Pieces* is perhaps inevitable.[58] However, the suitability of romantic sentiment and lyricism in a Holocaust novel is a vigorously debated subject. Méira Cook asserts that in many places Michaels fails to combine lyricism and narrative successfully, because "when brutality, love-making, and the pragmatism of daily living are all described in Michaels' habitual mode of high lyricism, a prevailing flatness results."[59] Marchand complains of a similar flatness in the tone of *The English Patient,* and although chapter titles such as "The Holy Forest" – an allusion to Robin Blaser's lifelong poem, *The Holy Forest* (1993), which Ondaatje edited – invite readers to approach Ondaatje's writing from a serial perspective, the fault in these novels lies in their failure to mobilize all the rhythmic possibilities and orthogonal shifts made viable by the lyric voice in the twentieth century.[60] By gravitating toward a uniform narrative tone, *Fugitive Pieces* and *The English Patient* conform more to realist conventions than lyric ones.

Larger ethical questions swirl around the use of the lyric voice in narratives of the Second World War, however. Both Cook and D.M.R. Bentley begin essays on *Fugitive Pieces* by weighing the relative merits of two famous quotations and opposing viewpoints on writing in the lyric voice after the Holocaust. The first is Theodor Adorno's assertion in a 1949 essay (collected in 1955) that to "write poetry after Auschwitz is barbaric."[61] Cook argues that *Fugitive Pieces* "is, in many ways, a response to Adorno's implicit challenge: if it is no longer possible to write after Auschwitz is the only alternative to remain silent?"[62] While examining the different valencies of silence (as defensive bulwark, veiled aggression, and social paralysis), Michaels attempts to reclaim the lyric voice as a means of promoting empathy and responsibility. Unlike Adorno, who was outraged that poets would publish so shortly after escaping the prison camps, Michaels confronts the fading presence of the events of the Second World War and uses the lyric to sharpen that dulled awareness. Similarly, Kimberly Verwaayen argues that Michaels's collection of lyric sequences, *Miner's Pond* (1991), constitutes a "deeply committed post-holocaust testament to memory" in the face of collective denial.[63] The same can be said of *Fugitive Pieces,* Michaels's subsequent publication. Although no one poem in *The Weight of Oranges* (1986) or *Miner's Pond* suggests a template for *Fugitive Pieces,* her reader witnesses Michaels stretch her short lyric forms into extended sequences, and nearly every sequence in the early books develops a theme (geology, piano lessons, the redeeming power of memory, the survivor's impulse to flee) which she weaves into her novel.

Before Cohen approached the novel, he also explored the question of writing poetry after Auschwitz and, like Michaels, he rejected silence. In Cohen's "Lines From My Grandfather's Journal" the grandfather seems to be reduced to a silence that prohibits metaphor in the aftermath of the atrocities in Poland:

Desolation means no angels to wrestle ... Desolation means no ravens, no black symbols. The carcass of the rotting dog cannot speak for you.

The ovens have no tongue. The flames thud against the stone roofs. I cannot claim that sound.
Desolation means no comparisons ... [64]

Yet the persistence of metaphor even in this passage (the tongue of the ovens) and the fact that the poem continues beyond the ellipsis indicate that Cohen contemplates the ban on poetry and rejects it: "Who dares disdain an answer to the ovens? Any answer."[65] Likewise, in *Flowers for Hitler*, Cohen refuses to collaborate in the dictator's program to silence his generation. Michael Q. Abraham therefore reads "Lines from My Grandfather's Journal" as a "gentle manifesto" in which "artistic creativity" is defined as "a compromise between an unattainable ideal and an unacceptable nullity, an essential comparison of, and struggle between, opposite visions."[66] When Cohen wrestles with these issues in *The Favourite Game*, he comes to the conclusion that the hope of the next generation lies in the practice of comparison and the celebration of alterity in a relational matrix.

The second oft-cited quotation about writing after the Holocaust comes from a 1958 speech delivered by Paul Celan, in which the Jewish poet explains to a German audience how language might overcome calamity. Although Henighan states that critics who perceive "*Fugitive Pieces* as courageous because it raises the question of writing poetry after Auschwitz ha[ve] not read Paul Celan," Bentley speculates that the character of Jakob Beer might be modelled on Celan.[67] The discussion of silence in Celan's Bremen speech might also explain why Klein's silence had such a radicalizing impact on Cohen: "Only one thing remained reachable, close and secure amid all losses: language. Yes, language. In spite of everything, it remained secure against loss. But it had to go through its own lack of answers, through terrifying silence, through the thousand darknesses of murderous speech. It went through. It gave me no words for what was happening, but went through it. Went through and could resurface, 'enriched' by it all."[68] The opening sentence of this passage supplies the title of Carson's *Economy of the Unlost: Reading Simonides of Keos with Paul Celan*, although Carson translates Celan's word "*unverloren*" differently: "Reachable, near and unlost amid the losses, this one thing remained: language. This thing, language, remained unlost, yes, in spite of everything."[69] For Carson, Michaels, and Celan, language reaffirms human interconnection even in the face of murder and travesty.

Celan's method of torturing diction and syntax is not that of Michaels, even though Jakob Beer contemplates a comparable style as he struggles to incorporate muteness and disappearance into his poems: "I thought of writing poems in this way, in code, every letter askew, so that loss would wreck the language, become the language."[70] However, Jakob finds that he cannot achieve the clarity he seeks by this means. Likewise, Michaels's poetry is haunted by the loss of her grandparents' Polish, but given that she did not, like Celan, endure the desacralization of her mother tongue, one must still ask: what, specifically, is unlost in *Fugitive Pieces*? The name of the poet in the novel suggests a number of possible answers. Jakob, in the Old Testament, is identified with the nation of Israel, and the trials and tribulations of Jakob in *Fugitive Pieces* may reflect the diasporic experience of European Jewry. However, as Bentley notes, Jakob's full name recalls "the nineteenth-century German composer who renamed himself Giacomo Meyerbeer after receiving a legacy from a relative called Meyer and achieving critical success with a series of operas in Italy."[71] This naming has important implications for two important themes in the book: love and music. The composer was born Yaakov Liebmann Beer (1791–1864) in Berlin and he moved from Germany to Italy and thence to France. The assimilation of Yaakov into Jakob and the loss of Beer's middle name ("Love-man") during this migration may well serve as an analogy for the much more sinister loss of love for one's fellow citizens and human beings that swept over these countries with the rise of fascism a century later.

The ability to love others and to communicate this love is a power that Jakob and Ben seek to reclaim after the trauma of their upbringings. Their struggle reflects Adorno's revised statements in *Negative Dialectics* (1966), where, as Kevin McNeilly points out, Adorno concedes that he "may have been wrong to say that after Auschwitz you could no longer write poems," because "perennial suffering has as much right to expression as a tortured man has to scream."[72] Adorno reaffirms his belief that art can mitigate suffering, yet he stresses that the more pressing question is "whether after Auschwitz you can go on living – especially whether one who escaped by accident, one who by rights should have been killed, may go on living."[73] Adorno sees in this question a crisis of "bourgeois subjectivity," because the death camp survivors must return to the quotidian state of affairs that masked the atrocities of the camps and cope with "the drastic guilt" of having been "spared."[74] This characterization succinctly describes Ben's father, whose sorrow and emotional difficulties Ben inherits.

However, Adorno's new question finds earlier and more eloquent expression in a letter from Uncle Melech in *The Second Scroll* that rewrites the first stanza of Klein's lyric "Meditation upon Survival":

I bless the Heavenly One for my rescue. It is wonderful to be alive again; to know that the trouble, the astonishment, the hissing is over; to eat, not husks or calories, but food; to have a name; and be of this world. Even now I do not know how it happened or by what merit it was I who was chosen, out of the thousands who perished, to escape all of the the strange deaths that swallowed up a generation. At times I feel – so bewildered and burdened is my gratitude – that the numbered dead run through my veins their plasma, that I must live their unexpired six million circuits, and that my body must be the bed of each of their nightmares. Then, sensing their death wish bubbling the channels of my blood, then do I grow bitter at my false felicity – the spared one! – and would almost add to theirs my own wish for the centigrade furnace and the cyanide flood. Those, too, are the occasions when I believe myself a man suspect, when I quail before the eyes of my rescuers wondering *Why? Why did this one escape? What treaty did he strike with the murderers? Whose was the blood that was his ransom?* I try to answer these questions, but my very innocence stutters, and I end up exculpating myself into a kind of guilt.[75]

In *The Second Scroll* Melech writes to his Canadian nephew "as one who having fled from out a burning building runs up and down the street to seek, to find, to embrace the kinsmen who were with him in that conflagration and were saved," but in *Fugitive Pieces* Ben's father withdraws from the world.[76] He avoids the Jewish ghetto near Spadina Avenue, suffers a lifetime of food anxieties, and chooses not to name his son in the hope of tricking the angel of death. The father's story represents the crisis of bourgeois subjectivity transported to the suburbs of Toronto. And yet Michaels sees hope, not in the glory of the coming of the Messiah, but in the modest achievements of subsequent generations of Canadians: in the scholar who writes the Talmudic accompaniment to Beer's scroll and in a revised notion of social circuitry. Like the Telephone Dance that emerges as a response to colonial brutality in *Beautiful Losers*, this mode of contact takes the circuits of Klein's nightmare and reconfigures them as a network of empowerment. According to John Moss, a confrontation with similar historical and philosophical issues led Bowering to "conceive fiction as the interpenetration of personalities," including those of the author-as-reader and the reader-as-author.[77]

By thinking comparatively, Ben finally realizes how he might regain the power to love at the conclusion of *Fugitive Pieces*. On the airplane back to

Canada, having cheated on his wife in Greece, Ben reconsiders the legacy of his father and the survivor's eating disorder:

> But now, from thousands of feet in the air, I see something else. My mother stands behind my father and his head leans against her. As he eats, she strokes his hair. Like a miraculous circuit, each draws strength from the other.
> I see that I must give what I most need.[78]

Thus, as in the Torah, the conclusion is a beginning. There is no definitive before and after, but only a process of overcoming. And, as in the New Testament, the concept of love that facilitates this overcoming is paradoxical: one must incur loss for gain. Ben's vision through the airplane window suggests a way in which he might return from physical and emotional exile and reconcile himself with the WASPish background of his Canadian wife, Naomi. The epiphany changes Ben from a lost soul into a member of a complex multi-ethnic and multi-generational network that transforms the crisis of contact into an interpersonal charge that helps to heal the wounds of trauma. True to the motif of the double exposure, Ben "only understands [this story] at second sight," as Barbara Estrin points out.[79]

Consciously or not, Michaels also reconfigures a number of Cohen's key motifs from *The Favourite Game* in the conclusion to *Fugitive Pieces*. Michaels equates intimacy with scarring, and Ben abandons his lover Petra – who, like Tamara, is "perfect, not a blemish or a scar"[80] – because he recognizes that his love for the wounded Naomi runs deeper.[81] Returning to Canada, he soothes his emotional scars by remembering Naomi's favourite game: "When you were a little girl you had a favourite bowl, with a design painted on the bottom. You wanted to eat everything, to find the empty bowl full of flowers."[82] The bowl anecdote domesticates the bouquet in Breavman's backyard, and helps to re-contextualize a disturbing memory from Ben's childhood: "Once, I saw my father sitting in the snow-blue kitchen. I was six years old. I came downstairs in the middle of the night. There had been a storm while I slept. The kitchen glowed with new drifts piled against the windows; blue as the inside of a crevasse. My father was sitting at the table, eating. I was transfixed by his face. This was the first time I had seen food make my father cry."[83] Much as Breavman's epiphany arose from the aftermath of Martin's death, Ben's epiphany stems from his struggle to understand his father's suicide. The flower and snow passages lead to the conclusion, where Michaels redefines Bertha's spinning game as a "miraculous circuit" of touch, in which Ben's mother strokes her husband's hair in much the same way that Jakob's mother had combed Bella's hair at the outset of the novel. This motivic repetition and the debt Ben owes to Beer for awakening his final realization demonstrate that while the family unit is a recursive formation, the notion of family in Michaels is not limited to blood lines. Ben retraces Beer's artistic and spiritual path and adopts him as a father figure whose failures with Alex he must not repeat, and whose happiness with Michaela he strives to recreate.

Fugitive Pieces may be read as a movement from a dystopic version of Cohen's social vision in *The Favourite Game* to a concluding gesture of hope for the future. The opening scene of the principal narrative portrays young Jakob playing with his sister, Bella, in his parents' home. Jakob's mother takes a break from sewing buttons on his shirt in order to brush Bella's hair, and Jakob, seeking attention, crams his body inside a cupboard in a game of hide and seek. At that moment, soldiers burst into the living room and assassinate the parents, whose twisted bodies fall in a "flesh-heap."[84] Jakob eventually emerges from his hiding place and is traumatized by the sight of his murdered parents. He then experiences a second devastating fall, as he runs for his life, buries himself in underbrush, and forgets to care for Bella, whose disappearance and probable rape haunt him for the rest of his life (even more vigorously than Bertha's fall haunts Breavman).[85] This section establishes a range of images (Bella's hair and the disinterred body) and phrases (from Bella's sheet music and piano lessons) that recur throughout the text. Thus the adult Jakob keeps a bowl of buttons on his desk because he becomes a poet and translator whose project is to fashion connective devices.

Despite the echoes of Cohen, Henighan sees *Fugitive Pieces* as a "shameless imitation of Ondaatje's metaphor-laden aesthetic."[86] Certainly, the impress of Ondaatje's work on *Fugitive Pieces* is unmistakable. When Alex invites Jakob to hear a concert at the Workers' Education Association, for example, the scene so closely resembles the one that brings Patrick to Alice's theatre performance in the Waterworks in *In the Skin of a Lion* that Michaels embeds an acknowledgement in the narrative. When Alex says "So long," Jakob replies punningly, "Ceylon," invoking the country of Ondaatje's birth.[87] Yet even here one encounters, not the straightforward patrilineage of influence, but rather a kind of playful feedback loop in which Michaels rewrites the Jewish visions of Klein and Cohen via Ondaatje, whose own writing was a secular response to Cohen. At the very least, these connections should force Solecki to rethink his claim that, "whether thought of as Canadian or as Sri Lankan, [Ondaatje is] an isolated and nearly autochthonous figure in both cultures: influenced by writers in neither country and without obvious influence on the next generation."[88] Solecki himself provides ample evidence of Cohen's influence on Ondaatje in *Ragas of Longing*, and Michaels's mythologization of the Humber River (in Toronto's West End) is clearly a response to Ondaatje's mythologization of the Don River (in Toronto's East End) in *In the Skin of a Lion*.

However, contradictions abound within Michaels's network of literary and musical allusions, facts, and fictions. The emphasis on romance and high drama in Giacomo Meyerbeer's operas greatly influenced the work of Richard Wagner, whom Meyerbeer aided personally while Wagner was struggling to earn a reputation in Paris. Despite this personal and artistic debt, Wagner remained an anti-Semite who demanded the prohibition of operas by Jews, beginning with those of Meyerbeer, who was at one time the most popular composer of operas in Europe. Wagner's heady combination of romance and ethnic nationalism was embraced by the Nazis, who rewrote history to cover up the debt of German society to Jewish innovations. On the other hand, Wagner's treatment of harmony broke down the conventional hierarchy of tones and his treatment of the *leitmotif* led to the development of Schoenberg's twelve-tone method. The fact that several of the chapter titles in *Fugitive Pieces* appear twice (and not quite in the same order) might suggest a musical sense of the serial in which each "piece" forms an independent part of a larger sequence that evolves through variations on a set of "notes." This interpretation would explain why the final chapter of *Fugitive Pieces* bears the name "The Way Station," rather than "The Terminus," because "The Way Station" had already appeared in chapter 4 and may yet appear again in relation to a different journey and carrying a different connotation. Since Schoenberg was a Jewish poet and intellectual who was driven into exile in California by the Nazis in 1933, this interpretation might seem attractive.

However, the musicians named in *Fugitive Pieces* are the pre-twentieth-century masters; Beethoven and Brahms are Bella's favourites to play on the piano, and the stormy details of Beethoven's life story are woven into the biography of Ben's father, a piano teacher and former conductor. Through the father's music, Michaels emphasizes the agonizing contradiction between the Jewish artists' love for German high culture and their utter revulsion for the Nazi-era state. She confirms that these stories are inextricably linked through repeated references to "the swirls and eddies of Brahms's Intermezzo No. 2" on Bella's piano.[89] An intermezzo is a short piece of music that is played between scenes of an opera and usually takes the form of a linked series. Intermezzi are fugitive pieces, conduits from one place to the next. However, under Michaels's hand, the musical form functions as a structural principal and the linked series becomes the narrative, instead of merely facilitating it. In this kind of lyric opera, "every moment is two moments," because temporal judgements are relational, as Michaels emphasizes by quoting Einstein: "All our judgements in which time plays a part are always judgements of simultaneous events. If, for instance, I say the train arrived here at seven o'clock, I mean: the small hand of my watch pointing to seven and the arrival of the train are simultaneous events ... The time of the event has no operational meaning" unless it is related to perception and spatial coordinates.[90] Michaels therefore organizes the time of her novel relative to human perception and correspondences between historical moments, rather than aligning it with a fixed temporal arc.

Critics have noted these iterations in *Fugitive Pieces*, but because they hunt for a conventional narrative arc within the novel they find the pattern of echoes perplexing.[91] Cook lists some of the affinities between Michaels's descriptions of settings, characters, and events, but concedes in a footnote that "it is difficult to know what to make of these correspondences except to view them in the light of annotated similes by means of which characters are linked by a series of linguistic contrivances."[92] In *Fugitive Pieces* the interlinking power of metaphor transforms from a descriptive tool into a multidirectional narrative force that connects Beer, Bella, Ben, Beethoven, and Brahms much as it had joined Bolden, Bellocq, Nora Bass, the Brewitts, and Webb in *Coming Through Slaughter*, a novel about a musician who "played nearly everything in B-Flat."[93] The effect of this patterning is unparalleled in Holocaust literature, according to Zeitlin: "Images and metaphors seem to rise, unbidden, out of the text from some secret inner space like a kind of vibrant 'soul-music' that captures the subtle intensities of sadness, love, guilt, and longing. Nothing in Holocaust literature comes close to the richness and density of the huge imagination at work here: the intricate symmetries, the bold interlayering of art and science, nature and poetry, history and music, as well as the expansion of horizons – both temporally and spatially, in height as in depth, in geology as in geography – which no brief summary can hope to convey. Throughout a single note plays with infinite variations: What is the meaning of death? What happens to the dead when the memory of them is still lodged in the living, acutely present, and they reside in a twilight space between ghost and flesh?"[94]

Since it is clear from *Fugitive Pieces* and Michaels's interview statements that she has studied the "narrative moves" of Ondaatje and other

Canadian poet-novelists very carefully, instead of deeming *Fugitive Pieces* "shapeless showing-off" critics would do better to read the novel as Michaels's careful effort to situate herself in a literary tradition.[95] In Michaels's essays on her craft, one finds succinct observations on style and technique that may serve as a recapitulation of the ideas I have discussed in the previous chapters.[96] Henighan is therefore justified in linking Michaels's highly metaphorical style to Ondaatje and other Canadian poet-novelists, but his dismissal of her work unfairly collapses all difference between these authors.

One might infer from the subtitle of Henighan's salvo, "Free Trade Fiction, or the Victory of Metaphor over History," that Henighan believes metaphor has no place in historical novels. Henighan praises Margaret Atwood for her "carefully developed imagery" in the early portion of his book and later names her among Canada's strongest social documentarians.[97] However, he condemns Atwood's *Surfacing* (1972) because "the poet-turned-novelist etch[es] the values of a generation in metaphor."[98] Henighan identifies *Surfacing* as a precursor to *Fugitive Pieces*, largely because Michaels and Atwood make the mistake (according to Henighan) of finding metaphors that reflect the values of middle-class Torontonians. His disdain for Canada's largest city and class becomes the grounds for his rejection of novels that reflect their values, even as he argues that poet-novelists fail to engage with society. The implication is that social documentation makes a novel "authentic," unless the novelist makes use of metaphors, which are inauthentic. Yet in this same essay, Henighan names Robert Musil's *The Man Without Qualities* among the three great works of European modernism because "in Musil the crumbling of the certainties of nineteenth-century rationalism and the disintegration of the Austro-Hungarian empire become elaborate metaphors for one another."[99] What, then, is the place of metaphor in historical novels?

While Henighan approves of structural parallels in narrative, he does not like to encounter actual metaphors in prose. He claims, for instance, that the "opening four paragraphs of *The English Patient*, describing Hana walking into the villa as she feels the rain coming on, display a pitch-perfect ear for prose rhythms. Only that garish, attention-grabbing image of the 'penis sleeping like a sea horse' mars the tone."[100] Marchand also considers this simile "strikingly inappropriate,"[101] although the scorched Almásy is an explorer known for his archaeology of an ancient seabed in the desert; although sex is consistently equated with water imagery in the novel and the love of Almásy's life will die in the Cave of Swimmers; although Almásy will die in part from his addiction to morphine, a version of the street drug "horse"; although male sea horses expel their young from a brood pouch in their tail, much as the young lovers in the novel are nurtured and then repulsed by Almásy's tale; and despite the fact that when Hana pauses to consider the phallus she foreshadows the choice she will eventually make between her natural and adoptive father-figures, Patrick (the lion) and Almásy (the sea horse) respectively. While there are many gratuitous metaphors in both *The English Patient* and *When Words Deny the World*, the sea horse metaphor strikes me as more than appropriate.[102] It is a carefully placed prolepsis, a synchronic glimpse of Almásy's life story.

Henighan centres his argument against metaphor in his objection to a key passage in *Fugitive Pieces*. He perceives a contradiction in Michaels's statement that the Nazis "annihilated metaphor, turning humans into objects," and her observation that "Non-Aryans were never to be referred to as human, but as 'figuren,' 'stücke' – 'dolls,' 'wood,' 'merchandise,' 'rags.' Humans were not being gassed, only 'figuren,' so ethics weren't being violated."[103] Henighan concludes that metaphor facilitated the Nazi atrocities, but he overlooks the fact that these depersonalized terms were valuable to the Nazis precisely because they had lost their properties as metaphors. The terms were not supposed to maintain disparity, although Michaels notes slippages in the Nazis' logic. The terms were supposed to ossify into denotations and deny the humanity of the Jews. Thus, the concern for constructing a metaphorical frame of reference in the poet's novel is usually matched by a drive to unframe the analogy and prevent it from ossifying into an unquestioned cognitive paradigm. Chris Jennings argues that "translation is [Carson's] master trope" because it "invokes metaphor's 'ability to hold in equipoise two perspectives at once,'"[104] and Barbara Estrin identifies a similar logic in Michaels's writing: "Translation, Jakob writes, is 'like the immigrant,' someone who moves between places but who struggles to identify the connection between where he has been and what he is. Recognizing the middle interlude between the lines, the immigrant neither returns to the beginning nor hearkens too easily toward the end ... Translation confers on the act of naming the saving miracle of a new structure, one with ties to the previous one but freed from the confines of a deadly and fixed construct."[105] Although Henighan claims that the best writing on the Holocaust employs "scientific precision" and "objectivity," these terms were also used by the Nazis to justify their theories of racial superiority and heroic genealogy, as Athos's discussion of Nazi archaeology in *Fugitive Pieces* demonstrates.[106]

One can see how quickly these perceptual ossifications occur by reconsidering Muybridge's photography, its claims to objectivity, and its impact on realist art. Muybridge's technological innovations facilitated the scientific aspirations of realism in the late nineteenth century, and Muybridge's collaborator, the realist painter Tomas Eakins, incorporated their findings into his portraiture, which was considered exemplary in nineteenth-century America. Muybridge intended to correct the anatomical errors of traditional portraiture with his photographic grids, but the symmetrical aesthetics of his grid trumped his scientific principles. Muybridge mixed and matched the photographs in his series such that the "relationship of the images, in some 40 percent of the plates, is not what Muybridge states it to be."[107] Consequently, Marta Braun does not consider Muybridge's photographic output a correction to painterly tradition, but rather "a reiteration of contemporary pictorial practice, and a compendium of social history and erotic fantasy. Most often Muybridge was not using his camera as an analytic tool at all but was using it for narrative representation."[108] Perhaps because Muybridge depended on the revenues of his public lectures and book publishing, his well-received medium of representation quickly triumphed over his pretense to objectivity. Braun rejects the assumption that "Muybridge was photographing movement in time" and concludes that he was really "telling stories in space – giving us fragments of the world, fragments that could be expanded into stories."[109] Braun overstates her case somewhat, because, by her own estimate, sixty percent of Muybridge's photographs are still recordings of temporal passage. But her research into Muybridge's overlooked falsifications demonstrates that spatial configurations such as the linear grid influence the perception of time in narrative and create readerly expectations that solidify into generic expectations. Notions of authenticity quickly gel around these expectations, particularly when associations with science come into play, as in the naturalist branch of the novel.

Poet-novelists deliberately flout the conventions that equate realist technique with objectivity and authenticity in narrative. They disrupt linear chronologies, insert gaps into the causal succession of events, and shun sequential character development. They exchange Aristotle's beginning-middle-end theory of plot for a narrative style based on stylized juxtapositions; but by a further inversion, his sequential formula persists on the meta-fictive level of composition. Embedded within most of these novels is a fairly linear narrative of the metafictional author's quest for a new narrative form, and this quest includes a crisis, conflict resolution, and ultimately the achievement of a desired end. There is a linear teleology, but it is in the subtext.

Fugitive Pieces underscores the difficulty of writing criticism in a multicultural society whose readers cannot always be counted on to recognize formal patterns from another cultural inheritance, whether Jewish, Greek, or Sri Lankan. For example, Henighan describes the shift between books in *Fugitive Pieces* as "the novel's most ungainly lurch" and states that the change in narrator was necessitated by Beer's weakness as a character, not by the Talmudic model of scroll and commentary favoured by Klein and Cohen.[110] Henighan complains that the novel is "imagistically scattered," but he does not acknowledge such themes as the golem myth that bind the diasporic lives.[111] He tries to excuse John Berger's endorsement of Michaels by speculating on a romantic liaison between the authors and suggests that the dedication "for J." refers to Berger (whose novels appear in *Fugitive Pieces*). However, Michaels's novel suggests that the dedication refers to "the 'J' stamped on a passport," which in mid-twentieth century Europe "could have the power of life or death."[112] Henighan deems Michaels's lyrical tone inappropriate for a story featuring so many deaths, but Naomi stresses that singing a prayer for the dead is a traditional response: "The only thing you can do for the dead is sing to them. The hymn, the miroloy, the kaddish."[113] Whereas the kaddish for Uncle Melech performed at the climax of *The Second Scroll* celebrates an epic hero, Michaels seems to perform a common prayer for the Jewish dead. Yet, by writing novels, both Canadian authors demonstrate that there are innovative ways in which one can perform such songs.

John Moss offers a more balanced appraisal of *Fugitive Pieces* than Henighan, but in the negative half of his catalogue he lists some of the same grievances: "I am genuinely disconcerted by my response to this novel. There is writing here so poetic I was left gasping for breath; there is narrative dexterity as plots elliptically collide that is astonishingly sophisticated; there are brief glimpses into human misery, the tortured human soul, that chill to the bone. Yet the self-conscious aphorisms and contrived profundity, mawkish exploitation of horrific events, vapid characterization and self-conscious cosmopolitanism left me cold."[114] Henighan objects also to Michaels's aphorisms, and in the midst of complaining that *Fugitive Pieces* is formless he criticizes one of the rhetorical patterns he notices: "A typical scene begins with an aphorism, often containing a metaphor, slips into recollection, then, as the scene's momentum wanes, coughs up a fresh aphorism and starts over again."[115] In defense of Michaels's aphorisms, one should note that Klein identifies the very method that Henighan outlines as the classic mode of Yiddish narrative: "now a text from Holy Writ, now a proverb, now an anecdote, all essences much relished by the people, the true hallmark of the classic style."[116] Still, even according to these criteria, the use of aphorisms in *Fugitive Pieces* is excessive, as many of them do not even get this exegetical treatment. Certain pages recall the aristocratic parlour games of eighteenth-century France, where the players could only speak in proverbs. At these moments, one can practically hear a Richler protagonist grumbling in the background and wondering aloud whether Michaels and her friends subscribe "to the same chief rabbi of platitudes[.] Had they been issued with similar condolence kits on graduation from yeshiva?"[117]

In *Fugitive Pieces*, readers also confront a growing and related problem with the Canadian poet's novel – namely, the "museumification" of lived experience. Key supporting characters in *Fugitive Pieces* (Maurice and Michaela) are museum curators, and Henighan argues persuasively that "the Canadian novel of the 1990s evolved from an artistic work engaged with language and history into an *objet d'art*."[118] The zeal for pop culture and current events in *Beautiful Losers* disappears in favour of historical narratives that present the past as precious fragments on display. Michaels takes the notion of reframing the past too literally and the result is often stuffy and unstreetworthy. This is a condition that Cohen warned readers against in *The Favourite Game*. His description of a metropolis where "there is no present tense ... only the past claiming victories" casts an unflattering light on some of the double exposures of Michaels's Toronto.[119]

The failure to engage with popular culture and the specificities of Canadian history, both recent and distant, results in what Henighan describes as the "steamrolling" of "Canadian history."[120] While I have established that this claim is overstated, in *Fugitive Pieces* Michaels's preoccupation with Europe trumps local concerns whenever she addresses the history of Native peoples. In one exemplary scene, Athos begins to draw an interesting parallel between Native and Polish history when he explains that "the Laurentian People were contemporaries of the inhabitants of Biskupin."[121] On a visit to the grounds of a former Seneca village in Toronto's well-heeled Baby Point, Athos complains to Jakob that the archaeological record in Biskupin was altered to suit Aryan theories of racial superiority, such that "the Reich could feel justified in copying our [Greek] temples for their glorious capital."[122] As the two scholars wander among mansions in search of Native artifacts, the reader expects Athos to follow the course of his analogy to its logical conclusion and consider the decimating impact of European colonization on the People of the Long House. As Dalia Kandiyoti notes, the translators' archaeological efforts create out of the Toronto site a "counter-*topos* that overturns the perception of the city as the 'new' world."[123] However, I cannot endorse the assertion of Kandiyoti and Meredith Criglington that this comparison ultimately empowers Native readers and historians, because the characters back away from an indictment of French, British, and Canadian colonization.

Jakob, who worships the Greek sun and who has infinite patience for the grotesqueries of Jewish Holocaust accounts, finds the day on Baby Point rather hot and the images of burning flesh in Canada disturbing. The pair abandon their enquiry and take a taxi home. They do not want to think about how the brother of their Greek friend Constantine might be complicit in the displacement of the Seneca through his operation of the Royal Diner. Worse, when Jakob "imagine[s] an Iroquois attack on the affluent neighbourhood, flaming arrows soaring above patio furniture," he positions the Seneca in the role of genocidal attackers.[124] Athos compounds this impression by invoking the "murder of fur trader Étienne Brûlé. Auto da fe."[125] The translators' professional sympathy for Brûlé, who mediated between the Huron and the French, diminishes the fact that he was tried as a heretic, not for being white or Christian, but for betraying Huron trading interests to the Seneca. The violent death of one European in 1633 arrests the discussion of what, if interpreted in a continental context (which is the way that Michaels treats the Jewish Holocaust), constitutes one of the largest genocides in human history.

This kind of evasion of the hard questions confronting Canada in the decade of the Oka standoff and the second referendum on Quebec independence laid the grounds for a backlash against Canadian poet-novelists. Even the Jewish Canadian critic David Solway dismisses Michaels (along with Ondaatje and Bowering) as a "media cynosure."[126] Although Canadian bookstores and prize lists in the 1990s were saturated with poet's novels, a sense of fatigue is evident in more recent reviews. For example, Darryl Whetter expresses relief that Bowering's short story collection *Standing on Richards* (2004) "transfers the poet's obsession with searing language into the private tic and talk of multiple, varied narrators without trafficking in any of the precious, dewy observations about light or time or liminality which too often cloud the (Canadian?) poet's turn to fiction."[127] For the most part, the poet's novel has lost its street cred, and young writers who grew up on this fiction express surprise and delight that other literatures depict characters who listen to contemporary music and like TV and do drugs without the aid of nurses.[128]

Henighan addresses these lacunae in his own novel *The Streets of Winter* (2004), which is set in Montreal in the 1990s. To a certain extent, Henighan's attack on the poet's novel prepares the critical ground for the reception of *The Streets of Winter*. The novel brings together a number of troubled characters in a bleak political atmosphere that is appropriate to the mood of anglophone Montreal in the shadow of the Quebec referendum. In Henighan's rendering, the French-English divide proves unmanageable, immigrant dreams are dashed, interracial marriages fail, monumental ambitions prove ruinous, and political movements are crushed. Even though the shifts in perspective between the predominantly male characters must be buttressed by an interpretive key at the beginning of each chapter, the novel is an engaging read. Henighan offers convincing depictions of working-class immigrant experiences, but one still hesitates to endorse his larger social vision because the diverse array of cultural inheritances in *The Streets of Winter* converge into a sequence of cause and effect that leads to a final, apocalyptic conflagration. The concluding image of a young man's corpse being buried by a backhoe warns that platitudinous notions of multiculturalism in a global economy mask grave social problems. But if the poet-novelists who sought alternatives to this apocalyptic scenario are irrelevant, why does Henighan cite, without acknowledgment, passages from Klein's "Heirloom" and Cohen's "The Genius"?[129] Why, if "authentic" novels should constrain their focus to the concerns of one nation, does Henighan derive his title from a Chilean poem? Why does he select an epigraph from the lyrical novel *Les Faux-Monnayeurs*? Plainly, even Henighan cannot establish a strict division between poetry and prose. However, his sense that the end-of-the-millennium offerings from Canada's major publishing houses fail to represent the destructive creation of a rapidly transforming economy resonates with many observers.

Into this void in the 1990s leapt Lynn Crosbie, a veteran of the Toronto goth scene who grew up busking on the streets of Montreal with a future member of Cirque du Soleil. Crosbie's poetry, novels, and criticism signify an important evolution in the development of the poet's novel by a younger generation. Shortly after Carson won the Griffin Poetry Prize in 2001, Crosbie published an outspoken article in the *Globe and Mail* entitled "Something New, Please, O Universe." In this article, Crosbie lashes out at the Griffin judges and at the contest's mission statement, which asserts that the aim of the prize is "to raise public awareness of the crucial role poetry must play in society's cultural life."[130] "With all due respect to the genuinely gifted Anne Carson," Crosbie writes in a measured moment (after having composed a satirical poem out of the more staid fragments of the nominees' poetry), the "cultural life" evoked in the poetry of the Griffin nominees "is overly rarefied."[131] Of course, it is not Carson's fault that she was awarded a prize whose mission statement may or may not reflect her writing style, but Crosbie is adamant that writers must engage explicitly with popular culture.[132] In addition to her books of poetry and reviews,

Crosbie contributes a regular column, "Pop Rocks," to the *Globe and Mail*, and runs an advice column in *Flare* magazine. From this perspective, Crosbie regards Carson's style and subject matter in *Men in the Off Hours* as overly weighted with tradition – in stark contrast to the reviewer of *Plainwater* in *The New York Review of Books*, who declares that Carson has "created an individual form and style for narrative verse ... Seldom has Pound's injunction 'Make It New' been so spectacularly obeyed."[133]

On the level of content, I am sympathetic to Crosbie's demands for more explicitly popular settings and subjects. However, Crosbie's argument falters in a theoretical sense because it depends on the high culture / low culture distinction that she has spent her career dismantling. She underestimates the manner in which Carson's poetry critiques the media of popular culture in her "TV Men" series, or the ways in which Carson's poetry feeds into a broader cultural miasma. For example, Richard Siken sees Geryon as a literary expression of a pop cultural tendency to represent desire as monstrosity (King Kong, vampires, etc.).[134] Moving in the other direction of influence, the American actress Jennifer Connelly cites Carson's poem "Flatman (1st draft)," from *Men in the Off Hours*, as the inspiration for her attempts to bring a comic book character to life in the 2003 Hollywood movie *The Hulk*.[135] Connelly rewrote her character for the film with screenwriter James Shamus, who maintains that "Carson's themes shed light on the nature of pop culture."[136] A copy of Carson's *Eros the Bittersweet* also played a pivotal role in the first season of *The L Word*, a Showtime series about lesbians in Los Angeles.[137]

The scope of Crosbie's literary world, which is populated with villains and divas lifted from the pages of tabloids, is also limited in its own way. Her standard technique, followed in collections and long poems such as *VillainElle* (1994), *Presley* (1998), and *Missing Children* (2003), is to take an anecdote from a tabloid clipping and invest the poetic voice with kitsch, horror flick, and high lyric sentiments in rapid succession.[138] Alternatively, she takes quotations from the English canon and reverse-engineers their vaunted sentiments back to the morass of infamy, vanity, and greed from which they derived, as in *Pearl* (1996). She thereby injects a kind of verve and danger into her poetry that, for as long as it confined its subject matter to B-movies or the carnival of Toronto's Queen Street, was quietly praised by critics. However, by choosing a serial format to tell the story of the serial killers Paul Bernardo and Karla Homolka in her first novel, *Paul's Case: The Kingston Letters* (1997), Crosbie treads a stylistic path already blazed by Ondaatje in *The Collected Works of Billy the Kid* (1970) and Dennis Cooley in *Bloody Jack* (1984), which features an epigram from *Billy*.

Crosbie has also paid homage to *The Collected Works of Billy the Kid* on several occasions, but unlike Ondaatje she dares to bring the serial killer out of the mythic American west and situate him in the Southern Ontario milieu that is the subtext of Ondaatje's long poem.

If Crosbie distinguishes herself from Ondaatje and Michaels in her choice of contemporary subject matter, the serial form of her novel compels critics to affiliate her prose with these same authors. In the conclusion to "Confession and Critique: The Work of Lynn Crosbie," Philip Marchand expresses his reservations about lyrical fiction in Canada and Crosbie's novels in particular: "With [Crosbie's] novels, we confront a much larger issue – that of fiction written by Canadian poets, notably Michael Ondaatje and Anne Michaels. Works such as *The English Patient* and *Fugitive Pieces* are, in a sense, disastrous literary successes embraced by readers in spite of the novels' failure to reconcile the lyrical impulse with the traditional demands of realistic fiction for credible characterization and narrative. *Dorothy L'Amour* by no means solves this question – the narrator remains a consciousness unrooted in a recognizable character. As in the work of Ondaatje and Michaels, there are moments of brilliant imagery and striking perception, but the moments do not cohere."[139] Marchand recommends that poets stick to poetry: "It may well be that Crosbie's forte is to continue as a dramatic monologuist in verse, refining and expanding her gifts as a poetic chronicler of our nightmare world."[140] Marchand's conclusion thus encapsulates the standard argument against lyrical fiction, because it seeks to judge serial forms according to realist criteria.

To recapitulate: Marchand's idea of a credible narrator in the novel is one who meets "the traditional demands of realistic fiction." He prefers descriptive continuity to "moments of brilliant imagery." He prefers detailed characterizations to striking insights into a particular character's mode of perception. Most tellingly, he feels that if these moments do not cohere in a continuous sense, then they are incoherent in a readerly sense. Yet, as Marchand concedes, readers have embraced many works of lyrical fiction. Rather than consider the novels by Canadian poets as "disastrous literary successes" because of their failure to meet "the traditional demands of realist fiction," it is time to acknowledge that the success of these narratives derives, at least in part, from their ability to establish their own terms of reference and create new kinds of coherence. These novels are more than simply attempts to sustain on the lyre the weight of epic song; they are efforts to change the tune. To esteem the novels solely on the basis of their realism is at once a category mistake and a flagrant refusal to contemplate the particularity of the authors' projects and stated aims. Henighan looks

among the poet-novelists for a Canadian Dickens, and not surprisingly he
fails to find one because these authors seek alternatives to nineteenth-
century artistic models, as Michaels's rethinking of Meyerbeer's music and
Bowering's play on the term "serial" make explicit. Stephen Scobie begins
to establish this new frame of reference in his rebuttal to critics of *The English Patient*, "The Reading Lesson: Michael Ondaatje and the Patients of
Desire," where he states that Ondaatje's "poetic novels" demand that "the
logic of imagery tak[e] precedence over the logic of [realist] characterization."[141] However, these novels also move beyond imagism.

In surveying the development of the poet's novel over the last half-
century, one witnesses changing notions of what constitutes narrative continuity. While Klein's early admirers qualified their enthusiasm for the
language and imagery of *The Second Scroll* by judging it as a "kind of novelistic failure," Klein's novel seems much more successful when read in the
context of novels by Canadian authors who responded to it (and met with
similar reviews).[142] Within a Canadian context, Stan Dragland observes
that "postmodernist fiction slowly grew up around *Beautiful Losers*, help-
ing to make its discontinuities legible."[143] Yet even within these clusters of
influence there is always dissension. Crosbie's critique of Carson in "Something New, Please, O Universe" is illustrative, because Crosbie passes
judgement on the very same writers with whom she has aligned herself (in
the case of Ondaatje, who is a Griffin trustee) and with whom critics such
as Marchand have positioned her.

AN ALTERNATIVE READING

In the interest of embracing dissension and opening up a different interpretation of the relation between Canadian poetry and the novel from the one
I propose, it is useful to consider Christian Bök's afterword to *Ground
Works: Avant-Garde for Thee* (2002). This anthology, produced in collaboration with Margaret Atwood, surveys avant-garde publications in Canada from 1965 to 1985 and places emphasis on prose productions issued
by small presses. The title of Bök's anthology derives, not from *Groundwork* by Jakob Beer, but from a passage in "The Pretty Good Canadian
Novel" chapter of *A Short Sad Book*, where Bowering discusses Coach
House Press and interjects: "Forgive this ranting. It is the middle of the
novel, where all the axes are ground. It is the ground work."[144] Bök clearly
has an axe to grind with what he sees as the dominance of realist (not lyrical) fiction in Canada, and he compiles "a brief encyclopaedia of millenary
potential" to counter it.[145] The resulting anthology begins with the final

book of Cohen's *Beautiful Losers* and includes the comic book insert from Ondaatje's *The Collected Works of Billy the Kid* and the "Night (Merida" chapter of Marlatt's *Zócalo*. Yet as my introduction demonstrates, many critics believe that the once avant-garde works of Cohen, Ondaatje, Bowering, and Marlatt now constitute the mainstream.

Although Atwood first identified the need for a historical anthology of avant-garde productions in Canada, she called on Bök to select the authors. Explaining the rationale behind this anthology, Bök asserts that avant-garde prose has principally influenced experimental poetry in Canada, and not the other way around:

> While the stories here constitute some of the most adventurous fiction yet written in this country, much of it has, nevertheless, languished in obscurity, doing more perhaps to inspire the next wave of avant-garde poetlings than to inspire the next wave of avant-garde novelists. While the classic, mimetic novel may still dominate the modern milieu of literature, such realist fiction often does so at the expense of indigenous innovation. Many avant-garde writers must contend with tepid support from a community of indifferent, if not uninitiated, peers, many of whom might dismiss experimentation as nothing more than an excuse for lousy prose. The American novelist Brion Gysin has averred that writing lags at least fifty years behind painting, and his comments about the philistine sensibility of literature apply all the more aptly to Canada at the very moment when our writers have begun to receive unprecedented international acclaim. The work in this anthology, however, reminds us that to explore the limits of language, literature must often put its own most elementary principles at risk.[146]

I do not share Bök's wholesale disdain for realist fiction, and the entire thrust of this study has been to demonstrate that the relation of poetry to prose in Canada has principally been the inverse of the one he states. However, his observations shed light on his own development as a writer and emphasize that the interactions between poetry and prose are indeed dynamic and reciprocal.

NATIONAL LITERATURE AND THE POET'S NOVEL

The affinities between Canadian poets and novelists are thus numerous, but still the question remains: What role can the poet's novel play in a national literature? Henighan asserts that poet's novels have no staying power, but the fact that Ondaatje's *In the Skin of a Lion* became a bestseller fifteen years after its publication (when it won the inaugural Canada Reads contest in 2002) would seem to deflate this argument. No doubt Henighan would argue that the prize system is part of the Toronto-centric cultural apparatus that sustains our national illness. The fact that Hubert Aquin's *Prochain épisode* won the subsequent contest would not confirm the Toronto-centrism of his thesis, but would augment his distaste for the inter-mingling of lyricism and nationalism, even Québécois nationalism. Attuned to the lyrical traditions of French prose, Aquin's 1965 novel displays many of the features that Henighan says define a Toronto novel in the 1990s – a lyrical tone, a fondness for enigmatic imagery, a self-conscious narrative framework, and foreign settings in which cultures (Cuban, Swiss, Québé-cois, and English Canadian) are juxtaposed through metaphor. Indeed, most of these elements present themselves in the first two sentences: "Cuba coule en flammes au milieu du lac Léman pendant que je descends au fond des choses. Encaissé dans mes phrases, je glisse, fantôme, dans les eaux névrosées du fleuve et je découvre, dans ma dérive, le dessous des surfaces et l'image renversée des Alpes."[147] The multilayered form of the poet's novel is not the offspring of "TorLit" decadence, as Henighan asserts, but a broader response to the complexity of living in a society where cultural frames of reference conflict, inspire, frustrate, and seduce. As with Klein's multiple exposures in *The Second Scroll*, the doubled images in Aquin's novel function as a symbolic means of thinking through issues of culture clash.

Henighan would also have difficulty explaining the growing popularity of Cohen's *The Favourite Game*, which, although not available in a Cana-dian edition for the first seven years of its existence, concluded the century on T.F. Rigelhof's list of the top ten Canadian books.[148] *The Favourite Game* continues to enjoy a revival in the new millennium, having been adapted to film by a largely francophone cast and production company, who re-situated the story in a working-class part of Montreal.[149] Perhaps *The Favourite Game* is an anomaly in Canadian literature, because Cohen's poems and songs have drawn readers to his novels, and not the other way around. However, it seems that Henighan's narrow view of the "vital inter-linking" that constitutes "authentic art" inhibits him from recognizing the social concerns that underlie the fragmented and metaphoric aspects of the poet's novel.

Poet-novelists have also influenced realist dimensions of Canadian litera-ture in ways that Henighan does not recognize. Henighan praises the inno-vative narrative structure of Richler's *St. Urbain's Horseman*, but he does not acknowledge that the novel rewrites the quest narrative of *The Second Scroll* from the perspective of a diasporic Jew, according to Michael Hurley and Andy Belyea.[150] *St. Urbain's Horseman* also contests the outcome of certain scenes in Cohen's novels, in particular the Palais d'Or fight.[151] Although Henighan would cut off the poetic branch of the Canadian novel, it is plainly twined around others that he admires. One thinks, for example, of the endorsement from Alice Munro that appears on some of Carson's jacket covers: "*Autobiography of Red* is amazing – I haven't discovered any writing in years that's so marvelously disturbing."[152]

I have developed this study by focusing on a specific group of writers at the heart of the literary canons defined by the likes of Bök and Hutcheon. However, it is important in addition to note the leading role that the poet's novel has played in reformulating notions of canonicity and Canadian history along more ethnically diverse lines. Joy Kogawa's *Obasan* (1981) greatly increased the profile of Japanese Canadian literature and history in the 1980s, as well as having a decisive impact on the movement to offer redress to Japanese Canadian families whose ancestors were interned as enemy aliens during the Second World War. Similarly, George Elliott Clarke's *Whylah Falls* (1990) has been instrumental in drawing attention to Black Nova Scotian and African Canadian writing, and the tenth anniversary re-issue of *Whylah Falls* demonstrates the enduring success of this project. *Whylah Falls* is predominantly a collection of lyrics, but it is listed as a "poem novel" in the liner notes to Clarke's 2001 collection, *Blue*, and it marks Clarke's most explicit attempt to write the epic of what he sometimes calls the "state" of Africadia (a fusion of Africa and Acadia).[153] (I will elaborate on the achievements of these authors in a forthcoming chapter of the *Cambridge History of Canadian Literature*.)

By turning to the novel, Canadian poets have overcome the limitations of poetry's audience. They have also created a literary climate in which the history of the Canadian novel since the Second World War cannot be understood without a thorough understanding of contemporaneous developments in poetry. Perhaps, as Henighan asserts, the sheer volume and prestige of poet's novels in Canada is anomalous, but that does not invalidate these novels as fiction or as Canadian cultural productions. On the contrary, fans and critics of the form should now recognize the elaborate web of friendships, presses, collaborations, critical traditions, language issues, art influences, historical concerns, and urban geographies that have shaped the poet's novel in this country.

Examining these networks also reveals that innovative writing is often disseminated by ingenious means. *Tish* made use of new printing technologies and a voluntary subscription basis to create a market for postmodern poetics in Canada. Bowering's *Imago* and Ondaatje's *The Long Poem Anthology* defied publishing standards by reproducing only long poems. Marlatt and the *Tessera* collective avoided the high cost of maintaining an independent journal by publishing their material through special issues in like-minded journals. Carson has raised the profile of classical scholarship in North America, even as it is under siege institutionally, by composing hybrid narratives out of non-narrative fragments, and through her use of experimental media such as an internet opera. Cohen's move from poetry to the novel to the album may be the most famous example of poetic metamorphosis in Canada, but the transformation of novels by Cohen and Ondaatje into film was facilitated by the fact that these authors spent years translating the logic of photography and cinema into poetry and prose. The announcement that *Fugitive Pieces* would open the Toronto International Film Festival in 2007 emphasized the uncanny ability of these supposedly inchoate works to metamorphose into popular narrative media.[154]

Like Dude Botley listening to Buddy Bolden, anyone who spends considerable time pondering these novels will begin to apprehend formal patterns that dispel the initial impression of formlessness, which was simply a challenge to audience expectations. The authors' formal deviations are not purely random, but are motivated by identifiable aesthetic and sociopolitical concerns. To perform a variation on the Gould epigram that began this chapter, the poet-novelists have developed a prose form that expresses the limitations of realist narrative and which takes as its point of departure the terror of formlessness from a realist perspective and converts this energy into an aesthetic opportunity.[155] The authors have had to develop alternative narrative strategies to make their novels intelligible, and over time these narrative strategies have become conventions in themselves. Unfortunately, most Canadian criticism on the poet's novel focuses on how authors break genre conventions, and not on how they also establish them. On the other hand, the Canadian conventions are often unfamiliar to international readers, and in surveying foreign reviews of the poet's novel, one could be forgiven for thinking that Cohen was simply a Beat poet, or that Ondaatje exists solely by virtue of Salman Rushdie. I hope I have dispelled this impression by demonstrating that stylistic trends in the Canadian novel are buttressed by particular material and personal supports: mentors, anthologies, urban geographies, editors and presses, clusters of enthusiastic and hostile critics, and a mixture of homage and transformation by a subsequent generation of writers. Younger authors such as Crosbie have begun to challenge both the realist and lyrical traditions in Canada, and new poet-novelists will undoubtedly make their mark by fashioning alternatives to the narrative strategies detailed here.

Notes

INTRODUCTION

1 Fraser Sutherland, "Jane Urquhart's Painterly Poetry," *Globe and Mail*, 28 October 2000, sec. D, p. 13.

2 For Marlatt's response to the poem/novel controversy, see *Readings from the Labyrinth*, 55.

3 Aristotle argues that introducing elements of poetry into prose narrative results in "frigidity." See the chapter on frigidity in Aristotle, *On Rhetoric: A Theory of Civic Discourse*, 3.3. For a modern objection to poetic prose, see David Solway, *Director's Cut*, 186–7.

4 Allan Hepburn, "Lyric and Epic Fiction," 32. Note that Hepburn favours epic fiction in this review because he argues that it communicates a broader social vision.

5 George Murray, "The Verse Has Just Begun," *Globe and Mail*, 1 Sept. 2000, sec. D, p. 7.

6 Although Bakhtin was skeptical about the possibility that the long poem could achieve the polyphonic character of the novel, he made an exception for Pushkin's *Eugene Onegin*, which bears the appropriate subtitle, "a novel in verse." See M.M. Bakhtin, *Speech Genres and Other Late Essays*, 135. The belief that contemporary Canadian long poems move in the direction of the polyphonic novel is a commonplace of criticism on the long poem. See for example Laurie Ricou, "Poetry," *Literary History of Canada: Canadian Literature in English*, 4:26; see also Douglas Barbour, *Michael Ondaatje*, 7.

7 The Marlatt quotation is from a taped interview with Fred Wah reported in his introduction to *Net Work*, by Daphne Marlatt, 9.

8 Michael Ondaatje, "Introduction to Robin Blaser's 'Hello,'" 454.

9 Idem, "An Interview with Michael Ondaatje (1984)," by Sam Solecki, *Spider Blues*, 326.

10 Marlatt, quoted in Wah's introduction to *Net Work*, 9.

11 Anne Michaels, "Narrative Moves: An Interview with Anne Michaels," 17.

12 George Bowering, "Once Upon a Time in the South: Ondaatje and Genre," *Re-Constructing the Fragments of Michael Ondaatje's Works*, edited by Jean-Michel Lacroix, 36.

13 Ibid., 30

14 George Bowering, "Author's Statement," *The New Long Poem Anthology*, edited by Sharon Thesen, 351.

15 Ondaatje writes in his afterword to Howard O'Hagan's *Tay John* (271) that the first Canadian novel to affect him was Sheila Watson's *The Double Hook* (1959). The nickname "Kip" for the character Kirpal Singh in Ondaatje's *The English Patient* is perhaps an allusion to the outrider in Watson's novel.

16 James Reaney, "Long Poems," 118.

17 The Ottawa conference proceedings were published as *Bolder Flights: Essays on the Canadian Long Poem* and edited by Frank M. Tierney and Angela Robbeson.

18 Bowering, *A Short Sad Book*, 140.

19 Frank Davey, "The Language of the Contemporary Canadian Long Poem," 192.

20 Dave Carley, "The Survivor: Margaret Atwood," *Time* (Cdn. ed.), 16 December 2002, p. 44.

21 Gordon Teskey, "The Love Poet: Anne Carson," *Time* (Cdn. ed.), 16 December 2002, p. 46.

22 Ibid., 47. Fraser Sutherland also draws a comparison between the "appositional leaps" of Carson's writing and those of Ondaatje's work in "Addressing the Empress," 8.

23 Pico Iyer cites the affinity between Ondaatje's Asian-Canadian themes and those of Mistry's fiction in "The New Arrival: Rohinton Mistry," *Time* (Cdn. ed.), 16 December 2002, p. 47.

24 Christian Bök, *Ground Works: Avant-garde for Thee*, 231.

25 Stephen Henighan, *When Words Deny the World*, 146.

26 Solway, *Director's Cut*, 149.

CHAPTER ONE

1 Michael Ondaatje, "Interview with Michael Ondaatje," by Eleanor Wachtel, 256.

2 Paul Ricoeur, *Time and Narrative*, 1:8. See also Daniel Albright, *Lyricality in English Literature*, ix; W.R. Johnson, *The Idea of Lyric*, 77; Smaro Kamboureli, *On The Edge of Genre*, 157; Margot Kaminski, "Questioning the Canon: Early Long Poems by Canadian Women," 57.

3 Jed Rasula, "A Gift of Prophecy," 187.

4 See Northrop Frye, *Anatomy of Criticism*, 272.

5 Albright, *Lyricality in English Literature*, ix.

6 Friedrich Nietzsche, *The Birth of Tragedy & The Genealogy of Morals*, 19, 8.

7 Albright, *Lyricality in English Literature*, 2.

8 Aristotle, *Poetics*, 4.2.

9 Margaret Atwood, Introduction To *The New Oxford Book of Canadian Verse in English*, xxxiii.

10 Kamboureli, *On the Edge of Genre*, 188.

11 George Bowering, preface to *Burning Water*, n.p.

12 Brian Trehearne, *The Montreal Forties: Modernist Poetry in Transition*, 250.

13 Daphne Marlatt, *Readings from the Labyrinth*, 80.

14 William Rogers, *The Three Genres and the Interpretation of Lyric*, 81, 84.

15 Gerard Manley Hopkins, *The Note-books and Papers of Gerard Manley Hopkins*, 249; see also Mary Ann Caws, *Reading Frames in Modern Fiction*, 6.

16 Michael Ondaatje, "the gate in his head." *Rat Jelly*, 62.

17 Ibid.

18 Sharon Cameron, *Lyric Time: Dickinson and the Limits of Genre*, 204.

19 Anne Carson, "Poetry Without Borders," 57.

20 Jack Spicer, *After Lorca*, n.p.

21 Frye, *Anatomy of Criticism*, 303.

22 Ibid., 271.

23 Carson, "Poetry Without Borders," 57.

24 Roland Greene, *Post-Petrarchism: Origins and Innovations of the Western Lyric Sequence*, 80.

25 Barbara Godard, "Epi(pro)logue: In Pursuit of the Long Poem," 313.

26 D.M.R. Bentley, "Colonial Colonizing," *Bolder Flights: Essays on the Canadian Long Poem*, 9; Henry Kelsey, "Now Reader Read ..." *Early Long Poems on Canada*, ed. D.M.R. Bentley, 5–7.

27 Adam Hood Burwell, "Talbot Road," *Early Long Poems on Canada*, edited by D.M.R. Bentley, 109–27.

28 Adam Kidd, "The Huron Chief," *Early Long Poems on Canada*, edited by D.M.R. Bentley, 297–365.

29 Frye, "The Narrative Tradition in English-Canadian Poetry," 155.

30 Ibid., 156.

31 Ibid., 157.

32 See the commentary on Meredith in Philip Marchand, *Marshall McLuhan: The Medium and the Messenger*, 32.

33 In *McLuhan in Space*, Richard Cavell reads *Through the Vanishing Point* as the final installment of a trilogy of critical works (including *The Gutenberg Galaxy* and *Understanding Media*) that McLuhan completed before devoting himself to artist books. See the second half of *McLuhan in Space*.

34 McLuhan, *Through the Vanishing Point*, 250.

35 Ed Jewinski, *Michael Ondaatje: Express Yourself Beautifully*, 133.

36 Cavell, *McLuhan in Space*, 94.

37 See the original cover of Michael Ondaatje's *Coming Through Slaughter* (Toronto: Anansi, 1976).

38 McLuhan, *The Gutenberg Galaxy*, 276.

39 Erving Goffman, *Forms of Talk*, 8.

40 Deborah Tannen, "What's in a Frame?" *Framing in Discourse*, 53.

41 Northrop Frye, "The Narrative Tradition in English-Canadian Poetry," 151–2.

42 Dorothy Livesay, "The Documentary Poem: A Canadian Genre," 281.

43 Ibid., 267

44 Ibid., 269. For Livesay's retraction see Dorothy Livesay, "The Canadian Documentary: An Overview," 127.

45 For instance, Roy Miki argues that the narrative frame of Livesay's best-known documentary poem, "Call My People Home" (1950), "becomes a representational device that enables the translation of Japanese Canadian experience ('the objective facts') into a public discourse ('subjective feelings of the poet'), in this instance, a radio drama which displaces the specificity of internment through 'thematic'

abstraction ... The thematic message conveyed to its non-Japanese Canadian readers (and listeners, since it was aired on the radio) is that internment and forced dispersal, despite the hardships, has 'allowed' Japanese Canadians to assimilate" (Miki, *Broken Entries: Race, Subjectivity, Writing*, 102–3; Livesay, "Call My People Home," *The Documentaries*, 34–48).

46 bp Nichol, "The Medium Was the Message," 299.

47 Ibid., 298–9. Nichol relates these thought probes to his own passion for the hypothetical systems of Alfred Jarry's 'pataphysics, which is the subject of Christian Bök's treatise '*Pataphysics: The Poetics of an Imaginary Science* (2002).

48 Nichol, "The Medium Was the Message," 300.

49 Edward Foster, *Jack Spicer*, 13.

50 Ibid., 11.

51 Robin Blaser, "Statement," *The Long Poem Anthology*, edited by Michael Ondaatje, 323. Rilke's lyricism, in turn, profoundly influences Ondaatje's *Tin Roof* (1982) and Bowering's *Kerrsdale Elegies* (1984).

52 Spicer, *After Lorca*, n.p.

53 Ibid., n.p.

54 Ibid., n.p.

55 Ibid., n.p.

56 Jack Spicer, *Billy the Kid*, in *The Collected Books of Jack Spicer*, 77–83.

57 Robin Blaser, "The Fire," *The Poetics of the New American Poetry*, 236.

58 Ibid., 237–8.

59 George Bowering, *Imago* 1 (1964), 2.

60 Ondaatje, *The Long Poem Anthology*, back cover.

61 Idem, introduction to *The Long Poem Anthology*, 11.

62 Robin Blaser, "The Practice of Outside," *The Collected Books of Jack Spicer*, 270–329; Robin Blaser, "The Moth Poem," *The New Long Poem Anthology*, edited by Sharon Thesen, 17–37.

63 Douglas Barbour, *Lyric/Anti-Lyric*, 7.

64 Robin Blaser, "Statement," *The Long Poem Anthology*, 323.

65 Lewis Ellingham and Kevin Killian, ed., *Poet Be Like God*, x.

66 Both poems appear in *The Collected Books of Jack Spicer*. For a reading of Spicer in terms of musical theory, see Stephanie A. Judy, "'The Grand Concord of What': Preliminary Thoughts on Musical Composition in Poetry," 267–85.

67 Blaser, "The Practice of Outside," 278.

68 *Encarta Electronic Encyclopedia*, 1998, s.v. "serial"; see also John Vander Weg, *Serial Music and Serialism*, 1–11.

69 M.J. Grant, *Serial Music, Serial Aesthetics: Compositional Theory in Post-War Europe*, 68. This change in outlook was partly a response to the catastrophic rage for order in Nazi-era Germany, partly the inspiration of developments in information theory, and partly the result of the composers' attraction to – and awareness of problems posed by – abstract art in the period (Grant 34–8).

70 Glenn Gould, "'I'm a Child of Nature,'" *The Art of Glenn Gould*, 44. For the 1955 recording, see Johann Sebastian Bach, *The Goldberg Variations*, by Glenn Gould, Columbia Records ML 5060. For the 1981 recording, see Johann Sebastian Bach, *Goldberg Variations*, by Glenn Gould, CBS IM 37779.

71 See in particular Gould's sound collage, *The Idea of North*, in *Glenn Gould's Solitude Trilogy*, CBC Records PSCD 2003–3.
72 Ira Nadel, *Various Positions*, 124.
73 Nancy Huston's *Les variations Goldberg* (1981) is the most obvious example of Gould's influence on the novel.
74 Glenn Gould, "An Argument for Music in the Electronic Age," *The Art of Glenn Gould*, 228. Note that the posthumous Glenn Gould prize for contributions to music and recording was awarded to Pierre Boulez in 2002.
75 Idem, "Forgery and Imitation in the Creative Process," *The Art of Glenn Gould*, 213.
76 Reginald Smith Brindle argues that the "happy mean between change and repetition [that] is the fundamental basis of so many sonata and rondo movements ... is also the basis of a great deal of serial music, though the repetitions are usually skillfully disguised" (Reginald Smith Brindle, *Serial Composition*, 102).
77 Gould, "An Argument for Music in the Electronic Age," *The Art of Glenn Gould*, 229.
78 Michael Jarrett, "Writing Mystery," 32.
79 Robert Duncan, preface to *Medieval Scenes*, n.p.
80 Paul Cobley, *Narrative*, 242.
81 Ibid., 242.
82 Daphne Marlatt, *What Matters: Writing 1968–70*, 155.
83 Robin Blaser, "The Translator: A Tale," *The Long Poem Anthology*, 179.
84 George Bowering, "Interview," interview by Caroline Bayard and Jack David, 93.
85 Idem, "Vancouver as Postmodern Poetry," *Vancouver: Representing the Postmodern City*, edited by Paul Delany, 135.
86 Michael Ondaatje, "An Interview with Michael Ondaatje," interview by Stephen Scobie and Douglas Barbour, 12. Ondaatje and Marlatt, along with many others, also contributed to "A Celebration of Roy Kiyooka" published as a special issue of *Brick* 48 (spring 1994): 13–33.
87 Daphne Marlatt, introduction to *Mothertalk*, 5. See also Susanna Egan and Gabriele Helms, "The Many Tongues of *Mothertalk: Life Stories of Mary Kiyoshi Kiyooka*," 44–77.
88 Roy Kiyooka, *Long Beach to Peggy's Cove*, in *All Amazed: For Roy Kiyooka*, 94–9.
89 Roy Kiyooka, *Van Gogh and the Bird of Paradise*, in *All Amazed*, 110–1.
90 Sheryl Conkelton, "Roy Kiyooka: '....The Sad and Glad Tidings of the Floating World....'," in *All Amazed*, 107.
91 Roy Kiyooka, *Powell Street Promenade*, in *All Amazed*, 100.
92 Idem, *The Fontainebleau Dream Machine: 18 Frames from a Book of Rhetoric*, in *Pacific Windows: Collected Poems of Roy K. Kiyooka*, 110, 112, 124, 127.
93 Robin Blaser, "The Moth Poem," *The New Long Poem Anthology*, 17–37.
94 Idem, "Statement," *The Long Poem Anthology*, 323.
95 Christian Bök, "Oneiromechanics: Notes on the Dream Machines of Roy Kiyooka," 24.
96 Eva-Marie Kröller, "Roy Kiyooka's 'The Fontainebleau Dream Machine': A Reading," 47.

97 Frye, *Anatomy of Criticism*, 274.
98 Carson, "Woman of Letters," 29.
99 Robert Kroetsch, "Stone Hammer Poem," *Completed Field Notes*, 1–7.
100 George Bowering, "Stone Hammer Narrative," *Imaginary Hand*, 172.
101 Robert Kroetsch, "For Play and Entrance: The Contemporary Canadian Long Poem," *The Lovely Treachery of Words*, 118, 117.
102 Linda Hutcheon gives Kroetsch this nickname in *The Canadian Postmodern*, 160. The comment on Homer appears in Kroetsch, "For Play and Entrance," *The Lovely Treachery of Words*, 126.
103 M.L. Rosenthal and Sally M. Gall, *The Modern Poetic Sequence*, 9.
104 Kamboureli, *On the Edge of Genre*, 64.
105 Ibid., 75.
106 Joseph Riddel, "A Somewhat Polemical Introduction," 466.
107 Ibid., 467.
108 Kamboureli, *On the Edge of Genre*, 49.
109 Ibid., 67.
110 Heather Murray, "The Impossible Genre," 97.
111 Greene, *Post-Petrarchism*, 13.
112 M.H. Abrams, *A Glossary of Literary Terms*, 130.
113 J.A. Cuddon, *A Dictionary of Literary Terms*, 430.
114 Marlatt, *Ana Historic*, 67.
115 Malcolm Bradbury, *The Novel Today*, 8.
116 Ondaatje, "Michael Ondaatje: An Interview," by Catherine Bush, 245.
117 Cobley, *Narrative*, 91.
118 George Becker, *Realism in Modern Literature*, 37, 103–4.
119 Friedrich von Schlegel, *Dialogue on Poetry and Literary Aphorisms*, 140–1.
120 Michael Ondaatje, quoted in Melanie Rehak, "Things Fall Together," *New York Times Magazine*, p. 38.
121 Hermann Hesse, quoted in Ralph Freedman, *The Lyrical Novel*, 42.
122 Freedman, *The Lyrical Novel*, vii.
123 Ibid., 7–8.
124 Ibid., 8.
125 Ibid., 7.
126 Ibid., 8.
127 Joseph Frank, "Spatial Form in Modern Literature," 3–62.
128 Idem, "Spatial Form: Thirty Years After," 202–43.
129 Idem, "Spatial Form in Modern Literature," 8.
130 Ibid., 49.
131 Ibid., 9.
132 See Cavell, *McLuhan in Space*, 8–9.
133 Ibid., 17, 21, 23, 25.
134 Frank, "Spatial Form: Thirty Years After," 214.
135 Frank was originally influenced in this mythic direction by *The Structure of the Novel* (1925) by Edwin Muir, whose poetry is the subject of Ondaatje's Master's thesis: "Mythology in the Poetry of Edwin Muir" (Queen's University, 1967). Frank himself concludes *Spatial Form in Narrative* by suggesting that the theories of space and orality outlined by Marshall McLuhan and Walter J. Ong

(McLuhan's former student) would be fruitful avenues of further investigation. Another critic in the volume attempts to reconcile Frank's ideas with the myth criticism of Northrop Frye.

136 Spicer, *After Lorca*, n.p.
137 Idem, *The Tower of Babel*, 73.
138 Marlatt, *Readings from the Labyrinth*, 50.
139 Ondaatje, "An Interview with Michael Ondaatje (1975)," 24.
140 Daphne Marlatt and Betsy Warland, *Double Negative*, 38.
141 Ibid., 36, 37. As Sidonie Smith observes in her fine reading of this poem, Marlatt resolves to "untrain" her stereotypical reading of the trope and "traine" it anew in the feminine (154).
142 Marlatt and Warland, *Double Negative*, 38.
143 Sidonie Smith, *Moving Lives*, 154.
144 W.F. Garrett-Petts and Donald Lawrence, *Photographic Encounters*, 1.
145 Bowering, *A Short Sad Book*, 95.
146 Ibid., 93.
147 Ibid., 157.
148 Bowering's references to Curnoe are in *A Short Sad Book*, 143, 160; the allusion to Spicer, 50; the term "serial novel," 139.
149 Robin Myers and Michael Harris, introduction to *Serials and Their Readers 1620–1914*, vii.
150 Laurel Brake, "'The Trepidation of the Spheres': The Serial and the Book in the 19th Century," 84.
151 Bowering, *A Short Sad Book*, 137.
152 Michael Ondaatje, "Michael Ondaatje: An Interview," by Catherine Bush, 242.
153 Bowering, *A Short Sad Book*, 142.
154 Barbara Godard, "Stretching the Story: The Canadian Story Cycle," 32.

CHAPTER TWO

1 Leonard Cohen, *The Favourite Game*, 32.
2 Leonard Cohen, *The Songs of Leonard Cohen*, Columbia Records, WCK 9533.
3 Ira Nadel, *Various Positions: A Life of Leonard Cohen*, 16.
4 Ibid., 57; Leonard Cohen, "Last Dance at the Four Penny," *The Spice-Box of Earth*, 65–6.
5 Cohen discusses his father's death and shows excerpts from the home movies in *Songs from the Life of Leonard Cohen*, Sony Music, 1988, 70 minutes.
6 Cohen, *Beautiful Losers*, 18.
7 Nadel, *Various Positions*, 41.
8 J.A. Wainwright, "The Favourite Game: Canadian Literature In and Out," 244.
9 Ibid.
10 Leon Edel, "Marginal *Keri* and Textual *Chetiv*: The Mystic Novel of A.M. Klein," 16.
11 Cohen, *The Favourite Game*, 7.
12 Naïm Kattan, *A.M. Klein: Poet and Prophet*, 21.
13 A.M. Klein, "To Keats," *Complete Poems*, 1:4; idem, "Heirloom," ibid., 1:298.
14 A.M. Klein, *The Rocking Chair and Other Poems*, 11–2, 4, 29–31.

15 Pierre Anctil, "A.M. Klein: The Poet and His Relations with French Quebec," 352.
16 Ibid., 356–7.
17 A.M. Klein, "Montreal," *Selected Poems*, 89.
18 Klein, quoted in Seymour Mayne, Afterword to *The Second Scroll* by A.M. Klein, 137.
19 See Klein's letter to A.J.M. Smith, cited by Mayne in his afterword to *The Second Scroll*, 139–40.
20 Klein, *The Second Scroll*, 42.
21 Ibid., 76–7.
22 Ibid., 68.
23 Seth Lerer, "Medieval English Literature and the Idea of the Anthology," 1254–5.
24 Klein, *The Second Scroll*, 89.
25 Klein, quoted in Mayne, Afterword to *The Second Scroll*, 138.
26 Michael Hurley and Andy Belyea, "A.M. Klein," *The Encyclopedia of Literature in Canada*, 583–5. See also Tom Marshall, Introduction to *A.M. Klein*, x.
27 Klein, *The Second Scroll*, 55.
28 Ibid., 78.
29 Coleman Klein discusses his father's legacy in the film *A.M. Klein: The Poet as Landscape*, dir. David Kaufman, Ergo Media, 1987, 58 minutes.
30 Edel, "Marginal *Keri*," 29.
31 Kattan, *A.M. Klein: Poet and Prophet*, 80.
32 Roger Hyman, *Aught from Naught: A.M. Klein's* The Second Scroll, 30–4; Rachel Feldhay Brenner, *A.M. Klein, The Father of Canadian Jewish Literature*, ii.
33 Klein in a letter to Edel, quoted in Mayne, afterword to *The Second Scroll*, 138.
34 See Coleman Klein's discussion of his father's political career in *A.M. Klein: The Poet as Landscape*.
35 Leonard Cohen, quoted in Nadel, *Various Positions*, 67.
36 Ibid., 67; Winfried Siemerling, "Leonard Cohen. 'Loneliness and History: A Speech Before the Jewish Public Library,'" *Take This Waltz*, edited by Michael Fournier and Ken Norris, 143–53.
37 Leonard Cohen, "A Political Constituency that Really Exists in the World: An Interview with Leonard Cohen," by Winfried Siemerling, *Take This Waltz*, 156.
38 Siemerling, "Leonard Cohen. 'Loneliness and History,'" 147.
39 A.M. Klein, "In Praise of the Diaspora (An Undelivered Memorial Address)," *Beyond Sambation: Selected Essays and Editorials (1928–1955)*, 463–77.
40 Nadel, *Various Positions*, 67; Siemerling, "Leonard Cohen. 'Loneliness and History,'" 150.
41 Nadel, *Various Postions*, 9.
42 Ibid., 46.
43 Michael Ondaatje, *Leonard Cohen*, 7.
44 Stephen Scobie, *Leonard Cohen*, 22.
45 Leonard Cohen, "For Wilf and His House," *Let Us Compare Mythologies*, 3.
46 Ondaatje, *Leonard Cohen*, 19.
47 Ibid., 43–4; Scobie, *Leonard Cohen*, 56.
48 Clint Burnham, "How Postmodern Is Cohen's Poetry?" 65.
49 Cohen, "As the Mist Leaves No Scar," *The Spice-Box of Earth*, 56.

50 Idem, "True Love Leaves No Traces," *Stranger Music*, 216; idem, *Death of a Ladies' Man*, Columbia Records, WCK 44286.

51 Cohen, "True Love Leaves No Traces," *Stranger Music*, 216.

52 Leonard Cohen, "Poem, en Prose," CIV/n: *A Literary Magazine of the 50's*, edited by Aileen Collins (Montreal: Véhicule Press, 1983), 112; idem, "Friends," *Let Us Compare Mythologies*, 21.

53 Nadel, *Various Positions*, 12.

54 Cohen, "Lines from My Grandfather's Journal," *The Spice-Box of Earth*, 80.

55 A.M. Klein, "Portraits of a Minyan," *Selected Poems*, 6. This test of erudition was clarified for me, via Nathalie Cooke, in a private email from Rabbi Leigh Lerner of Montreal, 3 September 2003.

56 Cohen, "Lines from My Grandfather's Journal," *The Spice-Box of Earth*, 81.

57 Ibid., 84.

58 Ibid., 84.

59 Cohen, "To a Teacher," *The Spice-Box of Earth*, 21.

60 Ondaatje, *Leonard Cohen*, 15; George Bowering, "Inside Leonard Cohen," *Leonard Cohen: The Artist and His Critics*, edited by Michael Gnarowski, 34.

61 Cohen, "Lines from My Grandfather's Journal," *The Spice-Box of Earth*, 86.

62 Nadel, *Various Positions*, 99.

63 Stephen Scobie, "Racing the Midnight Train: Leonard Cohen in Performance," 54.

64 Robert Fulford, "On Books: A Rich Vein of Satire in this Fall's Canadian Novels," *Maclean's*, 5 October 1963, p. 79.

65 George Woodcock, "The Song of the Sirens: Reflections on Leonard Cohen," *Leonard Cohen: The Artist and His Critics*, edited by Michael Gnarowski, 160. See also Joan Crate's poetic meditation on this subject in "The Mistress' Reply to the Poet."

66 Dagmar de Venster, "Leonard Cohen's Women," *Mother Was Not a Person*, edited by Marguerite Andersen, 97.

67 Roy Kervin, "Leonard Cohen Tries His Hand at a Novel," *Montreal Gazette*, p. 47.

68 Ed Kleiman, "Blossom Show," review of *The Favourite Game*, by Leonard Cohen, *Alphabet* 9 (November 1964), 78.

69 See Leonard Cohen, "Leonard Cohen: The Poet as Hero: 2," 56.

70 See the video clip of the Clarkson interview with Cohen in the CBC online archive <http://archives.cbc.ca/ 300c.asp?IDCat=68&IDDos=93&IDLan=1&IDMenu=68>

71 Charles Poore, "Young Bohemians – Canadian Style," review of *The Favourite Game*, by Leonard Cohen, *New York Times*, 12 September 1963, p. 35.

72 *Mambo Italiano*, dir. Émile Gaudreault, Samuel Goldwyn Films, 2003.

73 Gilles Hénault, "'The Favourite Game,' ou le jeu de l'amour et du hasard," 7. [Like Breavman, they destroy ancient myths to make new ones better suited to their situation, while retaining a nostalgia of belonging to an ethnic group, its culture and traditions. After all, one must first repudiate a tradition to valorize it.]

74 Sherry Simon, "Crossing Town: Montreal in Translation," 17.

75 Mordecai Richler, *St. Urbain's Horseman*, 142.

76 Cohen, *The Favourite Game*, 47.

77 Ibid., 49.

78 Nadel introduces Cohen as a poet *"maudit"* (2) in *Various Positions* and later cites a letter in which Cohen laments from Greece: "It is hard to be a poet *maudit*

when you have a good tan" (114). Of Breavman, Hénault writes in his review of *The Favourite Game*: "c'est Rimbaud cherchant à 'posséder la vérité dans une âme et un corps'" (7).

79 Cohen, *Beautiful Losers*, 127.
80 Ibid., 130.
81 Cohen, *The Favourite Game*, 6–7.
82 Ibid., 109.
83 Ibid., 125.
84 Poore, "Young Bohemians," 35.
85 Cohen, *The Favourite Game*, 147.
86 Ibid., 229.
87 Leonard Cohen, quoted in Nadel, *Various Positions*, 109–10.
88 Ibid., 116.
89 Ibid., 116–7.
90 Ibid., 118.
91 Cohen, "Leonard Cohen: The Poet as Hero: 2," 50.
92 Leonard Cohen, quoted in Nadel, *Various Positions*, 141.
93 Cohen, *The Favourite Game*, 4.
94 Michael Greenstein, *Third Solitudes*, 124.
95 Ondaatje, *Leonard Cohen*, 24.
96 Ibid., 23.
97 Cohen, *The Favourite Game*, 5–6.
98 Stan Dragland, "F.ing through *Beautiful Losers*," *Take This Waltz*, edited by Michael Fournier and Ken Norris, 55.
99 Linda Hutcheon, *Leonard Cohen and His Works*, 10.
100 Ian Adam, "The Human Centre," 127, 128.
101 Ibid., 127, 128.
102 T.F. Rigelhof, "The Fiction of Leonard Cohen," 141.
103 Cohen, *The Favourite Game*, 80.
104 Cohen, "The Party Was Over Then Too," *Book of Longing*, 26.
105 Cohen, *The Favourite Game*, 105.
106 Ibid., 27.
107 Ondaatje, *Leonard Cohen*, 26.
108 Michael Ondaatje, "The Vault," *There's a Trick With a Knife*, 66–7. See also Stephen Scobie, "His Legend a Jungle Sleep: Michael Ondaatje and Henri Rousseau," 42–60.
109 Cohen, *The Favourite Game*, 59.
110 Ondaatje, *Leonard Cohen*, 34.
111 Cohen, *The Favourite Game*, 108.
112 Ibid., 193.
113 Ibid., 222–3.
114 Ibid., 182.
115 Ibid., 73.
116 Ibid., 73.
117 Ibid., 78.
118 Ibid., 78.
119 Ibid., 235.

120 Ibid., 236.
121 Cohen, "Lines from My Grandfather's Journal," *The Spice-Box of Earth*, 86.
122 Idem, *The Favourite Game*, 4.
123 See Carmen Ellison, "'Not My Real Face': Corporeal Grammar in *The Favourite Game*," 67.
124 Nadel, *Various Positions*, 88.
125 Cohen, *The Favourite Game*, 226.
126 Ibid., 244.
127 Patricia Morley, *The Immoral Moralists*, 78.
128 Anne Carson, *Autobiography of Red*, 75.
129 Cohen, *The Favourite Game*, 244.
130 Ibid., n.p.
131 Ibid., 144, 133.
132 Patricia Morley, "'The Knowledge of Strangerhood'; 'The Monuments Were Made of Worms,'" *Leonard Cohen: The Artist and His Critics*, edited by Michael Gnarowski, 134.
133 Morley, *The Immoral Moralists*, 73.
134 Loranne Dorman and Clive Rawlins, *Leonard Cohen: Prophet of the Heart*, 113.
135 Winfried Siemerling, *Discoveries of the Other*, 52.
136 Desmond Pacey, "Cohen as a Literary Phenomenon," *Leonard Cohen: The Artist and His Critics*, edited by Michael Gnarowski, 83.
137 Cohen, *The Favourite Game*, 9.
138 Ibid., 10.
139 Ibid., 10.
140 Ibid., 15.
141 Ibid., 23.
142 Ibid., 19.
143 Ibid., 72.
144 Ibid., 116.
145 Cohen disapproves of institutionalized Christianity and in *Beautiful Losers* accuses the Jesuits, the Company of Jesus, of a host of violent crimes. But in his poems and songs (most famously in the second verse of "Suzanne"), Cohen has maintained a longstanding interest in Jesus as a Jewish prophet of love (whom the grandfather in "Lines" also attempts to reclaim). Thus, the coda to *The Favourite Game* is not simply a vision of lost innocence. It offers a test pattern against which to compare Breavman's ideas of connection on the facing page, and it underscores the emotional poverty of Breavman's adult behaviour.
146 George Bowering, *A Short Sad Book*, 44; Cohen, *Beautiful Losers*, 101–2.
147 Klein, *The Second Scroll*, 98.
148 Ibid., 99.
149 Ibid., 98.
150 Ibid., 100.
151 Cohen, "The Genius," *The Spice-Box of Earth*, 78.
152 Idem, *The Favourite Game*, 10.
153 Ibid., 7. See the very different portrait of Jewish-German sexual contact in Richler's *St. Urbain's Horseman*.
154 Klein, *The Second Scroll*, 80.

155 Ibid., 81.
156 Ibid., 87.
157 Cohen makes this remark in the film *Songs from the Life of Leonard Cohen*.
158 A.M. Klein, "The Chanukah Dreidel," *Short Stories*, 43–8.
159 Roger Hyman, *Aught from Naught*, 101.
160 Ibid., 101.
161 Cohen, *The Favourite Game*, 33. I owe the word origins of the names to Joseph Shipley's *Dictionary of Word Origins*.
162 Morley, "'The Knowledge of Strangerhood'; 'The Monuments Were Made of Worms,'" *Leonard Cohen*, edited by Michael Gnarowski, 134.
163 Cohen, *Beautiful Losers*, 101.
164 Poore, "Young Bohemians," 35; Milton, "Beyond Agonistics," 244.
165 Nadel, *Leonard Cohen*, 60.
166 Cohen, *Beautiful Losers*, 172. The appellations "I" and "IF" were employed early in Cohen criticism by Scobie and Barbour and have now become standard designations.
167 Cohen, *Beautiful Losers*, 28.
168 Ibid., 198.
169 Ibid., 205–6.
170 Ibid., 31.
171 For a slightly different take on this scene, see Nicole Markotic's "The Telephone Dance & Mechanical Ecstasy in Leonard Cohen's *Beautiful Losers*."
172 This Messianic notion of time and social circuitry is vital to Michaels's world view in *Fugitive Pieces*, as I illustrate in my conclusion.
173 Milton, "Beyond Agonistics," 236.
174 Cohen, *The Favourite Game*, 39.
175 Morley, *The Immoral Moralists*, 13.
176 See John Allemang, "The Original Canadian Idol," *Globe and Mail*, 23 August 2003, sec. F, p. 2.
177 Pacey, "Cohen as a Literary Phenomenon," 78, 85.
178 Ondaatje, *Leonard Cohen*, 49.
179 Cohen, *The Favourite Game*, 103.
180 Idem, *Beautiful Losers*, 98.
181 Ibid., 99.
182 Ibid., 45.
183 Cohen, *The Favourite Game*, 85. The second novel also portrays Lawrence of Arabia being whipped and fondled in a more violent version of the scenario Breavman and Lisa acted out. See Cohen, *Beautiful Losers*, 250.
184 Idem, *Beautiful Losers*, 45.
185 Ibid., 44. The ensuing debate anticipates the argument between Patrick Lewis and Commissioner Harris in the Waterworks at the conclusion of Ondaatje's *In the Skin of a Lion*.
186 Idem, *The Favourite Game*, 211–12.
187 Idem, *Beautiful Losers*, 167. See the chant illustrated by Sarah Perkins and Ian Jackson in Leonard Cohen, *God is Alive, Magic is Afoot*.
188 See the liner notes and photograph in Buffy Sainte-Marie, *Up Where We Belong*, EMI 72438350592.

189 Cohen, *The Favourite Game*, 213.
190 Hutcheon, *The Canadian Postmodern*, 26.
191 Ibid., 26.
192 Cohen, *Beautiful Losers*, 3.
193 Ibid., 3.
194 Cohen, *The Favourite Game*, 183. This passage establishes a precedent for the triptych of dolphin sonographs in *Coming Through Slaughter*, where Ondaatje investigates the power of dolphins to emit whistles and echolocation clicks simultaneously.
195 Cohen, *Beautiful Losers*, 117. However, he misses the precedent established in *The Favourite Game*.
196 Cohen, *Beautiful Losers*, 139–40. This mantra has prompted Sylvia Söderlind to interpret *Beautiful Losers* as a Canadian version of *The Book of Changes*. See Sylvia Söderlind, *Margin/Alias: Language and Colonization in Canadian and Québécois Fiction*, 54.
197 Cohen, *Beautiful Losers*, 9–10.
198 Ibid., 199.
199 Söderlind, *Margin/Alias*, 49.
200 Cohen, *Beautiful Losers*, 161.
201 Ibid., 174–5.
202 Norman Ravvin, "Writing Around the Holocaust," 30, 28.
203 Ibid., 15.
204 Ibid., 15.
205 Ibid., 12–13.
206 Ibid., 195. This translation derives from Scobie, *Leonard Cohen*, 107.
207 Cohen, *Beautiful Losers*, 104–5.
208 Scobie, *Leonard Cohen*, 106–7.
209 Dennis Lee, *Savage Fields*, 95.
210 Cohen, *Beautiful Losers*, 251.
211 Ibid., 237.
212 Ibid., 252.
213 Ibid., n.p.
214 Söderlind, *Margin/Alias*, 64.
215 See Nadel, *Various Positions*, 269.
216 Cohen, *Beautiful Losers*, 172.
217 Ibid., 258.
218 Ibid., 5.
219 Ibid., 259.
220 Leslie Monkman, "Beautiful Losers: Mohawk Myth and Jesuit Legend," 57.
221 Siemerling, *Discoveries of the Other*, 56–7.
222 Cohen, *Beautiful Losers*, 223. See Hutcheon, *Leonard Cohen*, 24.
223 Cohen, *Beautiful Losers*, 60. F. appears to write in English, but he repeatedly spells Argentina in the French manner, with a final "e," and Davey has noted that the English on the page could simply be a novelistic convention akin to the English transcriptions of the dialogue between Catherine's aunts.
224 Cohen, *Beautiful Losers*, 227.
225 Ibid., 59.

226 Greenstein, *Third Solitudes*, 139.
227 Ibid., 141.
228 Cohen, *Beautiful Losers*, 260.
229 Ibid., 260. The triple sense of "miss me" – of longing, of not finding, of gender transformation – in the final complex underscores the processes of desire and deferral that becomes central to Carson's aesthetic.
230 Nadel, *Various Positions*, 135.
231 Cohen, "A Note to the Chinese Reader," *Book of Longing*, 196.
232 Leonard Cohen, "Un Canadien Errant," *Recent Songs*, Columbia Records, WCK 36264. Note that Cohen's long poem *Death of a Lady's Man* began as a novel in manuscript.
233 Antoine Gérin-Lajoie, "Un Canadien Errant," 17.
234 Cohen, "Reading to the Prime Minister," *Book of Longing*, 104.
235 Cohen, "Titles," *Book of Longing*, 159.
236 Cohen, *Book of Longing*, 172.
237 Cohen, "The Best," *Book of Longing*, 141.
238 Tom Robbins, "Tom Robbins Considers the Man in the Tower," liner notes to *Tower of Song: The Songs of Leonard Cohen*, A&M Records, 3145402592, n.p.
239 Ondaatje, *Leonard Cohen*, 45.
240 Ibid., 45.
241 Ibid., 49.
242 Cohen, *Beautiful Losers*, 18.
243 Ibid., 18.
244 Ibid., 158.
245 According to *La Presse*, a group of architects banded together in 1927 to prevent new construction of the exterior balconies, deeming them "inasthétiques." The balconies were popular because they provided respite from the summer heat, enabled social interaction, and could not be taxed as part of the square footage of the house. A law passed that prohibited balconies in neighbourhoods where less than 60 per cent of the houses already had them. This law is still on the books in some quarters. See Isabelle Audet and Rémi Lemée, "Raconte-moi l'histoire de Montréal," *La Presse*, 19 July 2003, sec. J, p. 3. See also the novels of Michel Tremblay and David Fennario's play *Balconville* (Vancouver: Talonbooks, 1980). Cohen cites the performance of *Balconville* at the Centaur Theatre in Montreal as an inspiring event that led to the adaptation of his poems and novels to the stage by Centaur in *The Leonard Cohen Show*. See Dane Lanken, "The Leonard Cohen Show," *The Gazette*, 24 May 1980, p. 98.
246 Randolph Lewis, *Alanis Obomsawin*, 17; *Kanehsatake: 270 Years of Resistance*, dir. Alanis Obomsawin, National Film Board, 1993.

CHAPTER THREE

1 Michael Ondaatje, in Sam Solecki, "An Interview with Michael Ondaatje (1984)," 322.
2 Andrew Pyper, "In the Morgue of the Imagination," sec. D, p. 22.
3 Ondaatje, in Solecki, "An Interview with Michael Ondaatje (1984)," 325. Ondaatje cites Kingsley Amis's *Lucky Jim*, Salinger's *The Catcher in the Rye*, and

Hemingway's *The Old Man and the Sea* as examples of the kinds of novels he was writing against when he wrote *Coming Through Slaughter*.

4 Ondaatje, in Solecki "An Interview with Michael Ondaatje (1984)," 322, 324.
5 Linda Hutcheon, *The Canadian Postmodern*, 47–8; see also Perry Nodelman, "The Collected Photographs of Billy the Kid," 68.
6 Anne Blott, "'Stories to Finish': *The Collected Works of Billy the Kid*," 189.
7 Ondaatje, *The Collected Works of Billy the Kid*, 84.
8 Ondaatje, "Where the Personal and the Historical Meet: An Interview with Michael Ondaatje," 4–5.
9 Michael Ondaatje, "Spider Blues," *There's a Trick with a Knife I'm Learning to Do*, 62–63. The poet-spider is perhaps an allusion to the West African trickster figure, Anansi, after whom the Toronto publishing house is named. Ondaatje published *The Collected Works of Billy the Kid* with Anansi.
10 Ibid., 62–3.
11 Steven Heighton, "Approaching 'That Perfect Edge,'" 227.
12 Michael Ondaatje, "The gate in his head," *Rat Jelly*, 62.
13 George Bowering, "Ondaatje Learning To Do," *Imaginary Hand*, 164.
14 Ibid., 164.
15 Michael Ondaatje, "Moving to the Clear," 139, 143.
16 Heighton, "Approaching 'That Perfect Edge,'" 226.
17 Michael Ondaatje, "The gate in his head," *There's a Trick with Knife*, 64.
18 Eluned Summers-Bremner, "Reading Ondaatje's Poetry," *Comparative Cultural Studies and Michael Ondaatje's Writing*, edited by Steven Tötösky de Zepetnek, 104.
19 Michael Ondaatje, "House on a Red Cliff," *Handwriting*, 67.
20 Idem, "King Kong Meets Wallace Stevens," *There's a Trick with a Knife*, 61.
21 Sam Solecki, "Nets and Chaos: The Poetry of Michael Ondaatje," 94.
22 Ondaatje, *Handwriting*, 68.
23 Idem, "Letters & Other Worlds," *There's a Trick with a Knife*, 46.
24 Idem, "Moving to the Clear," 140.
25 Idem, "An Interview with Michael Ondaatje," by Scobie and Barbour, 12.
26 Idem, "An Interview with Michael Ondaatje (1975)," 20.
27 Idem, *the man with seven toes*, 44; see Colin MacInnes, Introduction to *Sidney Nolan*, 21–2.
28 Arun Mukherjee, *Oppositional Aesthetics: Reading from a Hyphenated Space*, 99.
29 Michael Alexander, *Mrs Fraser on the Fatal Shore*, 131.
30 Beverley Curran, "Ondaatje's *The English Patient* and Altered States of Narrative," *Comparative Cultural Studies and Michael Ondaatje's Writing*, 19.
31 Elwyn Lynn, *Sidney Nolan: Myth and Imagery*, 38.
32 Ondaatje, *the man with seven toes*, 9.
33 Ibid., 13.
34 Robin Blaser, "The Practice of Outside," 278.
35 Lynn, *Sidney Nolan*, 7.
36 Ibid., 8.
37 Bryan Robertson, "Biography, and Chronology of the Pictures," 37.
38 Ondaatje, *the man with seven toes*, 23.

39 Sam Solecki, "Point Blank: Narrative in *the man with seven toes*," *Spider Blues*, 138; Lynn, *Sidney Nolan*, 43.

40 Ondaatje, "An Interview with Michael Ondaatje," by Scobie and Barbour, 12.

41 Andrew Sayers, *Sidney Nolan: The Ned Kelly Story*, 23.

42 Lynn, *Sidney Nolan*, 23.

43 Ibid., 23.

44 See Michael Ondaatje, "'The Germ of Document,'" 49–50.

45 Lynn, *Sidney Nolan*, 34.

46 Michael Ondaatje, Afterword to *Tay John*, 266–7.

47 Idem, *the man with seven toes*, 11, 13.

48 Ibid., 16.

49 Ibid., 19.

50 Ibid., 32, 31.

51 Ibid., 41.

52 John Donne, "Elegy 19," *Norton Anthology of English Literature*, 5th ed., edited by M.H. Abrams et al. (New York: Norton, 1986), 1:1084–5.

53 Ondaatje, *the man with seven toes*, 41.

54 Travis Lane, "Dream as History," review of *the man with seven toes*, by Michael Ondaatje, *The Fiddlehead* 86 (Aug.–Sept.–Oct. 1970), 159.

55 Sigmund Freud, *The Interpretation of Dreams*, 449.

56 See Tanya Lewis, "Myth-Manipulation through Dismemberment in Michael Ondaatje's *the man with seven toes*," *Studies in Canadian Literature*, 100–13.

57 Ondaatje, "An Interview with Michael Ondaatje (1975)," 22. The themes of castration, mutilation, and adultery in the desert compel critics such as Beverly Curran to read *the man with seven toes* as the precursor to the desert wanderings of *The English Patient*.

58 Lane, "Dream as History," 159.

59 Max Harris, Introduction to *Angry Penguins and Realist Painting in Melbourne in the 1940s*, 16.

60 Patrick Corbally Stourton, ed., *Songlines and Dreamings: Contemporary Australian Aboriginal Painting*, 21.

61 Ibid., 17.

62 Solecki, "Point Blank," 138.

63 In addition to the series by Nolan and Ondaatje, the Mrs Fraser story inspired a plan for an opera with music by Peter Sculthorpe, sets by Nolan, and a libretto by Patrick White intended to be performed at the opening of the Sidney Opera House. Although the project was never completed, White used the story as the basis for his acclaimed novel, *A Fringe of Leaves* (1976). A range of works also explore the Mrs Fraser story from historical and critical perspectives, including John Curtis's *Shipwreck of the Stirling Castle* (1838) and Michael Alexander's *Mrs Fraser on the Fatal Shore* (1971).

64 Ondaatje, *the man with seven toes*, 20.

65 Roslynn Haynes, *Seeking the Centre: The Australian Desert in Literature, Art and Film*, 33.

66 Note that Ondaatje gives the title "What is in the Pot" to his introduction to *The Long Poem Anthology*. Following a presentation of part of this chapter at the University of Ottawa (26 Jan. 2003), John Moss suggested to me that the name

Potter could also refer to the protagonist James Potter in Watson's *The Double Hook*.

67 Ondaatje, *the man with seven toes*, 42.
68 Ibid., 42.
69 Ibid., 42.
70 Ibid., 42.
71 Michael Ondaatje, "Interview with Michael Ondaatje," *Manna*, 21.
72 Ondaatje, "An Interview with Michael Ondaatje (1975)," 20.
73 Lynn, *Sidney Nolan*, 48.
74 Ibid., 48.
75 Ibid., 39.
76 Ondaatje, *The Collected Works of Billy the Kid*, 5.
77 Sidney Nolan, Mrs Fraser (1947), in Sidney Nolan: Landscapes and Legends, edited by Jane Clark, 41–2.
78 Lynn, *Sidney Nolan*, 29.
79 Ondaatje, "Where the Personal and the Historical Meet," 4.
80 Idem, *The Collected Works of Billy the Kid*, 5.
81 Douglas Barbour, *Michael Ondaatje*, 222.
82 See Joe Clark, *Tennessee Hill Folk*, essay by Jesse Stuart (Nashville: Vanderbilt University Press, 1972).
83 Ondaatje, *The Collected Works of Billy the Kid*, 17.
84 Barbour, *Michael Ondaatje*, 52.
85 See Ed Jewinski, *Michael Ondaatje*, 88.
86 Sam Solecki, *Ragas of Longing*, 14.
87 Ondaatje, *The Collected Works of Billy the Kid*, 21.
88 Ibid., 21.
89 Nodelman, "The Collected Photographs of Billy the Kid." 76.
90 Ondaatje, *The Collected Works of Billy the Kid*, 68.
91 Ibid., 50.
92 Michael Ondaatje, "Interview with Michael Ondaatje," *Manna*, 21.
93 Ibid., 20.
94 Ondaatje, *Billy*, 6.
95 Idem, "White Dwarfs," *Rat Jelly*, 70–1.
96 Idem, *The Collected Works of Billy the Kid*, 41.
97 T.D. MacLulich, "Ondaatje's Mechanical Boy: Portrait of the Artist as Photographer," 107.
98 John Welchman, "In and Around the 'Second Frame,'" *The Rhetoric of the Frame: Essays on the Boundaries of the Artwork*, 213.
99 Ondaatje, The Collected Works of Billy the Kid, 13.
100 Manina Jones, *That Art of Difference: 'Documentary-Collage' and English-Canadian Writing*, 74.
101 Michael Ondaatje, Afterword to "Peter," *How Do I Love Thee: Sixty Poets of Canada (and Quebec) Select and Introduce Their Favourite Poems from Their Own Work*, edited by John Robert Colombo, 149.
102 Ondaatje, *The Collected Works of Billy the Kid*, 85.
103 Ibid., 37.
104 Ibid., 23, 45, 91.

105 Stephen Scobie was the first to identify the uncredited photograph in his 1972 essay "Two Authors in Search of a Character: bp Nichol and Michael Ondaatje," 191.

106 Eadweard Muybridge, *Animals in Motion*, n.p.

107 James Sheldon, *Motion and Document – Sequence and Time: Eadweard Muybridge and Contemporary American Photography*, 15.

108 Jack Spicer, *After Lorca*, n.p.

109 See the chapters dedicated to Modernist art based on serial photography in Sheldon's *Motion and Document* and Marta Braun's *Picturing Time*.

110 Ondaatje, *The Collected Works of Billy the Kid*, n.p.

111 In an open letter to Marey published in the journal *La Nature*, Marey suggested developing "a kind of *photographic gun*, to seize the bird in ... the successive phases of the movement of its wings." The letter is quoted in Braun, *Picturing Time*, 47.

112 Michael Ondaatje, "the gate in his head," *There's a Trick with a Knife I'm Learning to Do*, 64. The photographs of the gull are reproduced in Braun, *Picturing Time*, 60, 62.

113 Braun, *Picturing Time*, 66.

114 Jed Rasula, "Spicer's Orpheus and the Emancipation of Pronouns," *Boundary 2*, 74.

115 Michael Ondaatje, *The Conversations: Walter Murch and the Art of Editing Film*, xvii.

116 Ibid., xvii.

117 MacLulich, "Ondaatje's Mechanical Boy," 108–9.

118 Nodelman, "The Collected Photographs of Billy the Kid," 70; see Ondaatje, *The Collected Works of Billy the Kid*, 27.

119 Ondaatje, "An Interview with Michael Ondaatje (1975)," 20.

120 Ibid., 16.

121 Idem, Introduction to *The Long Poem Anthology*, 15.

122 Idem, "An Interview with Michael Ondaatje (1984)," 324.

123 Barbour, *Michael Ondaatje*, 62–3.

124 Ondaatje, "An Interview with Michael Ondaatje (1975)," 26.

125 See, respectively, *The Collected Works of Billy the Kid*, 20, 90; 15; 60, 67; 99–102.

126 Ibid., 89.

127 Jones, *That Art of Difference*, 76.

128 Ondaatje has not published "silver bullet," but he mentions it in the *White Pelican* interview, 8–9.

129 Ondaatje, *Divisadero*, 16, 17.

130 Ibid., 9. Curnoe's work has enjoyed a revival in the new millennium, including a major retrospective exhibition at the Art Gallery of Ontario in the spring of 2001, entitled *Greg Curnoe: Life & Stuff*.

131 Joan Vastokas, introduction to *Worlds Apart, The Symbolic Landscapes of Tony Urquhart*, by Tony Urquhart, 7.

132 Tony Urquhart, *Box With Six Landscape Shards* (1970), in *Worlds Apart, The Symbolic Landscapes of Tony Urquhart*, 51.

133 Nichol makes this observation in a letter quoted by Stephen Scobie, "Two Authors in Search of a Character," *Spider Blues*, 205.
134 Michael Ondaatje, "What Lightning Was Like in the 1970s," *Paterson Ewen*, edited by Matthew Teitelbaum, 4.
135 The couple's son, Vincent, did not speak for his first five years but proved to be a child prodigy who composed a series of thirty poems before the age of nine, some of which Louis Dudek and F.R. Scott published in adult reviews. (Ewen incorporates one of these poems into *Portrait of Vincent*).
136 Matthew Teitelbaum, "Paterson Ewen: Comets and Other Unknowable Things," *Paterson Ewen*, edited by Matthew Teitelbaum, 51.
137 Ibid., 59.
138 Ibid., 76.
139 Ondaatje, "What Lightning Was Like in the 1970s," 3.
140 Barbara Godard, "Stretching the Story: The Canadian Story Cycle," *Open Letter* 27–71.
141 Ondaatje, "An Interview with Michael Ondaatje (1984)," 327.
142 Idem, *The Collected Works of Billy the Kid*, 20.
143 Ibid., 20.
144 Ibid., 31; Barbour, *Michael Ondaatje*, 54.
145 The chase occurs on page 92 in *Billy*. The name "Poe" is authentic, but it evokes the legacy of another great theorist and practitioner of the long poem, Edgar Allan Poe. Stuart Mackinnon's "The Intervals" is collected in Ondaatje's *The Long Poem Anthology*, 45–80.
146 Ondaatje, *The Collected Works of Billy the Kid*, n.p.
147 Idem, "Moving to the Clear," 141.
148 Idem, *The Collected Works of Billy the Kid*, 60.
149 Kieran Simpson, ed., *Canadian Who's Who*, 718. Barbour uses this quotation as an epigram to his book on Ondaatje because the poet's interest in dogs, in particular the mongrel, is one of his defining idiosyncrasies.
150 *Sons of Captain Poetry*, dir. Michael Ondaatje, Mongrel Films/Canadian Film-Makers Distribution Centre, 1970.
151 This chapbook is collected in bp Nichol, *An H in the Heart*, 220–2.
152 Ondaatje, *The Collected Works of Billy the Kid*, 81, 84.
153 Ibid., 29.
154 The Four Horsemen, "Assassin," *Live in the West*, 1974. 24 March 2006 <http://www.ubu.com/sound/4h.html>.
155 Ondaatje, *The Collected Works of Billy the Kid*, 104.
156 Ibid., 104.
157 Ibid., 104.
158 Leonard Cohen, *Beautiful Losers*, 8.
159 Ondaatje, *The Collected Works of Billy the Kid*, 105.
160 Ibid., 71.
161 Kathleen Bethell, "Reading Billy: Memory, Time, and Subjectivity in *The Collected Works of Billy the Kid*," *Studies in Canadian Literature*, 77.
162 Bowering, "Ondaatje Learning to Do," 163.
163 Ibid., 163.

164 Michael Ondaatje, review of *A Controversy of Poets*, ed. Paris Leary and Robert Kelly, *Quarry* 15, no.2 (Nov. 1965), 45.
165 George Bowering, *Errata*, 6.
166 Edward Foster, *Jack Spicer*, 25–6. Note, however, that Dennis Dennisoff sees a strong undercurrent of "Homosocial Desire and the Artificial Man in Michael Ondaatje's *The Collected Works of Billy the Kid*."
167 Jewinski, *Michael Ondaatje*, 65.
168 Ondaatje, *Leonard Cohen*, 28.
169 Leonard Cohen, *The Favourite Game*, 105.
170 Ondaatje, *Coming Through Slaughter*, n.p.; see Peter Warshall, "The Ways of Whales," 140.
171 Ondaatje, *Coming Through Slaughter*, 9.
172 Ibid., 10, 38.
173 Ibid., 131, 130.
174 Ibid., n.p.
175 Ibid., 63.
176 Barry Maxwell, "Surrealistic Aspects of Michael Ondaatje's *Coming Through Slaughter*," 102.
177 George Bowering, "A Great Northward Darkness," 8.
178 Ondaatje, *Coming Through Slaughter*, 48.
179 Ibid., 18.
180 *Pretty Baby*, dir. Louis Malle, Paramount, 1978.
181 Donald Marquis, *In Search of Buddy Bolden: First Man of Jazz*, 7.
182 Ibid., 112–26.
183 Ondaatje, "White Dwarfs," *There's a Trick with a Knife*, 68; Ondaatje, *Coming Through Slaughter*, 61.
184 Ondaatje, *Coming Through Slaughter*, 55.
185 Ibid., 159.
186 Stephen Scobie, "*Coming Through Slaughter*: Fictional Magnets and Spider's Webbs," 12. Sidney Nolan is also a fan of Rousseau and claims that his Ned Kelly series is composed of "Kelly's own words, and Rousseau, and sunlight" (Sidney Nolan, qtd. in Colin MacInnes, Introduction to *Sidney Nolan*, 30).
187 Ondaatje, *Coming Through Slaughter*, 134.
188 Ibid., 136.
189 Ibid., 134.
190 Ibid., 135.
191 Hillger, *Not Needing All the Words*, 54–5.
192 Ondaatje, *Coming Through Slaughter*, 56.
193 Ibid., 51.
194 Ibid., 64.
195 Ibid., 64.
196 Michael Greenstein, *Third Solitudes*, 129.
197 Ondaatje, *Coming Through Slaughter*, 127.
198 Ibid., 89.
199 Ibid., 8.
200 Ibid., 10.

201 Ondaatje, *Leonard Cohen*, 33.
202 Bart Testa, "He Did Not Work Here for Long: Michael Ondaatje in the Cinema," 155.
203 Derek Finkle, "From Page to Screen: Michael Ondaatje as Filmmaker," 171.
204 Ondaatje, *Coming Through Slaughter*, 72.
205 Ibid., 110.
206 Ondaatje, "White Dwarfs," *There's a Trick with a Knife*, 69.
207 Ondaatje, *Coming Through Slaughter*, 78.
208 Ibid., 78.
209 Ibid., 91.
210 Ibid., 92, 91.
211 Ibid., 92.
212 Hutcheon, *The Canadian Postmodern*, 48.
213 This song was brought to my attention by Douglas Barbour in a private e-mail, 27 March 2001.
214 Ondaatje, *Coming Through Slaughter*, 139.
215 Ibid., 94, 38.
216 Maxwell, "Surrealistic Aspects," 108.
217 Ondaatje, *Coming Through Slaughter*, 93–4.
218 Ibid., 110–111.
219 Ibid., 32.
220 Ibid., 32–3.
221 Ibid., 160.
222 Ibid., 83.
223 Ibid., 148.
224 Ibid., 17.
225 Blaser, "The Practice of Outside," 278.
226 Solecki, *Ragas of Longing*, 20; Ondaatje, "An Interview with Michael Ondaatje (1984)," 324.
227 Ondaatje, "An Interview with Michael Ondaatje (1975)," 26.
228 Idem, "The Germ of Document," 50.
229 Ondaatje, *Coming Through Slaughter*, 99.
230 Bowering, "A Great Northward Darkness," 10.
231 Stephen Scobie, "Fictional Magnets," 5–6.
232 Ondaatje, *Leonard Cohen*, 49.
233 Hutcheon, *The Canadian Postmodern*, 84.
234 See Ondaatje, *Coming Through Slaughter*, 17, 105; ibid., 11, 82.
235 Ibid., 57.
236 Heighton, "Approaching 'That Perfect Edge,'" 241.
237 Ondaatje, *Coming Through Slaughter*, 82.
238 Smaro Kamboureli, "The Poetics of Geography in Michael Ondaatje's *Coming Through Slaughter*," 119.
239 Ibid., 119.
240 Ondaatje, *Coming Through Slaughter*, 141.
241 Robert Kroetsch, "For Play and Entrance: The Contemporary Canadian Long Poem," *The Lovely Treachery of Words*, 120.
242 Solecki, *Ragas of Longing*, 70.

243 Ondaatje, *Coming Through Slaughter*, 144.
244 Siemerling, *Discoveries of the Other*, 116.
245 Sally Bachner, "'He Had Pushed His Imagination into Buddy's Brain,' or, How to Escape History in *Coming Through Slaughter*," 218.
246 Ibid., 218.
247 Michael Ondaatje, "The Ondaatje Myth," 15.
248 Gary Kamiya, "Painting the Eyes of a God," review of *Anil's Ghost*, by Michael Ondaatje, 4 October 2000 <www.galon.com/books/2000/04/25/Ondaatje/index.html>.

CHAPTER FOUR

1 George Bowering, *A Short Sad Book*, 140.
2 Idem, *Baseball, a poem in the magic number 9*, in *George Bowering Selected*, 19–31.
3 Roy Miki, "Editor's Note," *George Bowering Selected*, 233.
4 Eva-Marie Kröller, *George Bowering: Bright Circles of Colour*, 115.
5 Bowering, Angela, George Bowering, David Bromige, and Michael Matthews, *Piccolo Mondo: A Novel of Youth in 1961 As Seen Somewhat Later*, 52. Bowering discusses his early prose style in a 1976 interview with Caroline Bayard and Jack David in *Out-Posts*, 81.
6 See Kröller, *George Bowering: Bright Circles of Colour*, 116.
7 Bowering explains in one of his versions of the *Tish* story that "when a bunch of us tyros was considering starting a monthly poetry newsletter, our regular mentor, Warren Tallman, cautioned caution, but Duncan, a guest in Tallman's house, told us to go ahead. What'll we call it, we wondered. Should we call it something like *The Vancouver Poetry Newsletter*? In the doorway between the front hall and the living room at 2527 West 37th Avenue, Duncan said, 'Call it *Tish*'" (George Bowering, *A Magpie Life*, 209).
8 Ibid., 26.
9 Bowering, "Vancouver as Postmodern Poetry," *Vancouver: Representing the Postmodern City*, edited by Paul Delany, 121.
10 Bowering, *A Magpie Life*, 27.
11 Ibid., 72.
12 *Poetry and the Colonized Mind* is a monument to the cultural monomania and isolationism it professes to deplore in American society, and is so entirely unconcerned with poetry that it manages to discuss the *Tish* movement without citing a single poem from founding editor Fred Wah or later editors such as Daphne Buckle (Marlatt). Richardson directs his tirade primarily at Bowering and Davey, but he accuses the entire group of espousing a "U.S. individualistic anarchism" that threatens Canadian traditions (29). Richardson seems as unaware of the irony involved in calling anarchism a national trait as he is of the fact that, in George Woodcock, the University of British Columbia already had a prominent anarchist in its employ. Woodcock became the first editor of *Canadian Literature*, but the journal certainly cannot be classified as anarchist. See also Robin Mathews, "In Search of a Canadian Poetic," 31–2.
13 David Dawson, *Tish* 20 (August 1963), 5.

14 Frank Davey, "Theory and Practice in the Black Mountain Poets" (Ph.D. diss., University of Michigan at Ann Arbor, 1968).
15 Bowering, *A Magpie Life*, 193.
16 Ibid., 201; George Bowering, *Imaginary Hand*, 163.
17 Bowering, "Interview," *Out-Posts*, 81.
18 There was Canadian literature on the UBC syllabus, but mainly the poetry of an older generation: Carman, Lampman, D.C. Scott. See also Daphne Marlatt, "Interview: There's This and This Connexion," 28.
19 Bowering, "Interview," *Out-Posts*, 81.
20 Idem, *Curious*, n.p.
21 Idem, *A Magpie Life*, 200.
22 See Roy Miki, "Was It a Real Book or Was It Just Made Up?" Afterword to *Sticks & Stones*, by George Bowering, 55.
23 Talonbooks re-issued *Sticks & Stones* in 1989, including the original companion drawings by Gordon Payne and the preface by Creeley, but no large-scale printing occurred before then.
24 Bowering, "Interview," *Out-Posts*, 90.
25 George Bowering, *Points on the Grid*, 66.
26 George Bowering, *West Window*, 141.
27 Idem, preface to *The Catch*, 9.
28 Idem, "Brown Globe," *In the Flesh*, 16.
29 R.M. Rilke, *Duino Elegies*, 5.
30 Roy Miki, "Editor's Note," *George Bowering Selected*, 232.
31 George Bowering, "Statement," *The New Long Poem Anthology*, edited by Sharon Thesen, 351.
32 In the Bayard and David interview, Bowering explains: "That long poem business, of starting the magazine, was naturally contemporaneous with my wanting to write long poems myself. Saying, OK, I've written all these lyrics, I've got to do something else" (92).
33 Bowering, "Statement," *The New Long Poem Anthology*, 351.
34 Bowering, "Interview," *Out-Posts*, 85.
35 See Bowering, "Statement," *The New Long Poem Anthology*, 351.
36 Bowering, *In the Flesh*, 8.
37 Bowering, "Statement," *The New Long Poem Anthology*, 351.
38 Idem, "Vox Crapulous (alternative title: J. Edgar Hoover)," *The Man in Yellow Boots*, 32.
39 Idem, *The Man in Yellow Boots*, 98.
40 Idem, *Seventy-One Poems for People*, 67–90.
41 See "Telephone Metaphysic" and its illustration (Bowering, *Sticks*, 22–3).
42 This citation from Bowering's unpublished papers derives from Kröller (*Bright*, 36). For all further citations from Bowering's unpublished letters, I am endebted to Miki's bibliography, *A Record of Writing*.
43 Bowering, *The Man in Yellow Boots*, 38, 52. See also George Bowering, "The Good Prospects," *100 Poets Against the War*, ed. Todd Swift (Cambridge, UK: Salt Publishing, 2003), 15.
44 The title comes from a description of a wheel in a Greg Curnoe painting in "Elegy Six" of Bowering's *Kerrisdale Elegies*. One of the many Curnoe wheels appears on

the cover of the second edition of *The New Long Poem Anthology*, ed. Sharon Thesen.

45 George Bowering, *Another Mouth*, n.p.
46 Bowering, "Interview," *Out-Posts*, 88.
47 Roy Kiyooka, "Pacific Windows," *Capilano Review* 2, no. 3 (fall 1990), n.p.
48 Bowering, *A Short Sad Book*, 167.
49 Jack Spicer, "Seven Poems for the Vancouver Festival," *The Collected Books of Jack Spicer*, 259.
50 Bowering, *Baseball, a poem in the magic number 9*, in *George Bowering Selected*, edited by Roy Miki, 29.
51 Ibid., 25.
52 For Bowering on the literary aspects of baseball, see *Imaginary Hand*, 47; idem, *A Magpie Life*, 99–107.
53 Bowering, *Imaginary Hand*, 165.
54 The back cover of *Smoking Mirror* shows Bowering admiring one of bissett's performance poetry recordings.
55 Bowering, "Interview," *Out-Posts*, 98.
56 Miki, *A Record of Writing*, 21.
57 Bowering, *A Short Sad Book*, 26.
58 Idem, "Interview," *Out-Posts*, 85.
59 Idem, *A Magpie Life*, 52.
60 See Miki, *A Record of Writing*, 13; M.H. Abrams, *A Glossary of Literary Terms*, 153.
61 For Bowering's first-person account of this beating, see George Bowering, "Support Your Local Police," *Seventy-One Poems for People*, 32–36. For a satirical version, see Angela Bowering et al., *Piccolo Mondo*, 138–9.
62 See Stendhal, *Le rouge et le noir* (Paris: Garnier, 1960), 76. See also Michael Ondaatje, *The English Patient*, 91.
63 Bowering, *Mirror on the Floor*, 62.
64 Ibid., 62.
65 Ibid., 63.
66 John Harris, *George Bowering and His Works*, 29.
67 "Sousterre" eventually appeared in *Smoking Mirror*, 39–53.
68 McClelland and Stewart Papers, McMaster University, qtd. in Miki, *A Record of Writing*, 48.
69 Ibid., 48.
70 Bowering, "Interview," *Out-Posts*, 92.
71 Idem, *The Concrete Island: Montreal Poems 1967–71*, n.p.; idem, *Another Mouth*.
72 Idem, "Interview," *Out-Posts*, 84.
73 Kröller, *George Bowering*, 65.
74 Fred Wah, "Bowering's Lines," 102.
75 Bowering, *Errata*, 34.
76 Johanne Saul, "Displacement and Self-Representation: Theorizing Contemporary Canadian Biotexts," 259–272.
77 Bowering, *A Magpie Life*, 37.
78 Idem, "bp Nichol on the Train," *Imaginary Hand*, 194.

79 Idem, *The Concrete Island*, n.p.
80 Idem, *Autobiology*, 103.
81 Kröller, *George Bowering*, 66.
82 Leonard Cohen, "Lines from My Grandfather's Journal," *The Spice-Box of Earth*, 80–6.
83 Bowering, "Interview," *Out-Posts*, 88.
84 Idem, *Autobiology*, 75.
85 Ibid., 7.
86 Ibid., 7.
87 Kröller, *Bright*, 66.
88 Bowering, *Autobiology*, 17–8.
89 Idem, "Dance to a Measure," *Imaginary Hand*, 141.
90 Bowering, *Autobiology*, 8.
91 Ibid., 8.
92 Ibid., 9.
93 Bowering, "Interview," *Out-Posts*, 90. These views on art are likely an application of Olson's opinions. See Charles Olson, "Equal, That Is, to the Real Itself," *Poetics of the New American Poetry*, 177.
94 Bowering, "Interview," *Out-Posts*, 87.
95 Robin Blaser, Introduction to *Selected Poems: Particular Accidents*, by George Bowering, 9.
96 Bowering, *Autobiology*, 23.
97 Ibid., 28.
98 Ibid., 80.
99 Ibid., 20.
100 Idem, *The Catch*, 51.
101 The 1974 edition of Spicer's *After Lorca* employs a similar design.
102 Kröller, *George Bowering*, 69.
103 Bowering, *Autobiology*, 38, 67; idem, *A Short Sad Book*, 151; idem, *Harry's Fragments*, 61, 115.
104 Bowering, *Autobiology*, 34; idem, *A Short Sad Book*, 87.
105 Idem, *Autobiology*, 71.
106 Gertrude Stein, *A Long Gay Book*, 152–253.
107 Bowering, *Autobiology*, 39.
108 Idem, *Allophanes*, n.p.
109 Idem, *Autobiology*, 95, 96.
110 Ibid., 101–2.
111 George Bowering, "Session 4: Personal Interview," by Roy Miki, 11 May 1988, cited in Miki, *A Record of Writing*, 36.
112 Bowering, "Session 2: Personal Interview," by Roy Miki, 9 March 1988, cited in Miki, *A Record of Writing*, 34.
113 Idem, "Interview," *Out-Posts*, 93.
114 Idem, "The Painted Window," 24.
115 Ibid., 24–5.
116 Bowering, *Errata*, 4.
117 Idem, "The Painted Window," 25.
118 Ibid., 25.

119 Ibid., 28, 32, 30, 28.
120 Ibid., 29.
121 Ibid., 30.
122 Ibid., 35.
123 Robin Blaser, Introduction to *Selected Poems: Particular Accidents*, by George Bowering, 15.
124 Bowering, *A Short Sad Book*, 134.
125 Ibid., 134–5.
126 Ibid., 134.
127 Ibid., 166. The critic Bowering mentions is perhaps D.G. Jones in *Butterfly on Rock: A Study of Themes and Images in Canadian Literature*.
128 Bowering, *A Short Sad Book*, 44.
129 Ibid., 132. The index attempts to dissociate "Al" from Al Purdy by making the poet "Al Purdy" a walk-on character who appears only on page 44.
130 Ibid., 71–2.
131 Ibid., 185.
132 Ibid., 184–5.
133 Bowering, "A Great Northward Darkness," 3.
134 Idem, "Sheila Watson, Trickster," *The Mask in Place*, 105.
135 Idem, *Allophanes*, n.p; Daphne Marlatt, *What Matters*, n.p.
136 Paul Ricoeur, "The Narrative Function," 278; Bowering, "A Great Northward Darkness," 6.
137 Bowering, *A Short Sad Book*, 74.
138 Ibid., 39.
139 Ibid., 174.
140 Ibid., n.p.
141 Ibid., n.p.
142 Ibid., 95.
143 Ibid., 15.
144 Ibid., 15.
145 Ibid., 15.
146 Ibid., 16.
147 Ibid., 52.
148 Kröller, *George Bowering*, 56.
149 Bowering, *A Short Sad Book*, 54.
150 Ibid., 91.
151 Richardson, *Poetry and the Colonized Mind: Tish*, 73; Bowering, "Interview," *Out-Posts*, 93.
152 Idem, *A Short Sad Book*, 113.
153 Ibid., 114–15.
154 Ibid., 163.
155 Bowering has produced popular histories such as *Bowering's BC: A Swashbuckling History* (1996), *Egotists and Autocrats: The Prime Ministers of Canada* (1999), and *Stone Country: An Unauthorized History of Canada* (2003).
156 Bowering, *A Short Sad Book*, 154.
157 Stein, *A Long Gay Book*, 153.

158 An encrypted reference to the writer Paul Claudel (1868–1955), who was known for his renderings of conflicting human passions. He was also the brother of the sculptor Camille Claudel.

159 Ulla Dydo, *A Stein Reader*, 152.

160 Blaser, Introduction to *Selected Poems* by George Bowering, 16–7.

161 Note that Stein herself does not believe in repetition: "There is the important question of repetition and is there any such thing. Is there repetition or is there insistence. I am inclined to believe that there is no such thing as repetition" (Gertrude Stein, "Portraits and Repetition," 99).

162 George Bowering, "14 Plums," *Capilano Review*, 101.

163 Idem, "Session 15," quoted in Miki, *Record*, 85.

164 Bowering, *Allophanes*, n.p.

165 Kröller, *George Bowering*, 54, 55.

166 Bowering, "Interview," *Out-Posts*, 88.

167 Idem, "No Solitudes," *The Concrete Island*, n.p.

168 Kröller, *George Bowering*, 55.

169 Ibid., 62.

170 See Greg Curnoe, *Canada* (Ottawa: National Gallery of Canada, 1976), 47.

171 Kröller, *George Bowering*, 64.

172 Bowering, "Uncle Louis," *West Window*, 127.

173 Bowering, "14 Plums," 88.

174 Blaser, Introduction to *Selected Poems*, by George Bowering, 14–5.

175 Bowering, *A Short Sad Book*, 26.

176 Ibid., 33.

177 Ibid., 58.

178 Ibid., 92.

179 Ibid., 101.

180 Ibid., 103.

181 Ibid., 52.

182 Ibid., 139.

183 Ibid., 16, 95.

184 Ibid., 164.

185 This citation from the Bowering Papers in the National library is quoted in Miki, *Record*, 34.

186 Bowering, *A Short Sad Book*, 89.

187 Ibid., 81.

188 Ibid., 140.

189 Bowering, *A Magpie Life*, 51.

190 Olson, "Projective Verse," 153.

191 Ibid., 148.

192 Ibid., 152.

193 Idem, "Equal, That Is, to the Real Itself," 181.

194 Olson appears in *A Short Sad Book* to debate his "special view of history" with that of historian and Confederation poet Charles G.D. Roberts (96–7).

195 Trent Keough, "The International Politics of Existentialism: From Sartre, to Olson, to Bowering," 49.

196 *Harry's Fragments* would make an interesting subject for further analysis. It
extrapolates from the fragments of Heraclitus in somewhat the same way that
Carson does from the fragments of Stesichoros. But Bowering's novel is fundamentally a detective story, where the typically male figure is "a core of rationality
or logic stepping into a world of chaos or the unknown anyway, stepping into the
wild logos and sorting it out, bringing order" (87). Nonetheless, it stresses the
maze of lyrical detours and puzzles.
197 Kröller, *George Bowering*, 99.
198 Bowering, *Errata*, 61.
199 Michael Ondaatje, Introduction to *From Ink Lake*, xvi.
200 See William Fenton, *Re-Writing the Past: History and Origin in Howard
O'Hagan, Jack Hodgins, George Bowering and Chris Scott*, 131.
201 Glenn Deer, "The Politics of Modern Literary Innovation: A Rhetorical Perspective," 371.
202 Russell Brown, "Words, Places, Craft: Bowering's Critical Voice," 33.
203 Marlatt, "Interview: There's This and This Connexion," 30.

CHAPTER FIVE

1 Daphne Marlatt, *Ana Historic*, 31.
2 Daphne Marlatt, *Readings from the Labyrinth*, 1.
3 George Bowering, "Language Women: Post-anecdotal Writing in Canada," 103,
105.
4 Fred Wah, Introduction to *Net Work*, by Daphne Marlatt, 8.
5 Daphne Marlatt, "Given this Body: An Interview with Daphne Marlatt," 35.
6 Ibid., 55.
7 Marlatt, *Readings from the Labyrinth*, 145.
8 Sabrina Reed, "'*Against* the Source': Daphne Marlatt's Revision of Charles
Olson," *Studies in Canadian Literature*, 133.
9 Marlatt, "Given this Body," 59.
10 Idem, *Readings from the Labyrinth*, 15.
11 Idem, *What Matters: Writing 1968–70*, 23.
12 Idem, "Given this Body," 87–8.
13 Ibid., 49. See also Jack Silver, "Moving into Winter," 90–101.
14 Marlatt, *What Matters*, 35.
15 Christina Cole, "Daphne Marlatt as Penelope, Weaver of Words: A Feminist
Reading of *Steveston*," *Open Letter*, 7.
16 Miriam Nichols, "Subjects of Experience: Post-Cognitive Subjectivity in the Work
of bpNichol and Daphne Marlatt," *Studies in Canadian Literature*, 116.
17 Ibid., 112.
18 Deborah O, "Coded Spaces/Signifying Bodies," *Open Letter*, 76.
19 Marlatt, *Frames of a Story*, 1.
20 Ibid., 2.
21 Andersen, *The Snow Queen*, 234.
22 See Garry Morse's comparison of Marlatt and Bowering in "From 'Take Out: An
All You Can Eat Smorgasbord of Vancouver Poetics,'" *West Coast Line*, 87–90.

23 Marlatt, "Given this Body," 40.
24 Idem, *Frames of a Story*, 4.
25 Idem, "Given this Body," 37.
26 Bowering, "Language Women," 102; Cole, "Daphne Marlatt as Penelope," 6.
27 Marlatt, "Given this Body," 44.
28 Idem, *Frames of a Story*, 37, 5, 38–9, 37.
29 Robert Lecker, "Daphne Marlatt's Poetry," 59.
30 Marlatt, *Frames of a Story*, 5.
31 Idem, "Given this Body," 46.
32 Idem, *Frames of a Story*, 39.
33 Idem, "Interview: There's This and This Connexion," 29.
34 Idem, *Frames of a Story*, 7.
35 Douglas Barbour, *Daphne Marlatt and Her Works*, 19.
36 Charles Olson, "Projective Verse," *Poetics of the New American Poetry*, 156.
37 Caroline Rosenthal, "'You Can't Even Imagine?': Monstrous Possibilities of Female Identity in Daphne Marlatt's *Ana Historic*," 67.
38 Marlatt, *Frames of a Story*, 27.
39 Ibid., 28.
40 Ibid., 10.
41 Ibid., 15.
42 Ibid., 29.
43 Julie Beddoes, "Mastering the Mother Tongue: Reading Frank Davey Reading Daphne Marlatt's *How Hug a Stone*," 87; Nichols, "Subjects of Experience," 113; Susan Knutson, *Narrative in the Feminine: Daphne Marlatt and Nicole Brossard*, 53–65.
44 Lecker, "Daphne Marlatt's Poetry," 56.
45 Daphne Marlatt, *This Tremor Love Is*, 28.
46 Lecker, "Daphne Marlatt's Poetry," 56.
47 George Bowering, *The Catch*, 9.
48 Susan Knutson, "Daphne Marlatt and Nicole Brossard: Writing Metanarrative in the Feminine," 29.
49 Marlatt, *Readings from the Labyrinth*, 60.
50 De Lauretis, "Desire in Narrative," 119.
51 Ibid., 109.
52 Ibid., 109.
53 Marlatt, *Frames of a Story*, 43.
54 Ibid., 46.
55 Ibid., 47.
56 Idem, "Interview: There's This and This Connexion," 32.
57 Idem, *Frames of a Story*, 48.
58 Ibid., 48.
59 Ibid., 50.
60 Marlatt, "Given this Body," 50.
61 Idem, *Frames of a Story*, 52.
62 Ibid., 62.
63 Ibid., 62.

64 Ibid., 62.
65 Hans Christian Andersen, *The Snow Queen*, trans. R.P. Keigwin (New York: Atheneum, 1968), 94.
66 Marlatt, "Given this Body," 40–1.
67 Marlatt, *Frames of a Story*, 63.
68 Ibid., 63.
69 Ibid., 63.
70 Ibid., 63.
71 Marlatt, *Ana Historic*, 152.
72 Idem, *What Matters*, n.p.
73 Idem, *Ana Historic*, 126, 125.
74 Idem, "The Measure of the Sentence," 90.
75 Idem, "Given this Body," 36,
76 Ibid., 36.
77 Marlatt, *Readings from the Labyrinth*, 55.
78 Idem, *How Hug a Stone*, 184.
79 Idem, "Given this Body," 80.
80 Idem, *How Hug a Stone*, 131.
81 Ibid., 135.
82 Ibid., 182.
83 Ibid., 184.
84 Daphne Marlatt, "Musing with Mothertongue," 28.
85 Marlatt, *How Hug a Stone*, 131.
86 Ibid., 139.
87 Lecker, "Daphne Marlatt's Poetry," 65.
88 Roy Kiyooka, *Pear Tree Pomes*, in *Pacific Windows: Collected Poems of Roy K. Kiyooka*, 199.
89 Kiyooka, *Pear Tree Pomes*, in *Pacific Windows*, 196.
90 Marlatt, *Reading from the Labyrinth*, 202.
91 Ibid., 202.
92 Marlatt, *Zócalo*, 1.
93 Sigmund Freud, *The Interpretation of Dreams*, 57.
94 Marlatt, "Given this Body," 47.
95 Idem, "Second Thoughts: What I'd Be If I Were Not a Writer?" *Brick*, 28; see also Marlatt, "Given this Body," 77.
96 Marlatt, *Zócalo*, 6.
97 Ibid., 6.
98 Ibid., 6–7.
99 Wah, Introduction to *Net Work*, 14.
100 In her choice of setting, Marlatt may be responding to a 1955 lyric by her creative writing teacher, Earle Birney, entitled "Six-Sided Square: Actopan." The lyric is constructed as a rather condescending dialogue between a worldly poet and an inquiring "Lady." It depicts aspects of a typical *zócalo* and is framed on the page by a hexagonal outline (Earle Birney, "Six-Sided Square: Actopan," in *The Collected Poems of Earle Birney* [Toronto: McClelland & Stewart, 1975], 2:11).
101 Marlatt, *Zócalo*, 8.
102 Ibid., 34.

103 Ibid., 34.

104 Marlatt, "The Measure of the Sentence," 91.

105 Idem, *Zócalo*, 34.

106 Ibid., 34.

107 Ibid., 10.

108 Nichols, "Subjects of Experience," 113–14.

109 Marlatt, *Zócalo*, 10; Nichols, "Subjects of Experience," 113.

110 Marlatt, *Zócalo*, 10–1.

111 Ibid., 27.

112 Ibid., 11.

113 Ibid., 22.

114 Ibid., 44.

115 Marlatt, "Impossible Portraiture," *This Tremor Love Is*, 97; idem, *Readings from the Labyrinth*, 24.

116 Later the woman asserts her preference for her own medium: "Do you want to use the camera, he asks, offering her what he is here for. No, she waves the guide-book, I'll stick with this" (Marlatt, *Zócalo*, 45).

117 Ibid., 40–1.

118 Ibid., 41.

119 Ibid., 41, 42.

120 Freud, *The Interpretation of Dreams*, 471, 492, 471.

121 Marlatt, *Zócalo*, 43.

122 Ibid., 43.

123 Ibid., 43.

124 Ibid., 43.

125 Freud, *The Interpretation of Dreams*, 490.

126 Marlatt, *Zócalo*, 44.

127 Ondaatje, *The Collected Works of Billy the Kid*, 21; George Bowering, "Frame," *In the Flesh*, 42.

128 Marlatt, *Zócalo*, 44–5.

129 Ibid., 45.

130 Ibid., 45.

131 Ibid., 46.

132 Ibid., 46.

133 Ibid., 47.

134 Idem, *Frames of a Story*, 47.

135 Idem, *Zócalo*, 48–9.

136 Ibid., 50.

137 Ibid., 57, 56.

138 Ibid., 56.

139 Ibid., 56.

140 Ibid., 56.

141 Ibid., 58, 59.

142 Ibid., 59.

143 Ibid., 59.

144 Ibid., 59.

145 Ibid., 60.

146 *Webster's New Collegiate Dictionary*, 8th ed., s.v. "Meridian."
147 Laurie Ricou, "Phyllis Webb, Daphne Marlatt and Similitude," *A Mazing Space*, 207.
148 Marlatt, *Zócalo*, 61.
149 Ibid., 62.
150 Ibid., 62.
151 Ibid., 47, 40.
152 Ibid., 62.
153 Jeff Derksen, "Sites Taken As Signs: Place, the Open Text, and Enigma in New Vancouver Writing," *Vancouver: Representing the Postmodern City*, 156.
154 Marlatt, *Zócalo*, 62.
155 Ibid., 63.
156 Ibid., 64.
157 Ibid., 43.
158 Ibid., 66.
159 Ibid., 66.
160 Ibid., 68.
161 Ibid., 68.
162 Ibid., 68.
163 Ibid., 68.
164 Ibid., 73.
165 Ibid., 18.
166 Ibid., 74.
167 Marlatt, *Ana Historic*, 150.
168 Ibid., 47.
169 Ibid., 139, n.p.
170 Ibid., 59, 16.
171 Ibid., 29.
172 Ibid., 31.
173 Ibid., 48.
174 Idem, *Readings from the Labyrinth*, 26.
175 Keith Green and Jill LeBihan, "The Speaking Object: Daphne Marlatt's Pronouns and Lesbian Poetics," 432.
176 Marlatt, *Readings from the Labyrinth*, 116.
177 Ibid., 116.
178 Marlatt, *What Matters*, 43.
179 Idem, *Readings from the Labyrinth*, 125.
180 Annette Lönnecke, "Postmodern Canadian Autobiography: Daphne Marlatt's *How Hug a Stone* and Michael Ondaatje's *Running in the Family*," 45.
181 Consider, for example, the romantic misadventures of the history professor Jim Dixon in Kingsley Amis's *Lucky Jim*. Ondaatje mentions in endnote 113 of chapter three that he was writing against the style of Amis's novel, but Marlatt suggests an alternative to its plot, as well as to its portrait of Margaret, who has "cracked up" (Kingsley Amis, *Lucky Jim* [1953; reprint. New York: Viking, 1969], 12).
182 Marlatt, *Ana Historic*, 140.
183 Ibid., 31.

184 Ibid., 9.
185 Ibid., 9.
186 Ibid., 10.
187 Heather Zwicker, "Daphne Marlatt's 'Ana Historic': Queering the Postcolonial Nation," 170–1.
188 Marlatt, *Ana Historic*, 17.
189 Ibid., 25.
190 Ibid., 52, 82.
191 Ibid., 50.
192 Ibid., 49.
193 Ibid., 59.
194 Ibid., 56.
195 Ibid., 10.
196 Ibid., 141.
197 Ibid., 141.
198 Ibid., 141.
199 Ibid., 141, 142.
200 Ibid., 131.
201 Ibid., 142.
202 Leonard Cohen, *Beautiful Losers*, 17.
203 Ibid., 186.
204 Ibid., 186, 187.
205 Marlatt, *Ana Historic*, n.p.
206 Ibid., 67.
207 Anne Carson, *Eros the Bittersweet*, 10.
208 Marlatt, *Ana Historic*, 48–9.
209 Marlatt describes this kind of conversion as a "lyric strategy: Take words at 'face value' in their idiomatic currency, and, through an investigation of their sources and cognates, subvert their negative meaning, trace an other linguistic history that generates affirming ones" (Marlatt, *Readings from the Labyrinth*, 167).
210 Ibid., 46.
211 Idem, *Ana Historic*, 17.
212 Ibid., 90.
213 Marlatt, *Readings from the Labyrinth*, 117.
214 Ibid., 10.
215 Marlatt, "Dorothy Black Lectures," University of British Columbia, Vancouver, 14–15 February 2000.
216 Idem, "Eratic/Erotic Narrative: Syntax and Mortality in Robin Blaser's 'Image Nations,'" *The Recovery of the Public World: Essays on Poetics in Honour of Robin Blaser*, edited by Charles Watts and Edward Byrne, 98.
217 Idem, *Ana Historic*, 37.
218 Idem, *Readings from the Labyrinth*, 37.
219 Ibid., 58.
220 *Webster's New Collegiate Dictionary*, 8th ed., s.v. "Anacoluthon."
221 Rosenthal, "'You Can't Even Imagine,'" *Narrative Deconstructions*, 73.
222 Marlatt, *Readings from the Labyrinth*, 58.
223 *Encarta Electronic Encyclopedia*, 1998 ed., s.v. "Anabaptists."

224 Peter Dickinson, "Towards a Transnational, Translational Feminist Poetics: Lesbian Fiction/Theory in Canada and Quebec," 131–55.

225 Jun Ling Khoo, "Inter-translation / *Transformation* in Nicole Brossard and Daphne Marlatt's 'Mauve' and 'Character / Jeu de letters,'" 217–28.

226 Dickinson explores word plays that link Ana's name with anecdotes, analogies, psychoanalysis, and its gendered impact on historiography – the "Ana Hysteric" (146). Marlatt mobilizes these tools toward an analytical form of theory fiction. Dickinson, *Here is Queer*, 154, 155.

227 Marlatt, *Ana Historic*, 45.

228 Ibid., 45.

229 Ibid., 46.

230 Ibid., 49.

231 Ibid., 148; see also 88.

232 Carson, *Eros the Bittersweet*, 152.

233 Marlatt, *Ana Historic*, 152.

234 Ibid., 152.

235 Idem, *Frames of a Story*, 50.

236 Idem, *Ana Historic*, 152.

237 Idem, *Frames of a Story*, 52.

238 Green and LeBihan, "The Speaking Object," 432.

239 Marlatt, *Ana Historic*, 129.

240 Green and LeBihan, "The Speaking Object," 441.

241 Daphne Marlatt, "The recent," *Vancouver Poems*, n.p.

242 Idem, *Ana Historic*, n.p.

243 George Bowering, *A Short Sad Book*, 174.

244 Gillian Whitlock, "White Diasporas: Joan (and Ana) Make History," 98.

245 Green and LeBihan, "The Speaking Object," 437.

246 Ibid., 436.

247 Daphne Marlatt, "Between Continuity and Difference: An Interview with Daphne Marlatt," *Beyond Tish*, 106.

248 Glen Lowry, "Cultural Citizenship and Writing Post-Colonial Vancouver: Daphne Marlatt's *Ana Historic* and Wayde Compton's *Bluesprint*," 27.

249 Knutson, "Daphne Marlatt and Nicole Brossard," 29.

250 Marlatt, *Ana Historic*, 90.

251 Ibid., 150.

252 Marlatt, *Taken*, 95.

253 Ibid., 129.

254 Ibid., 130.

255 Ibid., 130.

256 Marlatt, "History and Place: An Interview with Daphne Marlatt," by Sue Kossew, *Canadian Literature*, 49–50.

257 Zwicker, "Daphne Marlatt's 'Ana Historic,'" 166.

258 Marlatt, *Ana Historic*, 24.

259 Teresa de Lauretis, "Feminist Studies/Critical Studies: Issues, Terms, and Contexts," 14.

260 Marlatt, "Musing with Mothertongue," 28.

CHAPTER SIX

1 Anne Carson, "The *Matrix* Interview," by Mary di Michele, *Matrix*, 10.
2 Idem, "A Talk with Anne Carson," 19–20.
3 I published an early version of this chapter as "'Dazzling Hybrids': The Poetry of Anne Carson" in *Canadian Literature* 166 (autumn 2000): 17–41.
4 Manina Jones, *That Art of Difference*, 14.
5 Daphne Marlatt, "A Poignant Critique in a Playful Mixing of Genres," 41–3. The Ondaatje blurb appears on the front cover of Carson's *Autobiography of Red*.
6 Michael Ondaatje, "An Interview with Michael Ondaatje (1984)," 329. I am fully aware that in discussing the serial novel I am contributing to this categorizing phenomenon. However, as I have demonstrated, there is considerable flexibility in the form.
7 Anne Carson, "Readings from *Short Talks*; *Men in the Off Hours*; and *The Beauty of the Husband*," University of British Columbia, Vancouver, 2 November 2001.
8 Carson clarified the publication history of *Short Talks* for me in a private email, 1 February 2002.
9 Sam Solecki, *Ragas of Longing*, 14.
10 Guy Davenport, Introduction to *Glass, Irony and God*, x, ix.
11 Ibid., x.
12 Daphne Marlatt, "On Salvaging: A Conversation with Daphne Marlatt," 33.
13 Anne Carson, "Mimnermos: The Brainsex Paintings," *Plainwater*, 3–26.
14 Jeff Hamilton, "This Cold Hectic Dawn and I," 117.
15 Carson, "Interview," *Matrix*, 12–13.
16 Jeff Hamilton, "This Cold Hectic Dawn and I," 114.
17 Anne Carson, "A Talk with Anne Carson," 19.
18 Ibid., 19.
19 Carson, "Mimnermos," *Plainwater*, 4.
20 Leonard Cohen, *Beautiful Losers*, 182.
21 Carson, "Mimnermos," *Plainwater*, 12.
22 Ibid., 12.
23 Carson, *Autobiography of Red*, 93.
24 Idem, "Mimnermos," *Plainwater*, 12.
25 Ibid., 12.
26 For more on Muybridge's pseudonym, see Gordon Hendricks, *Eadweard Muybridge: Father of the Motion Picture*, 34.
27 Carson, "Mimnermos," *Plainwater*, 12.
28 B. Renner, "Anne Carson's *Autobiography of Red* and 'Mimnermos: The Brainsex Paintings,'" review of *Autobiography of Red* and *Plainwater*, by Anne Carson, *Electronic Literary Magazine* 4 <http://elimae.com/reviews/carson/carson.html>.
29 Archibald Allen, *The Fragments of Mimnermus: Text and Commentary*, 21.
30 Carson, "Mimnermos," *Plainwater*, 24.
31 Ibid., 26.
32 Carson, "Mimnermos," *Plainwater*, 18–19. This passage could also refer to the long poem "The Anthropology of Water," which constitutes the latter half of *Plainwater*.

33 Carson, "Mimnermos," *Plainwater*, 26.

34 Idem, "A Talk with Anne Carson," 22.

35 Ibid., 19.

36 Carson, *Glass, Irony and God*, 41.

37 Chris Jennings, "The Erotic Poetics of Anne Carson," 929.

38 Anne Carson, *Economy of the Unlost*, viii.

39 Ibid., viii.

40 Ibid., vii, viii.

41 Anne Carson, Introduction to *Short Talks*, 9.

42 Carson, *Short Talks*, 9.

43 Melanie Rehak, "Things Fall Together," 39.

44 Ibid., 37.

45 Mark Halliday, "It's Not Easy Being Red," *Boston Phoenix*, 29 June 1998 <http:// weeklywire.com/ww/06-29-98/boston_books_1.html>.

46 Calvin Bendient, "Celebrating Imperfection," p. 44; Julie Bruck, "Timelines," p. 98; Carl Wilson, "What Anne Carson Thinks About," sec. D, p. 19.

47 Oliver Reynolds, "After Homer, Before Stein," p. 24.

48 Karl Miller, "International Books of the Year – and the Millennium," p. 6.

49 William Logan, "Vanity Fair," *New Criterion On-Line*, 20 Jan. 2000 <http://www. newcriterion.com/archive/17/jun99/logan.htm>; Mark Halliday, "It's Not Easy Being Red," *Boston Phoenix*, 29 June 1998 <http:// weeklywire.com/ww/06-29-98/boston_books_1.html>.

50 Carson cites the earlier date in *Autobiography of Red*, 3. J.A. Davison cites the later one in *From Archilochus to Pindar*, 197.

51 Carson, *Autobiography of Red*, 3, 5.

52 Ibid., 5. In translation, at least, "The Red Place" is a noun. However, the confusion of nouns and adjectives plays a key role in Carson's treatment of the epithetic proper noun "Stesichoros."

53 Carson, *Autobiography of Red*, 6.

54 Malcolm Davies, "Stesichorus' Geryoneis and Its Folk-Tale Origins," 277.

55 Willis Barnstone, *Greek Lyric Poetry*, 109.

56 Quintilian, quoted in Andrew Miller, *Greek Lyric*, 77; Carson, *Autobiography of Red*, 4.

57 Alison Dale Maingon, "Stesichoros and the Epic Tradition," 1.

58 Malcolm Davies, "Monody, Choral Lyric, and the Tyranny of the Handbook," 60; David Campbell, *Greek Lyric*, 2:262.

59 Maingon, "Stesichoros and the Epic Tradition," 355.

60 Carson, *Autobiography of Red*, 60, 147.

61 Ibid., 4.

62 Ibid., 4.

63 Ibid., 4, 5.

64 Davison, *From Archilochus to Pindar*, 200.

65 Carson, *Autobiography of Red*, 5.

66 Homer, *The Iliad*, trans. Richmond Lattimore (Chicago: University of Chicago Press, 1961), 3.180. Also translated as "whore that I am" (Robert Fagles, *The Iliad* [New York: Viking 1990], 3.128) or "shameless bitch / that I am" (Stanley

Lombardo, *Iliad* [Indianapolis: Hackett, 1997], 3.190-1). It should be noted that the translators make no attempt to lessen the pungency of these remarks. On the contrary, Lattimore's use of "slut" in a 1951 translation suggests a certain relish in the task.

67 Homer, *The Iliad*, trans. Richmond Lattimore, 6.344; also translated as "bitch that I am, vicious, scheming" (Homer, *Iliad*, trans. Robert Fagles, 6.408) or "scheming, cold-blooded bitch" (Homer, *Iliad*, trans. Stanley Lombardo, 6.362).
68 *Oxyrhynchus Papyri*, edited by E. Lobel, vol. 46 (London: 1967), 43.
69 Maingon, "Stesichoros and the Epic Tradition," 86.
70 Ibid., 87.
71 Carson, *Autobiography of Red*, 3.
72 Richard Kostelanetz, Introduction to *The Yale Gertrude Stein*, xiv.
73 Ibid., xiv.
74 Carson, *Autobiography of Red*, 4.
75 Ibid., 6–7.
76 Idem, *Glass, Irony and God*, 121.
77 Ibid., 121.
78 Ibid., 121.
79 Idem, "Dirt and Desire: Essay on the Phenomenology of Female Pollution in Antiquity," *Men in the Off Hours*, 133.
80 Ibid., 133.
81 Carson, *Economy of the Unlost*, 28.
82 Idem, *Autobiography of Red*, 10.
83 Ibid., 13.
84 Miller, *Greek Lyric*, 77.
85 Carson, *Autobiography of Red*, 37.
86 Davies, "Stesichorus' *Geryoneis* and Its Folk-Tale Origins," 279, 278, 279.
87 Carson, "The *Matrix* Interview," 12.
88 Norma Lorre Goodrich, *The Ancient Myths*, 30.
89 Ibid., 30.
90 Hesiod, *The Homeric Hymns. And Homerica*, 101.
91 Goodrich, *The Ancient Myths*, 33.
92 Plutarch, *De Iside et Osiride*, 165.
93 Ibid., 145.
94 Ibid., 121.
95 Carson, "Interview," *Matrix*, 14–15.
96 Carson, *Autobiography of Red*, 6.
97 Carson, "Mimnermos," *Plainwater*, 20.
98 Ibid., 22–3.
99 Carson, *Autobiography of Red*, 15.
100 Idem, "Mimnermos," *Plainwater*, 3; Idem, *Economy of the Unlost*, 118.
101 Idem, *Autobiography of Red*, 17.
102 Maingon, "Stesichoros and the Epic Tradition," 300.
103 Euripides, *Electra*, 149.
104 Anne Carson, "Helen," *Boston Review* 23, 15 June 1999 <http://www-polisci.mit.edu/ BostonReview/BR23.3/carson.html>.

105 Maingon, "Stesichoros and the Epic Tradition," 307; A.M. Dale, Introduction to *Helen*, xxiii.
106 Plato, *The Republic*, 9.586c.
107 Robert Meagher, *Helen: Myth, Legend, and the Culture of Misogyny*, 10.
108 Hesiod, *The Homeric Hymns. And Homerica*, 123.
109 Jed Rasula, "A Gift of Prophecy," 188.
110 Carson, *Autobiography of Red*, 18, 19.
111 Martin Robertson, "Geryoneis: Stesichoros and the Vase-Painters," note 210.
112 John Boardman, *Greek Art*, 77; "Geryon," Virtual Sculpture Gallery, 20 Jan. 2000 <http://www.eekman.com/virtual_gallery/ sculptures/geryon.shtml>. Note that some critics consider this sculpture a representation of Orthos's father, Typhon, who had a hundred heads instead of three. See Michael Grant and John Hazel, *Gods and Mortals in Classical Mythology*, 412.
113 Carson, *Plainwater*, 189.
114 Idem, *Glass, Irony and God*, 30, 30–1.
115 Idem, *Autobiography of Red*, 75.
116 Idem, "Irony Is Not Enough: Essay on My Life as Catherine Deneuve (2nd draft)," *Men in the Off Hours*, 119–26.
117 Idem, *Red*, 79.
118 Idem, *Eros the Bittersweet*, 78.
119 Idem, *Autobiography of Red*, 39.
120 Ibid., 144.
121 Ibid., 32, 90.
122 Teresa de Lauretis, "Desire in Narrative," 109.
123 Maingon, "Stesichoros and the Epic Tradition," 292.
124 Carson, *Autobiography of Red*, 129.
125 Idem, "Woman of Letters," 31.
126 Ibid., 30.
127 Jefferey Beam, *Oyster Boy Review* 9, 02 Feb. 2000 <http://www.levee67.com./obr/09/beam.html>.
128 See the front cover of Will Aitken's *Realia*.
129 Anne Carson, "The Art of Poetry No. 88: Anne Carson," 190–226.
130 Carson, *Autobiography of Red*, 46.
131 Ibid., 129.
132 Ibid., 128.
133 Jan Schoo, *Hercules' Labors: Fact or Fiction?* 86.
134 Maingon, "Stesichoros and the Epic Tradition," 60.
135 Joanne Dobson, *Dickinson and the Strategies of Reticence*, 107.
136 Carson, *Autobiography of Red*, 22.
137 See, for example, #1651, #1686 – though not always (see #1606). Emily Dickinson, *The Complete Poems of Emily Dickinson*.
138 Carson, *Autobiography of Red*, 35.
139 Ibid., 60.
140 Ibid., 22.
141 Sharon Cameron, *Lyric Time: Dickinson and the Limits of Genre*, 4.
142 Carson, *Autobiography of Red*, 144.
143 Ibid., 93.

144 Ibid., 145.
145 Ibid., 145.
146 Ibid., 146.
147 Ibid., 105.
148 Ibid., 57.
149 Ibid., 57.
150 Carson, "The *Matrix* Interview," 17.
151 Idem, *Plainwater*, 123.
152 Idem, "The *Matrix* Interview," 14.
153 Idem, *Plainwater*, 120.
154 Marlatt, "A Poignant Critique in a Playful Mixing of Genres," 42.
155 Carson, *Autobiography of Red*, 67.
156 Ibid., 147.
157 Ibid., 147.
158 Elizabeth Macklin, review of *Autobiography of Red*, by Anne Carson, *Boston Review* 23, 20 Jan. 2000 <http:// bostonreview.mit.edu/BR23.6/ macklin.html>.
159 Jacques Derrida, "Parergon," *The Truth in Painting*, 71.
160 Ibid., 58.
161 Carson, *Autobiography of Red*, 149.
162 Maingon, "Stesichoros and the Epic Tradition," 359.
163 Schoo, *Hercules' Labors*, 7.
164 S.C. Neuman, *Gertrude Stein: Autobiography and the Problem of Narration*, 17.
165 Carson, *Glass, Irony and God*, 137.
166 Goodrich, *The Ancient Myths*, 27.
167 Carson, *Autobiography of Red*, 148.
168 Plutarch, *De Iside et Osiride*, 131.
169 Carson, "The Unbearable Lightness of Being Anne Carson," sec. R, p. 5.
170 Anne Carson, *The Beauty of the Husband*, 137. See also 141.
171 Ibid., 15.
172 Ibid., 38.
173 Daphne Merkin, "'The Beauty of the Husband': Anne Carson's Elusive Tangos," *New York Times*, 30 September 2001 <wysiwg://79/http://www.nytimes.com/2001/09/30/books/review/30MERKINTW.html>.
174 Carson, *The Beauty of the Husband*, 129–30.
175 Ibid., 115.
176 Ibid., 74.
177 Carson, *Eros the Bittersweet*, 16.
178 Ibid., 51.
179 Ibid., 79.
180 Monique Tschofen, "'First I Must Tell About Seeing': (De)monstrations of Visuality and the Dynamics of Metaphor in Anne Carson's *Autobiography of Red*," 49.
181 Line Henrikson, "The Verse Novel as a Hybrid Genre: Monstrous Bodies in Anne Carson's *Autobiography of Red* and Les Murray's *Freddy Neptune*," 36.
182 Ibid., 42.
183 See Gary Saul Morson and Caryl Emerson, *Mikhail Bakhtin: Creation of a Prosaics*, 327–8.

184 Lampman quoted in D.M.R. Bentley, Introduction to *The Story of an Affinity*, in *Early Long Poems on Canada*, edited by D.M.R. Bentley, 553.
185 Marta Dvorak, "Fiction," 161.
186 Marlatt, "On Salvaging," 32.
187 Ibid., 32.
188 Sylvia Söderlind, *Margin/Alias*, 42, 48.
189 Cohen, *Beautiful Losers*, 43.
190 Stephen Scobie, "Racing the Midnight Train: Leonard Cohen in Performance," 67.
191 Cohen, *The Favourite Game*, 113.
192 Carson, *Autobiography of Red*, 30.
193 Andre Furlani, "Reading Paul Celan with Anne Carson: 'What Kind of Withness Would That Be?'" *Canadian Literature*, 176 (spring 2003): 84–104.
194 Michael Greenstein, "Subverting Westmount: Leonard Cohen's New Jews," 134.
195 Beverley Curran, "Ondaatje's *The English Patient* and Altered States of Narrative," 18.
196 The conclusion to Jennings's essay discusses the importance of this anecdote to Carson's aesthetic, as does the introduction to Robert Stanton, "'I am writing this to be as wrong as possible to you': Anne Carson's Errancy," 28–43.
197 Carson, *Eros the Bittersweet*, xi.
198 Carson, *The Beauty of the Husband*, 99.
199 Guy Davenport, introduction to *Glass, Irony and God*, ix.
200 Carson, *Economy of the Unlost*, viii.
201 Carson, *Autobiography of Red*, 149.
202 Jeet Heer, "Poet or 'Prize-Reaping Machine'?," *National Post*, 31 January 2002, sec. B, p. 5+; Sandra Martin, "Who's Afraid of Anne Carson?," *Globe and Mail*, 2 February 2002, sec. R, p. 3.
203 David Solway, "The Trouble with Annie: David Solway Unmakes Anne Carson." *Books in Canada* 30, no.1 (July 2001), 26.
204 Robert Potts, "Neither Rhyme nor Reason," *Guardian UK*, 26 January 2002 <www.guardian.co.uk.Archive/Article/0,4273,4342945,00.html>.
205 Note, however, that Carson's 2005 offering, *Decreation*, has received a lukewarm response. See, for example, André Alexis, "More Ambition Than Execution," review of *Decreation*, by Anne Carson, *Globe and Mail*, 17 September 2005, sec. D. p. 24.
206 Carson, *The Beauty of the Husband*, 15; Fraser Sutherland, "It Takes Two to Tango," *Globe and Mail*, 10 February 2001, sec. D, p. 3; Merkin, "'The Beauty of the Husband': Anne Carson's Elusive Tangos"; Solway, "The Trouble with Annie," 26.
207 Merkin, "'The Beauty of the Husband': Anne Carson's Elusive Tangos."
208 Carl Wilson, "What Anne Carson Thinks About," sec. D, p. 18.

CHAPTER SEVEN

1 Glenn Gould, *The Glenn Gould Reader*, 379.
2 W.R. Johnson, *The Idea of Lyric*, 149–50.
3 Stephen Henighan, *When Words Deny the World*, 155.

4 Ironically, in an earlier volume of the Porcupine's Quill series, Montreal critic T.F. Rigelhof combatted Toronto-centrism by making a passionate argument for the recognition of Cohen as "a novelist to be reckoned much higher than a footnote appended to Michael Ondaatje's career." See T.F. Rigelhof, *This Is Our Writing*, 151.

5 George Bowering, quoted on the *Director's Cut* page of the Porcupine's Quill website, 14 May 2004 <http://www.sentex.net/~pql/directors.html>.

6 For a detailed response to Solway's attack on Carson, see Ian Rae, "Anne Carson and the Solway Hoaxes."

7 Henighan, *When Words Deny the World*, 140. See also Philip Marchand, *Ripostes*, 34.

8 Martin Levin, "B.C. Booster," *Globe and Mail*, 23 August 2003, sec. D, p. 13.

9 Sam Solecki, *Ragas of Longing*, 163.

10 Henighan, *When Words Deny the World*, 134.

11 *The English Patient*, dir. Anthony Minghella, Miramax Films, 1996.

12 Henighan, *When Words Deny the World*, 171.

13 Katherine Acheson, "Anne Wilkinson in Michael Ondaatje's *In the Skin of a Lion*: Writing and Reading Class," 107; Ondaatje, *In the Skin of a Lion*, 196–203.

14 Acheson, "Anne Wilkinson," 112.

15 Lorraine York, "Whirling Blindfolded in the House of Women: Gender Politics in the Poetry and Fiction of Michael Ondaatje," 85.

16 See Dean Irvine's discussion of this passage in his introduction to *Heresies: The Complete Poems of Anne Wilkinson 1924–1961*, 24–5.

17 Ondaatje, *The English Patient*, 288.

18 Irvine, introduction to *Heresies*, 24.

19 Ondaatje, *In the Skin of a Lion*, 182, 228; Annick Hillger, *Not Needing All the Words: Michael Ondaatje's Literature of Silence*, 121–2. Receiving the gift from Al in *In the Skin of a Lion*, Caravaggio complains that he has nothing to give and Al replies: "Remember my name" (182). Caravaggio then ponders his name on the following page, where "*Al*" appears in italics. Ondaatje seems to be calling attention to the legacy of Purdy in the region around Belleville.

20 Irvine, Introduction to *Heresies*, 35, 19.

21 Journal, 16 June 1951. Anne Wilkinson, *Tightrope Walker: Autobiographical Writings of Anne Wilkinson*, 89.

22 Irvine, introduction to *Heresies*, 38.

23 Brian Trehearne, "Critical Episodes in Montreal Poetry of the 1940s," *Canadian Poetry*, 21–52.

24 Hillger, "The Young Poet and the Fathers of Can.lit," *Not Needing All the Words*, 97–109.

25 Ondaatje, "Interview with Michael Ondaatje," *Manna*, 20.

26 Solecki, *Ragas of Longing*, 73, 35.

27 Ondaatje, "Song to Alfred Hitchcock and Wilkinson," *The Dainty Monsters*, 17.

28 Ondaatje, "White Dwarfs," *Rat Jelly*, 70.

29 Journal, October 28, 1951. Wilkinson, *Tightrope Walker*, 96.

30 Alice Brittan, "War and the Book: The Diarist, the Cryptographer, and *The English Patient*," PMLA, 208.

31 Anne Michaels, *Fugitive Pieces*, 253.
32 Ibid., 204.
33 Ibid., 159.
34 Winfried Siemerling, "Leonard Cohen. 'Loneliness and History: A Speech Before the Jewish Public Library,'" *Take This Waltz: A Celebration of Leonard Cohen*, edited by Michael Fournier and Ken Norris, 146–7.
35 Michaels, *Fugitive Pieces*, 79.
36 Ibid., 55, 257, 100.
37 Ibid., 209, 211; Anne Michaels, "Cleopatra's Love," *Poetry Canada*, 14.
38 Michaels, *Fugitive Pieces*, 140.
39 Ibid., 159.
40 Ibid., 253.
41 Solecki, *Ragas of Longing*, 175.
42 Monika Fludernik, "Chronology, Time, Tense and Experientiality in Narrative," *Language and Literature*, 132.
43 Ibid., 126.
44 Ibid., 127.
45 Ibid., 129.
46 Ondaatje, *The English Patient*, 278.
47 Fludernick, "Chronology, Time, Tense and Experientiality in Narrative," 130.
48 Vernon Provencal, "The PseudoHerodotean Origins of *The English Patient*," *English Study in Canada*, 139.
49 Lisa Pace Vetter, "Liberal Political Inquiries in the Novels of Michael Ondaatje," *Perspective on Political Science*, 27–36.
50 Amy Novak, "Textual Hauntings: Narrating History, Memory, and Silence in *The English Patient*," *Studies in the Novel*, 206.
51 Froma Zeitlin, "New Soundings in Holocaust Literature: A Surplus of Memory," *Catastrophe and Meaning: The Holocaust and the Twentieth Century*, edited by Moishe Postone and Eric Sautner, 189.
52 Annick Hillger, "'Afterbirth of Earth': Messianic Materialism in Anne Michaels' *Fugitive Pieces*," *Canadian Literature*, 29. Hillger quotes from Walter Benjamin's "Theses on the Philosophy of History."
53 Nicola King, "'We Come After': Remembering the Holocaust," *Literature and the Contemporary Fictions and Theories of the Present*, edited by Roger Luckhurst and Peter Marks, 104; Michaels, *Fugitive Pieces*, 18.
54 Zeitlin, "New Soundings in Holocaust Literature," 202.
55 Dalia Kandiyoti, "'Our Foothold in Buried Worlds': Place in Holocaust Consciousness and Anne Michaels's *Fugitive Pieces*," *Contemporary Literature*, 315.
56 Ibid., 318.
57 Susan Gubar, "Empathic Identification in Anne Michaels's *Fugitive Pieces*: Masculinity and Poetry after Auschwitz," 272–3.
58 Carson, *Eros the Bittersweet*, 79.
59 Méira Cook, "At the Membrane of Language and Silence: Metaphor and Memory in *Fugitive Pieces*," *Canadian Literature*, 16.
60 Daniel Albright argues that the lyric operates according to an "orthogonal principal" in which language attains its lyrical character by shifting radically out of one register into another (*Lyricality in English Literature*, 259). Usually this shift in

tone moves from low to high, but when an elevated tone becomes the norm, it also moves effectively from high to low.

61 Theodor Adorno, "Cultural Criticism and Society," 34.

62 Cook, "At the Membrane of Language and Silence," 12–13.

63 Kimberly Verwaayen, "Re-Membering the (W)holes: Counter-memory, Collective Memory, and Bergsonian Time in Anne Michaels' *Miner's Pond*," *Canadian Poetry*, 69.

64 Leonard Cohen, "Lines from My Grandfather's Journal," *The Spice-Box of Earth*, 84–5.

65 Ibid., 81.

66 Michael Q. Abraham, "Neurotic Affiliations: Klein, Layton, Cohen, and the Properties of Influence," 109, 110, 110.

67 Henighan, *When Words Deny the World*, 149; D.M.R. Bentley, "Anne Michaels' *Fugitive Pieces*," *Canadian Poetry*, 8.

68 Paul Celan, "Speech on the Occasion of Receiving the Literature Prize of the Free Hanseatic City of Bremen," *Collected Prose*, 34.

69 Carson, *Economy of the Unlost*, 29.

70 Michaels, *Fugitive Pieces*, 111.

71 Bentley, "Anne Michaels' *Fugitive Pieces*," 7–8.

72 Kevin McNeilly, "All Poets Are Not Jews: Transgression and Satire in A.M. Klein," *English Studies in Canada*, 425–6; Theodor Adorno, *Negative Dialectics*, 362.

73 Adorno, *Negative Dialects*, 363.

74 Ibid., 363.

75 Klein, *The Second Scroll*, 24–5; idem, "Meditation upon Survival," *Selected Poems*, 135–6.

76 Klein, *The Second Scroll*, 24.

77 John Moss, "Life/Story: The Fictions of George Bowering," 87.

78 Michaels, *Fugitive Pieces*, 294.

79 Barbara L. Estrin, "Ending in the Middle: Revisioning Adoption in Binjamin Wilkomirski's *Fragments* and Anne Michaels's *Fugitive Pieces*," *Tulsa Studies in Women's Literature*, 294.

80 Michaels, *Fugitive Pieces*, 279.

81 Ibid., 231.

82 Ibid., 294.

83 Ibid., 294.

84 Ibid., 7.

85 Although there is no etymological connection, Beer's surname also constitutes the first half of two German verbs, *beerben* (to bury) and *beerdigen* (to inherit from), that are crucial to the story.

86 Henighan, *When Words Deny the World*, 146.

87 Michaels, *Fugitive Pieces*, 128. Compare with Ondaatje, *In the Skin of a Lion*, 114.

88 Solecki, *Ragas of Longing*, 164.

89 Ibid., 125. For further intermezzo references see 141, 164, 167–8.

90 Ibid., 161–2. Michaels also repeats the phrase "every moment is two moments" on pages 138, 140, and 143.

91 See, for example, Bentley, "Anne Michaels' *Fugitive Pieces*," 13–14.
92 Cook, "At the Membrane of Language and Silence," 30–1.
93 Ondaatje, *Coming Through Slaughter*, 12. The alliterations in Ondaatje's novel are highlighted by Susan MacFarlane in "Picking Up the Pieces: *Coming Through Slaughter* as Paradigm," 82.
94 Zeitlin, "New Soundings in Holocaust Literature," 186. While I rejoice in such bold endorsements of Canadian literature by critics abroad, it is disappointing that Klein's name rarely appears in surveys of Holocaust literature.
95 Henighan, *When Words Deny the World*, 150.
96 See Anne Michaels, "Cleopatra's Love," 15.
97 Henighan, *When Words Deny the World*, 36, 180.
98 Ibid., 146.
99 Ibid., 136.
100 Ibid., 140.
101 Philip Marchand, *Ripostes*, 41.
102 Consider, for example, the self-defeating metaphors in Henighan's polemic: "Rather than feasting, vulture-like, on the putrid flesh – and how putrid it is! – of the history of the last decade, many of our most prominent novelists have collaborated in rewriting history as a stately foreign pageant, fleeing the gnarled corruption of our slow subsiding into the hide of the elephant to our south for a realm of noble metaphors" (137).
103 Henighan, *When Words Deny the World*, 149; Michaels, *Fugitive Pieces*, 143, 165.
104 Chris Jennings, "The Erotic Poetics of Anne Carson," *University of Toronto Quarterly*, 923, 926. See also Anne Carson, *Eros the Bittersweet*, 73.
105 Barbara L. Estrin, "Ending in the Middle," 296.
106 Henighan, *When Words Deny the World*, 148.
107 Marta Braun, *Picturing Time*, 237.
108 Ibid., 249.
109 Ibid., 251.
110 Henighan, *When Words Deny the World*, 148.
111 Ibid., 152. Although Klein rejected the golem as an embodiment of violence, Mordecai Richler praises him in *St. Urbain's Horseman* as a "sort of Jewish Batman ... the body without a soul. He was made out of clay by Rabbi Judah Ben Bezalel in the sixteenth century to defend the Jews of Prague from a pogrom and, to my mind, still wanders the world, turning up wherever a defender is most needed" (282–3). According to legend, the golem's Adamic clay comes from a river. Michaels's hero emerges from the ancient riverbed of Biskupin, wanders the world, and eventually defends his people through writing that rescues Ben, who emerges from the flooded banks of the Humber to defend the legacy of Beer.
112 Michaels, *Fugitive Pieces*, 207.
113 Ibid., 241. The kaddish occupies such a central place in Jewish religious practice that even the secular Jakob Hersh in *St. Urbain's Horseman* suffers nightmares from worrying that his half-*goy* son will fail to perform this ceremony in his memory.
114 John Moss, *The Paradox of Meaning: Cultural Poetics and Critical Fictions*, 171.
115 Henighan, *When Words Deny the World*, 150.

116 A.M. Klein, *Beyond Sambation: Selected Essays and Editorials 1928–1955*, 233.

117 Richler, *St. Urbain's Horseman*, 409.

118 Henighan, *When Words Deny the World*, 134.

119 Cohen, *The Favourite Game*, 125.

120 Henighan, *When Words Deny the World*, 172.

121 Michaels, *Fugitive Pieces*, 102.

122 Ibid., 104.

123 Dalia Kandiyoti, "'Our Foothold in Buried Worlds,'" *Contemporary Literature*, 324.

124 Michaels, *Fugitive Pieces*, 105.

125 Ibid., 105. Jakob's lover, Michaela, also fears the "ghosts of Indians" and the history of their ritual fires on Manitoulin Island (Michaels, *Fugitive Pieces*, 187).

126 Solway, *Director's Cut*, 159.

127 Darryl Whetter, "Sterling Stories Don't Need Tricks," *Globe and Mail*, 8 May 2004, sec. D, p. 8.

128 See Rob Payne, "Give Me Tasmanian Babes, Give Me Telemarketing Hell, Give Me Something Funny," *Globe and Mail*, 26 January 2002, sec. D, p. 4.

129 Stephen Henighan, *The Streets of Winter*, 234, 293.

130 "Griffin Poetry Prize," 22 October 2001 <http://www.GriffinpoetryPrize.com/welcome-page.htn>.

131 Lynn Crosbie, "Something New, Please, O Universe," *Globe and Mail*, 16 June 2001, sec. D, p. 7.

132 Note that Crosbie's article changes the verbs in the mission statement from the imperative "must play" to the present tense "plays," thus making Carson's classicism seem less relevant to popular culture. Crosbie would probably dismiss the imperatives, like the rest of the prize material, as "Griffin propaganda" (sec. D, p. 7).

133 See the back cover of the Vintage, 2000, edition of *Men in the Off Hours*.

134 Richard Siken, "Seeing Red: Anne Carson's Classical Return to the Monster Tale Comprises her Best Work Yet," review of *Autobiography of Red*, by Anne Carson, *Tucson Weekly*, 29 June 1998 <http://www.weeklywire.com/ww/06-29-98/tw_book1.html>.

135 Michael Snayerson, "The Intriguing Miss Connelly," *Vanity Fair* (September 2002), 374.

136 Ibid., 374.

137 See Meghan O'Rourke, "Hermetic Hotties: What is Anne Carson Doing on *The L Word*?" 10 May 2004 <http://slate.msn.com/id/2095317/>.

138 Lynn Crosbie, *Presley*, in *Queen Rat*, 9–29.

139 Philip Marchand, "Confession and Critique: The Work of Lynn Crosbie," ECW, 149.

140 Ibid., 149.

141 Stephen Scobie, "The Reading Lesson: Michael Ondaatje and the Patients of Desire," 92, 96.

142 Leon Edel, "Marginal *Keri* and Textual *Chetiv*: The Mystic Novel of A.M. Klein," 24. See also Tom Marshall, introduction to *A.M. Klein's Symposium*, vi.

143 Stan Dragland, "F.ing through *Beautiful Losers*," *Take This Waltz*, ed. Michael Fournier and Ken Norris, 49.

144 George Bowering, *A Short Sad Book*, 141. See also Michaels, *Fugitive Pieces*, 165, 206, 266.
145 Bök, afterword to *Ground Works*, 230.
146 Ibid., 231.
147 Hubert Aquin, *Prochain Épisode*, 9.
148 T.F. Rigelhof, "Enough Said," *Globe and Mail*, 22 January 2000, sec. D, p. 22.
149 *The Favourite Game*, Dir. Bernard Hébert, Ciné Qua Non Films, 2003.
150 Michael Hurley and Andy Belyea argue that *The Second Scroll* is echoed in "form and conception ... by Richler's *St. Urbain's Horseman*" ("A.M. Klein," *Encyclopedia of Literature in Canada*, 585).
151 In addition to the Palais d'Or and shoe-stuffing scenes that invoke *The Favourite Game*, there are perhaps allusions to *Beautiful Losers* in Richler's novel. Uncle Abe's critique of Jewish children who sympathize with French-Canadians, wear "Indian headbands," smoke pot, and dream about being black, could be read as a rebuke to Cohen and his ilk (Richler, *St. Urbain*, 428).
152 Munro's endorsement appears on the cover of the copies of *Autobiography of Red* and *Men in the Off Hours* that I have worked from in this study.
153 George Elliott Clarke, *Fire on the Water*, n.p.
154 *Fugitive Pieces*, dir. Jeremy Podesla, Serendipity Point Films, 2007.
155 Glenn Gould, *The Glenn Gould Reader*, 379.

Bibliography

Abraham, Michael Q. "Neurotic Affiliations: Klein, Layton, Cohen, and the Properties of Influence." *Canadian Poetry* 38 (spring/summer): 88–129.

Abrams, M.H. *A Glossary of Literary Terms*. 6th ed. Orlando, FL: Harcourt Brace, 1993.

Acheson, Katherine. "Anne Wilkinson in Michael Ondaatje's *In the Skin of a Lion*: Writing and Reading Class." *Canadian Literature* 145 (summer 1995): 107–19.

Adam, Ian. "The Human Centre." Review of *The Favourite Game*, by Leonard Cohen. *Edge: An Independent Periodical* 2 (spring 1964): 129–30.

Adorno, Theodor. "Cultural Criticism and Society." 1949. In *Prisms,* translated by Samuel and Sherry Weber, 17–34. Cambridge, Massachusetts: MIT, 1981.

– *Negative Dialectics*. 1966. Reprint. New York: Continuum, 1995.

Aitken, Will. *Realia*. 2000. Reprint. Toronto: Vintage Canada, 2001.

Alexander, Michael. *Mrs Fraser on the Fatal Shore*. New York: Simon and Schuster, 1971.

Alexis, André. "More Ambition Than Execution." Review of *Decreation*, by Anne Carson. *Globe and Mail*, 17 September 2005, sec. D, p. 24.

Albright, Daniel. *Lyricality in English Literature*. Lincoln: University of Nebraska Press, 1985.

Allen, Archibald. *The Fragments of Mimnermus: Text and Commentary*. Stuttgart: Franz Steiner, 1993.

Allen, Donald and Warren Tallman, ed. *Poetics of the New American Poetry*. New York: Grover, 1973.

Anctil, Pierre. "A.M. Klein: The Poet and His Relations with French Quebec." In *The Canadian Jewish Studies Reader,* edited by Richard Menkis and Norman Ravvin, 350–72. Calgary: Red Deer Press, 2004.

Andersen, Hans Christian. "The Snow Queen." In *The Complete Fairy Tales and Stories*, translated by Erik Christian Haugaard, 234–62. 1844. Reprint. New York: Doubleday, 1974.

Aquin, Hubert. *Prochain Épisode*. 1965. Reprint. Montréal: Leméac, 1992.

Aristotle. *On Rhetoric: A Theory of Civic Discourse*. Translated by George Kennedy. New York: Oxford University Press, 1991.

– *Poetics*. Translated by Malcolm Heath. New York: Penguin, 1996.

Atwood, Margaret. Introduction to *The New Oxford Book of Canadian Verse in English*, edited by Margaret Atwood, xxvii–xxxix. 1982. Reprint. Don Mills, Ontario: Oxford University Press, 1983.

– *Oryx and Crake*. Toronto: McClelland & Stewart, 2003.

– *Surfacing*. Toronto: McClelland & Stewart, 1972.

– *Survival*. Toronto: Anansi, 1972.

Bachner, Sally. "'He Had Pushed His Imagination into Buddy's Brain', or, How to Escape History in *Coming Through Slaughter*." *Rethinking History* 9, no.2/3 (June/Sept. 2005): 197–220.

Bahti, Timothy. *Ends of the Lyric: Direction and Consequence in Western Poetry*. Baltimore: Johns Hopkins University Press, 1996.

Bakhtin, M.M. *Speech Genres and Other Late Essays*. Translated by Vern McGee. Austin: University of Texas Press, 1986.

Barbour, Douglas. *Daphne Marlatt and Her Works*. Toronto: ECW, 1992.

– *Lyric/Anti-Lyric*. Edmonton: NeWest, 2001.

– *Michael Ondaatje*. Toronto: Maxwell Macmillan, 1993.

Barnstone, Willis. *Greek Lyric Poetry*. Bloomington: Indiana University Press, 1962.

Becker, George. *Realism in Modern Literature*. New York: Frederick Ungar Publishing, 1980.

Beddoes, Julie. "Mastering the Mother Tongue: Reading Frank Davey Reading Daphne Marlatt's *How Hug a Stone*." *Canadian Literature* 155 (winter 1997): 75–87.

Bendient, Calvin. "Celebrating Imperfection." Review of *Autobiography of Red*, by Anne Carson. *New York Times Book Review*, 14 May 2000, p. 44.

Bentley, D.M.R. "Anne Michaels' *Fugitive Pieces*." *Canadian Poetry* 41 (fall-winter 1997): 5–20.

– "Colonial Colonizing: An Introductory Survey of the Canadian Long Poem." In *Bolder Flights: Essays on the Canadian Long Poem*, edited by Frank Tierney and Angela Robbeson, 7–29. Ottawa: Ottawa University Press, 1998.

– ed. *Early Long Poems on Canada*. London, Ontario: Canadian Poetry Press, 1993.

Bethell, Kathleen. "Reading Billy: Memory, Time, and Subjectivity in *The Collected Works of Billy the Kid*." *Studies in Canadian Literature* 28, no.1 (2003): 71–89.

Birney, Earle. *David, and Other Poems*. Toronto: Ryerson Press, 1942.

– *The Collected Poems of Earle Birney*. Toronto: McClelland & Stewart, 1975.

Blaser, Robin. "The Fire." In *The Poetics of the New American Poetry*, edited by Donald Allen and Warren Tallman, 235–46. New York: Grove, 1973.

– *The Holy Forest*. Toronto: Coach House, 1993.

– "The Practice of Outside." In *The Collected Books of Jack Spicer*, 271–329. 1975. Reprint. Santa Rosa, California: Black Sparrow Press, 1999.

Blott, Anne ."'Stories to Finish': *The Collected Works of Billy the Kid*." *Studies in Canadian Literature* 2, no.2 (summer 1977): 188–202.

Boardman, John. *Greek Art*. New York: Praeger, 1973.

Bök, Christian and Margaret Atwood, ed. *Ground Works: Avant-Garde for Thee*. Toronto: Anansi, 2002.

– *Eunoia*. Toronto: Coach House Books, 2001.

– "Oneiromechanics: Notes on the Dream Machines of Roy Kiyooka," *West Coast Line* 16 (spring-summer 1995): 24–8.

– '*Pataphysics: The Poetics of an Imaginary Science*. Evanston, Illinois: Northwestern University Press, 2002.

– "The Secular Opiate: Marxism as an Ersatz Religion in Three Canadian Texts." *Canadian Literature* 147 (winter 1995): 11–22.

Bowering, Angela, George Bowering, David Bromige, and Michael Matthews. *Piccolo Mondo: A Novel of Youth in 1961 as Seen Somewhat Later*. Toronto: Coach House Press, 1998.

Bowering, George. "A Great Northward Darkness: The Attack on History in Recent Canadian Fiction." In *Imaginary Hand*. Edmonton: NeWest, 1988. 1–21.

– *A Magpie Life: Growing a Writer*. Toronto: Key Porter, 2001.

– *A Short Sad Book*. Vancouver: Talonbooks, 1977.

– *Allophanes*. Toronto: Coach House Press, 1976.

– *Another Mouth*. Toronto: McClelland & Stewart, 1979.

– *At War with the U.S.* Vancouver: Talonbooks, 1974.

– *Autobiology*. Vancouver: Georgia Straight Writing Supplement, 1972.

– *Bowering's BC: A Swashbuckling History*. Toronto: Viking, 1996.

– *Burning Water*. 1980. Reprint. Toronto: Penguin, 1994.

– *Curious*. Toronto: Coach House Press, 1973.

– *Egotists and Autocrats: The Prime Ministers of Canada*. Toronto: Viking, 1999.

- *Errata*. Red Deer, AB: Red Deer College Press, 1988.
- "14 Plums." Interview by Bill Schermbrucker, Sharon Thesen, David McFadden, and Paul de Barros. *Capilano Review* 15, no.1 (January 1979): 86–107.
- *Genève*. Toronto: Coach House Press, 1971.
- *George, Vancouver*. Toronto: Weed/Flower Press, 1970.
- *Harry's Fragments*. Toronto: Coach House Press, 1990.
- *Imaginary Hand: Essays by George Bowering*. Edmonton: NeWest, 1988.
- *Imago* 1 (1964).
- *In the Flesh*. Toronto: McClelland & Stewart, 1974.
- "Interview." 1976. In *Out-Posts,* edited by Caroline Bayard and Jack David, 78–99. Erin, Ontario: Porcépic, 1978.
- *Kerrisdale Elegies*. Toronto: Coach House Press, 1984.
- "Language Women: Post-anecdotal Writing in Canada." In *Imaginary Hand*, 99–109. Edmonton: NeWest, 1988.
- *Mirror on the Floor*. Toronto: McClelland & Stewart, 1967.
- *Points on the Grid*. Toronto: Contact, 1964.
- *Rocky Mountain Foot*. Toronto: McClelland & Stewart, 1968.
- *Selected Poems: Particular Accidents*, edited by Robin Blaser. Vancouver: Talonbooks, 1980.
- *Seventy-One Poems for People*. Red Deer, Alta.: Red Deer College Press, 1985.
- *Shoot!* Toronto: Key Porter Books, 1994.
- *Smoking Mirror*. Edmonton: Longspoon Press, 1982.
- *Sticks & Stones*, with drawings by Gordon Payne. 1962. Reprint. Vancouver: Talonbooks, 1989.
- *Stone Country: An Unauthorized History of Canada*. Toronto: Penguin, 2003.
- "Stone Hammer Narrative." In *Imaginary Hand*, 171–83. Edmonton: NeWest, 1988.
- *The Catch*. Toronto: McClelland & Stewart, 1976.
- *The Concrete Island: Montreal Poems 1967–71*. Montreal: Véhicule, 1977.
- *The Gangs of Kosmos*. Toronto: Anansi, 1969.
- *The Man in Yellow Boots*. Special Issue of *El Corno Emplumado* 16 (Oct. 1965).
- *The Mask in Place*. Winnipeg: Turnstone, 1982.
- "The Painted Window: Notes on Post-Realist Fiction." *University of Windsor Review* 13, no. 2 (spring-summer): 24–35.
- *The Silver Wire*. Kingston, Ontario: Quarry Press, 1966.
- "Vancouver as Postmodern Poetry." In *Vancouver: Representing the Postmodern City*, edited by Paul Delany, 121–43. Vancouver: Arsenal, 1994.
- *West Window: The Selected Poetry of George Bowering*. Toronto: General, 1982.

Bradbury, Malcolm. *The Novel Today*. Glasgow: Fontana, 1977.

Brake, Laurel. "'The Trepidation of the Spheres': The Serial and the Book in the
19th Century." In *Serials and Their Readers 1620–1914*, 83–101. Newcastle,
Delaware: Oak Knoll, 1993.

Braun, Marta. *Picturing Time*. Chicago: University of Chicago Press, 1992.

Brenner, Rachel Feldhay. *A.M. Klein, The Father of Canadian Jewish Literature*.
Queenston, Ontario: Edwin Mellen Press, 1990.

Brindle, Reginald Smith. *Serial Composition*. New York: Oxford University Press,
1966.

Brittan, Alice. "War and the Book: The Diarist, the Cryptographer, and *The
English Patient*." PMLA 121, no.1 (Jan. 2006): 200–13.

Brown, Russell. "Works, Places, Craft: Bowering's Critical Voice." *Essays on
Canadian Writing* 38 (summer 1989): 30–52.

Bruck, Julie. "Timelines." Review of *Autobiography of Red*, by Anne Carson.
Time Magazine, Canadian ed., 10 April 2000, p. 98.

Burnham, Clint. "How Postmodern Is Cohen's Poetry?" *Canadian Poetry* 33
(fall/winter 1993): 65–73.

Cameron, Sharon. *Lyric Time: Dickinson and the Limits of Genre*. Baltimore:
John Hopkins, 1979.

Campbell, David. *Greek Lyric*. Cambridge, Massachusetts: Harvard University
Press, 1988.

Carney, Lora Senechal, et al. "A Celebration of Roy Kiyooka." *Brick* 48 (spring
1994): 13–33.

Carson, Anne. "A Talk with Anne Carson." By John D'Agata. *Brick* 57 (fall
1997): 14–22.

– *Autobiography of Red*. 1998. Reprint. New York: Knopf, 1999.

– *Decreation*. Toronto: Knopf Canada, 2005.

– *Economy of the Unlost: Reading Simonides of Keos with Paul Celan*.
Princeton, New Jersey: Princeton University Press, 1999.

– *Eros the Bittersweet*. 1986. Reprint. Normal, Illinois: Dalkey Archive Press,
1998.

– *Glass, Irony and God*. New York: New Directions, 1995.

– *Men in the Off Hours*. New York: Knopf, 2000.

– *Plainwater*. 1995. Reprint. New York: Vintage, 2000.

– "Poetry Without Borders." Interview by Stephen Burt. *Publishers' Weekly* 247,
no.14 (3 April 2000): 56–7.

– *Short Talks*. London, Ontario: Brick Books, 1992.

– "The Art of Poetry No. 88: Anne Carson." Interview by Will Aitken. *Paris
Review* 171 (fall 2004): 190–226.

– *The Beauty of the Husband*. New York: Knopf, 2001.

- "The Matrix Interview." By Mary di Michele. *Matrix* 49: 10–17.
- "The Unbearable Lightness of Being Anne Carson." Interview by Sarah Hampson, *Globe and Mail*, 14 Sept. 2000, sec. R, p. 5.
- "Woman of Letters." Interview by Sam Difalco. *Canadian Writer's Yearbook* (2001): 28–31.

Cavell, Richard. *McLuhan in Space*. Toronto: University of Toronto Press, 2002.

Caws, Mary Ann. *Reading Frames in Modern Fiction*. Princeton: Princeton University Press, 1985.

Celan, Paul. "Speech on the Occasion of Receiving the Literature Prize of the Free Hanseatic City of Bremen." In *Collected Prose*. Translated by Rosemarie Waldrop, 33–5. Riverdale-on-Hudson, New York: Sheep Meadow, 1986.

Clark, Joe. *Tennessee Hill Folk*. Nashville: Vanderbilt University Press, 1972.

Clarke, George Elliott. *Blue*. Vancouver: Polestar, 2001.
- *Fire on the Water: An Anthology of Black Nova Scotian Writing*. Porter's Lake, Nova Scotia: Pottersfield, 1991.
- *Whylah Falls*. Victoria, B.C.: Polestar, 1990.

Cobley, Paul. *Narrative*. New York: Routledge, 2001.

Cohen, Leonard. *Beautiful Losers*. 1966. Reprint. Toronto: McClelland & Stewart, 1991.
- *Book of Longing*. Toronto: McClelland & Stewart, 2006.
- *Death of a Lady's Man*. Toronto: McClelland & Stewart, 1978.
- *Flowers for Hitler*. Toronto: McClelland & Stewart, 1964.
- *God is Alive, Magic is Afoot*. Illustrations by Sarah Perkins and Ian Jackson. Toronto: Stoddart, 2000.
- "Leonard Cohen: The Poet as Hero: 2." Interview by Michael Harris. *Leonard Cohen: The Artist and His Critics*, edited by Michael Gnarowski, 46–56. Toronto: McGraw-Hill Ryerson, 1976.
- *Let Us Compare Mythologies*. Montreal: Contact Press, 1956.
- *Stranger Music: Selected Poems and Songs*. 1993. Reprint. Toronto: McClelland & Stewart, 1994.
- *The Spice-Box of Earth*. Toronto: McClelland & Stewart, 1961.
- *The Favourite Game*. 1963. Reprint. Toronto: McClelland & Stewart, 2000.

Cole, Christina. "Daphne Marlatt as Penelope, Weaver of Words: A Feminist Reading of *Steveston*." *Open Letter* 6, no.1 (spring 1985): 5–19.

Cook, Méira. "At the Membrane of Language and Silence: Metaphor and Memory in *Fugitive Pieces*." *Canadian Literature* 164 (spring 2000): 12–33.

Cooley, Dennis. *Bloody Jack*. Winnipeg: Turnstone Press, 1984.

Crate, Joan. "The Mistress' Reply to the Poet." *Canadian Poetry* 33 (fall/winter 1993): 55–64.

Criglington, Meredith. "The City as a Site of Counter-Memory in Anne Michaels's *Fugitive Pieces* and Michael Ondaatje's *In the Skin of a Lion.*" *Essays on Canadian Writing* 81 (2004): 129–51.

Crosbie, Lynn. "Artful Impatience." *Globe and Mail*, 18 May 2002, sec. D, p.4.

– *Dorothy L'Amour.* Toronto: HarperFlamingo Canada, 1999.

– *Missing Children.* Toronto: McClelland & Stewart, 2003.

– *Paul's Case: The Kingston Letters.* Toronto: Insomniac Press, 1997.

– *Pearl.* Concord, Ontario: Anansi, 1996.

– *Queen Rat.* Toronto: Anansi, 1998.

– "Something New, Please, O Universe." *Globe and Mail*, 16 June 2001, sec. D, p. 7.

– *VillainElle.* Toronto: Coach House, 1994.

Cobley, Paul. *Narrative.* New York: Routledge, 2001.

Conkelton, Sheryl. "Roy Kiyooka: '...The Sad and Glad Tidings of the Floating World...'" In *All Amazed: For Roy Kiyooka*, edited by John O'Brian, Naomi Sawada, and Scott Watson, 101–15. Vancouver: Arsenal Pulp Press, Morris and Helen Belkin Art Gallery, Collapse, 2002.

Cuddon, J.A. *A Dictionary of Literary Terms.* 1977. Reprint. New York: Penguin, 1979.

Curran, Beverly. "Ondaatje's *The English Patient* and Altered States of Narrative." *Comparative Cultural Studies and Michael Ondaatje's Writing*, edited by Steven Tötösy de Zepetnek, 16–26. West Lafayette, Indiana: Purdue University Press, 2005.

Curtis, John. *Shipwreck of the Stirling Castle.* London: G. Virtue, 1838.

Dale, A.M. Introduction to *Helen*, by Euripides. Oxford: Clarendon, 1967.

Davenport, Guy. Introduction to *Glass, Irony and God*, by Anne Carson. New York: New Directions, 1995.

Davey, Frank. "The Language of the Contemporary Canadian Long Poem." In *Surviving the Paraphrase*, 183–93. Winnipeg: Turnstone, 1983.

Davison, J.A. *From Archilochus to Pindar.* New York: Macmillan, 1968.

Davies, Malcolm. "Monody, Choral Lyric, and the Tyranny of the Handbook." *Classical Quarterly* 38 (1988): 52–64.

– "Stesichorus' *Geryoneis* and Its Folk-Tale Origins." *Classical Quarterly* 38 (1988): 277–90.

Deer, Glenn. "The Politics of Modern Literary Innovation: A Rhetorical Perspective." *Dalhousie Review* 70, no.3 (fall 1991): 351–73.

Dennisoff, Dennis. "Homosocial Desire and the Artificial Man in Michael Ondaatje's *The Collected Works of Billy the Kid.*" *Michael Ondaatje Issue.* Ed.

Karen Smythe. Special issue of *Essays on Canadian Writing* 53 (summer 1994): 51–70.

Derksen, Jeff. "Sites Taken As Signs: Place, the Open Text, and Enigma in New Vancouver Writing." In *Vancouver: Representing the Postmodern City*, edited by Paul Delany, 144–61. Vancouver: Arsenal, 1994.

Derrida, Jacques. "Parergon." *The Truth in Painting*. Translated by Geoff Bennington and Ian McLeod, 15–147. Chicago: University of Chicago Press, 1987.

Dickens, Charles. *Oliver Twist*. 1837. Reprint. London: Penguin, 1985.

Dickinson, Emily. *The Complete Poems of Emily Dickinson*, edited by Thomas Johnson. Boston: Back Bay, 1961.

Dickinson, Peter. "Towards a Transnational, Translational Feminist Poetics: Lesbian Fiction/Theory in Canada and Quebec." In *Here is Queer*, 131–55. Toronto: University of Toronto Press, 1999.

Dobson, Joanne. *Dickinson and the Strategies of Reticence*. Bloomington: Indiana University Press, 1989.

Dorman, Loranne and Clive Rawlins. *Leonard Cohen: Prophet of the Heart*. London: Omnibus Press, 1990.

Dragland, Stan. "F.ing through *Beautiful Losers*." In *Take This Waltz: A Celebration of Leonard Cohen*, edited by Michael Fournier and Ken Norris, 48–69, Ste Anne de Bellevue, Quebec: The Muses' Company, 1994.

Duncan, Robert. *Medieval Scenes*. Kent, Ohio: Kent State University Libraries, 1978.

Dvorak, Marta. "Fiction." In *Cambridge Companion to Canadian Literature*, edited by Eva-Marie Kröller, 155–76. Cambridge: Cambridge University Press, 2004.

Dydo, Ulla, ed. *A Stein Reader*. Evanston, Illinois: Northwestern UP, 1993.

Edel, Leon. "Marginal *Keri* and Textual *Chetiv*: The Mystic Novel of A.M. Klein." In *The A.M. Klein Symposium*, edited by Seymour Mayne, 15–29. Ottawa: University of Ottawa Press, 1975.

Egan, Susanna and Gabriele Helms. "The Many Tongues of Mothertalk: Life Stories of Mary Kiyoshi Kiyooka." *Canadian Literature* 163 (winter 1999): 44–7.

Ellingham, Lewis and Kevin Killian, ed. *Poet Be Like God: Jack Spicer and the San Francisco Renaissance*. Hanover: Wesleyan University Press, 1998.

Ellison, Carmen. "'Not My Real Face': Corporeal Grammar in *The Favourite Game*." *Essays on Canadian Writing* 69 (winter 1999): 64–72.

Estrin, Barbara L. "Ending in the Middle: Revisioning Adoption in Benjamin Wilkomirski's *Fragments* and Anne Michaels's *Fugitive Pieces*." *Tulsa Studies in Women's Literature* 21, no. 2 (2002): 275–300.

Euripides. *Electra*. Translated by Philip Vellacott. Harmondsworth, England: Penguin Books, 1963.

Fagles, Robert, trans. *The Iliad*. New York: Viking, 1990.

Fenton, William. *Re-Writing the Past: History and Origin in Howard O'Hagan, Jack Hodgins, George Bowering and Chris Scott*. Rome: Bulzoni, 1988.

Finkle, Derek. "From Page to Screen: Michael Ondaatje as Filmmaker." *Michael Ondaatje Issue*. Ed. Karen Smythe. Special issue of *Essays on Canadian Writing* 53 (summer 1994): 167–85.

Fludernik, Monika. "Chronology, Time, Tense and Experientiality in Narrative." *Language and Literature* 12, no. 2 (2003): 117–34.

Foster, Edward. *Jack Spicer*. Boise, Idaho: Boise State University Press, 1991.

Fournier, Michael and Ken Norris, ed. *Take This Waltz: A Celebration of Leonard Cohen*. Ste. Anne de Bellevue, Quebec: The Muses' Company, 1994.

Frank, Joseph. "Spatial Form: Thirty Years After." In *Spatial Form in Narrative*, edited by Jeffrey Smitten and Ann Daghistany, 202–43. Ithaca: Cornell University Press, 1981.

– "Spatial Form in Modern Literature." In *The Widening Gyre: Crisis and Mastery in Modern Literature*, 1–9. New Brunswick, New Jersey: Rutgers University Press, 1963.

Freedman, Ralph. *The Lyrical Novel*. Princeton, New Jersey: Princeton University Press, 1963.

Freud, Sigmund. *The Interpretation of Dreams*. Translated by James Strachey. 1900. Reprint. New York: Penguin, 1991.

Frye, Northrop. *Anatomy of Criticism*. 1957. Reprint. Princeton, New Jersey: Princeton University Press, 2000.

– "The Narrative Tradition in English-Canadian Poetry." *The Bush Garden*. 1971. Reprint. Toronto: Anansi, 1995.

Fulford, Robert. "On Books: A Rich Vein of Satire in this Fall's Canadian Novels." *Maclean's*, 5 Oct. 1963, 79.

Furlani, Andre. "Reading Paul Celan with Anne Carson: 'What Kind of Withness Would That Be?'" *Canadian Literature* 176 (spring 2003): 84–104.

Garrett-Petts, W.F., and Donald Lawrence. *Photographic Encounters: The Edges and Edginess of Reading Prose Pictures and Visual Fictions*. Edmonton: University of Alberta Press, 2000.

Geddes, Gary, ed. *Canadian Poets × 2*. Toronto: Oxford University Press, 1990.

Gérin-Lajoie, Antoine. "Un Canadien Errant." *The Oxford Book of Canadian Verse*, edited by A.J.M. Smith, 117. 1960. Reprint. London: Oxford, 1961.

Gide, André. *Les faux-monnayeurs*. Paris: Gallimard, 1925.

Gnarowski, Michael, ed. *Leonard Cohen: The Artist and His Critics*. Toronto: McGraw-Hill Ryerson, 1976.

Godard, Barbara. "Epi(pro)logue: In Pursuit of the Long Poem." *Open Letter* 6, no.2–3 (summer-fall 1985): 300–35.

– "Stretching the Story: The Canadian Story Cycle." *Open Letter* 7, no.6 (fall 1989): 27–71.

Goffman, Erving. *Forms of Talk*. Philadelphia: University of Pennsylvania Press, 1981.

Goodrich, Norma Lorre. *The Ancient Myths*. New York: Mentor, 1960.

Gould, Glenn. *The Art of Glenn Gould Reflections of a Musical Genius*, edited by John P.L. Roberts. Toronto: Malcolm Lester Books, 1999.

– *The Glenn Gould Reader*, edited by Tim Page. Toronto: Lester & Orpen Dennys, 1984.

Grant, Michael and John Hazel. *Gods and Mortals in Classical Mythology*. Springfield Mass.: G. & C. Merriam, 1973.

Grant, M.J. *Serial Music, Serial Aesthetics: Compositional Theory in Post-War*. Cambridge: Cambridge University Press, 2001.

Gray, Robert William. "Melancholic Poetics: The Vagaries and Vicissitudes of Identity in Three Canadian Poetic Novels and Various Psychoanalytic Works." Ph.D. diss., University of Alberta, 2003.

Green, Keith and Jill LeBihan. "The Speaking Object: Daphne Marlatt's Pronouns and Lesbian Poetics." *Style* 28, no.3 (fall 1994): 432–44.

Greene, Roland. *Post-Petrarchism: Origins and Innovations of the Western Lyric Sequence*. Princeton, New Jersey: Princeton University Press, 1991.

Greenstein, Michael. "Subverting Westmount: Leonard Cohen's New Jews." In *Third Solitudes: Tradition and Discontinuity in Jewish-Canadian Literature*, 119–41. Montreal: McGill-Queen's University Press, 1989.

Gubar, Susan. "Empathic Identification in Anne Michaels's *Fugitive Pieces*: Masculinity and Poetry after Auschwitz." *Signs* 28, no.1 (2002): 249–276.

Gunew, Sneja. *Framing Marginality*. Carlton, Victoria: Melbourne University Press, 1994.

Gunnars, Kristjana. *The Substance of Forgetting*. Red Deer, Alberta: Red Deer College Press, 1992.

Hamilton, Jeff. "This Cold Hectic Dawn and I." Review of *Plainwater* and *Glass, Irony and God*, by Anne Carson. *Denver Quarterly* 32, no.1–2 (summer-fall 1997): 105–24.

Harris, John. *George Bowering and His Works*. Toronto: ECW, 1980.

Harris, Max. Introduction to *Angry Penguins and Realist Painting in Melbourne in the 1940s*. London: Hayward Gallery, 1988.

Haynes, Roslynn. *Seeking the Centre: The Australian Desert in Literature, Art and Film*. Melbourne: Cambridge University Press, 1998.

Heer, Jeet. "Poet or 'Prize-Reaping Machine'?" *National Post*, 31 Jan. 2002, sec. B, p.5+.

Heighton, Steven. "Approaching 'That Perfect Edge': Kinetic Techniques in the Poetry and Fiction of Michael Ondaatje." *Studies in Canadian Literature* 13, no.2 (1988): 223–43.

Hénault, Gilles. "'The Favourite Game,' ou le jeu de l'amour et du hasard." Review of *The Favourite Game*, by Leonard Cohen. *La Presse*, 7 Dec. 1963, p. 7.

Hendricks, Gordon. *Eadweard Muybridge: Father of the Motion Picture*. New York: Grossman, 1975.

Henighan, Stephen. *The Streets of Winter*. Saskatoon: Thistledown Press, 2004.

– *When Words Deny the World*. Erin, Ontario: Porcupine's Quill, 2002.

Henrikson, Line. "The Verse Novel as a Hybrid Genre: Monstrous Bodies in Anne Carson's *Autobiography of Red* and Les Murray's *Freddy Neptune*." *Belgian Journal of English Language and Literatures* 3 (2005): 35–47.

Hepburn, Allan. "Lyric and Epic Fiction." In *Canadian Notes & Queries* 60 (2001): 30–2.

Hesiod. *The Homeric Hymns. And Homerica*. Translated by Hugh Evelyn-White. 1914. Reprint. Cambridge, Massachussets: Harvard University Press, 1982.

Hesse, Hermann. *Der Steppenwolf*. Zürich: Büchergilde Gutenberg, 1927.

Hiebert, Paul. *Sarah Binks*. Toronto: Oxford University Press, 1947.

Hilger, Stephanie M. "Ondaatje's *The English Patient* and Rewriting History." In *Comparative Cultural Studies and Michael Ondaatje's Writing*, edited by Tötösy de Zepetnek, 38–48. West Lafayette: Purdue University Press, 2005.

Hillger, Annick. "'Afterbirth of Earth': Messianic Materialism in Anne Michaels' *Fugitive Pieces*." *Canadian Literature* 160 (1999): 28–45.

– *Not Needing All the Words: Michael Ondaatje's Literature of Silence*. Montreal: McGill-Queen's University Press, 2006.

Homer. *The Iliad*. Translated by Richmond Lattimore. Chicago: University of Chicago Press, 1961.

Hopkins, Gerard Manley. *The Note-books and Papers of Gerard Manley Hopkins*, edited H. House. London: Oxford University Press, 1937.

Hsuan Hsu. "Post-Nationalism and the Cinematic Apparatus in Minghella's Adaptation of Ondaatje's *The English Patient*." *Comparative Cultural Studies and Michael Ondaatje's Writing*, edited by Tötösy de Zepetnek, 49–61. West Lafayette: Purdue University Press, 2005.

Huk, Romana. Introduction to *Assembling Alternatives: Reading Postmodern Poetics Transnationally*, edited by Romana Huk, 1–37. Middletown: Wesleyan University Press, 2003.

Hurley, Michael and Andy Belyea. "A.M. Klein." *The Encyclopedia of Literature in Canada*, edited by W.H. New, 583–5. Toronto: University of Toronto, 2002.

Huston, Nancy. *Les Variations Goldberg*. Paris: Seuil, 1981.

– *Plainsong*. Toronto: McArthur and Company, 1993.

Hutcheon, Linda. *A Poetics of Postmodernism*. New York: Routledge, 1988.

– *Leonard Cohen and His Works*. Toronto: ECW Press, 1989.

– *The Canadian Postmodern*. Toronto: Oxford University Press, 1988.

Hyman, Roger. *Aught from Naught: A.M. Klein's* The Second Scroll. Victoria, B.C.: University of Victoria, 1999.

Irvine, Dean. Introduction to *The Complete Poems of Anne Wilkinson 1924–1961*. Montreal: Véhicule, 2003.

Jarrett, Michael. "Writing Mystory: Michael Ondaatje's *Coming through Slaughter*." *Michael Ondaatje Issue*. Ed. Karen Smythe. Special issue of *Essays on Canadian Writing* 53 (summer 1994): 27–42.

Jennings, Chris. "The Erotic Poetics of Anne Carson." *University of Toronto Quarterly* 70, no.4 (fall 2001): 923–36.

Jewinski, Ed. *Michael Ondaatje: Express Yourself Beautifully*. Toronto: ECW Press, 1994.

Jollimore, Troy and Sharon Barrios. "Beauty, Evil, and *The English Patient*." *Philosophy and Literature* 28, no.1 (April 2004): 23–40.

Johnson, W.R. *The Idea of Lyric: Lyric Modes in Ancient and Modern Poetry*. Berkeley: University of California Press, 1982.

Jones, D.G. *Butterfly on Rock: A Study of Themes and Images in Canadian Literature*. Toronto: University of Toronto Press, 1970.

Jones, Manina. *That Art of Difference: 'Documentary-Collage' and English-Canadian Writing*. Toronto: University of Toronto Press, 1993.

Judy, Stephanie A. "'The Grand Concord of What': Preliminary Thoughts on Musical Composition in Poetry." *Boundary* 2 6, no.1 (fall 1977): 267–85.

Kamboureli, Smaro. *On The Edge of Genre: The Contemporary Canadian Long Poem*. Toronto: University of Toronto Press, 1991.

– "The Poetics of Geography in Michael Ondaatje's *Coming Through Slaughter*." *Descant* 42 (fall 1983): 112–26.

Kaminski, Margot. "Questioning the Canon: Early Long Poems by Canadian Women." In *Bolder Flights: Essays on the Canadian Long Poem*, edited by Frank Tierney and Angela Robbeson, 53–64. Ottawa: Ottawa University Press, 1998.

Kandiyoti, Dalia. "'Our Foothold in Buried Worlds': Place in Holocaust Consciousness and Anne Michaels's *Fugitive Pieces*." *Contemporary Literature* 45, no.2 (2004): 300–30.

Kattan, Naïm. *A.M. Klein: Poet and Prophet*. Translated by Edward Baxter. Lantzville, B.C.: XYZ Publishing, 2001.

Keough, Trent. "The International Politics of Existentialism: From Sartre, to Olson, to Bowering." *Mosaic* 29, no.1 (March 1996): 37–56.

Kervin, Roy. "Leonard Cohen Tries His Hand at a Novel." Review of *The Favourite Game*, by Leonard Cohen. *Montreal Gazette*, 21 Sept. 1963, p. 47.

Khoo, Jun Ling. "Inter-translation / *Transformation* in Nicole Brossard and Daphne Marlatt's 'Mauve' and 'Character / Jeu de lettres,'" 217–28. In *Intercultural Journeys / Parcours Interculturels*, edited by Natasha Dagenais and Joanna Daxell. Baldwin's Mills, Quebec: Editions Topeda Hill, 2003.

King, Nicola. "'We Come After': Remembering the Holocaust." In *Literature and the Contemporary Fictions and Theories of the Present*, edited by Roger Luckhurst and Peter Marks, 94–108. New York: Longman, 1999.

Kiyooka, Roy. *All Amazed: For Roy Kiyooka*, edited by John O'Brian, Naomi Sawada, and Scott Watson. Vancouver: Arsenal Pulp Press, Morris and Helen Belkin Art Gallery, Collapse, 2002.

– "Inter-Face: Roy Kiyooka's Writing: A Commentary / Interview." By Roy Miki. In *Roy Kiyooka*. Vancouver: Artspeak and Or Gallery, 1991.

– *Mothertalk: Life Stories of Mary Kiyoshi Kiyooka*, edited by Daphne Marlatt. Edmonton: NeWest, 1997.

– *Pacific Windows: Collected Poems of Roy K. Kiyooka*, edited by Roy Miki. Vancouver: Talonbooks, 1997.

Kleiman, Ed. "Blossom Show." Review of *The Favourite Game*, by Leonard Cohen. *Alphabet* 9 (November 1964): 78.

Klein, A.M. *Beyond Sambation: Selected Essays and Editorials 1928–1955*, edited by M.W. Steinberg and Usher Caplan. Toronto: University of Toronto Press, 1982.

– *Complete Poems*, edited by Zailig Pollock. Toronto: University of Toronto Press, 1990.

– *Hath Not a Jew*. New York: Behrman's Jewish Bookhouse, 1940.

– *Selected Poems*, edited by Zailig Pollock, Seymour Mayne, and Usher Caplan. Toronto: University of Toronto Press, 1997.

– *Short Stories*, edited by M.W. Steinberg. Toronto: University of Toronto Press, 1983.

– *The Hitleriad*. New York: New Directions, 1944.

– *The Rocking Chair and Other Poems*. Toronto: Ryerson, 1948.

Knutson, Susan. "Daphne Marlatt and Nicole Brossard: Writing Metanarrative in the Feminine." *Signature* 3 (summer 1990): 28–43.

– *Narrative in the Feminine: Daphne Marlatt and Nicole Brossard*. Waterloo, Ontario: Wilfrid Laurier University Press, 2000.

Kogawa, Joy. *Obasan*. New York: Penguin, 1981.

Kossew, Sue. "History and Place: An Interview with Daphne Marlatt." *Canadian Literature* 178 (2003): 49–56.

Kostelanetz, Richard. Introduction to *The Yale Gertrude Stein*. New Haven: Yale University Press, 1980.

Kröller, Eva-Marie. *George Bowering: Bright Circles of Colour*. Vancouver: Talonbooks, 1992.

– "Roy Kiyooka's 'The Fontainebleau Dream Machine': A Reading." *Canadian Literature* 113–14 (summer-fall 1987): 47–58.

Kroetsch, Robert. *Completed Field Notes: The Long Poems of Robert Kroetsch*. Toronto: McClelland & Stewart, 1989.

– *The Hornbooks of Rita K.* Edmonton: University of Alberta Press, 2001.

– *The Lovely Treachery of Words*. Toronto: Oxford University Press, 1989.

Kuester, Martin. *Framing Truths: Parodic Structures in Contemporary English-Canadian Historical Novels*. Toronto: University of Toronto Press, 1992.

Lacroix, Jean-Michel, ed. *Re-Constructing the Fragments of Michael Ondaatje's Works*. Paris: Presses de la Sorbonne nouvelle, 1999.

Lane, Travis. "Dream as History." Review of *the man with seven toes*, by Michael Ondaatje. *The Fiddlehead* 86 (Aug.–Sep.–Oct. 1970): 158–62.

Lanken, Dane. "The Leonard Cohen Show." *The Gazette*, 24 May 1980, p. 98.

Lauretis, Teresa de. *Alice Doesn't: Feminism, Semiotics, Cinema*. Bloomington: Indiana University Press, 1984.

– ed. *Feminist Studies/Critical Studies*. Bloomington: Indiana University Press, 1986.

Lecker, Robert. "Daphne Marlatt's Poetry." *Canadian Literature* 76 (spring 1978): 56–67.

Lee, Dennis. *Savage Fields*. Toronto: Anansi, 1977.

Lee, Sky. *Disappearing Moon Café*. Vancouver: Douglas & McIntyre, 1990.

Lerer, Seth. "Medieval English Literature and the Idea of the Anthology." *PMLA* 118, no.5 (Oct. 2003): 1251–67.

Lewis, Randolph. *Alanis Obomsawin: The Vision of a Native Filmmaker*. Lincoln: University of Nebraska Press, 2006.

Lewis, Tanya. "Myth-Manipulation through Dismemberment in Michael Ondaatje's *The Man with Seven Toes*." *Studies in Canadian Literature* 24, no.2 (1999): 100–13.

Livesay, Dorothy. "The Canadian Documentary: An Overview." *Open Letter* 6, no.2–3 (summer/fall 1985): 127–30.

– *The Documentaries*. Toronto: Ryerson Press, 1968

– "The Documentary Poem: A Canadian Genre." In *Contexts of Canadian Criticism*, edited by Eli Mandel, 34–48. Toronto: University of Toronto Press, 1971.

Lombardo, Stanley. *Iliad*. Indianapolis: Hackett, 1997.

Longfellow, Henry Wadsworth. *Evangeline*. In *Poetical Works*, 142–73. London: Oxford University Press, 1973.

Longus. *Daphnis and Chloe*. Translated by Ronald McCail. New York: Oxford University Press, 2002.

Lönnecke, Annette. "Postmodern Canadian Autobiography: Daphne Marlatt's
    How Hug a Stone and Michael Ondaatje's *Running in the Family*." In *The
    Guises of Canadian Diversity: New European Perspectives/Les Masques de la
    diversité canadienne: Nouvelles Perspectives Européennes*, edited by Serge
    Jaumain and Marc Maufort, 39–46. Amsterdam: Rodopi, 1995.

Lowry, Glen. "Cultural Citizenship and Writing Post-Colonial Vancouver:
    Daphne Marlatt's *Ana Historic* and Wayde Compton's *Bluesprint*." *Mosaic: A
    Journal for the Interdisciplinary Study of Literature* 38, no.3 (2005): 21–39.

Lynn, Elwyn. *Sidney Nolan: Myth and Imagery*. London: Macmillan, 1967.

MacFarlane, Susan. "Picking Up the Pieces: *Coming Through Slaughter* as
    Paradigm." *Open Letter* 7, no. 6 (fall 1989): 72–83.

MacInnes, Colin. Introduction to *Sidney Nolan*, edited by Kenneth Clark, Colin
    MacInnes, and Bryan Robertson. London: Thames and Hudson, 1961.

MacLennan, Hugh. *Two Solitudes*. 1945. Reprint. Toronto: Stoddart, 1993.

MacLulich, T.D. "Ondaatje's Mechanical Boy: Portrait of the Artist as
    Photographer." *Mosaic* 14, no.2 (spring 1982): 107–19.

Maingon, Alison Dale. "Stesichoros and the Epic Tradition." Ph.D. diss.,
    University of British Columbia, 1978.

Malina, Debra. *Breaking the Frame: Metalepsis and the Construction of the
    Subject*. Columbus: Ohio State University Press, 2002.

Marchand, Philip. "Confession and Critique: The Work of Lynn Crosbie." *Essays
    on Canadian Writing* 73 (spring 2001): 141–50.

– *Ripostes*. Erin, Ontario: Porcupine's Quill, 1998.

– *Marshall McLuhan: The Medium and the Messenger*. 1989. Reprint. Toronto:
    Vintage Canada, 1990.

Markotic, Nicole. "The Telephone Dance & Mechanical Ecstasy in Leonard
    Cohen's *Beautiful Losers*." *Canadian Poetry* 33 (fall/winter 1993): 32–9.

Marlatt, Daphne. "A Poignant Critique in a Playful Mixing of Genres." Review
    of *Autobiography of Red*, by Anne Carson. *Canadian Forum* (Sept. 1999):
    41–3.

– *Ana Historic*. 1988. Reprint. Toronto: Anansi, 1998.

– "Between Continuity and Difference: An Interview with Daphne Marlatt." By
    Brenda Carr. In *Beyond Tish*, edited by Douglas Barbour, 99–107. Edmonton:
    NeWest, 1991.

– "Dorothy Black Lectures." University of British Columbia, Vancouver, 14–15
    Feb. 2000.

– "Eratic/Erotic Narrative: Syntax and Mortality in Robin Blaser's 'Image
    Nations.'" In *The Recovery of the Public World: Essays on Poetics in Honour
    of Robin Blaser*, edited by Charles Watts and Edward Byrne, 95–100.
    Vancouver: Talonbooks, 1999.

- *Frames of a Story.* Toronto: Ryerson Press, 1968.
- "Given this Body: An Interview with Daphne Marlatt." Interview by George Bowering. *Open Letter* 4, no.3 (1979): 32–88.
- "History and Place: An Interview with Daphne Marlatt." Interview by Sue Kossew. *Canadian Literature* 178 (autumn 2003): 49–76.
- *How Hug a Stone.* 1983. In *Ghost Works,* 129–87. Edmonton: NeWest, 1993.
- "Interview: There's This and This Connexion." By David Arnason, Dennis Cooley, and Robert Enright. *CV/II* 3, no.1 (spring 1977): 28–33.
- *leaf leaf/s.* Los Angeles: Black Sparrow, 1969.
- "Musing with Mothertongue." In *Two Women in a Birth.* By Daphne Marlatt and Betsy Warland, 25–30. Toronto: Guernica, 1994.
- "Old Scripts and New Narrative Strategies." In *Readings from the Labyrinth,* 62–7. Edmonton: NeWest, 1998.
- "On Salvaging: A Conversation with Daphne Marlatt." Interview by Pauline Butling and Susan Rudy. *Poets Talk: Conversations with Robert Kroetsch, Daphne Marlatt, Erin Mouré, Dionne Brand, Marie Annharte Baker, Jeff Derksen and Fred Wah,* 23–41. Edmonton: University of Alberta Press, 2005.
- *Our Lives.* 1975. Reprint. Lantzville, B.C.: Oolichan, 1980.
- *Readings from the Labyrinth.* Edmonton: NeWest, 1998.
- *Rings.* Vancouver: Vancouver Community Press, 1971.
- *Taken.* Toronto: Anansi, 1996.
- "The Measure of the Sentence." *Open Letter* 5, no.3 (summer 1982): 90–2.
- *This Tremor Love Is.* Vancouver: Talonbooks, 2001.
- *Vancouver Poems.* Toronto: Coach House Press, 1972.
- *What Matters: Writing 1968–70.* Toronto: Coach House Press, 1980.
- "What Would You Be If You Weren't a Writer?" *Brick* 51 (winter 1995): 28.
- *Zócalo.* 1977. In *Ghost Works,* 1–74. Edmonton: NeWest, 1993.

Marlatt, Daphne and Betsy Warland. *Double Negative,* with collages by Cheryl Sourkes. Charlottetown, P.E.I.: Gynergy Books, 1988.

Marlatt, Daphne and Robert Minden. *Steveston.* Vancouver: Talonbooks, 1974.

Marquis, Donald. *In Search of Buddy Bolden: First Man of Jazz.* Baton Rouge: Louisiana State University Press, 1978.

Marshall, Tom. Introduction to *A.M. Klein,* edited by Tom Marshall. Toronto: Ryerson, 1970.

Martin, Sandra. "Who's Afraid of Anne Carson?" *Globe and Mail,* 2 Feb. 2002, sec. R, p. 3.

Mathews, Robin. "In Search of a Canadian Poetic." *Canadian Forum* 62, no.723 (Nov. 1982): 31–2.

Maxwell, Barry. "Surrealistic Aspects of Michael Ondaatje's *Coming Through Slaughter.*" *Mosaic* 18, no.3 (summer 1985): 101–15.

Mayne, Seymour. Afterword to *The Second Scroll*, by A.M. Klein. 1951. Reprint. Toronto: McClelland & Stewart, 1994.

McLuhan, Marshall. "George Meredith as a Poet and Dramatic Novelist." Master's thesis, University of Manitoba, 1934.

– *The Gutenberg Galaxy.* 1962. Reprint. Toronto: University of Toronto Press, 1995.

– "The Place of Thomas Nashe in the Learning of His Time." Ph.D. diss., Cambridge University, 1943.

– *Understanding Media: The Extensions of Man.* New York: McGraw-Hill, 1964.

McLuhan, Marshall and Harley Parker. *Through the Vanishing Point: Space in Poetry and Painting.* New York: Harper & Row, 1968.

McLuhan, Marshall, Quentin Fiore and Jerome Agel. *The Medium Is the Massage.* New York: Random House, 1967.

McNeilly, Kevin. "All Poets Are Not Jews: Transgression and Satire in A.M. Klein." *English Studies in Canada* 28, no.3 (Sept. 2002): 413–45.

Meagher, Robert. *Helen: Myth, Legend, and the Culture of Misogyny.* New York: Continuum, 1995.

Michaels, Anne. "Cleopatra's Love." *Poetry Canada* 14, no.2 (spring 1994): 14–15.

– *Fugitive Pieces.* Toronto: McClelland & Stewart, 1996.

– "Narrative Moves: An Interview with Anne Michaels." Interview by Anonymous. *Canadian Notes & Queries* 50 (1986).

– *The Weight of Oranges / Miner's Pond.* Toronto: McClelland & Stewart, 1997.

Miki, Roy. *A Record of Writing: An Annotated and Illustrated Bibliography of George Bowering.* Vancouver: Talonbooks, 1990.

– *Broken Entries: Race, Subjectivity, Writing.* Toronto: Mercury, 1998.

– "Editor's Note." *George Bowering Selected.* By George Bowering, 231–4. Toronto: McClelland & Stewart, 1993.

Miller, Andrew. *Greek Lyric.* Indianapolis: Hackett, 1996.

Miller, Karl. "International Books of the Year – and the Millennium." *London Times Literary Supplement*, 3 Dec. 1999, p. 6.

Milton, Paul. "Beyond Agonistics: Vertiginous Games in the Fiction of Leonard Cohen." *Essays on Canadian Writing* 69 (winter 1999): 235–59.

Monkman, Leslie. "Beautiful Losers: Mohawk Myth and Jesuit Legend." *Journal of Canadian Fiction* 3, no.3 (1974): 57–9.

Morley, Patricia. *The Immoral Moralists: Hugh MacLennan and Leonard Cohen.* Toronto: Clarke, Irwin, 1972.

Morse, Garry. "From 'Take Out: An All You Can Eat Smorgasbord of Vancouver Poetics.'" *West Coast Line: A Journal of Contemporary Writing & Criticism* 39, no.2 (fall 2005): 87–90.

Morson, Gary Saul and Caryl Emerson. *Mikhail Bakhtin: Creation of a Prosaics.* Stanford: Stanford University Press, 1990.

Moss, John. *The Paradox of Meaning: Cultural Poetics and Critical Fictions.* Winnipeg: Turnstone, 1999.

– "Life/Story: The Fictions of George Bowering." *Essays on Canadian Writing* 38 (summer 1989): 85–98.

Mukherjee, Arun. *Oppositional Aesthetics: Reading from a Hyphenated Space.* Toronto: TSAR, 1994.

Murray, George. "The Verse Has Just Begun." *Globe and Mail,* 1 Sept. 2000, sec. D, p. 7.

Murray, Heather. "The Impossible Genre." Review of *On the Edge of Genre,* by Smaro Kamboureli. *Essays on Canadian Writing* 55 (spring 1995): 91–7.

Muybridge, Eadweard. *Animals in Motion.* New York: Dover, 1957.

Myers, Robin and Michael Harris. Introduction to *Serials and Their Readers 1620–1914.* Newcastle, Delaware: Oak Knoll, 1993.

Nadel, Ira. *Leonard Cohen: A Life in Art.* Toronto: ECW Press, 1994.

– *Various Positions: A Life of Leonard Cohen.* Toronto: Random House Canada, 1996.

Neuman, S.C. *Gertrude Stein: Autobiography and the Problem of Narration.* Victoria, B.C.: English Literary Studies, 1979.

Nichol, bp. *An H in the Heart,* edited by George Bowering and Michael Ondaatje. Toronto: McClelland & Stewart, 1994.

– "The Medium Was the Message." *Meanwhile: The Critical Writings of bp Nichol,* edited by Roy Miki, 298–300. Vancouver: Talonbooks, 2002.

Nichols, Miriam. "Subjects of Experience: Post-Cognitive Subjectivity in the Work of bpNichol and Daphne Marlatt." *Studies in Canadian Literature* 25, no.2 (2000): 108–30.

Nietzsche, Friedrich. *The Birth of Tragedy & The Genealogy of Morals.* Translated by Francis Golffing. Garden City, New York: Doubleday, 1956.

Nodelman, Perry. "The Collected Photographs of Billy the Kid." *Canadian Literature* 87 (winter 1980): 68–79.

Nolan, Sidney. *Sidney Nolan,* edited by Kenneth Clarke, Colin MacInnes, and Bryan Robertson. London: Thames and Hudson, 1961.

– *Sidney Nolan: Landscapes and Legends,* edited by Jane Clark. Sidney: Cambridge University Press, 1987.

Novak, Amy. "Textual Hauntings: Narrating History, Memory, and Silence in *The English Patient.*" In *Studies in the Novel* 36, no.2 (summer 2004): 206–32.

O, Deborah. "Coded Spaces/Signifying Bodies." *Open Letter* 10, no.7 (winter 2000): 69–81.

Olson, Charles. "Equal, That Is, to the Real Itself." In *Poetics of the New American Poetry*, edited by Donald Allen and Warren Tallman, 175–81. New York: Grove, 1973.

– "Projective Verse." In *Poetics of the New American Poetry*, edited by Donald Allen and Warren Tallman, 147–58. New York: Grove, 1973.

– *The Maximus Poems.* New York: Jargon/Corinth Books, 1960.

Ondaatje, Michael. Afterword to "Peter." In *How Do I Love Thee: Sixty Poets of Canada (and Quebec) Select and Introduce Their Favourite Poems From Their Own Work*, edited by John Robert Colombo, 149. Edmonton: Hurtig, 1970.

– Afterword to *Tay John.* By Howard O'Hagan, 265–72. 1960. Reprint. Toronto: McClelland & Stewart, 1989.

– "An Interview with Michael Ondaatje." Interview by Stephen Scobie and Douglas Barbour. *White Pelican* 1, no.2 (1971): 6–15.

– "An Interview with Michael Ondaatje (1975)." Interview by Sam Solecki. In *Spider Blues: Essays on Michael Ondaatje*, edited by Sam Solecki, 13–27. Montreal: Véhicule, 1985.

– "An Interview with Michael Ondaatje (1984)." Interview by Sam Solecki. *Spider Blues: Essays on Michael Ondaatje*, edited by Sam Solecki, 321–2. Montreal: Véhicule, 1985.

– *Anil's Ghost.* Toronto: McClelland & Stewart, 2000.

– *Coming Through Slaughter.* Toronto: Anansi, 1976.

– *Divisadero.* Toronto: McClelland & Stewart, 2007.

– ed. *From Ink Lake.* Toronto: Knopf, 1982.

– *Handwriting.* Toronto: McClelland & Stewart, 1998.

– *In the Skin of a Lion.* 1987. Reprint. New York: Penguin, 1988.

– "Interview with Michael Ondaatje." Interview by Anonymous. *Manna* 1 (March 1972): 19–22.

– "Interview with Michael Ondaatje." Interview by Eleanor Wachtel. *Essays on Canadian Writing* 53 (summer 1994): 250–61.

– "Introduction to Robin Blaser's 'Hello.'" In *The Recovery of the Public World: Essays on Poetics in Honour of Robin Blaser*, edited by Charles Watts and Edward Byrne, 454. Vancouver: Talonbooks, 1999.

– *Leonard Cohen.* Toronto: McClelland & Stewart, 1970.

– "Michael Ondaatje: An Interview." Interview by Catherine Bush. *Essays on Canadian Writing* 53 (summer 1994): 238–49.

– "Moving to the Clear." Interview by Jon Pearce. In *Twelve Voices: Interviews with Canadian Poets*, 139–43. Ottawa: Borealis, 1980.

- "Mythology in the Poetry of Edwin Muir." Master's thesis. Queen's University, 1967.
- *Rat Jelly*. Toronto: Coach House, 1973.
- Review of *A Controversy of Poets*, edited by Paris Leary and Robert Kelly. *Quarry* 15, no.2 (Nov. 1965): 44–5.
- *Running in the Family*. Toronto: McClelland & Stewart, 1982.
- *The Collected Works of Billy the Kid*. Toronto: Anansi, 1970.
- *The Conversations: Walter Murch and the Art of Editing Film*. Toronto: Vintage, 2002.
- *The Dainty Monsters*. Toronto: Coach House Press, 1967.
- *The English Patient*. Toronto: McClelland & Stewart, 1992.
- "'The Germ of Document': An Interview with Michael Ondaatje." By Gerry Turcotte. *Australian-Canadian Studies* 12, no.2 (1994): 49–54.
- *The Long Poem Anthology*. Toronto: Coach House Press, 1979.
- *the man with seven toes*. 1969. Reprint Toronto: Coach House Press, 1971.
- "The Ondaatje Myth." Interview by John Burns. *The Georgia Straight*, 13–20 April 2000, p. 15.
- *There's a Trick With a Knife I'm Learning to Do: Selected Poems 1963–78*. 1979. Reprint. Toronto: McClelland & Stewart, 1992.
- *Tin Roof*. Victoria, B.C.: Morris Print Co., 1982.
- "What Lightning Was Like in the 1970s." In *Paterson Ewen*, edited by Matthew Teitelbaum, 3–4. Toronto: Douglas & McIntyre, 1996.
- "Where the Personal and the Historical Meet: An Interview with Michael Ondaatje." Interview by Cary Fagan. *Paragraph* 12, no.2 (March 1990): 3–5.
Pacey, Desmond. "Cohen as a Literary Phenomenon." *Leonard Cohen: The Artist and His Critics*, edited by Michael Gnarowski, 74–93. Toronto: McGraw-Hill Ryerson, 1976.
Page, P.K. *The Glass Air: Selected Poems*. Toronto: Oxford University Press, 1985.
Payne, Rob. "Give Me Tasmanian Babes, Give Me Telemarketing Hell, Give Me Something Funny," *Globe and Mail*, 26 Jan. 2002, sec. D, p. 4.
Plato. *The Republic*. Translated by Paul Shorey, 2 vols. Cambridge, Mass: Harvard University Press, 1935.
Plutarch. *De Iside et Osiride*. Translated by J. Gwyn Griffiths. Cambridge: University of Wales Press, 1970.
Poore, Charles. "Young Bohemians – Canadian Style." Review of *The Favourite Game*, by Leonard Cohen. *New York Times*, 12 Sept. 1963, p. 35.
Pratt, E.J. *Brébeuf and His Brethren*. Toronto: MacMillan, 1940.
- *Towards the Last Spike*. Toronto: Macmillan, 1952.
Provencal, Vernon. "The PseudoHerodotean Origins of *The English Patient*." *English Studies in Canada* 29, no. 3–4 (Sept. and Dec. 2003): 139–65.

Pushkin, Alexander. *Eugene Onegin: A Novel in Verse.* Translated by Douglas Hofstadter. New York: Basic Books, 1999.

Pyper, Andrew. "In the Morgue of the Imagination." *Globe and Mail,* 4 Nov. 2000, sec. D, p. 22.

Rae, Ian. "Anne Carson and the Solway Hoaxes." *Canadian Literature* 176 (spring 2003): 45–65.

– "'Dazzling Hybrids': The Poetry of Anne Carson." *Canadian Literature* 166 (autumn 2000): 17–41.

Rasula, Jed. "A Gift of Prophecy." Review of *Autobiography of Red*, by Anne Carson. *Canadian Literature* 161/162 (summer/fall 1999): 187–9.

– "Spicer's Orpheus and the Emancipation of Pronouns." *Boundary* 2 6, no. 1 (fall 1977): 51–102.

Ravvin, Norman. "Writing Around the Holocaust: Uncovering the Ethical Centre of *Beautiful Losers.*" *Canadian Poetry* 33 (fall/winter 1993): 22–31.

Reaney, James. "Long Poems." *Open Letter* 6, no.2–3 (summer–fall 1985): 115–9.

Reed, Sabrina. "'*Against* the Source': Daphne Marlatt's Revision of Charles Olson." *Studies in Canadian Literature* 26, no.1 (2001): 132–44.

Rehak, Melanie. "Things Fall Together." *New York Times Magazine,* 26 March 2000, p. 36–9.

Reynolds, Oliver. "After Homer, Before Stein." *London Times Literary Supplement,* 3 Dec. 1999, p. 24.

Richardson, Keith. *Poetry and the Colonized Mind: Tish.* Preface by Robin Mathews. Oakville, Ontario: Mosaic, 1976.

Richler, Mordecai. *St. Urbain's Horseman.* 1971. Reprint. Toronto: McClelland & Stewart, 2001.

Ricoeur, Paul. "The Narrative Function." In *Hermeneutics & The Human Sciences,* edited and translated by John B. Thompson. Cambridge, UK: Cambridge University Press, 1981.

– *Time and Narrative.* Translated by Kathleen McLaughlin and David Pellauer. Chicago: Chicago University Press, 1985.

Ricou, Laurie. "Phyllis Webb, Daphne Marlatt and Similitude." In *A Mazing Space: Writing Canadian Women Writing*, edited by Shirley C. Neuman and Smaro Kamboureli. Edmonton: Longspoon/NeWest, 1986.

– "Poetry." In *Literary History of Canada: Canadian Literature in English*, edited by W.H. New, 2d ed., 4: 3–45. Toronto: University of Toronto Press, 1990.

Riddel, Joseph. "A Somewhat Polemical Introduction." *The Long Poem in the 20th Century.* Special issue, *Genre* 11, no.4 (winter 1978): 459–77.

Rigelhof, T.F. "Enough Said." *Globe and Mail,* 22 Jan. 2000, sec. D, p. 22.

– *This Is Our Writing.* Erin, Ontario: Porcupine's Quill, 2000.

Rilke, R.M. *Duino Elegies.* Translated by Edward Snow. New York: Farrar, Straus and Giroux, 2000.

Robertson, Bryan. "Biography, and Chronology of the Pictures." In *Sidney Nolan*, edited by Kenneth Clarke, Colin MacInnes, and Bryan Robertson, 36–50. London: Thames and Hudson, 1961.

Robertson, Martin. "Geryoneis: Stesichoros and the Vase-Painters." *Classical Quarterly* 19 (1969): 207–21.

Rogers, William. *The Three Genres and the Interpretation of Lyric*. Princeton, New Jersey: Princeton University Press, 1983.

Rose, H.J. *A Handbook of Greek Literature: From Homer to the Age of Lucian*. 1934. Reprint. Wauconda, Illinois: Bolchazy-Carducci Publishers, 1996.

Rosenthal, Caroline. "'You Can't Even Imagine?': Monstrous Possibilities of Female Identity in Daphne Marlatt's *Ana Historic*." In *Narrative Deconstructions of Gender in Works by Audrey Thomas, Daphne Marlatt, and Louise Erdrich*, 66–106. New York: Camdenhouse, 2003.

Rosenthal, M. L. and Sally M. Gall. *The Modern Poetic Sequence*. New York: Oxford, 1983.

Saul, Johanne. "Displacement and Self-Representation: Theorizing Contemporary Canadian Biotexts." *Biography* 24, no.1 (winter 2001): 259–73.

Sayers, Andrew. *Sidney Nolan: The Ned Kelly Story*. New York: Metropolitan Museum of Art, 1994.

Schaffer, Kay. *In the Wake of First Contact: The Eliza Fraser Stories*. New York: Cambridge University Press, 1995.

Schlegel, Friedrich von. *Dialogue on Poetry and Literary Aphorisms*. Translated by Ernst Behler and Roman Struc. London: Pennsylvania State University Press, 1968.

Schoo, Jan. *Hercules' Labors: Fact or Fiction?* Chicago: Argonaut, 1969.

Scobie, Stephen. "Coming Through Slaughter: Fictional Magnets and Spider's Webbs." *Essays on Canadian Writing* 12 (1978): 5–23.

– "His Legend a Jungle Sleep: Michael Ondaatje and Henri Rousseau." In *Spider Blues: Essays* on Michael Ondaatje, edited by Sam Solecki, 42–60. Montreal: Véhicule, 1985.

– *Leonard Cohen*. Vancouver: Douglas & McIntyre, 1978.

– "The Reading Lesson: Michael Ondaatje and the Patients of Desire." *Michael Ondaatje Issue*. Ed. Karen Smythe. Special issue of *Essays on Canadian Writing* 53 (summer 1994): 92–106.

– "Racing the Midnight Train: Leonard Cohen in Performance." *Canadian Literature* 152/153 (spring/summer 1997): 52–69.

– "Two Authors in Search of a Character: bp Nichol and Michael Ondaatje." *Spider Blues Essays on Michael Ondaatje*, edited by Sam Solecki, 185–210. Montreal: Véhicule, 1985.

Scott, F.R. "The Canadian Authors Meet." *The Collected Poems of F.R. Scott*, 248. 1981. Reprint. Toronto: McClelland & Stewart, 1982.

Sheldon, James. *Motion and Document – Sequence and Time: Eadweard Muybridge and Contemporary American Photography*. Andover: Massachusetts: Addison Gallery of American Art, 1991.

Shipley, Joseph. *Dictionary of Word Origins*. New York: Philosophical Library, 1945.

Siemerling, Winfried. *Discoveries of the Other: Alterity in the Work of Leonard Cohen, Hubert Aquin, Michael Ondaatje, and Nicole Brossard*. Toronto: University of Toronto Press, 1994.

– "Leonard Cohen. 'Loneliness and History: A Speech Before the Jewish Public Library.'" In *Take This Waltz: A Celebration of Leonard Cohen*, edited by Michael Fournier and Ken Norris, 143–53. Ste. Anne de Bellevue, Quebec: The Muses' Company, 1994.

Silver, Jack. "Moving into Winter." *Open Letter* 3, no.8 (spring 1978): 90–101.

Simon, Sherry. "Crossing Town: Montreal in Translation." PMLA: *Profession* (2002): 15–24.

– "Hybrid Montreal: The Shadows of Language." *Sites: The Journal of 20th-Century / Contemporary French Studies* 5, no.2 (fall 2001): 315–30.

Simpson, Kieran, ed., *Canadian Who's Who*, vol. 25. Toronto: University of Toronto Press, 1990.

Smith, A.J.M. ed., *The Oxford Book of Canadian Verse*. London: Oxford, 1960.

Smith, Sidonie. *Moving Lives: Twentieth-Century Women's Travel Writing*. Minneapolis: University of Minnesota Press, 2001.

Smitten, Jeffrey and Ann Daghistany, ed. *Spatial Form in Narrative*. Ithaca: Cornell University Press, 1981.

Söderlind, Sylvia. *Margin/Alias: Language and Colonization in Canadian and Québécois Fiction*. Toronto: University of Toronto Press, 1991.

Solecki, Sam. "Nets and Chaos: The Poetry of Michael Ondaatje." In *Spider Blues: Essays on Michael Ondaatje*, edited by Sam Solecki, 93–110. Montreal: Véhicule, 1985.

– "Point Blank: Narrative in *the man with seven toes*," *Spider Blues: Essays on Michael Ondaatje*, edited by Sam Solecki, 135–49. Montreal: Véhicule, 1985.

– *Ragas of Longing*. Toronto: University of Toronto Press, 2003.

Solway, David. *Director's Cut*. Erin, Ontario: Porcupine's Quill, 2003.

– "The Trouble with Annie: David Solway Unmakes Anne Carson." *Books in Canada* 30, no.1 (July 2001): 24–6.

Spicer, Jack. *After Lorca*. 1957. Reprint. San Francisco: Marco Polio, 1974.

– *The Collected Books of Jack Spicer*. 1975. Reprint. Santa Rosa, California: Black Sparrow Press, 1999.

– *The Heads of the Town Up to the Aether*. San Francisco: Auerhahn, 1962.

– *The Tower of Babel*. Hoboken, New Jersey: Talisman House, 1994.

Stanton, Robert. "'I am writing this to be as wrong as possible to you': Anne Carson's Errancy." *Canadian Literature* 176 (spring 2003): 28–43.

Stein, Gertrude. *A Long Gay Book*, in *A Stein Reader*, edited by Ulla Dydo. Evanston, Illinois: Northwestern University Press, 1993.

– *GMP (Matisse, Picasso and Gertrude Stein)*. 1933. Reprint. Barton: Something Else Press, 1972.

– "Portraits and Repetition." In *Writings and Lectures 1911–1945*, edited by Patricia Meyerowitz, 98–122. London: Peter Owen, 1967.

– *The Making of Americans*. 1925. Reprint. New York: Something Else Press, 1966.

Stourton, Patrick Corbally. Introduction to *Songlines and Dreamings: Contemporary Australian Aboriginal Painting*, edited by Nigel Corbally Stourton. London: Lund Humphries, 1996.

Sutherland, Fraser. "Addressing the Empress." *Literary Review of Canada* 8, no. 9 (Nov. 2000): 7–8.

– "Jane Urquhart's Painterly Poetry." *Globe and Mail*, 28 October 2000, sec. D, p. 13.

– "It Takes Two to Tango." *Globe and Mail*, 10 Feb. 2001, sec. D, p. 2+.

Summers-Bremner, Eluned. "Reading Ondaatje's Poetry." In *Comparative Cultural Studies and Michael Ondaatje's Writing*, edited by Steven Tötösky de Zepetnek. Indiana: Purdue University Press, 2005.

Tannen, Deborah, ed. *Framing in Discourse*. New York: Oxford University Press, 1993.

Taubin, Amy. "Doubled Visions." In *Michael Snow: almost Cover to Cover*, 98–109. London: Black Dog, 2001.

Teitelbaum, Matthew. "Paterson Ewen: Comets and Other Unknowable Things." In *Paterson Ewen*, edited by Matthew Teitelbaum, 35–86. Toronto: Douglas & McIntyre, 1996.

Teskey, Gordon. "The Love Poet: Anne Carson." *Time* (Cdn. ed.), 16 Dec. 2002, 47.

Testa, Bart. "He Did Not Work Here for Long: Michael Ondaatje in the Cinema." *Michael Ondaatje Issue*. Ed. Karen Smythe. Special issue of *Essays on Canadian Writing* 53 (summer 1994): 154–66.

Thesen, Sharon, ed. *The New Long Poem Anthology*. Toronto: Coach House Press, 1991.

– *The New Long Poem Anthology*. 2d ed. Vancouver: Talonbooks, 2001.

Thomas, Audrey. *Blown Figures*. Vancouver: Talonbooks, 1974.

Tierney Frank M. and Angela Robbeson, ed. *Bolder Flights: Essays on the Canadian Long Poem*. Ottawa: University of Ottawa Press, 1998.

Tötösky de Zepetnek, Stephen, ed. *Comparative Cultural Studies and Michael Ondaatje's Writing*. Indiana: Purdue University Press, 2005.

Townsend-Gault, Charlotte. "The Living of Modern Life – In Canada." In *Roy Kiyooka*. Vancouver: Artspeak and Or Gallery, 1991. ·

Trehearne, Brian. "Critical Episodes in Montreal Poetry of the 1940s." *Canadian Poetry* 41 (fall/winter 1997): 21–52.

– *The Montreal Forties: Modernist Poetry in Transition*. Toronto: University of Toronto Press, 1999.

Tschofen, Monique. "'First I Must Tell About Seeing': (De)monstrations of Visuality and the Dynamics of Metaphor in Anne Carson's *Autobiography of Red*." *Canadian Literature* 180 (spring 2004): 31–50.

Urquhart, Tony. *Worlds Apart, The Symbolic Landscapes of Tony Urquhart*. Windsor, Ontario: Art Gallery of Windsor, 1988.

Vander Weg, John. *Serial Music and Serialism*. New York: Routledge, 2001.

Venster, Dagmar de. "Leonard Cohen's Women." In *Mother was not a person*, edited by Marguerite Andersen, 96–7. Montreal: Content Publishing/Black Rose Books, 1972.

Verwaayen, Kimberly. "Re-Membering the (W)holes: Counter-memory, Collective Memory, and Bergsonian Time in Anne Michaels' *Miner's Pond*." *Canadian Poetry* 46 (spring–summer 2000): 69–85.

Vetter, Lisa Pace. "Liberal Political Inquiries in the Novels of Michael Ondaatje." *Perspectives on Political Science* 34, no.1 (2005): 27–36.

Wah, Fred. Introduction to *Net Work* by Daphne Marlatt. Vancouver: Talonbooks, 1980.

– "Bowering's Lines." *Essays on Canadian Writing* 38 (summer 1989): 101–6.

Wainwright, J.A. "The Favourite Game: Canadian Literature In and Out." *Essays on Canadian Writing* 71 (fall 2000): 241–8.

Warshall, Peter. "The Ways of Whales." In *Mind in the Waters*, edited by Joan McIntyre, 110–40. New York: Scribner's, 1974.

Watson, Sheila. *The Double Hook*. 1959. Reprint. Toronto: McClelland & Stewart, 1989.

Watt, Ian. *The Rise of the Novel*. 1957. Berkeley: University of California Press, 1964.

Welchman, John. "In and Around the 'Second Frame.'" In *The Rhetoric of the Frame: Essays on the Boundaries of the Artwork*, edited by Paul Duro, 203–22. Cambridge: Cambridge University Press, 1996.

Whitlock, Gillian. "White Diasporas: Joan (and Ana) Make History." *Australian and New Zealand Studies in Canada* 12 (Dec. 1994): 90–100.

Whyte, Jon. *Homage, Henry Kelsey*. Winnipeg: Turnstone, 1981.

Wilkinson, Anne. *Lions in the Way*. Toronto: Macmillan, 1956.

- *The Collected Poems of Anne Wilkinson and a Prose Memoir*, edited by A.J.M. Smith. Toronto: Macmillan, 1968.
- *Tightrope Walker: Autobiographical Writings of Anne Wilkinson*, edited by Joan Coldwell. Toronto: University of Toronto Press, 1992.

Wilson, Carl. "What Anne Carson Thinks About." *Globe and Mail*, 1 April 2000, sec. D, p. 19.

Woolf, Virginia. *The Waves*. New York: Harcourt Brace, 1931.

Yeats, W.B., ed. *Oxford Book of Modern Verse: 1892–1935*. Oxford: Clarendon Press, 1936.

York, Lorraine. "Whirling Blindfolded in the House of Women: Gender Politics in the Poetry and Fiction of Michael Ondaatje." *Michael Ondaatje Issue*. Ed. Karen Smythe. Special issue of *Essays on Canadian Writing* 53 (summer 1994): 71–91.

Zeitlin, Froma. "New Soundings in Holocaust Literature: A Surplus of Memory." In *Catastrophe and Meaning: The Holocaust and the Twentieth Century*, edited by Moishe Postone and Eric Sautner, 173–208. Chicago: University of Chicago Press, 2003.

Zwicker, Heather. "Daphne Marlatt's 'Ana Historic': Queering the Postcolonial Nation." *Ariel* 30, no.2 (April 1999): 161–75.

Permissions

Index